Subject Analysis in
Online Catalogs

Second Edition

Subject Analysis in Online Catalogs

Hope A. Olson
School of Library and Information Studies
University of Alberta

John J. Boll
School of Library and Information Studies
University of Wisconsin-Madison

2001
Libraries Unlimited
A Division of Greenwood Publishing Group, Inc.
Englewood, Colorado

Libraries Unlimited
A Division of Greenwood Publishing Group, Inc.
P.O. Box 6633
Englewood, CO 80155-6633
1-800-237-6124
www.lu.com

Library of Congress Cataloging-in-Publication Data

Olson, Hope A.
   Subject analysis in online catalogs.--2nd ed. / Hope A. Olson, John J. Boll.
      p. cm.
   Rev. ed. of: Subject analysis in online catalogs / Rao Aluri, D. Alasdair Kemp, John J. Boll 1991.
   Includes bibliographical references and index.
   ISBN 1-56308-800-2
      1. Online library catalogs--Subject access. 2. Subject cataloging--Data processing.
3. Online bibliographic searching. 4. Information retrieval. I. Boll, John J., 1921-
II. Aluri, Rao. Subject analysis in online catalogs. III. Title.

Z699.35.S92 A46 2001
025.3'132--dc21
                                                                                    2001029828

Contents

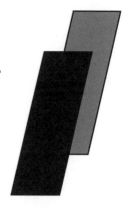

6—SUBJECT HEADINGS AND DESCRIPTORS (*continued*)

7—BIBLIOGRAPHIC CLASSIFICATION 153

Preface

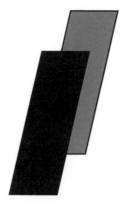

This book is based on the premise that subject access in online catalogs is a complex process involving interaction among a number of components that together form a subject access system. These components are the database of the online catalog, the languages used for subject analysis and the policies and principles of their application, the users, and the hardware and software that allow users to interact with the system. All of these components have to work together for successful subject retrieval. For example, the most powerful subject retrieval software and advanced hardware technology are of no great use if the database does not have adequate subject information. Likewise, an excellent database, high-quality indexing, and the most user-friendly software together cannot help users who are either unwilling or unable to exploit the subject retrieval features of the online catalog.

This book is about subject analysis and online catalogs and where they meet. It occupies the area of two overlapping sets in a sort of Venn diagram within the larger domain of information storage and retrieval.

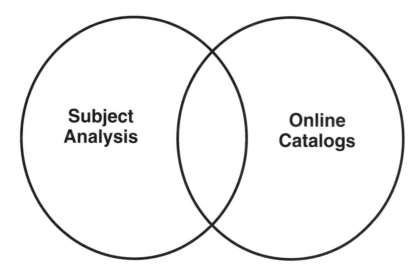

However, it is not primarily about online catalogs; nor is it primarily about subject analysis. The overlapping area concerning subject analysis and access to the content of online catalogs is far more complex and crucial than either area by itself. This book is designed to bridge the fields of bibliographic subject retrieval and online public access catalogs on a policy, characteristics, and methodological basis, in a historical framework where appropriate. Indexing vocabularies, as the basis irrespective of medium, are described specifically. Their use in online public access catalogs, and ways in which such catalogs operate, are described generally, with examples of the effects of changing media and changing policies. Any discipline can produce an interface to a database (although we tend to do it better in library and information science). No other discipline can organize the content as effectively as we can.

This book is arranged to reflect the notion of these interacting components. Chapter 2 explains the organization of the electronic files in an online catalog. The database is the most crucial component of the subject access system. The information it contains and its organization affect all other components. For the purpose of this book, the term "database" is used in a broad sense that includes not only the bibliographic file but also related files, notably the authority and inverted files, as explained in Chapter 2. Chapters 3 and 4, on language, serve as an overview and introduction to Chapters 5 through 8 on indexing and classification. They emphasize the fact that indexing vocabularies and classificatory schemes are languages and, therefore, follow linguistic rules. They also explore the differences between controlled and uncontrolled languages and their semantic and syntactic ramifications. Chapter 5 examines the indexing process and the policies governing it in terms of four factors—accuracy, exhaustivity, specificity, and consistency—that play a major role in determining the outcome of searching.

Chapter 6 explains the workings of two major verbal controlled vocabularies, the *Library of Congress Subject Headings* (LCSH) and the *Medical Subject Headings* (MeSH), the latter serving as a contrast to the former, which is the predominant standard in North America, as well as keywords. Chapters 7 and 8 discuss the principles of classification and the major classification schemes, the *Dewey Decimal Classification* (DDC) and the *Library of Congress Classification* (LCC). These are used not only in North America, but also elsewhere, particularly the DDC, which is the most widely used classification in the world. Chapter 9 examines different views of the concept of "user" and how they play a significant role in development of online systems. Chapter 10 looks at how users interact with a system through the languages of the system, its search functions, and its screen displays. Chapter 11 explains common approaches to research in information retrieval and online catalogs to provide background for critical reading of research findings and starting points for carrying out research projects in a professional context. Both of these activities should lead to effective evaluation of online catalogs.

We believe that this text brings together information about the various components of online subject access in a coherent and accessible way. It is our intent that the book provide readers with a general conception of online catalogs, grounded in evidence of current practice but applicable to future developments. It is trite to say, but vital to remember, that information technology is changing faster than we can write. Therefore, the principles of online subject access are the most useful contributions we can offer.

This book is primarily addressed to students who have some background in organizing information and are ready to focus on subject access. It is also addressed to librarians interested in subject access in online catalogs and in the adaptation of traditional methods of subject analysis to new information technologies.

Acknowledgments

We take this opportunity to thank Rao Aluri and Alasdair Kemp who shared with John J. Boll the authorship of the first edition. We also thank our friends and colleagues who have contributed ideas, verified facts, and reviewed texts, and the staff at Libraries Unlimited. Any errors or omissions are our own. Notable amongst those we wish to thank are Sharon Balazs, Julianne Beall, Pauline A. Cochrane, Karen Dahlen, Sharon DeJohn, Anne Giffey, Rebecca Guenther, Ingrid Hsieh-Yee, Rich Lane, Gregory New, Matthew J. Olson, Mary K. D. Pietris, Kendall G. Rouse, Athena Salaba, Christopher Schladweiler, Dennis B. Ward, Phyllis Holman Weisbard, Beacher J. E. Wiggins, Connie Winther, and Thompson Yee.

1

Introduction

The topic of subject analysis in online catalogs is an exciting one because of its many challenges and its constant change. It breaks down into two obvious areas of concern: subject analysis and online catalogs. Each is important alone, but their combination creates complexity that merits close study.

ONLINE CATALOGS

Online catalogs became widespread in North American libraries during the 1980s. Sometimes referred to as online public access catalogs (OPACs, or even just PACs), they are now the standard form of bibliographic access in the industrialized world and, increasingly, worldwide. Standards for creation of online databases are now established in an international context. Bibliographic utilities and local and regional consortia have built impressive databases based on these standards. Libraries have adopted integrated systems that combine online catalogs with other automated functions. Such systems prevent duplication of data between functions and allow linking of data for purposes such as public access to acquisition records and circulation status. Numerous vendors compete in this market. Online catalogs have definitely come of age.

However, there is always change on the horizon. The existing standards continue to evolve and expand to transfer more data more efficiently and to use that data more effectively. Effort is now being put into providing more flexible and useful interfaces between searchers and databases. New environments offer different opportunities. The World Wide Web (WWW) has enabled libraries to make their online catalogs freely available to an enormous audience through Web-based catalogs. The WWW has also made cataloging electronic documents commonplace. Furthermore, these electronic documents have begun to incorporate data about themselves, referred to as metadata, similar to the data in catalog records (Milstead and Feldman 1999). Metadata are discussed further in Chapter 2.

The boundaries of online catalogs are no longer clear. Many catalogs include interfaces to other databases such as indexes and collections of full-text journal articles. Whether these databases are part of the online catalog, or the latter simply provides a

1

gateway to them, is open to argument. Unlike library catalogs, other databases do not follow internationally accepted standards. Any individual catalog may offer access to other databases in a wide range of formats. This book focuses on library catalogs that provide access to a library's collection or the collections of a consortium of libraries, rather than the diffuse array of other databases available. However, the principles of subject access in library catalogs, if not the particular vocabularies, can also be applied to any of these databases.

Perceptions about what computers can do also raise problems. Some see keyword searching, the searching of all words in catalog records, as a panacea. Various types of automatic cataloging or indexing have been the subject of experiment for decades. More recently the increased power of computers has enabled these efforts to become practicable, raising questions about the value of human intellectual effort in organizing and retrieving information (Crawford 1992 and 1999). Experience with the WWW suggests to many of us that machine analysis of documents has not yet achieved the reliability of human analysis. However, rejection of these means could limit our ability to provide better service. All of these wider computer concerns also affect the particular area of subject access.

SUBJECT ANALYSIS

Early in the days of online catalogs it became apparent, especially through the very influential studies commissioned by the Council on Library Resources, that catalog users did more subject searching in online catalogs than they had done in card catalogs (Matthews, Lawrence, and Ferguson 1983; Lawrence 1984; Markey 1984). Subject access to documents in library catalogs has always been challenging, and the difficulties and opportunities offered by automation have added a further dimension. In card catalogs, subject access was limited to subject headings for retrieval through the catalog and classification for retrieval at the shelves. In online catalogs, the free text or keyword searching capabilities make every word in the catalog record a potential access point.

The capacity for various types of combined term searching, including Boolean searching and limiting by elements such as language and date, stretches the uses of library databases beyond anything a card catalog could provide. Such options have created concomitant problems in user education and information overload (Borgman 1983). They have not saved money, but they have made catalog information more widely and flexibly available than was possible with card catalogs. The current blurring of the lines between library catalogs, indexing and abstracting databases (often available online through library catalogs, as mentioned previously), and the WWW expands the application of subject access standards without leaving behind questions that have been matters of concern for decades.

The traditional concerns of subject analysis still apply in the online environment. Retrieval by subject or topic is a different and usually more difficult task than identifying and retrieving particular known items, for two reasons. The first is that documents have labels useful for searching as known items (for example, the author of the item is Jane Austen and the title is *Pride and Prejudice*) that can be recognized comparatively readily in most cases and can therefore be used in searching for those items. Second, in the case of known item retrieval, only rarely can there be doubt that the item found is or is not the one sought. The labels for the subjects of documents, on the other hand, are often imprecise and ambiguous. With more interpretation involved, there is more likelihood that two individuals will disagree on the subject of a book than on its author. Thus, it is not always possible to be sure that what was retrieved is what was wanted, or that it was the best possible response to the request.

Differences of interpretation in subject analysis make standardization of databases for predictable retrieval more difficult to attain. However, differences of interpretation may well address the needs of different communities. Weighing the advantages of standardization for purposes of cooperation against the advantages of difference for adapting to particular contexts has been a constant issue for subject analysis in particular. Critiques of the mainstream biases of subject access standards have arisen in the literature of cataloging since at least the 1960s (Olson and Schlegl in press). However, such standardization has been the key to successful cooperation and sharing of catalog records and to transferring records from one system to another. Addressing this tradeoff in an automated environment offers more possibilities for flexibility than have yet been tapped.

Adding issues of online access to these issues of subject analysis creates a more complex mix of problems but also a more varied array of approaches to solutions. For example, classification in North American libraries has been used almost exclusively for shelf arrangement since Charles Cutter and others moved us away from the classified catalog (in class number order) to the dictionary catalog (in alphabetical order) in the nineteenth century. Now we are seeing a reawakening of electronic browsing in the form of categories in WWW search engines (Dodd 1996). This development suggests that library classifications that developed over more than a century can provide a better means of subject access. Only online access makes a return to classified browsing feasible beyond library shelves.

Another area of possibility is the idea of using some vocabulary (or perhaps a classification) as a switching language to translate among different languages, vocabularies, and perspectives (Cochrane 1998). The potential for new developments rests on two factors: the powerful evolving electronic environment and the rich tradition of subject analysis in libraries. The theory, principles, and practice of the latter, used creatively, will guide us to better subject access and help us use the former to better do our job of linking people and information.

REFERENCES

Borgman, Christine L. 1983. Psychological factors in online catalog use, or why readers fail. In *Training users of public access catalogs*, edited by Marsha Hamilton McClintock, 23–34. Washington, DC: Council on Library Resources.

Cochrane, Pauline. 1998. Library of Congress Subject Headings: Critique. Talk given as part of One-size-fits-all Subject Access Systems: Tailoring General Schemes to Meet the Needs of Specific Communities of Searchers, sponsored by the Subject Access Committee of the Association for Library Collections and Technical Services at the American Library Association, Annual Conference, 27 June, Washington, DC.

Crawford, Walt. 1992. *The online catalog book: Essays and examples.* New York: G. K. Hall; Toronto: Maxwell Macmillan Canada; New York: Maxwell Macmillan International.

———. 1999. The card catalog and other digital controversies: What's obsolete and what's not in the age of information. *American Libraries* 30 (1): 53–58.

Dodd, David G. 1996. Grass-roots cataloging and classification: Food for thought from World Wide Web subject-oriented hierarchical lists. *Library resources & technical services* 40: 275–86.

Lawrence, Gary S. 1984. Lessons from the CLR public online catalog study. In *Crossroads: Proceedings of the First National Conference of the Library and Information Technology Association, 1983,* edited by Michael Gorman, 84–93. Chicago: American Library Association.

Markey, Karen. 1984. *Subject searching in library catalogs: Before and after the introduction of online catalogs.* (OCLC Library Information and Computer Science Series No. 4). Dublin, OH: OCLC.

Matthews, Joseph R., Gary S. Lawrence, and Douglas K. Ferguson, eds. 1983. *Using online catalogs: A nationwide survey.* New York: Neal-Schuman.

Milstead, Jessica, and Susan Feldman. 1999. Metadata: Cataloging by any other name. . . . *Online* 23(1). Available: http://www.onlineinc.com/onlinemag/OL1999/milstead1.html. (Accessed May 9, 2001).

Olson, Hope A., and Rose Schlegl. In press. Critiques of subject access bias: A meta-analysis. *Cataloging & Classification Quarterly* 32(2).

2

The Database

INTRODUCTION

The database of an online catalog consists of a number of files. The most important from the perspective of subject access are the bibliographic file, the authority file, and the inverted file. The retrieval of subject or other information is the result of interaction among these files. Therefore, it is useful to examine each in some detail.

BIBLIOGRAPHIC FILE

The heart of a library catalog is the bibliographic file. It consists of bibliographic records that are surrogates representing or standing in the place of actual documents. A document is an item containing recorded information. It is usually physically present in a collection, such as a book or periodical, but it may be accessible through the library or information center, such as a World Wide Web (WWW) page. In either case, a surrogate can be created to represent the document. The collection of surrogates makes up the bibliographic file. The surrogates or bibliographic records are complex entities, containing information such as author, title, physical description, subject, and holdings (what volumes or copies a library actually has). In an online catalog each of these records is coded for electronic storage and manipulation so that a bibliographic record can be retrieved by a variety of means.

The international standard for coding electronic bibliographic records is the Machine Readable Cataloging (MARC) bibliographic format. The use of the MARC format began in the late 1950s, when the Library of Congress, the Association of Research Libraries, and the Council for Library Resources recognized that computer processing of bibliographic information offered potential to accommodate the coding of bibliographic records for greater efficiency, better searchability of data, and record transfer between libraries. Henriette Avram undertook the development of MARC in a farsighted project housed at the Library of Congress. The result was a format that has proven to be accommodating and flexible.

In an international context, MARC comes in various formats developed largely along national lines (Campos et al.1995). There are currently more than twenty different MARC formats, most identified by country, such as USMARC, CAN/MARC, and UKMARC. To allow exchange between these formats an international format, UNIMARC, was developed by the International Federation of Library Associations in 1977 (International Federation of Library Associations and Institutions 1996). It is used primarily as a medium of translation between MARC formats. Efforts toward even greater compatibility are exemplified by the recent "harmonization" between USMARC and CAN/MARC, which eliminated the differences between the two formats over the course of a four-year project and implementation. Such changes must be undertaken carefully because they have the potential to affect thousands of catalogs containing millions of bibliographic records. The success of such projects reflects the basic soundness of MARC.

Another major change in MARC over the last several years has been format integration. MARC was originally developed for books, with variants for six other types of publications (serials, videorecordings, etc.) following over the years. During the 1990s the differences among these formats were gradually consolidated into one MARC for all bibliographic records (Glennan 1995). The result has simplified the cataloger's task by requiring knowledge of only one format. Integration has added some aspects with potential to further enhance retrieval but has been developed to ensure that previously coded bibliographic records will not be incompatible with records coded in the new format. As a result, individual libraries may choose whether to upgrade old records by weighing available resources against perceived advantages. Again, these changes indicate the flexibility of the MARC format although they do not directly affect subject access.

Because MARC is an international standard and has become the single standard used in library catalogs, it is to a library's advantage to make full use of it. Libraries import MARC records in the process of copy cataloging, downloading records from other libraries to adapt to their own catalogs. This process is the electronic version of the centuries-old tradition of sharing information between libraries. Libraries also export MARC records, not only as their contribution to sharing but also as they join networks or consortia or migrate from one online system to another. The systems employed to create the interface between databases and people can change as the software used incorporates new features. However, the database itself is much more difficult to change. Few libraries have the human resources to go back and change records created over the course of many years. Therefore, the flexibility and compatibility that MARC offers are extremely valuable in allowing the intellectual labor of cataloging to be moved and adapted to different contexts. A MARC record is like a well-organized soft-sided suitcase. It is portable, expands and contracts to fit its contents, fits into a car trunk or airplane hold with other suitcases, and keeps the contents organized so that they can be readily unpacked at the end of a journey if they were well-packed to begin with.

The following discussion of MARC is intentionally brief and focuses mainly on subject access. For a fuller discussion of MARC see Deborah Byrne (1998) or Walt Crawford (1982 and 1984); for a more general summary see Betty Furrie (1998).

Structure of the MARC Bibliographic Record

This flexible suitcase was designed with the following in mind:

> The philosophy behind MARC . . . was the design of one format structure (the physical representation in a machine-readable medium) capable of containing bibliographic information for all forms of material (books, serials, maps, music, journal articles, etc.) and related records (name and subject reference records, etc.). The *structure*, or "empty container," the *content designators* (tags, indicators, and subfield codes) used to explicitly identify or to additionally characterize the data elements, and the *content*, the data itself (author's name, titles, etc.), are the three components of the format. (Avram 1975, 7)

The structure, the first component of the MARC record, has three sections: a leader, a directory, and variable fields.

Leader

The leader is the first twenty-four characters of a MARC record. The purpose of the leader is to provide information necessary to process the record. That is, it tells the system how to read a particular record. Each character represents a piece of tightly coded information. For example, the first five characters represent the length of the record, the sixth character represents the record status, the seventh the type of material, and so forth.

Directory

The record directory is an index to the location of variable-length fields within the record. It consists of a variable number of fixed-length entries. Each of these entries is made up of three elements: a three-character field tag, a four-character field length, and a five-character starting position. The leader and directory facilitate the use of the MARC record in general, but they do not have a specific impact on subject access.

Variable Fields

The variable fields contain the bibliographic data that are displayed in a catalog along with more coded data relating to the record and the item cataloged. This information is divided into fields, each of which has a three-character *tag*. For example, a subject heading field for a topic is coded with the tag 650:

```
650 ƀ0 $aWomen travelers $zAfrica $vBiography.
```

One or two *indicators* may be used to provide the system with information about a particular field. These indicators are displayed immediately after the tag—in this case, ƀ0. Here, the second indicator is coded 0 to indicate the source of the subject heading, the *Library of Congress Subject Headings* (LCSH). In this and following examples ƀ indicates that the character position is blank; that is, either the indicator has no values or no information has been provided. Each field is further subdivided by *subfields,* which are identified by subfield codes consisting of a delimiter (in North America usually a $ or ≠) and a subfield value. In this example the subfields are $a, $z, and $v—each denoting a different type of content, as is discussed further later in this chapter. Indicators and subfields are specific to each field, so a second indicator of 0 in a 650 field does not mean the same thing as an indicator of 0 in another field.

The variable fields are grouped by function with the following tags (XX stands for numbers from 00 to 99):

```
0XX   Control information, identification and
      classification numbers, etc.

1XX   Main entries

2XX   Titles and title paragraph

3XX   Physical description, etc.

4XX   Series statements

5XX   Notes

6XX   Subject access fields

7XX   Added entries and linking fields

8XX   Series added entries, etc.

9XX   Other, including local
```

This structure of the variable fields corresponds roughly to the contents of a traditional catalog entry as developed in card catalogs. However, because automated catalog records can be searched in far more flexible ways than can card catalogs, subject access is not limited to the 6XX fields. Free text or keyword searching of most or all fields has both advantages and disadvantages, but it is certainly useful as an option for subject access made possible by automated catalog records (see Chapter 3 for a full discussion). The MARC format also makes electronic browsing by classification possible for general catalog users. It uses fields in the 0XX range for this purpose. Neither of these approaches was feasible in a manual environment.

MARC Fields for Subject Access

MARC bibliographic records have three types of subject access fields: the 6XX, containing standardized subject terms; fields 050 to 088, containing classification and call numbers; and most of the 2XX to 5XX fields of the description, offering potential for keyword searching (although other access point fields in 1XX and 7XX may also serve this purpose).

6XX Fields

The subject access fields coded 600 to 658 contain controlled vocabulary terms (except field 653) "that provide additional access to a bibliographic record through a heading or term that is constructed according to established subject cataloging or thesaurus-building principles and guidelines" (Library of Congress. Network Development and MARC Office, 1998a). The specific fields in this range are:

600	Subject added entry-Personal name
610	Subject added entry-Corporate name
611	Subject added entry-Meeting name
630	Subject added entry-Uniform title
650	Subject added entry-Topical term
651	Subject added entry-Geographic name
653	Index term-Uncontrolled
654	Subject added entry-Faceted topical terms
655	Index term-Genre form
656	Index term-Occupation
657	Index term-Function
658	Index term-Curriculum objective

For subject added entry fields 600–651, the second indicator denotes the subject heading system or thesaurus used to construct the heading:

0	Library of Congress Subject Headings/LC authority files
1	LC subject headings for children's literature
2	Medical Subject Headings/NLM authority files
3	National Agricultural Library subject authority file
4	Source not specified
5	Canadian Subject Headings/NLC authority file
6	Répertoire des vedettes-matière/NLC authority file
7	Source specified in subfield $2

This indicator is extremely important. It will tell a library if the headings in catalog records copied from another library are compatible with the standards it uses. For example, if a library in the United States copies a record from a library in Canada it is not likely to want headings with the second indicator 5, which means that they are from the *Canadian Subject Headings*. General libraries may not want to use subject headings coded 2 because they will be *Medical Subject Headings* (MeSH). However, most libraries in North America will be pleased to see headings coded 0, indicating that they are valid LCSH, and libraries using more specialized vocabularies will want to be able to identify headings from those vocabularies. Further, automated systems can be set to display subject headings from only certain sources. For example, a library that uses only LCSH has the option to display only LCSH, even if it has bibliographic records that contain other standards, by setting the system to display only headings with the second indicator 0. Other headings can be allowed to remain in the records yet not be displayed, saving work in editing and allowing for their display at some later date should that be desired. So a library that uses only English-language headings may simply not display entries with the second indicator 6 for the French translation of LCSH, *Répertoire des vedettes-matière*. If the same library should choose to have a bilingual catalog at a later date, those headings will not be lost but will display simply by changing the instructions to the system.

The first four fields in this range—600, 610, 611, and 630—are used to describe a document about a person, a corporate body (including a conference or other type of meeting), or a specific work. These headings are typically governed by the *Anglo-American Cataloging Rules*, 2d ed., 1988 Revision (AACR2R) in countries that use those rules. Their indicators give information about their content; for example, the first indicator in field 600 shows whether a personal name is a forename (0), surname (1), or family name (2). Their subfields also reflect the content of the cataloging rules, breaking down the 600 field, for example, into elements such as the personal name itself ($a), the dates associated with the name ($d), and the fuller form of the name ($q), as shown in the following examples, as well as many other possibilities:

```
600 10 $aEliot, T. S. $q(Thomas Stearns), $d1888-1965.
600 00 $aCher, $d1946-
```

Field 600 is used for works *about* a specific person, such as a biography or literary criticism, not for works *by* that person.

Corporate names have a first indicator coded to show that they are entered either indirectly (1) or directly (2) and a special subfield ($b) for their subdivisions:

```
610 10 $aUganda. $bMinistry of Gender and Community
       Development
610 20 $aInternational Federation of Library
       Associations and Institutions
```

Field 610 is used for works *about* a specific corporate body, such as its annual report or a history of the organization.

Likewise, documents may be *about* conferences or meetings and have headings with subfields to accommodate their specialized AACR2R form of entry:

```
611 20 $aInternational Conference on Cataloguing
       Principles $d(1961 : $cParis, France)
```

Uniform titles (standardized forms of titles used to gather different manifestations of the same work) have subfields to identify names of parts or sections of a work, languages of translation, or elements more specific to a given form:

```
630 ⌴0 $aTalmud. $pHorayot.
630 ⌴0 $aTalmud. $lEnglish.
```

The uniform titles for works with an author or creator are subfields of the personal name. Therefore, most works of music are coded in field 600 with a subfield $t for the uniform title and further subfields for other aspects of the work such as the key in which the music is written:

```
600 10 $aMozart, Wolfgang Amadeus, $d1756-1791.
        $tSerenades, $nK.250, $rDmajor. $pRondeau
```

Remember that these fields are subject headings and describe documents *about* these works.

The first indicator and the subfields for the 600, 610, 611, and 630 fields are the same as for main and added entries for personal names, corporate names, and uniform titles in the 1XX and 7XX fields. This parallel structure of the fields facilitates authority control, as discussed later in this chapter.

Field 650 is for topical terms. Its first indicator identifies the level of the subject, primary or secondary, although this information is often not supplied, as in the following examples. In subject cataloging practice, the primary subject heading describes the major focus of the document and usually corresponds to the subject represented by the classification number.

The main heading in a subject heading string is coded in subfield $a:

```
650 ᏏO $aWomen travelers

650 ᏏO $aClimatic changes

650 ᏏO $aAfrican literature
```

Field 651 is similarly formatted to contain the name of a geographic place used as a subject entry in its subfield $a:

```
651 ᏏO $aAfrica

651 ᏏO $aAmazon River

651 ᏏO $aContinental Divide National Scenic Trail
```

Subject added entry fields 600–651 also have four subfields specifically designed for the subdivisions of subject headings:

```
$v    Form subdivision
$x    General subdivision
$y    Chronological subdivision
$z    Geographic subdivision
```

These four subfields correspond to the four types of subdivisions in LCSH: form, topical, chronological, and geographic (see Chapter 6). The following examples show some of the many variations these MARC fields can accommodate:

```
600 00 $aGautama Buddha $vBiography $vEarly works to
        1800

610 10 $aUnited Nations $zAfrica

611 20 $aEpsom Derby, England (Horse race)$xHistory
        $y20th century

630 00 $aKoran $xCriticism, interpretation, etc.
        $xHistory $y19th century
```

```
650 ⊮0 $aSupermarkets $zFrance $xCheckout counters
651 ⊮5 $aSaskatchewan $xPolitics and government
       $y1971-1982
```

These coded headings will, of course, be displayed without the coding in online catalogs. The precise form of display may vary between online catalogs, but it will be
something like the following:

```
Gautama Buddha - Biography - Early works to 1800

United Nations - Africa

Epsom Derby, England (Horse race) - History - 20th century

Koran - Criticism, interpretation, etc. - History - 19th
   century

Supermarkets - France - Checkout counters

Saskatchewan - Politics and government - 1971-1982
```

The format and punctuation will depend on the options chosen by a library from those
offered by its vendor. The preceding discussion gives only a sample of coding for the
subject added entry fields. For more complex and unusual examples there are numerous other subfields.

The index term fields 653 and 655–658 are not commonly used in online catalogs at this time. Field 653 contains keywords supplied by a cataloger or indexer, but
not part of a controlled vocabulary such as a subject heading list or thesaurus (see
Chapter 3). It offers potential for considerable flexibility in augmenting subject access. Fields 655–658 allow indexing by genre, occupation, function, and curriculum
objective according to established vocabularies. Field 654 contains subject added entries constructed from faceted vocabularies such as the *Art and Architecture Thesaurus*. Fields 653–658 are used mainly for special types of collections that require
access to elements not commonly included in general controlled vocabularies such as
LCSH. The coming exception to this is the Library of Congress's intention to begin to
code field 655 indicating genre (Yee 1998).

Fields That Contribute to Keyword Searching

MARC bibliographic records contain a number of other fields that, although not
designed to be subject access points, do denote, at least to a degree, the subject contents of the works for keyword searching. Although any field in the MARC record
could conceivably assist in subject access, those that are primarily useful contain
titles and notes (see also Piternick 1985). In particular, the title proper and other title
information in field 245 $a and 245 $b often provide keywords that cannot be represented in a controlled vocabulary. For example, the phrase *unpaid labor* in the following title is not represented in the subject headings because there is no LCSH heading
for unpaid labor:

```
245 10 $aWomen's paid and unpaid labor : $bthe work
       transfer in health care and retailing / $cNona
       Y. Glazer.

650 ⊮0 $aWomen $xEmployment $zUnited States.
```

```
650 ƀ0 $aWomen $zUnited States $xEconomic conditions.

650 ƀ0 $aCapitalism $zUnited States.

650 ƀ0 $aSelf-service (Economics) $zUnited States.

650 ƀ0 $aService industries $zUnited States.

650 ƀ0 $aRetail trade $zUnited States.

650 ƀ0 $aMedical care $zUnited States.

650 ƀ0 $aHome care services $zUnited States.
```

The word *postcolonial* in the next title is not contained in the subject headings for this record for the same reason:

```
245 10 $aResistance in postcolonial African fiction /
        $cNeil Lazarus.

600 10 $aArmah, Ayi Kwei, $d1939- $xCriticism and
        interpretation.

650 ƀ0 $aAfrican fiction $y20th century $xHistory and
        criticism.

651 ƀ0 $aAfrica $xIntellectual life $y20th century.

650 ƀ0 $aDecolonization in literature.

650 ƀ0 $aRadicalism in literature.

651 ƀ0 $aAfrica $xIn literature.

651 ƀ0 $aGhana $xIn literature.
```

The 5XX notes fields also provide the opportunity for much more specific terms than are typically included in the subject entries (see Chapter 5 for a full discussion of specificity) as well as including keywords not occurring in the title. Including the table of contents of a document in field 505 is a common way of augmenting a biblio-graphic record for keyword searching. In an edited collection or conference proceed-ings, individual papers or chapters may not be reflected in the subject entries designed to cover the entire document. A contents note can provide more information on the actual contents. For example, the contents note in the following can be far more spe-cific than standard subject heading practice:

```
245 00 $aTropical rainfall anomalies and climatic
        change / $cHermann Flohn (ed.).

505 ƀ0 $aTeleconnections of tropical rainfall
        anomalies and the southern oscillation /
        H. Behrend — Teleconnections in the Caribbean
        and northern South America and the southern
        oscillation / C. Becker and H. Flohn — Zonal
        surface winds and rainfall in the equatorial
        Pacific and Atlantic / H. Flohn — Nauru rainfall,
        1893-1977 / H.-P. Junk — Oceanic upwelling and
        air-sea-exchange of carbon dioxide and water
        vapor as a key for large-scale climatic change?
        / K.-H. Weber and H. Flohn.
```

```
650 ƀ0  $aRainfall anomalies $zTropics.

650 ƀ0   $aClimatic changes $zTropics.
```

Field 520, the summary note, can provide similar access:

```
245 00 $aHistory and culture of Africa $h[transparencies]

520    $aPart 1 reveals the heights of civilization
       achieved in Africa by the empires of Egypt,
       Kush, Ethiopia, Sudan, ancient Gana, and Mali
       and the accomplishments of their great kings,
       scientists, and artists. Part 2 traces the
       emergence of Africa into the modern world, with
       emphasis on the effects of the slave trade and
       colonialism and the impact of Africa's leading
       political figures.

651 ƀ0 $aAfrica $xHistory.
```

One can quickly see from these examples that specific topics such as *teleconnections* or *slave trade* and specific places such as *Nauru* or *Kush* would not be included in subject headings representing the entire document because they make up only a relatively small part of each work, but they are potentially useful access points for people seeking these topics. However, combining *teleconnections* and *Nauru* in a search would erroneously retrieve the first record.

Classification Fields for Subject Access

Classification is usually thought of as a means of finding an item on the library shelf once the surrogate has been found in the catalog. However, just as classification provides for browsing at the shelf, it can also organize bibliographic records in an online catalog for electronic browsing. The most likely fields for this purpose are:

```
050   Library of Congress call number
055   Call number/Class number assigned in Canada
060   National Library of Medicine call number
070   National Agricultural Library call number
074   GPO item number
080   Universal Decimal Classification number
082   Dewey Decimal call number
084   Other classification number
086   Government document call number
```

A full discussion of how classification can be used in searching appears in Chapters 7 and 8. It is sufficient to note here that the MARC bibliographic format, as it currently exists, can facilitate subject access through classification. It is our belief that this form of access has been underutilized and will become more prominent in the near future as people accustomed to searching the simplistic classifications of the WWW search engines come to realize the potential of the much more sophisticated library classifications.

Flexibility and the Future of the
MARC Bibliographic Format

The MARC format for bibliographic records has proven to be revolutionary. The development of bibliographic utilities in particular and the growth of library automation in general can be largely attributed to this bibliographic standard. There are, of course, criticisms of the format. The major and most valid criticism is that the MARC bibliographic format is simply an automation of catalog cards. Indeed, new technologies in general tend to begin by mimicking their predecessors and only develop their own potential over time. However, in the case of MARC it is probably more appropriate to note that the layout of the variable fields reflects cataloging standards rather than catalog cards. Fields for bibliographic description and main and added entries are based on the principles codified at the 1961 International Conference on Cataloguing Principles (commonly referred to as the Paris Principles, they have their roots in centuries of library cataloging) and the International Standard Bibliographic Description (ISBD) developed at the 1969 International Meeting of Cataloguing Experts in Copenhagen.

The MARC variable fields dealing with subject access have the potential to reflect a large number of different standards. The second indicator of fields 600–651, discussed previously, shows the wide range of vocabularies that can be accommodated in these fields. The other 6XX fields offer coding for vocabularies beyond the scope of typical library catalogs. The fields for classification numbers previously discussed add to this range of options. Finally, the flexibility of what can be included in the 5XX notes fields allows enhancement through free text for keyword searching. It is difficult to imagine what type of subject access information could not be contained in the MARC bibliographic record format. This is not to say that improvement is not possible; for example, finer coding of classification numbers could allow for searching their individual facets. However, MARC has shown flexibility in its revisions in the past and offers that potential for the future.

If anything can make MARC less pervasive it is likely to be recent interest in using metadata for a variety of different information resources, especially electronic documents on the WWW (for speculation about the use of different models within systems, see Green 1996). *Metadata* is often defined as data about data. Metadata are akin to the information in a catalog record, basic information that acts as a surrogate for the document itself. On the WWW, metadata are data attached to a document to make it more searchable by representing the attributes of that document (whether text, graphic, or sound) in a standardized form. Metadata currently overlap with cataloging in the bibliographic control of electronic documents. However, there is no fundamental conceptual difference between bibliographic records and metadata.

Various metadata standards such as the Dublin Core were developed during the 1990s (Caplan and Guenther 1996; Milstead and Feldman 1999). The Association of Library Collections and Technical Services of the American Library Association has a Metadata Task Force. Metadata include the standard types of information such as author/creator, title, source, and some kind of locator (e.g., a Uniform Resource Locator or URL, which is the address of a WWW document), but also include subject access information. Whether this will ultimately be classification or subject headings or thesauri is unclear at the moment, although much is being done in the area of classification.

Metadata usually refers to recently developed standards for creating surrogates to stand in the place of and to summarize the characteristics of larger items such as documents and graphics. However, metadata are both simpler and more complex than that. Metadata in a broad sense are what we have been doing in our field for centuries. Catalog records and index entries are metadata. The principles that apply to our traditional forms of organizing information will also apply in new ways to new formats for metadata.

The least explored aspect of metadata is subject access. Typically, metadata standards enumerate the types of information that will be contained in a record. These standards are much like the ISBD or the Paris Principles for access points in catalog records. For example, the Dublin Core has fifteen elements (*Dublin Core metadata element set,* 2000):

Title	Format
Creator	Identifier
Subject	Source
Description	Language
Publisher	Relation
Contributor	Coverage
Date	Rights
Type	

However, unlike cataloging standards, metadata standards do not necessarily prescribe how the content will be formatted. For example, when a subject field is defined in the Dublin Core, a specific vocabulary (controlled or natural) is not specified. From the heights of sophisticated cataloging we might see these new metadata standards as undeveloped. Yet, they offer opportunities for standardized representation of a much wider range of materials and in a much wider range of contexts than does current cataloging practice. Whether controlled subject access vocabularies become an integral part of these standards remains to be seen.

An important distinction to be made among the different standards discussed as metadata is between those that outline content and those that encode it. Metadata standards such as the Dublin Core and specialized archival, visual arts, geographical, and other standards generally identify the elements to be included in a surrogate. Other standards such as SGML, HTML, and XML encode those elements into machine-readable form. The encoding standards are more like MARC except that they tend not to have as specialized a purpose.

Because MARC is a specialized encoding standard, the metadata standards often seem to be parallel to it. However, it is important to note that although MARC is flexible in terms of what it can contain, it was originally designed to hold catalog records constructed according to ISBD, the Paris Principles, and the kinds of controlled vocabularies (subject headings and classifications) discussed in subsequent chapters of this book. Although Dublin Core designates categories of content, MARC reflects and contains categories of content. Bearing in mind this distinction, a comparison of the two is still useful for seeing the similarities and differences.

A significant question for the future is how metadata standards will evolve in relation to subject access. It is too early to be certain, but calls are already being made for controlled vocabularies to apply in the many metadata contexts. Traditional library vocabularies may be useful for some of these purposes. Undoubtedly, the principles embodied in traditional vocabularies will be useful if metadata developers are not going to waste their energies reinventing the wheel instead of developing what is already available into more adaptable standards.

Whether library catalogs are likely to stay separate from metadata for electronic documents or whether the boundary between the two will continue to blur is also not predictable. The latter seems most likely given the current trend toward linking online catalogs with electronic indexes and other databases and the increasing frequency with which online catalogs are being mounted on the WWW. Work has already been done on mapping the Dublin Core and other metadata formats to MARC (Library of Congress. Network Development and MARC Standards Office 1997). Even more directly related to the relations between conventional cataloging in MARC format and metadata such as Dublin Core is the Cooperative Online Resource Catalog (CORC) project at OCLC. In a growing union database, records are being established for WWW pages. These records can be imported or exported as MARC, Dublin Core, or other formats and can be combined into different kinds of products such as electronic pathfinders (OCLC 2000). This area will be an exciting one to watch or, better yet, be involved in, in the near future.

AUTHORITY FILE

The previous discussion covered the bibliographic records that constitute a file of surrogates for individual documents. Each record in the bibliographic file represents a unique document. A second file works alongside the bibliographic file: the authority file. From the perspective of subject access, the subject heading authority records contain the authorized forms of subject headings, their synonyms, and their related headings. The authorized form or authoritative heading is a particular term in a particular form which has been designated to represent one concept or topic (see the discussion of controlled vocabulary in Chapter 3 and Auld 1982; Avram 1984; Clack 1988 and 1990; Malinconico 1985; Micco 1996a and 1996b; Tillett 1989). Each authority record represents one authoritative subject heading and gives information about that heading and its relation to other terms and headings. The purposes of an authority record are 1) to maintain consistency in the choice and form of heading used to represent a given concept and 2) to relate that concept to others in the database. Controlled vocabularies are, in essence, the content of authority files. Authority records are the electronic manifestations of controlled vocabularies.

The manner in which an authority file operates varies from one system to another. However, the common factor is that each subject heading in each bibliographic record is verified against the authority file. In some systems the cataloger must instruct the system to find a heading in the authority file. Other systems will do this automatically and report any discrepancies to the cataloger. In either case the authority record "controls" the heading.

MARC Authority Records

Just as bibliographic records are commonly found in catalogs in MARC bibliographic format, so authority records are typically in MARC authority format. MARC authority format has an overall structure similar to bibliographic records: leader, directory, and variable fields (Library of Congress 1998b). The leader and directory have the same purposes as in the bibliographic record. The major differences are in the variable fields. Here the most significant field is the 1XX, which contains the authoritative heading. The first digit, 1, indicates that it is the authoritative heading; the second and third digits indicate what kind of heading it is, as in the bibliographic records:

```
X00    Personal name
X10    Corporate name
X11    Meeting name
X30    Uniform title
X50    Topical heading
X51    Geographic name
```

A topical subject heading will be in field 650 in a bibliographic record and it will be in field 150 in the authority record. Matching the second and third digits allows a system to match topical headings in bibliographic records to topical headings in authority records. The same is true for other types of headings, so a main (100) or added (700) entry for a personal name in a bibliographic record and a subject heading (600) for that personal name will all match the same authority record. In the authority record the authoritative form of the personal name will be coded 100.

Synonyms and other forms of a heading not used as authoritative headings will be coded 4XX. So in the authority record

```
150 ʋ0 $aWomen travelers
450 ʋ0 $wnnen $aTravelers, Women
550 ʋ0 $wgnnn $aTravelers
```

the 450 (nonauthoritative form of the heading) will produce a reference to the 150 (authoritative heading) in the online catalog, saying something like "for *Travelers, Women* see *Women travelers.*"

Relationships between authoritative headings are also coded in MARC authority records. Broader, narrower, and related terms are in the 5XX fields. Again, the second and third digits indicate the type of heading, so the 550 *Travelers* is a reference to another topical heading.

These 4XX and 5XX fields all contain a subfield $w that gives information about the type of reference in its first character. It is of particular interest in relation to controlled vocabularies in the 5XX fields, where $wg . . . indicates a broader heading, $wh . . . represents a narrower heading, and $wn . . . does not specify the type of relationship and is usually interpreted as an associative or related term heading. The $wh . . . narrower heading is not coded by the Library of Congress and most other libraries because the $wg . . . of the broader heading can be used to consistently create the reciprocal reference to the narrower heading (this relationship is explained more fully in Chapter 6 on LCSH). For example, "550 b0 $wgnnn $aTravelers" indicates that *Travelers* is a broader term in relation to *Women travelers*. It will produce a reference in the catalog saying something like "*Travelers* see also narrower term *Women travelers*" and the reciprocal reference "*Women travelers* see also broader term *Travelers*."

The inclusion of 4XX and 5XX fields in MARC authority records to accommodate references means that instead of references from subject headings having to be repeated each time a heading is used in a bibliographic record, they need be entered into the catalog only once, through the authority records. That is, no matter how many records use the heading *Women travelers*, the references from *Travelers, Women* and *Travelers* appear only in the authority record and it is from the authority record that the references that appear in the online public catalog are derived. The potential for different types of display of references is illustrated in Figures 2.1 and 2.2, which show the current two-stage process for viewing references in the Library of Congress's catalog (http://lcweb.loc.gov/catalog/).

Figure 2.1 shows the result of a subject search for *Travelers*. Clicking on "MORE INFO" takes the searcher to the next screen, shown in Figure 2.2. It gives the narrower and related terms for *Travelers*. A more direct approach is shown in Figure 2.3, page 21, from the University of Alberta's catalog (http://gate.library.ualberta.ca). References are displayed in the browsable list of headings and further information about a heading (reflecting the MARC authority record) is available by clicking on *(about)* where it occurs. Headings without an authority record have no *(about)* on which to click. These two displays are not the only possibilities, but serve to demonstrate how flexible the MARC record can be within the context of an online catalog.

Figure 2.1. Library of Congress subject browse results.

LIBRARY OF CONGRESS ONLINE CATALOG

Database New Headings Titles Account Request Help Search Start
Name Search List List Status an Item History Over

Database Name: Library of Congress Online Catalog
Information for: Travelers

See, See Also, and Narrower Term References:
* *Broader Terms not currently available*

Reference Information
Narrower Term:Church work with tourists, travelers, etc.
Narrower Term:Visitors, Foreign
See Also:Voyages and travels
Narrower Term:Women travelers
Narrower Term:Muslim travelers

Database · New Search · Headings List ·Titles List ·Help (Contents) · Account Status · Help (This Screen)

Figure 2.2. Library of Congress display of references.

A recent development in authority control is the decision to make authority records for the subdivisions that can be added to subject headings. (See Chapter 6 for an explanation of the usage of subdivisions in LCSH.) The subdivisions in these authority records will be coded 18X:

```
180   Topical subdivisions
181   Geographic subdivisions
182   Chronological subdivisions
185   Form subdivisions
```

These authority records correspond to the subfields $v, $x, $y, $z used in fields 600–651 in bibliographic records as described above (Library of Congress. Cataloging Policy and Support Office 1998). The Library of Congress began distribution of these authority records in 1998 (Yee 1998). This advance makes authority control more flexible, enabling control over the individual building blocks of subject heading strings (Drabenstott 1992).

Further, to match the intention of including genre headings more often in field 655 of bibliographic records, the Library of Congress has begun creating authority records for form/genre headings, with these authoritative headings coded 155.

TRAVELERS

- Travelers. (LC) (about) (17 titles)
  - *Search also under:* Commuters.
  - *Search also under:* Visitors, Foreign.
  - *Search also under:* Voyages and travels.
  - *Search also under:* Women travelers.
- Travelers -- Africa -- Biography. (LC) (1 title)
- Travelers, African -- History -- 16th century. (LC) (1 title)
- Travelers, Aged. (LC)
  - *Search under:* Aged -- Travel.
- Travelers Aid Association of America. (LC) (about)
- Travelers -- Alberta. (LC) (2 titles)
- Travelers, American. (LC) (2 titles)
- Travelers -- Arabian peninsula. (LC) (1 title)
- Travelers -- Arabian Peninsula -- Biography. (LC) (1 title)
- Travelers -- Asia -- Biography -- Juvenile literature. (LC) (1 title)
- Travelers -- Asia, Southeastern. (LC) (1 title)
- Travelers -- Attitudes. (LC) (1 title)
- Travelers -- Belgium. (LC) (1 title)
- Travelers -- Biography. (LC) (5 titles)
- Travelers -- Bosnia and Hercegovina. (LC) (1 title)
- Travelers -- British Columbia. (LC) (4 titles)
- Travelers -- British Columbia -- Statistics. (LC) (1 title)
- Travelers -- Canada. (LC) (6 titles)
- Travelers -- Canada -- Statistics. (LC) (3 titles)
- Travelers -- Canada -- Statistics. (LC) (1 title)

(next)

Figure 2.3. University of Alberta GATE subject browse.

MARC Classification Format

An additional file that has become available only recently can be created using the MARC format for classification (Library of Congress 1998c). It is similar to the MARC authority format used for subject headings in that it contains the terms of a controlled vocabulary, in this case a classification. Each record represents one classification number and information related to it. The MARC classification format was developed in 1990 and has been used to automate *Library of Congress Classification* (LCC), completed in 1995 (Guenther 1996). The *Dewey Decimal Classification* (DDC) was automated prior to completion of the MARC classification format, but it is in a roughly compatible format. Should classification become more commonly used as a subject access device, as seems likely, the MARC classification format will become increasingly important.

Obviously, the sophistication of MARC in relation to subject access is continuing to grow. It will be interesting to observe over the next several years whether this continuing flexibility addresses the needs of increasing electronic publishing and electronic access or if some other form of metadata will take precedence.

INVERTED FILE

A final type of database, the inverted file, exists in online systems to enable efficient retrieval. The bibliographic files previously discussed are of a type referred to as "sequential," "direct," or "linear." In such a file the records are located in a sequence much like the books on a shelf. The efficiency of this arrangement for retrieval is limited because each element of each record must be searched to gather the records that correspond to a particular search. Inverted files are created automatically by the system to make this process quicker. In an inverted file individual elements are extracted from each bibliographic record and put into a separate file. This file is never seen by the online catalog user but is read by the system. Each entry in the inverted file may consist of a field, a subfield, or a word. So for the following record

```
050 00 $aDT476.23.K56 $bB58 1994
082 00 $a916.604/312 $220
100 1  $aBlunt, Alison.
245 10 $aTravel, gender, and imperialism : $bMary
       Kingsley and West Africa / $cAlison Blunt.
260    $aNew York : $bGuilford Press, $c1994.
300    $ax, 190 p. : $bill., map ; $c24 cm.
440 ʙ0 $aMappings
504    $aIncludes bibliographical references
       (p. 165-181) and index.
600 10 $aKingsley, Mary Henrietta, $d1862-1900
       $xJourneys $zAfrica, West.
650 ʙ0 $aWomen travelers $zAfrica $vBiography.
651 ʙ0 $aAfrica, West $xDescription and travel.
```

the inverted file for searching keywords might include the following:

Blunt	Africa
Alison	Guilford
travel	Henrietta
gender	journeys
imperialism	women
Mary	travelers
Kingsley	biography
West	description

However, an inverted file for searching subject headings as a controlled vocabulary rather than keywords would include only three entries for this record:

Kingsley, Mary Henrietta, 1862-1900 Journeys Africa, West

Women travelers Africa Biography

Africa, West Description and travel.

A list of all elements from all records in the database is compiled by the system and codes are automatically attached to indicate which records contain a given element. Each record in the bibliographic database will have a unique code that will be attached to the entries in the inverted file. So of the following abbreviated records used as examples in this chapter we might say that the numbers are:

record 1   245 10 $aTravel, gender, and imperialism

          600 10 $aKingsley, Mary Henrietta, $d1862-1900
                 $xJourneys $zAfrica, West.

          650 ᗺ0 $aWomen travelers $zAfrica $vBiography.

          651 ᗺ0 $aAfrica, West $xDescription and travel.

record 2   245 10 $aResistance in postcolonial African fiction

          651 ᗺ0 $aAfrica $xIntellectual life $y20th century.

          651 ᗺ0 $aAfrica $xIn literature.

record 3   245 00 $aHistory and culture of Africa

          651 ᗺ0 $aAfrica $xHistory.

record 4   245 10 $aWomen's paid and unpaid labor

          650 ᗺ0 $aWomen $xEmployment $zUnited States.

          650 ᗺ0 $aWomen $zUnited States $xEconomic
                 conditions.

In the inverted file for subject keyword searching the following entries would gather these records (other entries in the inverted file would retrieve only one of these records, e.g., travelers 1, or history 3):

          Africa   1,2,3
          women   1,4

If a searcher entered the word *Africa* the system would search the inverted file, find the entry "Africa 1,2,3," and retrieve the bibliographic records numbered 1, 2, and 3. Similarly, if the word *women* were searched the system would find the appropriate entry in the inverted file and retrieve the bibliographic records linked to that entry, numbers 1 and 4.

Because the inverted file gathers all the instances of a particular element, it has done part of the retrieval task before a search is even performed. Therefore, it expedites searching efficiency. Because the inverted file is created and saved in the system, it requires more storage space. Fortunately, storage space is of less concern than it was in the past, although response time is still an issue in online catalogs. The inverted file is still, on balance, a useful means of facilitating searching and retrieval.

In choosing and setting up a system for subject searching, it is important to consider how the inverted file will be defined. Will there be separate files for subject keyword searching and subject heading searching? Will all individual words be included (except for a stopword list of articles, conjunctions, and prepositions), or will some entries be phrases? How large will stopword lists be? Which fields and subfields of the MARC bibliographic record will be included in which inverted file? Each of these decisions will affect the system's subject searching capabilities. What is in the bibliographic record can only be searched if the system is set up to do so.

CONCLUSION

Subject access in online catalogs employs three types of files: bibliographic, authority, and inverted. The bibliographic and authority files typically use MARC format as the international standard. The bibliographic file contains a record for each unique document in a collection or to which a particular catalog is giving access (for example, it could also be a WWW document). A bibliographic record is a surrogate that stands in the place of an actual document. The records in the authority file represent headings rather than documents. These headings are the authoritative forms of access points used to maintain consistency in choice and form of term. For subject analysis, the authority records represent subject headings, subdivisions of subject headings, or terms in other types of vocabularies. A similar type of record is the MARC classification format that accommodates entries for classification numbers.

The inverted files in an online catalog are digested versions of the bibliographic files. They do not provide intellectual content as the bibliographic and authority files do, but they allow for more efficient searching.

The labor-intensive nature of cataloging, especially subject cataloging, is good motivation for following international standards such as the MARC format. The ability to exchange records, sharing bibliographic data, is based on compatible systems. For now, deviation from MARC format will hinder this exchange and should not be considered lightly. However, in the future other types of formats such as those implied by various metadata projects may influence either the further evolution of MARC or migration to some other format. The nature of catalog databases will continue to be an arena of change.

REFERENCES

Auld, Larry. 1982. Authority control: An eighty year review. *Library Resources & Technical Services* 26: 319–30.

Avram, Henriette D. 1975. *MARC: Its history and implication.* Washington, DC: Library of Congress.

———. 1984. Authority control and its place. *Journal of Academic Librarianship* 9: 331–35.

Byrne, Deborah J. 1998. *MARC manual: Understanding and using MARC records*. 2d ed. Englewood, CO: Libraries Unlimited.

Campos, Fernanda M., M. Inês Lopes, and Rosa M Galvão. 1995. MARC formats and their use: An overview. *Program* 29: 445–59.

Caplan, Priscilla, and Rebecca Guenther. 1996. Metadata for Internet resources: The Dublin Core Metadata Elements Set and its mapping to USMARC. *Cataloging & Classification Quarterly* 22: 43–58.

Clack, Doris H. 1988. Authority control and linked bibliographic databases. *Cataloging & Classification Quarterly* 8: 35–46.

———. 1990. *Authority control: Principles, applications, and instructions*. Chicago: American Library Association.

Crawford, Walt. 1982. Library standards for data structures and element identification: U.S. MARC in theory and practice. *Library Trends* 31: 265–81.

———. 1984. *MARC for library use: Understanding the USMARC formats*. White Plains, NY: Knowledge Industry Publications.

Drabenstott, Karen M. 1992. The need for machine-readable authority records for topical subdivisions. *Information Technology and Libraries* 11: 91–104.

Dublin Core metadata element set, version 1:1: Reference description. 2000. Available: http://purl.oclc.org/dc/documents/rec-dces-19990702.htm. (Accessed May 9, 2001).

Furrie, Betty. 1998. *Understanding MARC bibliographic: Machine-readable cataloging*. 5th ed., reviewed and edited by the Network Development and MARC Standards Office, Library of Congress. Washington, DC: Cataloging Distribution Service, Library of Congress, in collaboration with The Follett Software Company. Available: http://lcweb.loc.gov/marc/umb/. (Accessed May 9, 2001).

Glennan, Kathryn P. 1995. Format integration: The final phase. *MC Journal: The Journal of Academic Media Librarianship* 3: 1–31. Available: http://wings.buffalo.edu/publications/mcjrnl/v3n2/glennan.html. (Accessed May 9, 2001).

Green, Rebecca. 1996. The design of a relational database for large-scale bibliographic retrieval. *Information Technology and Libraries* 15: 207–21.

Guenther, Rebecca S. 1996. Bringing the Library of Congress Classification into the computer age: Converting LCC to machine readable form. In *Knowledge Organization and Change: Proceedings of the Fourth International ISKO Conference, 15–18 July 1996, Washington, DC, USA*, edited by Rebecca Green, 26–32. Frankfurt/Main: INDEKS Verlag.

International Federation of Library Associations and Institutions. 1996. Universal Bibliographic Control and International MARC Core Programme. 1996. UNIMARC: An introduction. Available: http://www.ifla.org/VI/3/p1996-1/unimarc.htm. (Accessed May 9, 2001).

Library of Congress. Cataloging Policy and Support Office. 1998. Subdivision authority records (18X). Available: http://lcweb.loc.gov/catdir/cpso/subdauth.html. (Accessed January 17, 1999).

Library of Congress. Network Development and MARC Standards Office. 1997. Dublin Core/MARC/GILS crosswalk. Available: http://www.loc.gov/marc/dccross.html. (Accessed May 9, 2001).

———. 1998a. USMARC concise bibliographic: Subject access fields (6xx). Available: http://www.loc.gov/marc/bibliographic/ecbdsubj.html. (Accessed May 9, 2001).

———. 1998b. USMARC concise authority. MARC 21 concise format for authority data. Available: http://www.loc.gov/marc/authority/. (Accessed May 9, 2001).

———. 1998c. USMARC concise bibliographic: Classification and call number fields (05X-08X). Available: http://www.loc.gov/marc/bibliographic/ecbdclas.html. (Accessed May 9, 2001).

Malinconico, S. Michael. 1985. The role of a machine based authority file in an automated bibliographic system. In *Foundations of Cataloging: A Sourcebook*, edited by Michael Carpenter and Elaine Svenonius, 208–33. Littleton, CO: Libraries Unlimited. First published in *Automation in Libraries: Papers Presented at the CACUL Workshop on Library Automation, Winnipeg, June 22–23, 1974* (Ottawa: Canadian Library Association, 1975).

Micco, Mary. 1996a. Subject authority control in the world of Internet: Part 1. *Libres* 6. Available: ftp://curtin.edu.au/pub/libres/LIBRE6N3/MICCO_1. (Accessed May 9, 2001).

———. 1996b. Subject authority control in the world of Internet: Part 2. *Libres* 6. Available:ftp://ftp.curtin.edu.au/pub/libres/LIBRE6N3/MICCO_2. (Accessed May 9, 2001).

Milstead, Jessica, and Susan Feldman. 1999. Metadata projects and standards. *Online* 23 (1). Available: http://www.onlineinc.com/onlinemag/OL1999/milstead1.html#projects. (Accessed May 9, 2001).

OCLC. 2000. Boost your library's Net value with CORC. Available: http://www.oclc.org/oclc/promo/10520corc/index.htm. (Accessed May 9, 2001).

Piternick, Anne B. 1985. Use of names and titles in subject searching. *Database* 8: 22–28.

Tillett, Barbara B., ed. 1989. *Authority control in the online environment: Consideration and practices*. New York: Haworth.

Yee, Thompson. 1998. Subject authority data elements and form/genre implementation: LC report to ALA ALCTS CCS Subject Analysis Committee (SAC) Subcommittee on Form Headings/Subdivisions Implementation. Available: http://lcweb.loc.gov/catdir/cpso/formgenr.html. (Accessed May 9, 2001).

3

Language in Infor-
mation Retrieval

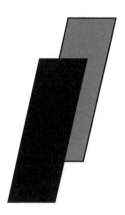

INTRODUCTION

Information retrieval involves the use of language, especially if the information—however defined—is in documentary form. Users express their needs as inquiries in linguistic form (even if the need is met by a nonverbal document such as a printed map or an audiotape); most documents are in verbal form or have a name in verbal form; and language plays an important role in the retrieval process itself, that is, in the process of describing, locating, and retrieving information, especially when retrieval is based on content rather than authorship.

Language in general, and individual languages in particular, can be viewed from many angles and as serving apparently different, but interrelated, purposes. For example

■ In the lexical sense as a body of words and methods of combining them and "other language elements" in a way that the resulting product can be understood by designated groups;

■ In the psychological sense as a means, vocal or other, of expressing or communicating feelings or thoughts, including the use of words in human conversation; inarticulate sounds by which animals express their feelings; the suggestion, by objects, actions, or conditions, of ideas associated therewith (such as "the language of flowers," body language); and

■ In the philosophical sense as a tool for communication.

Like other languages, indexing languages also serve as tools for communication, means of expressing feelings or thoughts, and methods of combining a group of words or word-like symbols so that they can be understood by the designated end users. Like other languages (French, Swedish, etc.), each indexing language is a separate entity that nevertheless shares some characteristics with other members of its language group. It has words or word-like symbols (vocabulary), rules for combining them (grammar), and by definition is a means of communication. The process of communication involves a source, a message, a means or channel of transmission, and the receiver. At any stage of the process some "noise" can affect it negatively: The source may use fuzzy thinking, the message may be inappropriate for the transmission channel used, the means of transmission may not be up to transmitting even a precisely phrased message, or the receiver may attach a meaning to the message that the originator had not intended. Effective communication requires that source and receiver understand the message in the same way. Ideally, they should be on the same wavelength. Indexing and retrieval are linked; the indexing language and the retrieval technique are interdependent.

The retrieval process involves two separate but interdependent stages. First is the "input stage," that is, the representation of the topical contents of documents in terms of verbal or notational symbols. The phrase *library architecture* or the notation *Z699* are such representations. This process is called "subject cataloging" or, sometimes, "indexing," the contents of the documents and is typically done by a professional cataloger or indexer. The second process, which is really the reverse of the first process, is the "retrieval stage," that is, the transformation of the user's needs into a retrieval query. This is typically done by the user, often with the help of a reference librarian. A query is the representation of the user's information need in a form acceptable to the information retrieval system such as the online catalog. For example, most currently available online catalogs cannot answer queries in text form, such as: "Is Eugene, Oregon a pleasant place to live in?" Instead, this information need is transformed into a query such as, "Find subject *Eugene, Oregon–Description and Travel*" or "Find *Eugene, Oregon*," which is then presented to the system. For retrieval to be successful, there must be some match between the indexing terminology employed in the system and the user's query.

LANGUAGE CHARACTERISTICS

At the input and retrieval stages of the indexing process the phenomena of language, indexing languages, and communication in general should be considered at three levels:

- The meaning or semantic level, that is, the meaning of the individual language element and of the complete statement;

- The structural or syntactic level, that is, the way in which the individual language elements are joined together to form statements; and

- The effective or pragmatic level, that is, the intended or unintended effects statements have on the recipients.

Semantics

Semantics is the study of meaning as expressed in means of communication such as words. Words have two kinds of meanings. "Denotative" meaning is a commonly accepted meaning based on definition; "connotative" meaning is an implied meaning based on ideas associated with the commonly accepted definition and on individual reaction to it. (For example, *home* denotes a place in which to live and connotes comfort, having to mow the lawn, security, love, real estate taxes.) Denotative meaning is, and must be, shared among members of the society in which the words are used, otherwise communication would be impossible. Connotative meaning is far more nebulous, varied, personal, arbitrary, and changeable. (For example, *cat* denotes a small furry domesticated quadruped of the *Felidae* family but connotes hairballs, purring, a feeling of pleasure, allergic reactions—sometimes all of these and more to one person at the same time.) Differences in connotative meanings are usually not based on the word itself but on the attitudes individuals have toward the object described.

The distinction between denotative and connotative meanings is reflected in the fact that some subjects or disciplines have an essentially "hard" vocabulary in which there is little or no disagreement about what the words mean. These terms will have the same import for the author of the document, the indexer, and the inquirer. Other subjects or disciplines have a high proportion of comparatively "soft" terms that may be used in different senses by different users or even by the same user at different times. This obviously reduces the value of these words for indexing and retrieval purposes. In literature, words may be used to convey ideas that do not directly relate to the author's purpose. To say that *The Old Man and the Sea* is about fishing, for example, is to miss the point; to index it as though it were prevents those who wish to read the novel from finding it and makes it likely that it will be retrieved when it is not wanted.

An aspect of meaning that has particular relevance for indexing because of its bearing on vocabulary control is the relationships between meanings and therefore between the denotations of words used to represent them. Three categories of bibliographic relationships are generally recognized:

Equivalent

Hierarchical

Affinitive/associative

Two expressions are equivalent when they mean the same thing. Synonyms are an obvious case of equivalence, as are variations in spelling and word form, and acronyms and abbreviations. Examples of such equivalences are *I.D. cards* and *Identification cards; Colour pigeons* and *Color pigeons*. In indexing vocabularies synonyms usually cause no conceptual problems although they may cause technical problems. Note, however, that there are degrees of equivalence and near-equivalence. Translated words are usually equivalent, but often with more than one meaning depending on context; some words overlap the meaning of others but do not mean the same thing, such as *salary* and *honorarium*. If the distinction is more than minimal (however that is defined) the relationship is affinitive rather than synonymous.

The two commonly recognized hierarchical relationships are genus/species and whole/part. For example, *Homo sapiens* is a species of the genus *Homo*. All of *Homo sapiens* belongs to the genus *Homo,* but only some of the species that belong to the genus *Homo* belong to the species *Homo sapiens*. Two examples of whole/part relationships are *Camera* and *Camera lens*; and *Foot* and *Toes*. A less obvious whole/part relationship is the instance (or generic topic/proper-named example) relationship, for example: *Mountain ranges* and *Himalayas*, or *Bavarian lakes* and *Ammersee* (a lake in Bavaria).

An example of a group of words and concepts that bears affinitive relationships is *animals* and *zoology.* Another one includes *teachers, teaching,* and *learning.* A teacher is someone engaged in the profession or activity called teaching. Teaching may bear a cause-and-effect relationship to learning, but that does not mean that one is a subunit of the other. The difficulty that arises with such relationships is that, unlike equivalence and hierarchical relationships, affinitive relationships depend on context. Decisions about affinitive relationships cannot easily and automatically be built into the indexing language or into the system of which the language is a part; they should be based on a general policy but must be created on an individual basis.

When indexing or searching for concepts, it is very important to bear in mind the exact concept with which we are dealing, in a semantic, hierarchical, and affinitive context. In designing, evaluating, and using online catalogs, indexing languages, and their indexing/retrieval capabilities we must also pay considerable attention to the needs of the clientele for whom they are created and to their likely use of, and reaction to, indexing terminology. We must concern ourselves with the end users, because their relationships to the language and to each other are likely to affect search results. All three levels—semantic, syntactic, and pragmatic—are important in information retrieval, because they affect the use and the effectiveness of an information retrieval system.

Syntactics

Syntactics is the study of that part of grammar that deals with sentence structure, that is, syntax. Syntax treats the arrangement and relative positions and mutual relationships of words in a sentence or statement as required by established usage and grammatical rules of the language being used. In other words, like semantics, syntax is concerned with clearness of expression, with efficient and unambiguous communication, and is language-dependent.

In English, syntactic relationships may be shown in several ways. One of these is order or sequence. Typically, a given group of words will make sense, or at least better sense, only in one sequence: *The lady is smiling; The smiling is lady.*

The second method of showing syntactic relationships is the use of "markers." For example, in the English language markers may take the form of inflections (such as *'s*) or prepositions (such as *of*) to indicate the possessive relationship: *The dog's hair; The hair of the dog.*

Although they can be differentiated, these two methods of showing syntactic relationships are interdependent and are often used together. In natural language the markers may determine the order of the language elements: *The hair dog's* as against *The dog's hair*; *Of the dog the hair* as against *The hair of the dog.*

Among artificially created "languages" such as indexing and bibliographic retrieval vocabularies, markers and order of language elements are just as language-dependent and in several, sometimes conflicting, ways. They are affected by the semantic and syntactic rules of the indexing language itself, those of the natural language (English, French, etc.) that links them to indexer and end user; the medium and format in which they are used (on catalog cards, on printed page, electronic display screen), and their purpose. These rules are described, in general and with respect to specific indexing languages, in Chapters 6, 7, and 8.

In "inflected" natural languages such as French, German, and Italian, "relative positions and mutual relationships" mean that articles, pronouns, and adjectives change in form to correspond in gender, number, and case with their respective nouns. English is a largely uninflected language and has relatively few instances in which inflection is of major importance. Nevertheless, in indexing languages that use English terminology decisions must be made at least with respect to multi-word terms, words that require some kind of clarification to avoid ambiguity, and especially at the retrieval stage, with query phrasing.

Semantic and Syntactic Relationships

The differences between semantic and syntactic relationships are not absolute and precise. In general, a syntactic relationship exists only between terms within one statement or sentence, whereas semantic relationships can exist among terms wherever located. However, depending on circumstances and interpretation, the same relationship may be regarded as either semantic or syntactic. For example, we may consider the phrase *high schools* to consist of two elements, *high* and *schools,* which are syntactically related, or we may consider it to be a single element, which is hierarchically related to a broader element, *schools,* and to a narrower element, *junior high schools.* Because such terms are also indexing and retrieval terms, it is essential that indexers and searchers be aware of such relationships and of the many ways in which, and points of view from which, searchers can view a topic.

The notions of semantics and syntax from the perspective of information retrieval are explored in Chapter 4, Section " 'Control' at the Indexing (Input) Stage: Semantics and Syntactics."

FOUR CATEGORIES OF
INFORMATION RETRIEVAL SYSTEMS

The many information retrieval systems that exist can be divided into four major groups. Three of these groups index and retrieve works on the basis of their subject, that is, what they are about. The fourth group works on other bases, for example, on the basis of having one work list another work as a source, such as in a footnote (citation indexing), or on a nonverbal basis.

Of the three groups that are based on the work's subject matter, the first indexes works with the actual words used in the document being indexed and/or its title and/or its abstract. This group uses what is called "uncontrolled" or "natural language." The only control exercised is that the computer is programmed by means of a "stopwords list" to *not* retrieve the document under terms that are obviously unsuitable as retrieval terms, such as articles, prepositions, pronouns, and conjunctions: *the, a, with, from, her, he, or, in, and,* and so forth.

The other two groups that index works on the basis of their subject matter use "controlled," that is, "prescribed," indexing languages. "Controlled indexing languages are indexing languages in which both the terms that are used to represent subjects, and the process whereby terms are assigned to particular documents, are controlled or executed by a person" (Rowley 1994, 109). One of these groups uses prescribed words to describe a work's subject. For example, for a work about professionals in the field of law, the prescribing authority might authorize the word *lawyers* as a retrieval term but not the words *attorneys* or *barristers.* (The reason for this technique is described in "Controlled Vocabularies" in this chapter.) The other group uses notations, that is, numbers or letters or combinations (alphanumeric notations) to express subject matter: *723.1; RpMsEn; NA7115.* This group uses notational, or classed, systems.

Some Inherent Characteristics
of Alphabetical and Classed Systems

Because the sequence in which topics are listed and can be accessed affects their use, it is important to visualize the basic differences between the alphabetical and the classed arrangements of a file. In a file that is arranged alphabetically by subject-words, subjects (and works about them) are listed in alphabetical order, by spelling:

```
Apes, Apparitions, Aquariums, Baboons, Beaches,
Chimpanzees, Condominiums, Demons, Diseases, Exorcism,
Fly-casting, Ghosts, Gibbons, Gift wrapping,
Gorillas, Haunted houses
```

In a classed scheme, the same subjects and the same works are listed in groups, subgroups, and sub-subgroups, that is, in hierarchies, by likeness and relatedness rather than by spelling:

```
Ape     [a biological family]
    Orangutan     [a genus]
    Chimpanzee     [a genus]
        Pygmy chimpanzee [a species]
        Common chimpanzee [a species]
    Gorilla [a genus]
Occultism
    Haunted houses
    Apparitions
        Ghosts
    Demons
        Exorcism of demons
```

To keep the various groups, subgroups, etc., in the desired order, a non-linguistic label which will do so is then assigned to each, such as 732.5, AB27, etc.

Even in an alphabetical arrangement subjects that are conceptually related can be listed near each other in two ways: 1) by happenstance, by what may be called "the accident of the alphabet" (for example, *Diet* and *Dietitian*, *Magnetic Pole* and *Magnetism*); or 2) by manipulating the alphabetical label so as to achieve within the alphabetical sequence a classed subarrangement (for example, *Librarians—Biography*; *Librarians—Education*; *Librarians—Japan*; *Art—History*; *Art, Medieval*). But the predominant alphabetical sequence is by spelling rather than by meaning. The different arrangements of the same subjects—alphabetical or classed—affect information retrieval.

Literary Warrant, Inquiry Warrant

The order in which subjects and subtopics are arranged, listed, and accessible in a file is also interconnected with the choice of names for these subjects. Regardless of format (classed or alphabetical) or medium (paper or screen), the terms and groupings used in an indexing system are a means of communication and should be familiar and transparent to authors, indexers, and searchers to aid indexing as well as retrieval. This is especially important in new and interdisciplinary fields that have their own slant and terminology. One attempt to achieve transparency is to select as controlled indexing terms professional words and concepts used in the respective literature; this is called "literary warrant." The indexing terms used should reflect the wording, the specificity, and the slant of the respective literature. When the indexing system is a classification scheme, literary warrant also refers to the idea that the classes, sub-classes, and specificity of subdivision should reflect the way in which the subject breaks down "naturally" as presented in its literature. Users should find material in the groupings that they tend to think of, and any group or subgroup should be small enough to permit easy scanning on the shelves, in a paper-based file, or on the screen. Classification schemes based on this principle are sometimes also called "practical," as opposed to "theoretical," schemes.

Another attempt to make indexing vocabularies transparent for input as well as output (retrieval) is based on the concept of "inquiry warrant" or "user warrant." Whereas literary warrant refers to the professional literature from which the information is to come, inquiry warrant refers to the way in which professionals search for information in their literature. The two sources employ usually the same concepts and terms, except when controversy, "political correctness," new technology, or other matters cause one or the other source to view its field in new ways or use new terms. These two methods are, in effect, complementary pragmatic (and partial) approaches to creating effective communication between indexer and searcher: "pragmatic" because they reflect not only the topic itself but also on how it is presented and viewed and accessible. They are sensible and helpful guidelines, but we must not lose sight of the reality that the passage of time, the medium and file format in which they are used, and technological developments can affect their usefulness and implementation.

Indexing Systems and Technology

Possible interaction between technology and indexing systems reaches, of course, beyond selecting useful indexing terms. Technological developments some-times make existing techniques obsolete and sometimes cause existing systems and approaches to be questioned. But they also often permit new approaches, raise expectations, and enable what had been previously theoretically desirable but practicably impossible to achieve. A case in point is the old debate over the relative merits of different file sequences and indexing languages.

The technical ability and abstract concept of employing alphabetical and classed sequences for mutual support in one list or file progressed from embryonic beginnings, in halting and circuitous steps, over many centuries. By the nineteenth century the classed and alphabetical systems had been increasingly refined and their reciprocity coordinated more or less effectively, for example in the format of the "classed catalog" with alphabetical indexes to the classed (and major) section. Several methods of using uncontrolled title-derived or text-derived words for subject access had also been in use, at least since the early nineteenth century. All, however, took (and typically still take) a format in which each sequence is separate, with one providing additional access to the separate, major section, such as an alphabetical index to a topically arranged text, both in print form.

Classed and alphabetical file arrangements, controlled and uncontrolled subject indexing languages all have advocates, and their relative merits have been studied for more than half a century. J. Aitchison and Alan Gilchrist (1987) and C. P. R. Dubois (1987) review the arguments from several angles; Elaine Svenonius (1986) and Jennifer Rowley (1994) describe the history of this controversy, which involved philosophical and economic concerns and was at least partly due to the difficulty or inability to integrate, amalgamate, and blend—rather than only coordinate—different controlled alphabetical and notational, along with uncontrolled, indexing terms in one paper-based sequence. In the 1960s the technology and professional thinking on combining and integrating (rather than only coordinating) controlled and uncontrolled indexing languages effectively in one system or one database were just being developed. But the reality, and most professional thinking on the topic, was still in "either/or" terms: A library or documentation center could use either controlled or uncontrolled alphabetical terminology in any one file, not both; selecting one was important. (The "Cranfield" experiments, mentioned in Chapter 4, Section "Controlled and Uncontrolled Indexing Vocabularies," dealt partly with this concern.)

Only the development of computer software and online public access catalogs (OPACs) has enabled the (from the searcher's point of view) seamless combination of different indexing languages in one database. Not all programs and OPACs have reached this state, but they have the potential to do so. This ability conforms to what seems to be the present consensus: that controlled as well as uncontrolled systems should be easily available in OPACs because they tend to complement each other.

Viewed from a historical perspective, technology has been a great, continuous, and mostly beneficial factor in the development of information retrieval. We should encourage and employ it imaginatively but not automatically; its capabilities should not entrance us, for example, to the extent of adopting features that impose unnecessary barriers to communication, such as cryptic or nonexisting screen instructions or features that are ineffective in a given environment. On the other hand, we should recognize that arguments for or against a particular indexing language or technique are often based on the technology available at the time, sometimes intertwined with developing professional philosophy. Many such arguments are, therefore, time-bound. That does not necessarily make them invalid, but it affects their relative importance.

Figure 3.1 lists the major information retrieval systems on the basis of 1) whether they approach a document by its subject or by other methods and 2) if by subject, whether by controlled or uncontrolled indexing language. Figure 3.1 and the "Thumbnail Sketches" that follow it can be a guide and road map to those systems. Although searchers often use more than one indexing system and language during one searching process, usually sequentially, each group and system is described separately for reasons of clarity, so that its characteristics stand out more precisely. Major systems from each group are discussed more fully in Chapters 6, 7, and 8.

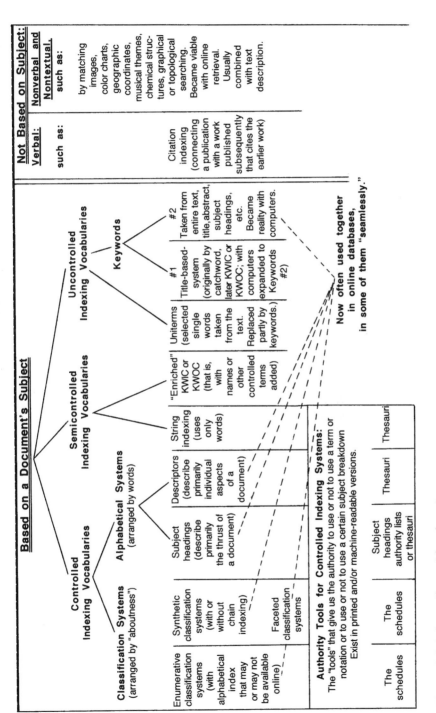

Figure 3.1. Information retrieval systems.

THUMBNAIL SKETCHES
OF MAJOR INDEXING SYSTEMS

See Figure 3.1 for the respective positions of the indexing systems in the cluster of information retrieval systems.

Citation indexing is not an indexing system as commonly understood but rather a "bibliographic references" system that uses bibliographic citations (that is, document surrogates) to connect a document with subsequent documents that refer to, or cite from, the earlier document. It is based on the premise that a document and its derivatives have something in common, typically the subject. It projects concepts forward, whereas bibliographies attached to documents project concepts backward. (It falls outside the scope of this work.)

Classification system. See *Enumerative classification system* and *Synthetic classification systems.*

Descriptor system is word-based and designed to assign controlled separate words or phrases to every aspect of a work to analyze it, along with one or more terms that describe the work as a whole. Descriptors may be precoordinated terms (which combine several otherwise independent concepts, like *Armed Forces and mass media,* or *Biological pest control agents industry*) or simple terms (like *Bashfulness,* or *Bugotu language*). Typically five to twenty-five descriptors are used per document. Like subject headings, descriptors are typically linked hierarchically and laterally into a cohesive vocabulary structure.

The term *descriptor* is sometimes misused in a generic sense to include subject headings, keywords, and sometimes even notations. What sets descriptors apart from these other systems is that 1) their primary function is to index a document conceptually, that is, to use a controlled vocabulary to describe concepts contained *in* a work rather than, like subject headings, the work as a whole or, like analytics, a specific part of a work; 2) unlike some subject headings, in most descriptor vocabularies multiple word descriptors use only direct word order (not *Psychology, Forensic* but *Forensic psychology*); 3) whereas subject heading systems are designed to use *only* the most specific authorized term to describe a topic, many descriptor systems are free to use the most specific term *plus* a term on a broader hierarchical level; (4) unlike keywords, descriptors are a controlled vocabulary; and (5) unlike notations descriptors are arranged in thesauri in several contexts, alphabetical, classed, and others. (For contrast, see *Subject headings system,* although the distinctions are becoming blurred.)

Enumerative classification system (examples are the Dewey Decimal Classification (DDC) and the Library of Congress Classification (LCC) lists in the schedules whatever concepts it authorizes. The indexer may not combine concepts at will. For example, the concept "Mathematics for aviators" can only be expressed if it is listed in the schedules with a notation. Otherwise it must be classed either as *Mathematics* or as *Aviation,* depending on the rules of the system. Some enumerative classification schemes, like the DDC, also have limited synthetic features (see Chapter 8). Enumerative classification as we know it was invented by Melvil Dewey around 1876.

Faceted classification system. See *Synthetic classification systems.*

Image-matching. See *Nonverbal indexing systems.*

Non-subject, nonverbal indexing systems. See *Citation indexing* and *Nonverbal indexing systems.*

Nonverbal indexing systems are based on describing and searching for concepts or documents by means other than text, such as color charts, chemical structures, geographic coordinates, or image matching. However, because most search engines are text-based, the systems are usually searchable by their accompanying text as well as by their respective nonverbal characteristic. They need not be subject-oriented. (They fall outside the scope of this work.)

Postcoordination. See *Precoordination* and *Postcoordination.*

Precoordination and *Postcoordination* methodologies involve two different concepts: the indexing or retrieval term *(vocabulary)* and the indexing or retrieval *system.* A precoordinated indexing term combines several otherwise independent concepts like *Games with music; Advertising, Magazine; Clocks and watches; Mountains in the Koran; Duets—Bibliography.* Some precoordinated terms consist of only one word, such as *Urinalysis* (analysis of urine) or *Phototherapy* (treatment of disease by means of light). Precoordinated terms can be words or notations or even (in the developing graphic systems) images.

A precoordinated system requires the indexer rather than the searcher to create a combined term that describes a complex concept. A postcoordinated system requires the searcher rather than the indexer to create a searching phrase that combines terms which are otherwise independent in that system (but which, themselves, may be precoordinated) into the desired complex concept. Because the searching phrase is temporary rather than part of a standard indexing vocabulary, it is usually referred to as a postcoordinated "searching phrase" or "searching string" rather than an indexing or searching "term."

If the software and hardware permit it, the use of Boolean techniques in OPAC and database searching permits postcoordinated retrieval regardless of whether the vocabulary system is a postcoordinated system. For maximum efficiency, however, the terms and the vocabulary system should be designed for postcoordinate retrieval.

String indexing system is a word-based system in which the indexer analyzes the various aspects of a complex subject treated in a document and records the aspects as words, along with "role operators" (that is, instructions to the computer). The computer program combines these words into a string of terms that is really a brief summary of the document's content. Then the program provides index entries by automatically recasting the string under every significant term that forms part of the string. As a result, the document summary is listed under every significant subject term. PRECIS is an example of a string indexing system.

Subject headings system is a word-based system designed to assign a controlled separate word or phrase to the document as a whole. If that is not grammatically possible, or if the work treats several independent topics or a topic that can be viewed from several angles, more than one subject heading may (must) be used. One to three subject headings per document used to be typical, but in 1996 Library of Congress (LC) policy changed to permit deeper indexing with up to ten subject headings, which blurs the distinction between subject headings and descriptors. The indexer may also assign additional, analytical subject headings designed to describe the content of a specific section in a work (for example, the name of a person in a collection of biographies).

Subject headings may be precoordinated concepts. Because subject headings are words they are listed in alphabetical order, but to keep specific aspects of a subject together individual headings are often subdivided by secondary alphabets, which introduces an element of classification into the alphabetical sequence.

Andrea Crestadoro (1856) invented the basic concept that topics should be described by a standardized vocabulary, and Charles Ammi Cutter (1876) first formulated this concept into a code. (For contrast, see *Descriptor system.*)

Synthetic classification systems are precoordinated systems. Their schedules tend to list not complete notations but language elements (numbers and/or letters), which the indexer combines into a complete notation according to the system's specific rules. The indexer is free to create notations that are as broad or as specific as seems suitable for a particular work and a particular collection or database. The best constructed synthetic schemes are faceted classification schemes, which break a field down into its component parts, that is, view it from all pertinent angles (like the facets of a diamond) and assign symbols to each angle, which the indexer then combines into a notation according to the particular system's precise guidelines.

In printed format the document descriptions (document surrogates) are typically listed in classed order by the first language element in the string, with a separate alphabetical subject index, which can take several forms, leading to them. This combination was designed to take advantage of the reciprocity of alphabetical and classed order and is reminiscent of the paper-based classed catalog that was popular in the nineteenth century and was used even in the early twentieth century by a few notable North American libraries (such as the Engineering Societies Library in New York and the John Crerar Library in Chicago) and especially in various formats by some academic libraries abroad.

CONTROLLED VOCABULARIES

A controlled indexing vocabulary

- authorizes only one term or notation for any one concept;

- establishes its size or scope (for example, whether the word *baseball* or the notation *796.357* are to include the concept *softball*);

- usually explicitly records its hierarchical and affinitive/associative relations;

- controls variant spellings; and

- explicitly identifies the multiple concepts expressed by homonyms, by means of adjectives, qualifiers, or phrases and precise terminology (Examples: *Security; Security (Law); Security (Psychology); Financial security; Computer security; Private security services; Computer networks—Security measures*).

The need to use far more precise terminology than one tends to use in daily conversation to search in a small, let alone a multimillion-documents file, surprises most beginning users of a retrieval system. Creating an effective indexing vocabulary and using it skillfully are demanding tasks: All terms/headings must be precise enough to preclude ambiguity; they should be known and used by people in the respective field to be helpful; they must be linked syndetically into a single structure; they must be grammatically understandable; and, even in the age of electronics, they must cluster related concepts in a structure that is helpful in paper-based files, in printouts, and when the "default" option is used. In the last example in the preceding list the designers evidently thought it more helpful to list the concept of *computer network security* next to other works on *computers* rather than next to other works on *security*.

The listed characteristics are designed to result in a visible "syndetic," that is, connective structure, which, among other things, is intended to enable indexers and searchers to find their desired topic more efficiently. For example, the indexing vocabulary might list relevant material under either the scientific nomenclature for species of animals or everyday terms *(bovidae* or *cattle),* but not under both. In paper-based files searchers who look under the term that is *not* authorized are referred to the authorized (used) term: *Bovidae,* see *Cattle.* In electronic systems this may also be the case, or the system automatically transfers the user who looks under *bovidae* to the listing under *cattle.* Only one out of (in this case) two synonyms is authorized to make sure that all material on cattle is listed under that term rather than being scattered under two terms or being listed twice, once under each term. Listing, or at least finding, together all documents that deal with the same topic is still an important principle of information retrieval, as discussed in Chapter 4, in "The Legacy of Paper-Based Rules." It permits overviewing in one spot the indexed material on the desired topic, provided the vocabulary's syndetic structure and the system's Boolean capacity enable access from many viewpoints. In a paper-based file, such as a card catalog, it also saves much preparation time and space, both major considerations in that environment and important even in the era of automation.

Advantages of Controlled Vocabularies

The design features can also be listed as advantages. The design features, in turn, are intended to result in other benefits of a more speculative nature. A controlled indexing vocabulary based on an authority list is intended to aid indexing and searching because:

- It increases the probability that both indexer and inquirer will express a particular concept in the same way, so as to improve the matching process, and enable the inquirer to find what is being looked for.

- It increases the probability that both indexer and searcher can be led to a desired topic by the syndetic features: "broader term," "narrower term," "related term," or *"see"* and *"see also."* (The terminology differs in some lists.)

- It increases the probability that the same term will be used by different indexers, or by the same indexer at different times, to ensure (inter-indexer) consistency.

- It helps to speed the indexing and especially the searching processes by making it unnecessary to imagine and to look up possible or likely synonyms if the term looked up initially is not in the database.

- It helps searchers to focus their thoughts when they approach the information system without a full and precise realization of what information they need.

Disadvantages of Controlled Vocabularies

Some arguments against the use of controlled vocabulary are:

- The high input cost: Controlled indexing is done typically by humans who must read the document, discern the various ideas it contains, then match these with appropriate terms in the authority list. That takes time.

- Human error in interpreting a document's subject matter.

- Incompatibility of different indexing languages, even within the same discipline or subject, making searching in different databases difficult but not impossible.

- The possibly out-of-date vocabulary: There is an inevitable time lag before new terms are added to the authority list or thesaurus.

- The possibly inadequate vocabulary. Indexer and searcher are limited to the terminology used, to the scope of each concept (term or notation), and to the structure of an existing system as determined by its designers. If this system does not match, or is not flexible enough to answer, the searcher's question adequately, it is not helpful for a given library or topic or clientele. (This explains the existence of hundreds of specialized alphabetical or classed schemes in addition to the well-known "general" indexing languages such as LCC, DDC, and Library of Congress Subject Headings [LCSH].)

A typical argument made against using controlled indexing vocabularies is that "the natural language of scientific prose is fully adequate for indexing and retrieval" (Klingbiel 1970). The language of science is, indeed, highly controlled and standardized because all sciences tend to be taxonomic in nature; taxonomy implies definition and, therefore, control of the meaning of words. However, it is wrong to generalize from science in particular to written language in general. Research has shown that precision of terminology used in a text, or in the title of a text (and therefore needed for uncontrolled retrieval) varies with the field. For example, A. B. Buxton and A. J. Meadows (1977) showed that the use of informative words in titles of articles (that is, the kinds of words that would be logical to use in uncontrolled retrieval) ranges from very high in journals of chemistry and botany to very low in the social sciences, with philosophy lowest. Many similar findings have been reported since then.

Authority Lists for Controlled Indexing Vocabularies

Printed authority lists are the paper-based predecessors of the MARC authority records for alphabetical and classed subject indexing vocabularies. Although very different with respect to technology and sophistication, both serve the same basic purpose: to provide a record and to control the use of every authorized (and therefore authoritative) indexing term in the context and framework of its vocabulary. A subject authority "list" is a source for authorized indexing terms whether or not they have been used in a particular catalog or database. A subject authority "file" is an internal tool for catalog or database management. It contains (see Chapter 2, "Authority File") those subject terms from the subject authority list that have been used in the respective catalog or database. It obviously grows and changes continuously. The terms "list" and "file" are sometimes used synonymously, but it is useful to keep the distinction in mind: Not every term in a generally available authority list is used or represented in a particular catalog's or database's authority file. In this section we are dealing with subject authority lists unless indicated otherwise.

Theoretically, anyone can create a controlled indexing vocabulary. Actually, only people or organizations that need to index documents even consider creating a list of authorized terms or notations, and then only when widely available ones are not suited to their needs. For the sake of interlibrary cooperation, and because creation of such lists is labor-intensive, requires linguistic and subject knowledge, and is affected by system capabilities, most libraries use existing nationally or internationally known lists. The *Library of Congress [List of] Subject Headings* (LCSH) (1998) and the *Dewey Decimal Classification* (DDC) (1996) are examples of general, internationally recognized, controlled indexing vocabularies. ("General" means that a system is intended to be suitable for all subjects.) The National Library of Medicine's *Medical Subject Headings* (MeSH) is an example of an internationally recognized specialized subject heading vocabulary. Hundreds of other controlled specialized indexing vocabularies exist, almost all of them alphabetical or notational. Control is exercised by assigning "authorized," or "authoritative" indexing terms (words or notations) to a document and by controlling the hierarchical, the semantic, and often the syntactic relationships within the system. For notations, the classification schedule serves as an authority list. Alphabetical subject headings are assigned from a subject headings authority list that lists topics in alphabetical sequence. For historical reasons, alphabetical and classed systems were created and developed separately and, even if they cover the same special topic, without organized, structured "interfaces" between the two systems. Some leading systems have tried to provide interfaces selectively, over time, on a term-by-term basis. But whereas classification schedules used alphabetical indexes merely as supporting devices and alphabetical subject headings lists used linguistic means (described in Chapter 6) to substitute in a limited way for classed order, the more recently invented thesauri developed into the first bibliographic control tool to coordinate alphabetical and classed structures and terms cohesively and on a system-wide, equal-access basis.

On the technical level, graphical user interfaces or Windows™ interfaces, or split screens, if available in a system, remove what used to be a controlled vocabulary's limitation on paper, and a highly annoying obstacle online: the need to consult a separate printed list or a separate screen to know the terms in the controlled vocabulary. If the system permits, it is now possible to view and manipulate an authority list in a window while simultaneously displaying a search profile or viewing bibliographic records on the screen's main section (Rowley 1994, 116).

Classification Schedules As Authority Tools

Classification schedules typically consist of at least two sections, neither designed or worded for public use. The principal, distinguishing section is the schedule itself, that is, a listing of authorized topics in classed order together with the respective notational symbols. Many notations are listed with instructions to the indexer regarding their scope, related concepts, and how to combine the notation with other parts of the schedule as needed. The second section is the alphabetical index to the classification schedule. (Chapters 7 and 8 deal in detail with classification.)

The schematic and very simplified example of a classification system shown here indicates hierarchical relations by means of indentations in the schedule; it indicates scope and affinitive/associative relations by instructions in the schedule and by the alphabetical index. The *MARC 21 Authority Format for Classification Data* permits all of these features and, because of its adaptability and electronic flexibility, many more. (See Chapter 8 for specifics.)

[Schedule, in classed sequence]

[In this schematic example verbal labels are in parentheses ( ) and instructions to the indexer in brackets [ ].]

```
380      (Commerce, communication, transportation)
         [Class regulatory and control aspects in 351]
385          (Railroad transportation)
             [Includes broad- and narrow gauge railways, monorailways,
             interurban, funicular, cogwheel railways, industrial
             railways.]
385.3            (Facilities)
385.36               (Locomotives)
386          (Inland waterways and ferry transportation
             [Class comprehensive works on water transportation
             in 387;
             Class comprehensive works on transportation in 388]
```

- -

[Alphabetical index to the schedule]

```
Ferry transportation                    386
    public administration               354
Inland water transportation             386
    engineering                         629
    law                                 343
    public administration               354
    transportation services            386
Locomotives                             385.36
    engineering                         625
    transportation services            385.36
Railroads
    engineering                         625.2
    transportation services            385
Transportation
    Commercial aspects                  380
        On inland waterways             386
    Government regulations              351
```

Subject Headings Authority Lists

Like classification schedules, subject headings authority lists are designed and worded for staff use. They are lists of authorized terms in alphabetical order, often with instructions to the indexer regarding a term's scope, related concepts, and whether or how to combine it with other terms. Most also contain some syndetic features in the form of cross-references. For internal use (for example to prevent "dead-end," circular, and other misleading cross-references) subject headings authority lists also record (the technical term is "trace") under the term *to* which a cross-reference refers, the term(s) *from* which the reference is made, using what amounts to professional shorthand symbols: *x* means "A *see*-reference should be made from the following term" and *xx* means "A *see-also* reference should be made from the following term."

Keeping a record (keeping "trace") of the references to be made in a catalog or bibliography is an important step in the development of subject headings authority lists; *see* references showed synonymous (equivalency) relationships clearly within the context of their vocabulary. But *see-also* references were used more generically to cover all other relationships: hierarchical, affinitive/associative, semantic, and syntactic. Their purpose was to direct indexers' (and secondarily searchers') imagination to terms or concepts that might more closely represent their wishes than the ones they had thought of. The more recently developed *thesauri* (described in the next section) indicate not only equivalent but also affinitive/associative, and especially hierarchical, relationships more precisely. They also tend to be worded "neutrally" for public as well as staff use and for indexing as well as retrieval. The most commonly used symbols are BT (Broader Term), NT (Narrower Term), RT (Related Term), UF (Use For, that is, use instead of); and USE (that is, use the following term).

The following examples do not represent the full range of relationships of the respective terms or concepts. They are intended to illustrate differences in symbols and wording. The left column illustrates the traditional subject headings authority list symbols, the central column illustrates the equivalent symbols used in the alphabetical section of thesauri, and the right column shows the equivalent MARC 21 format tags and indicators for either.

[Tracings symbols used in subj hdngs. authority lists]	[Tracings symbols used in thesauri]	[MARC 21 authority format tags and indicators]
Cookery	Cookery	150 ♭0 $a Cookery
x Cookbooks	*UF* Cookbooks	450 ♭0 $a Cookbooks
xx Home economics	*BT* Home economics	550 ♭0 $a Home economics $wg
xx Gastronomy *See also Gastronomy*	*RT* Gastronomy	550 ♭0 $a Gastronomy

The following examples represent the types of cross-references the above authority formats permit in the card catalog, in the OPAC, and in the authority list itself. Other, more complex types exist.

Cookbooks
    See Cookery
	Cookbooks
	    USE Cookery

Cookery
    See also Gastronomy
	Cookery
	    BT Home economics
	    RT Gastronomy

Gastronomy
    See also Cookery
	Gastronomy
	    RT Cookery

Home economics
    See also Cookery
	Home economics
	    NT Cookery

In card catalogs, cross-references had to be copied from the authority list and interfiled on separate cards. Because that was labor-intensive some libraries copied and interfiled only *see* references, some simply put a copy of the printed subject authority list next to the card catalog and encouraged patrons to check the list for cross-references. In many OPACs the situation is not much better. "De rigueur for effective subject access is a subject authority file linked to the bibliographic file, with full cross-reference structure that is searched on every subject search and with *see-also* references and scope notes displayed for users; such a system is surprisingly hard to come by, although there are a few, such as LC Access (developed at the Library of Congress." (Yee and Layne 1998, 146; see also 144–150.)

Thesauri

The merger of the United States Army, Navy, and Air Force departments into the U. S. Department of Defense in 1947 required, as a minor by-product, coordination and integration of three very different information retrieval systems. This, in turn, caused the United States Armed Services Technical Information Agency (ASTIA) to publish in 1960 the first authority list, named with some justification after, but not to be confused with, the traditional semantic thesauri such as *Roget's*: the *Thesaurus of ASTIA Descriptors* (Boll 1982, 6). It was published at a time when the library and documentalist professions had been theorizing and experimenting for almost two decades with very imaginative new indexing systems based on developing—but sometimes fiercely conflicting—indexing theories and technologies, and on the prospect of computers.

Initial confusion over the type of vocabulary to which thesauri could be applied gave way to the realization that their strength is coordinated precise control over an indexing vocabulary rather than over how this vocabulary is applied to individual documents. The National Information Standards Organization (NISO) defines a thesaurus as "a controlled [indexing language] vocabulary arranged in a known order and structured so that equivalence, homographic, hierarchical, and associative relationship indicators among terms are displayed clearly and identified by standardized relationship indicators that are employed reciprocally" (National Information Standards Organization 1993).

This definition pinpoints the essential characteristics but permits more than one display format. Since 1960, many thesauri have been created in fields ranging from alcoholism to music to psychology. Especially some early thesauri consist only of an alphabetical listing. Most, however, use what has become a distinguishing thesaurus characteristic: multiple display of, and equal access to, a concept from closely coordinated alphabetical and classed vocabulary structures. The display formats are continuing to develop as the need for newly developing subjects and viewpoints is recognized. Although typically designed for postcoordination, thesauri can also be used in precoordinate systems, and although designed for input and searching in controlled vocabulary systems, thesauri can also be helpful for searching unindexed, that is, natural language, databases.

Thesauri exist in printed and electronic formats that may differ from each other, for example in access and switching capability. The viewing medium presents other differences which should be taken into account when constructing or revising a thesaurus. "Viewing information on a screen differs from viewing printed information: with a screen, it is harder to browse and remember one's context; the screen is more difficult and tiring to view than printed media; and the available screen 'page' size can make it difficult to grasp information that is perfectly comprehensible in printed form" (National Information Standards Organization 1993, 25).

In printed format the three basic components of a thesaurus are *alphabetical*, showing all the immediate relationships of each term; *hierarchical*, showing all levels of hierarchies, and *permuted*, or *rotated*, which shows every term under every one of its component words in alphabetical order. Many versions of each list exist, as do other groupings. Online, the formats may differ, but the basic idea is the same. Also, some programs are beginning to permit switching seamlessly from one list to the other so that a searcher may not even be aware of the different groupings.

The alphabetical list in "flat format" thesauri shows for each term only three levels: the level of the term itself, the next broader, and the next narrower level:

```
Pueblo dolls
  UF Dolls, Pueblo    [UF = Used For, equivalent to the "x"
                       in subject heading lists]
  BT Dolls            [BT = Broader Term]
  NT Kachina dolls    [NT = Narrower Term]
```

A computer program can build a complete hierarchy from a "flat format" thesaurus. In "multilevel format" thesauri more than three hierarchical levels can be indicated in several ways in the alphabetical list, for example:

```
Federal Region IV         [authorized indexing term]
   BT1   USA              [BT1 = One level broader]
     BT2   North America  [BT2 = Two levels broader]
   NT1   Georgia          [NT1 = One level narrower]
     NT2   Atlanta        [NT2 = Two levels narrower]
   RT    Appalachia       [RT = Related term]
```

In the hierarchical lists a descriptor's complete hierarchy can be shown in several ways, for example:

```
Instruments                    [Broadest level]
. Musical instruments
. Optical instruments
. . Optical sensors
. . . Fiber optic sensors  [Narrowest level]
. . Refractometers
```

For an example of one version of a permuted list, see "Permuted Medical Subject Headings" in Chapter 6.

Thesauri As Linking Devices

Most thesauri are designed to control indexing vocabulary in one, typically rather specific, subject or field of interest, ranging from Agriculture to Vocational training and to the European Communities. Several thesauri are multilingual, but topical, or even only structural, coordination with thesauri in other, or related, topics or disciplines is usually not an objective. This can hamper searching for one topic in different sources that employ different controlled indexing languages. An annoyance in paper-based (and typically sequential) retrieval that "merely" demands professional searching dexterity, the lack of coordination became more visible when OPACs and the World Wide Web (WWW) began to enable access not only to local and other "Web catalogs," which tend to use the same or similar indexing languages and policies, but also other databases such as bibliographies and abstracting and indexing (A & I) services, which often use different indexing languages, structures, and policies. Attempted linguistic solutions usually involve some kind of adjustment, coordination, or integration of structures and/or terms, or "bridges" ("interfaces") between them.

The three thesauri discussed here illustrate coordination and adjustment and/or linguistic interfaces. Designed for information retrieval, they leave the location/call number task to other symbols. The *Art & Architecture Thesaurus* (A&AT 1994) was compiled partly from existing, often more specialized lists, and the editors adjusted and expanded the several scopes and viewpoints, and the very different terminologies, hierarchies, and syndetic structures, into one cohesive unit with multiple, but integrated, displays. In an effort to reduce fundamental barriers to the application of computers to medicine, the National Library of Medicine (NLM) issued in 1990 the original version of *Metathesaurus*, a compilation of terms drawn from more than thirty controlled vocabularies. James J. Cimino (1998) and Keith E. Campbell et al. (1998) describe the kind of multidisciplinary collaboration employed to create it; Betsy L. Humphreys et al. (1998) describe linguistic aspects. Of special interest is NLM's own thesaurus, MeSH *(Medical Subject Headings)*, which coordinates and integrates a wide range of medical topics, and aspects of topics, in multiple, innovative displays. It is described and discussed in Chapter 6 along with, and in contrast to, traditional subject headings authority lists.

"Keywords," uncontrolled language terms, which are described in the next section in this chapter, are commonly used to access controlled (and to the searcher unknown) indexing terms. If a thesaurus is not available as a linking device among several controlled indexing languages, keywords can serve in a limited way as partial substitutes.

UNCONTROLLED, OR NATURAL LANGUAGE, INDEXING SYSTEMS

An uncontrolled, or natural language, or free text, indexing system uses the actual words of a document or of some description of it such as its title or an abstract, as index terms. It is also called "derived indexing" because the terms used to retrieve the document are directly taken (or derived) from its text. No effort is made (or by definition could be made) to control or explain the semantic or hierarchical or affinitive/ associative relationships among uncontrolled indexing terms.

When subject indexing systems began to be studied in a precise and comparative way in the 1950s the concept "uncontrolled" included several then recently developed alphabetical systems such as "Uniterms" and "Keywords-in-Context." They differed greatly in underlying philosophy, technique, and resulting product, but all had in common that they depended on words from the title or the text itself. Their names no longer represent separate current indexing philosophies or techniques, but many of their basic characteristics are effectively incorporated in OPAC systems. Especially the term *keyword* has become identified with uncontrolled online alphabetical indexing systems. Although sometimes misused as a generic term to include the concepts of *subject heading* or *descriptor*, or even *class notation*, keywords are uncontrolled text-derived terms; subject headings and descriptors are used in prescribed form in controlled alphabetical indexing languages.

Keywords: KWIC, KWOC, Double KWIC

Based on the nineteenth-century technique of *catchword title indexing* (that is, recasting, in a bibliography or index, a document's title so that the word in its title that best expresses what the document is about is first), uncontrolled vocabulary indexing was reintroduced by Hans Peter Luhn of IBM in 1959 in the form of keyword-in-context (KWIC). By that time, the invention of center-punched cards (an early stage in the development of the computer) made it technically and financially feasible to multiple-list documents under every "significant" word (keyword) in their titles. In the early printed KWIC indexes every keyword served as an access point, printed in the middle of a line of type, with as many of the surrounding words of the title looped around the keyword as had room on that line of type, usually less than the complete title. Minor words such as articles, prepositions, and pronouns were printed as part of the title but were not keywords. The notation in the right margin typically referred to a complete bibliographic citation of the title, printed in a separate section. The KWIC example below is for two titles: *The impact of user charges on extended use of online information services*, and *Development and evaluation of reference services in agricultural libraries*. Other formats existed, some permitting limited postcoordination.

f reference services in	**agricultural** libraries. Development a	**S79**
ces. The impact of user	**charges** on extended use of online info	**M16**
s in agricultural libraries.	**Development** and evaluation of referen	**S79**
ries. Development and	**evaluation** of reference services in agric	**S79**
pact of user charges on	**extended** use of online information serv	**M16**
formation services. The	**impact** of user charges on extended use	**M16**
extended use of online	**information** services. The impact of use	**M16**
services in agricultural	**libraries**. Development and evaluation of	**S79**
es on extended use of	**online** information services. The impact	**M16**
ment and evaluation of	**reference** services in agricultural librarie	**S79**
se of online information	**services**. The impact of user charges on	**M16**
evaluation of reference	**services** in agricultural libraries. Develop	**S79**
r charges on extended	**use** of online information services. The im	**M16**
services. The impact of	**user** charges on extended use of online i	**M16**

A technical variant of KWIC was keyword-out-of-context (KWOC), which printed the keyword in the left margin of the first listed title in which it appeared and usually omitted it from titles in subsequent lines to speed visual scanning of titles in the printed list. A more basic variant was Double-KWIC, which combines keywords from the same title in pairs of two, presumably to improve retrieval. The results were, however, not always helpful.

Development of the computer, and especially of OPACs, permitted the KWIC technique to be expanded beyond the title. Now any term that is not on the database's stopwords list can be a keyword, whether taken from a document's title, abstract, contents note, from the controlled subject headings or descriptors assigned to it, or even from the text itself (fulltext indexing). Keywords are now an important retrieval device in most OPACs. Internet search services rely primarily on keywords rather than on controlled indexing terms. The format differs, but the concept remains. A preferred OPAC method is to display the sentence(s), paragraph(s), or MARC field(s) containing the desired keyword(s) with the keyword(s) highlighted.

Advantages of Uncontrolled Vocabularies

As mentioned previously, many descriptions and claims made for or against a particular indexing language or system reflect the technology and professional philosophy of their time. Although important, many are therefore time-bound. Except as indicated below, the following points are intended to reflect inherent rather than format-imposed features of uncontrolled vocabularies which, in an electronic environment, include, if not largely consist of, keywords:

- The human effort and cost involved in "natural language" indexing of an individual document tends to be minimal. Technical and linguistic skills are needed to set up the system, and to decide on the words to be stoplisted and the fields (such as title or abstract in the document surrogate and/or the document itself) to which the stopwords list should apply. But no professional examination of an individual document is needed to index it; no decision need be made as to what a document is about.

- No misinterpretation of the author's meaning by an indexer is possible.

- The vocabulary is up to date. Terms are used as soon as they have been invented.

- No effort, time, or expense need be expended to create for the vocabulary a syndetic structure, for example, to connect synonyms by means of cross-references such as *International politics,* see *World politics..*

- The user who may look under one of several synonyms or near-synonyms *(Parasites; Animal parasites; Entozoa; Epizoa; Pests)* has a fairly good chance of finding at least something under whichever term is selected as a retrieval term.

- Because most words in a document are access points, full text natural language indexing of an online document is much more exhaustive than indexing the document's surrogate (bibliographic description) by controlled or uncontrolled vocabularies. This creates the potential for a high recall of documents, although not necessarily documents that discuss the desired topic in detail.

- Uncontrolled alphabetical terms, conceived by a searcher, can serve as entry points to controlled indexing terms (alphabetical and/or notational), and to a syndetic structure that could help the searcher.

- Uncontrolled alphabetical terms, conceived by a searcher, can also serve as partial substitutes for a thesaurus to permit searching sequentially or simultaneously several controlled languages in more than one database.

Disadvantages of
Uncontrolled Vocabularies

Based on personal observation, Charles Bernier was an early voice to argue that "word indexing [that is, free-text indexing] leads to omission of entries, scattering of related information, and a flood of unnecessary entries" (1956, 223). The validity of the last point, "unnecessary entries" can be seen by examining the last sentence for words that would *not* be on a stop list, therefore used as keywords, but still not likely to be used by a searcher as access points for the topic raised in that sentence: *Based, claimed, leads, flood, omission.* Conversely, searchers interested in *floods* would be led to an item that has nothing to do with water. Many writers have made similar points since then.

Raya Fidel (1992, 211) lists the following attributes of a search term as not suitable for free text searching:

- If the search key has many synonyms,

- If the search key is ambiguous or vague, and

- If the search key's meaning depends on the context in which it appears.

Writing from a reference librarian-as-user viewpoint, Thomas Mann (1991) (not the German novelist, but then a reference librarian at the Library of Congress) wrote a rousing justification of the need for controlled indexing vocabularies. The occasion was LC's planned move toward "brief" or "minimal level" cataloging, with no or minimal subject control. Using several real-life examples, Mann showed that controlled subject headings and classification interact to provide subject access even if the searcher has no specific subject expertise, and that the traditional cataloging principles of "uniform heading" (one authorized term for one concept) and "specific entry" (use of the specific rather than a general term) permit greater retrieval relevance than keywords. Mann expanded and reinforced his exegesis of controlled indexing languages two years later in *Library Research Models,* in which he also joined the writers who argue for redesigning library services in the light of known user habits (Mann 1993).

Additional criticism of natural-language indexing includes the following points:

- Information that is implied but not overtly included in the text, which a skilled and subject-knowledgeable human indexer would discern, may be missed.

- Absence of vocabulary control moves the responsibility and the burden from the indexing system and the indexer to the searcher without providing the necessary tools or structural framework.

- A given concept may have been described by different terms in a collection of documents. Searchers must think of, and search under, as many likely variants of the desired concept as the topic and purpose of their search (casual, specific, exhaustive) requires. This includes synonyms, near-synonyms, related concepts, and special aspects. For example, depending on the context, the concept "Work" (in noun form) can also be described in the sense of—and therefore be called in a text—*Labor* (or *Labour*); *Occupation*; *Task*; *Job*; *Employment*; *Employee*; *Associate*; *Exertion*; *Effort*; and so forth. If the document happens to be written in German or French, terms like *Arbeit* and *travail* would be uncontrolled index terms. Searchers may also have to think of, and search under, terms that are more or less specific than the topic they had thought of initially, such as *Skilled labor*; *Labor law*. On the other hand, the word *Labor* in a text does not indicate by itself whether it is used in the sense of "work" or "giving birth."

- Mentioned previously as an advantage, up-to-dateness can also be a disadvantage. Searchers must be aware that names and terms in use at the time of a document's creation may differ from those used earlier or at the time of the search. Examples are *lasers*, originally known as *masers*, and country names such as *Sri Lanka*, formerly known as *Ceylon*.

- Although keywords work well as additions or access terms to controlled vocabulary, they also result in a high proportion of "false drops" and "information overload" (inapplicable records and too many records) unless searching precautions are taken.

- Unless systems have proximity capability (that is, the ability to search for more than one keyword within a specified distance from each other), the use of keywords in Boolean searching (that is, searching combinations of terms) may increase the number of "false drops" if the individual keywords are used in a different context in different record sections such as title or abstract, and the search parameter permits searching in both record sections.

■ Although automatic indexing by machine has made some headway it has, as of this writing, still far to go before it reaches the reliability and effectiveness of a good human indexer, such as selectiveness, showing unusual relationships of ideas, and so forth

CONCLUSION

This chapter provides an overview of major bibliographic subject indexing systems and languages, their characteristics, advantages, and disadvantages in general terms. Like languages in general, indexing languages are subject to semantic and syntactic rules, which are also briefly described. "Uncontrolled" indexing systems are briefly described as well as "controlled" systems and the bibliographic tools designed to control them. Chapter 4 deals primarily with bibliographic methods of using (or "controlling") subject indexing languages.

REFERENCES

[A&AT]. 1994. *Art & architecture thesaurus.* 2d ed. Toni Petersen, director. New York: Published on behalf of The Getty Art History Information Program [by] Oxford University Press.

Aitchison, J., and Alan Gilchrist. 1987. *Thesaurus construction.* 2d ed. London: Aslib.

Aitchison, Jean, Alan Gilchrist, and David Bawden. 1997. *Thesaurus construction and use: A practical manual.* 3d ed. London: Association for Information Management.

Bernier, Charles. 1956. Language and indexes. *American Documentation* 7: 222–24.

Boll, John J. 1982. From subject headings to descriptors: The hidden trend in Library of Congress subject headings. *Cataloging & Classification Quarterly* 1 (2/3): 3–28.

Buxton, A. B., and A. J. Meadows. 1977. The variation in the information content of titles of research papers with time and discipline. *Journal of Documentation* 33 (March): 46–52.

Campbell, Keith E., et al. 1998. The Unified Medical Language System; toward a collaborative approach for solving terminologic problems. *Journal of the American Medical Informatics Association* 5 (January/February): 11–16.

Cimino, James J. 1998. Auditing the Unified Medical Language System with semantic methods. *Journal of the American Medical Information Association* 5 (1, January/February): 41–51.

Crestadoro, Andrea. 1856. *The art of making catalogues.* London: British Museum. (Ann Arbor, MI: University Microfilms, 1968).

Cutter, Charles Ammi. 1876. *Rules for a printed dictionary catalog.* Washington, DC: Government Printing Office.

———. 1904. *Rules for a dictionary catalog.* 4th ed. Washington, DC: Government Printing Office.

[DDC]. 1996. *Dewey decimal classification and Relative index.* Devised by Melvil Dewey. Edition 21, edited by Joan S. Mitchell [et al.]. Albany, NY: Forest Press. 4v.

Dubois, C. P. R. 1987. Free text versus controlled vocabulary: a reassessment. *Online Review* 11 (August): 243–53.

Fidel, Raya. 1992. Thesaurus requirements for an intermediary expert system. In *Classification research for knowledge representation and organization,* edited by N. J. Williamson and M. Hudson. New York: Elsevier Science Publishers.

Humphreys, Betsy L., et al. 1998. The Unified Medical Language system: An informatics research collaboration. *Journal of the American Medical Informatics Association* 5 (1, January/February): 1–11.

Klingbiel, Paul H. 1970. *The future of indexing and retrieval vocabularies.* (AD 716 200). Alexandria, VA: Defense Documentation Center.

[LCSH]. *Library of Congress Subject Headings.* 19th ed. 1998. Prepared by the Cataloging Policy and Support Office, Library Services. Washington, DC: Library of Congress, Cataloging Distribution Service. 4v.

Mann, Thomas. 1991. *Cataloging quality: LC priorities, and models of the Library's future.* (Opinion Papers, no. 1). Washington, DC: Library of Congress, Cataloging Forum.

———. 1993. *Library research models: A guide to classification, cataloging, and computers.* New York: Oxford University Press.

[MeSH]. 1960 – . *Medical subject headings. Alphabetic list.* [With each January issue of *Index Medicus.* Also available online]; *Annotated alphabetical list.* [Annual]. Bethesda, MD: National Library of Medicine. [Also available online]; *Permuted medical subject headings.* [annual]. Bethesda, MD: National Library of Medicine. [Also available online]; *Tree Structure.* [Annual]. Bethesda, MD: National Library of Medicine. [Also available online].

[NISO]. National Information Standards Organization (U.S.). 1985. *Guidelines for the establishment and development of multilingual thesauri.* (ISO 5964). Geneva: International Organization for Standardization.

———. 1993. *Guidelines for the construction, format, and management of monolingual thesauri.* Approved August 30, 1993, by the American National Standards Institute. (ANSI/NISO Z39.19-1993). NISO Press.

O'Brien, Ann. 1994. Online catalogs: enhancements and developments. In *Annual review of information science and technology (ARIST)* vol. 29, 219–42. Medford, NJ: Published for the American Society for Information Science (ASIS) by Learned Information.

Rowley, Jennifer. 1994. The controlled versus natural indexing languages debate revisited: A perspective on information and retrieval practice and research. *Journal of Information Science* 20 (2): 108–19.

Svenonius, Elaine. 1986. Unanswered questions in the design of controlled vocabularies. *Journal of the American Society for Information Science* 37: 331–40.

Yee, Martha M., and Sara Shatford Layne. 1998. *Improving online public access catalogs.* Chicago: American Library Association.

4

Managing Information Retrieval Languages

INTRODUCTION

Like other languages, indexing languages consist of two parts: vocabulary (semantics, meaning) and syntax (structure). If we use terms as they appear in documents without semantic or syntactic modification, we are using an uncontrolled vocabulary, or uncontrolled or natural language. By exercising control over the terms used for recall (for example, over synonyms) we use a controlled vocabulary. By formalizing the flexible syntax of natural language and permitting only certain syntactic constructions we are using a structured language. A controlled vocabulary and formalized structure are features of an artificial indexing language, which enables us to use concept indexing rather than term indexing. In concept indexing, we try to establish a standard description for each concept and use that description at the indexing (input) stage each time it is appropriate, whether it has been used by the author or not. At the searching (output; retrieval) stage, we again use the standardized description and should be able to match these two more consistently and reliably. (Foskett 1996, 113–14).

"CONTROL": WHEN AND HOW?

The use of an artificial indexing language, that is, a controlled vocabulary and formalized structure, affects input (indexing) and output (retrieval). Semantic and/or syntactic control can be exercised at various stages and in several ways:

- At both the indexing (input) and searching (retrieval, output) stage. (Examples: The use of subject headings or descriptors for indexing and retrieval; and/or using classification combined with alphabetical indexing for input and retrieval.)

- At neither the indexing nor searching stage. (Example: Text published electronically in natural language and accessed (retrieved) by keywords, that is, uncontrolled terms. The program usually limits retrieval with "stoplisted" words.)

- At the input stage only. (An unexpected example is the instruction by journal editors to contributing authors to use in their descriptive abstract that precedes the article terms that are likely to be useful keywords for the article's topic.)

- At the retrieval (searching) stage only. Although natural language indexing systems typically exercise little or no control over the input process (except for the use of stopwords), several techniques and control systems have been developed to aid in the searching process. Some are described in the next section. Others are in process of development.

We should not, however, forget that as far back as the 1960s research studies (some of which are summarized later in this chapter and are technically evaluated in Chapter 11) showed that the qualities and the degree of use, rather than the type of indexing language and retrieval system, are important factors. In the 1990s Shirley Ann Cousins reflected similar ideas: "If an information need is to be satisfactorily met it is essential that the subject in question can be adequately represented in the index language being used. If it is not possible to provide an adequate representation of a user's subject query, then a search cannot be successful without considerable effort to adapt the query to match the controlled vocabulary" (1992, 293).

"CONTROL" AT THE
SEARCHING (RETRIEVAL) STAGE

A few of the methods and techniques developed to aid in the searching (retrieval) process are discussed in the following subsections. Used with natural language systems, they may be a partial substitute for the structure of controlled systems. Used with either controlled or natural language systems, some of them also permit searching for topics or for special aspects of topics that are too new or too specific to be represented by existing terms. The examples below range from "tried and true" to "potentially useful." Still others (not listed) are being invented as the need arises and technology permits.

Keywords for Access

Keywords, uncontrolled language terms, can be used as links to access controlled (and to the searcher unknown) indexing terms such as subject headings. Keywords help users over some of the difficulties of predicting the forms used by the controlled vocabulary. They can also be used to access concepts which (at least in the searcher's opinion) the existing controlled indexing language or indexing policy are not specific enough or are otherwise unable to handle. If a thesaurus is not available as a linking device among several controlled indexing languages, keywords can serve in a limited way as a partial substitute. "Keyword searching of subject headings provides a powerful mechanism to locate all headings containing a given word and all records containing a given word in the subject fields. However, it does so at the expense of the structure of the subject heading system which was designed to provide context with headings and subheadings" (Borgman 1996, 497). Karen Markey Drabenstott and Diane Vizine-Goetz describe different approaches to using keywords for subject access, and potentials and problems of different MARC fields and databases for keyword approach. (1994, 90–103, 276–93).

Keywords, used with or without "truncation" and with or without "Boolean operators" (both described in the next two sections) are well suited for full-text searching of electronic documents or electronic abstracts or annotations of documents. In this they resemble at the retrieval stage "deep indexing" at the input stage, except that the indexing process is controlled and results in some kind of recorded rigidity, whereas full-text retrieval by keyword(s) tends to be more transient and flexible according to the searcher's momentary desire and skill.

Truncation

Truncation, or "word stemming," allows the program to treat a question mark (?), or whichever symbol the program requires, as a substitute or "wildcat character" for one or more missing characters. Searchers thereby avoid the necessity of entering all variations of the truncated keyword.

"Right-hand" truncation allows a single expression to be used to represent a number of cognate words. For example, *theat?* can represent the variant spellings of the English language terms *theater* and *theatre*. Right-hand truncation "is similar to flipping through catalog cards before and after the one sought to look for variant endings" (Borgman 1996, 500). Most systems permit right-hand truncation, either implicitly, automatically at a predetermined spot such as after the seventh character, or explicitly, only when and where the searcher uses a wildcat character. "Left-hand" truncation can be used to allow matching regardless of the presence of prefixes. For example, *?natal* would match *paranatal*, *prenatal*, and *postnatal*. Similarly, if the computer program permits it, internal truncation can be used, so that *lab?r* matches both *labor* and *labour*.

Although it often improves subject searching, truncation is not the full solution. It does not provide access to broader or narrower terms, to synonyms or near synonyms *(pinnacle, summit, apex),* or to foreign-language equivalents, such as *Arbeit* or *travail* for *labor*. Nor, if British documents are involved, does it always provide access to British equivalents for North American terminology, such as *lift* for *elevator* or, in the case of our labor example, *trade* instead of *labor* for terms such as *trade unions* instead of *labor unions* or *labour unions*. For such cases, either the system must provide an interface, that is, an internal dictionary, or the user must think of appropriate terms if the vocabulary is uncontrolled.

Truncation also has its own problems and surprisingly often provides totally unexpected and irrelevant terms. For example, *labo?* will provide not only *labor*, *laborer*, *labour*, etc., but also *laboratory*. The command "FIND ?log?" can result in retrieving *allogamy, analogous, cataloging, catalogues, clogs, decalogue, dialogs, epilogue, flogging, illogical, monologue*, and other terms.

Boolean Searching; Proximity Operators

"Boolean searching," or "Boolean logic," is named after the English mathematician and logician George Boole (1815–1864), whose set logic is represented schematically by the Venn diagrams (named after the English logician John Venn, 1834–1923) mentioned in the Preface. "Boolean searching" is postcoordinate searching, where the searcher combines terms in a temporary searching phrase by means of the Boolean operators NOT, AND, and OR. The terms may themselves be precoordinated controlled terms, keywords, and/or, depending on system capabilities, truncated terms, notations, or even nonverbal images. The purpose of the temporary searching phrase is to search for concepts, or for aspects or interrelations of concepts, that do not have (or do not seem to have) an existing indexing label in the database being searched.

Postcoordination as a searching method was formalized from the 1940s onward, when then nontraditional retrieval theories and methods were being developed (such as uniterms) and being made viable by corresponding (but preelectronic) technologies (such as optical-coincidence, or peek-a-boo systems). Postcoordination came of age as computers began to be used in libraries for information retrieval, and especially with the development of online public access catalogs (OPACs).

The Boolean operator OR broadens a search, whereas AND and NOT (or BUT NOT) tend to limit it. "ORing" is especially helpful with full-text indexing, or when uncontrolled vocabulary is used, because it can be used for synonyms and near-synonyms such as "FIND *plant pathology* OR *plant disea*ses". "FIND *aged* OR *elderly*". It is also useful with controlled or uncontrolled languages if several terms (usually near-synonyms) are likely to produce acceptable results: "FIND *space exploration* OR *outer space research* OR *planetary exploration* OR *extraterrestrial exploration*".

If a more precise topic is desired, the search can be refined by using the Boolean operator AND. For example, to check whether something is available on any possible connection between speaking more than one language and being a naughty child, one might use the command: "FIND *Problem children* AND *Bilingualism*." (These are Library of Congress subject headings.) "ANDing" limits search results, up to a point. It cuts out all documents that are indexed under only one of these two subject headings, but it includes documents that are indexed under both of these terms plus any other terms that may be totally unrelated to the desired precise topic.

This is true for controlled and uncontrolled search terms, and even when only one search term and no Boolean operators are involved. A search for documents on the psychological aspects of education in general, which can be translated into the LC subject heading *Educational psychology,* retrieves documents that are listed only under this subject label, along with documents that have this label plus other subject labels such as *Creative ability; Education—Nigeria; Problem children; Science—Experimentation; Sex differences in education;* and others. (These examples may seem farfetched, but they are taken from real documents.) Clearly, some of these documents are too specialized to answer this search question. They represent "false drops," that is, unsuitable documents.

Even the NOT operator, a limiting operator, does not prevent false drops of unrelated items. NOT is used if material is wanted on a topic unless that topic is described with some emphasis on a specific other topic: "FIND *Recreational activities* BUT NOT *Social class*", for material that is indexed as dealing with recreational activities unless it is also indexed as dealing with social class. Although systems do not (and probably quite correctly) permit a command that says, "Find documents that are listed *only* under terms X and Y", they have begun to come close. In MARC bibliographic subject added entry field 650, and some others, the first indicator shows whether the listed subject term describes the main focus or a secondary aspect of the work being described. This is similar to systems like MeSH (Medical Subject Headings) (described in Chapter 6) and ERIC, which permit restricting searches to major descriptors while ignoring the many minor descriptors that record a work's secondary topics. It also corresponds somewhat to using the first subject heading in the 6XX USMARC field, which is typically used to describe the work's major topic or topics. Systems that permit combining call numbers and alphabetical terms in one Boolean search phrase would also come close, but at the time this is written, do not seem to be in demand.

In addition to the standard operators NOT, AND, OR, some systems such as Archivia Net of the National Archives of Canada use operators designed to decrease the number of "false drops," for example ADJ: *term X* ADJ [n 1-99] *term Y*, that is, within a specified number of words; SAME: *term X* SAME *term Y*, that is, within the same paragraph or subparagraph; NEAR: *term X* NEAR *term Y*, that is, in the same sentence.

Searchers should be aware not only of the undoubted benefits of Boolean searching but also of potential problems. Among them are the following:

- Different computer programs and OPACs of different age may handle multiple-word terms differently, leading to very different results for the same query. Most OPACs accept multiple-word terms such as *coaching football* as Boolean statements. The system may use implicit proximity operators (the word *coaching* adjacent to the word *football,* as a phrase), or it may use an implicit AND operator (*coaching* AND *football*), which would tend to yield more sets. Some use an implicit OR operator (*coaching* OR *football*), which would call up still more sets (Borgman 1996, 498).

- With respect to Boolean operators between (rather than implicitly within) the terms of a searching phrase, system capabilities also affect results. Many systems permit (or require) putting equivalents within parentheses that represent different fields:

  — FIND (terms *A* OR *B*) AND (term *C*) NOT (terms *D* OR *E*).

  — FIND (*libraries* OR *college libraries*) AND (*computers*) NOT (*recreational activities* OR *high school students*).

Systems that execute Boolean operators in algebraic order read the whole string, first executing statements within parentheses, then NOT, then AND, and then OR. This ensures that equivalents are treated as equivalents and is an important aspect of the Boolean field theory as applied to information retrieval. In contrast, many OPACs do not allow parentheses and simply execute words and operators from left to right, ignoring the algebraic hierarchy of operators. In such systems the phrasing of search questions may affect the results profoundly (Borgman 1996, 498). Searchers should also be aware that Boolean operators may be displayed transparently or implicitly on the screen.

Automatic Indexing and Retrieval; Relevance Ranking

An important element in the various attempts to aid in retrieving uncontrolled indexing vocabularies is the use of algorithms, that is, mathematical procedures. Algorithms are being increasingly used in many applications, but several researchers question their suitability as substitutes for, let alone improvements of, human indexing or searching. Robert Fugman, for example, does not think much of the research conducted in this area (1992) and writes: "It is the inherently *indeterminate nature of indexing* which . . . will continue to defy any *satisfactory* algorithmization" (emphasis in original) (Fugman 1995, 230).

For automatic indexing or retrieval, the terms in a document that are not on the stopwords list are stored in the inverted file (described in Chapter 2, Section "Inverted File"). On the assumption that the more frequently a term occurs in a document, the more likely it is that the document is about that term, retrieval is based on co-occurrence of the terms in the search query with the terms in the inverted file. To obtain relevance ranking, each term is given a weight in proportion to its ability to represent the document's content. The weight is derived from a statistical analysis based on the frequency of occurrence of the word in the document, possibly in relation to the frequency of the term elsewhere in the database and to the length of the document. Assigning appropriate weights to achieve useful relevance ranking is a crucial part of the system. Documents are listed in decreasing degree to which they match the searching phrase. Some systems also use syntactic analysis to make common links explicit between words.

Still in its infancy, relevance ranking is better suited for full text than bibliographic searching but has been used in a limited number of OPACs since about the mid-1990s. It is used on the Internet in searching Web search engines and is said to be a promising technique of searching by means of uncontrolled terms. Carol Tenopir and Pamela Cahn (1994) describe in detail several major databases that use it: West Publishing Corporation's WIN, DIALOG's TARGET, and Mead Data Central's FREESTYLE, introduced respectively in 1992, 1993, and 1994. They differ among themselves and, like all automatic indexing systems so far, are most effective for searching text or lengthy abstracts. But FREESTYLE has one feature that may make it useful for end-user searching of bibliographic citations: It permits searching in natural language, thus permitting even in bibliographic databases questions such as, "What are the public schools like in Middleton, Wisconsin?"

End-User Thesauri and Search Trees

For many decades some of the larger libraries put copies of the printed *Library of Congress's List of Subject Headings* (LCSH) (1998) next to the card catalog to help patrons find authorized terms. One problem with this is that LCSH abbreviations, explanations, and phraseology are designed for professional indexers and for the indexing process and are confusing to lay searchers. To avoid this obstacle and to improve the searching process, Marcia Bates and others began to suggest in the 1980s the creation of "user thesauri," or "end-user thesauri," quite different in design from the usual indexing thesauri, and containing far more of the alternative terms that searchers are likely to use to refer to a concept. End-user thesauri link vocabulary based on "user warrant," or "inquiry-warrant" (described in the section "Literary

Warrant, Inquiry Warrant" in Chapter 3) to the vocabulary (controlled or uncontrolled) that is in the database. They show hierarchical, associative, and other relationships and functions as part of the user/database interface. James D. Anderson and Frederick A. Rowley (1991) describe in some detail the structure and creation of two prototype end-user thesauri on the basis of Ranganathan's faceted classification and on terminology based on user-warrant. Their systems have menu and browsing ability as well.

A "search tree," or "subject tree," is, in effect, a condensation of a classification scheme (Woodward 1996, 198–203). It permits the searcher to see where in the scheme the desired topic is located and, in electronic form, to move instantly from one level of specificity to a more general or a more specific level (Example: *Songbirds, Birds, Canaries*). Search trees are being developed with different capabilities and in many formats and often also indicate the number of titles available on a given topic. An experimental variant is the query tree technique, which reformulates the query with each set of feedback documents retrieved from the previous query and which can also be transformed into a Boolean query (French et al. 1997).

On the Internet, several projects use search trees, some based on the *Dewey Decimal Classification* (DDC), the *Library of Congress Classification* (LCC), or the *Universal Decimal Classification* (UDC). Although search trees tend to avoid the dead ends that occur so often with keyword searches, the ones used on the Internet are, as of this writing, quite broad and would in no way provide as precise access to a specific item in a multimillion-volume collection as the major traditional classification schemes. Using a very promising different approach, OCLC began in 1996 a project to transform DDC captions (the descriptive terms and directions that go with the numbers in the schedule) into end-user language (Vizine-Goetz 1996).

Expert Systems

Also called "expert intermediary systems" or "knowledge-based systems," expert systems are a branch of artificial intelligence. They are computer programs composed of a "knowledge base" that contains the information in a very narrow field, gleaned from human experts and other sources such as print or databases, and an "inference engine" that applies the appropriate information from the knowledge base to a specific problem in that field. Expert systems are designed to perform tasks ordinarily requiring a specialist experienced in a given domain or subject, tend to be used with full-text documents, and perform at a level of competence that is better than that of nonexpert humans. In particular, they are able to handle incomplete information and are designed to perform problem-solving tasks based on judgmental and uncertain knowledge. Although conventional programs are executed according to a predefined algorithm and have only one solution path, expert systems use heuristic searching techniques that attempt to generate the "best possible" answer by exploring many solution paths (Morris 1992).

Work on expert systems began in the 1960s. Early versions began to enter the marketplace in the 1980s. Susan Gauch (1992) describes five different systems in the fields of cancer therapy, computer science, computer architecture, environmental pollution, and gardening. But it is still an emerging science and technology, albeit with promise and potential. Despite much progress on many fronts, difficult research problems remain unsolved, and much work remains to be done. More than one specialist even feels that "for the most part, language and ideas are simply too ambiguous for automated retrieval systems to properly identify and evaluate. It appears that artificial intelligence technologies will not meet this challenge in the near future" (Cataloguing and retrieval of information over network applications 1994). Martha M. Yee and Sara Shatford Layne agree and suggest an alternative: "[I]t is unlikely that algorithms will ever be developed that can figure out what a user wants—the searching process is just too complex. Instead, the user should always have at his or her fingertips a LOOK HARDER command or button that can be invoked at the user's discretion and suggest more complex types of searches and displays when the default searches and displays seem inadequate to the user. The user should be free to back out of these more complex approaches at any time" (1998, 8).

LINEARITY

We have so far dealt with subject indexing languages as such and with methods of using them for retrieving documents or topics contained in documents. This section provides a glimpse of the versatility with which subject indexing languages and systems can enrich the inherent limitations of the physical arrangement of books and other documents.

Books, as physical objects, are arranged on shelves piece by piece, in "linear" sequence. If the sequence is dictated by a classification scheme such as the DDC or LCC, the books are shelved in linear sequence according to the notations of that scheme. This works fairly well for books that deal with a single topic, such as "weaving" or "miniature golf," in LCC respectively *TT848* and *GV987*. But works that deal with the interrelationship of several topics, with more than one topic, or with special aspects of one or more topics are more of a problem. Does *weaving for allergy-sufferers* belong with works on *hand weaving* or with works on *respiratory diseases*? Should a work that deals with *the role of music in daily life today* be classed with *music* or with *sociology*; does a work with the title *Educational economics* belong with *education* or *economics*; if a book on *how social conflict is depicted in American literature* is classed and shelved with other books about literature, how do searchers who are interested in the *social conflict* aspect find it? For such works the linear sequence of shelving is insufficient as a retrieval device. Theoretically, the option exists of shelving different copies of a work under different notations, but for financial, space, and other reasons this is seldom a practical long-range solution.

The same problem arises for any kind of document (maps, floppies, sheet music), and in whatever order they are arranged or shelved (by size, date of publication, accession number, title, or any other order): Physical objects can be arranged in only one, linear, unidimensional sequence, whereas knowledge is multidimensional. This is also true for "hard copy," that is, paper-based files of document surrogates: card catalogs or printed bibliographies. Linearity means that a precoordinated indexing term can be filed, and thus provide access, only by one of its elements. Usually that is the first filing word in an alphabetical heading or the first part of a notation. If several indexing terms have the same first element, subarrangement is by the next word or the next element, and so forth.

To permit access to additional elements of a document or document surrogate the library profession, classificationists, and information scientists have developed several methods and techniques (described in the next section and in Chapters 6, 7, and 8). In general terms, they consist of codes of rules designed to coordinate input and output standards within a system and methods of assigning classed and alphabetical labels that permit multidimensional access to multidimensional works or topics.

They permit a flexible, individualized, subject approach that complements the "linear rigidity" of shelving. Many methods, like faceted classification, classed catalogs, chain indexing, and analytical subject headings, were developed long before electronics; others, like postcoordinate indexing, Boolean searching, and keyterms, were greatly improved by electronics; still others, like truncation, string indexing, and proximity operators, became feasible and effective only with electronics.

In this search for "multidimensional access" we must not forget, however, that not everybody, not every patron or library, needs or is helped by such specific, detailed, fine-toothed combing and fine-meshed combining of topics. In general, the larger the collection, the more research-oriented, the more specialized, the narrower its major focus, the smaller the physical units it contains (books as against research reports), the greater the need for multidimensional access. But for the "casual" user, for a public library branch, a more general, uncomplicated access to the collection seems to be more helpful. The profession has recognized this in the past, for example with the "reader interest classification," simplified subject headings authority lists for children's collections, abridged editions of the DDC or, more recently, providing DDC numbers with suggested cutoff marks for smaller collections.

"CONTROL" AT THE INDEXING (INPUT) STAGE: SEMANTICS AND SYNTACTICS

Subject indexing languages are "artificial" languages, that is, they are typically designed by a person or organization to achieve specified purposes. Typically phrased and intended for the "input," the indexing phase, the rules create a predictable structure of concepts and terms, a known pattern that is expected to facilitate communication through codes and standards that are equally understood by sender and receiver, by indexer/subject cataloger and searcher/user. The means of carrying out this basic purpose depend on the characteristics and purpose of the indexing system used and on the medium for which it is designed. These means change, improve, and expand with developing technology and professional expectations.

Although the rules are usually not phrased in such terms, they tend to follow semantic and syntactic principles. The most obvious semantic factor is the precise meaning and scope of a term or notation. For example, should the term or notation that describes the history of a country include only its political or also its social history? Or, should the term or notation for *Pathology of plants* be subdivided into more specific categories and, if so, by type of disease or by type of plant, or both, or by some other factors? The designer's semantic decisions about *whether* to subdivide depend on the size of the collection or database, on the topic, and other factors. Semantic rules tend to be policy matters and therefore more likely to vary among vocabularies even within one system, and to change over time within one vocabulary.

The designer's decisions about *how* to subdivide depend partly on the topic (*history, plants*) but are, as far as the technique is concerned, syntactic. Unlike semantic rules, syntactic rules are usually an inherent and therefore virtually unchangeable system element because they tend to make a system work. The syntactic factor operates in both classed and alphabetical systems but is most obvious in alphabetical systems. For example, in a precoordinated alphabetical system that combines topical and geographic terms (not all of them do), the geographic term is typically affixed to the topical term: *Education—Peru* rather than *Peru—Education*. However, this principle is not inviolate because other considerations may override it in specific situations. For example, when the geographic or political area is itself the topic its name precedes the qualifier: *Peru—History* rather than *History—Peru*. Similar considerations go into the design of classed systems. To list or shelve together material on a topic, the Dewey Decimal notation for a topic limited to a country adds the country symbol as an affix to the basic notation for the topic. For example, the DDC notation *725.1609495 (Post office buildings in Greece)* consists of *725.16 (Post office buildings)* and *09495 (in Greece)*. Not all classed systems are that clear.

Most of these rules were originally made for paper-based files and have typically a practical, multiple-use basis: In the previous examples they result in listing together the entries, and in shelving together works, for material on education wherever it takes place, and on post offices wherever they may be. But topics that deal with the essence of a country, such as its history, tend to be searched, and are therefore listed, under the country's name. Reflection will show that many of these rules are equally needed in an automated environment. This topic is discussed in "The Legacy of Paper–Based Rules" in this chapter.

Examples of
Semantic Indexing Rules (or Codes)

In 1914 a special committee of the American Library Association (ALA) issued a mimeographed *Code for Classifiers*. The ALA published it in a 128-page book in 1928 and in a second edition of 177 pages in 1939. (Merrill 1928 and 1939). Each edition was compiled with advice from leading librarians of the day, so that the *Code* represented something of a national consensus. Unfortunately, ALA did not keep it up. Three sample rules follow:

> Diplomatic relations of two countries:
>> Class under the country represented or expressed in the point of view of the author.

> Plants, Edible and non edible:
>> (a) Works on the cultivation of edible plants: Class in agriculture.
>> (b) Works on the cultivation of non edible plants: Class in horticulture. (Merrill 1928)

> Method vs. Subject matter:
>> A work treating of the results of applying a given method, hypothesis, or theory to the investigation of a given subject: Class under the subject investigated, not under the method of investigation. (Merrill 1939)

Such classification rules are semantic in nature because they define the scope, and therefore the meaning, of a notation. They are essential for any topic that can be viewed from more than one angle. Although phrased and intended primarily for the indexer or cataloger, they are equally essential guides for the searcher.

During the past few decades, the Library of Congress (LC) has formalized and codified its practices in the form of detailed subject heading and classification manuals. Originally intended primarily for LC catalogers, they have become an international standard (SCM:SH 1991; SCM:C 1992). Many are really precise syntactic and semantic rules, although LC does not use this terminology. Following is an LC subject heading rule, semantic in nature because it delineates the respective scopes of related terms:

> Assign the heading *Latin Americans* to works dealing with the citizens of Latin America. For works limited to Spanish speaking Latin Americans use *Spanish Americans (Latin America)*. Use the heading *Hispanic Americans* for United States citizens of Latin American descent. (SCM:SH, 1991, H985)

Especially during the period from the 1950s to 1980s, many other indexing manuals or guides were created for subject headings, and especially for descriptors. Most were created by bibliographical organizations, some even by nonbibliographical national or international organizations such as UNESCO or the American National Standards Institute (ANSI), in an attempt to create generally accepted standards. Following are two ANSI guidelines on word forms and word order for descriptors:

> In general, the singular form is used for processes, properties (attributes) and unique things; the plural for classes of things:
> Processes: Acidification; Painting
> Properties: Conductivity; Opacity
> Unique things: Earth; Oxygen
> Classes of things: Paintings; Stars; Teeth

> Direct entry: Terms consisting of two or more words should be entered in their natural word order, that is, the order normally used in English sentences: *Radar antennas*; rather than *Antennas, Radar* (NISO 1993).

As mentioned previously, semantic rules (especially scope rules) tend to be policy matters and likely to vary among vocabularies even within one system. The effect of different semantic rules within one controlled system (such as a subject headings system) can be to impede searching. For example, for a work on microbiological research, the authority list for one OPAC or database might authorize the subject heading *Microbiological research*, and for works respectively on microbiology and on research the two subject headings *Microbiology* and *Research*, whereas the authority list for another OPAC or database in the same discipline might authorize only the latter two terms. This forces the indexer using the second system to assign to a work on microbiological research either the term *Microbiology* or the term *Research,* or both, depending on the system's guidelines. Either alternative is feasible, but searchers can be excused for not knowing either alternative because system semantic rules and guidelines are typically not made public, or are made public only as general searching instructions. This is one of many instances in which postcoordinate keyword searching with Boolean techniques can help the searcher, sophisticated or not, better than controlled language searching in a paper-based file.

Figure 3.1 (page 35) groups subject-based information retrieval systems on the basis of whether the systems use controlled or uncontrolled indexing vocabularies. Another way of classifying information retrieval systems is to group them by who or what creates the semantics and syntax that permit retrieval: Is this the indexer, the

SYSTEMS WHICH REQUIRE OR PERMIT THE INDEXER TO PRECOORDINATE SUBJECT INDEXING TERMS, AND SYSTEMS WHICH MAY OR MAY NOT PERMIT THE SEARCHER TO POSTCOORDINATE RETRIEVAL TERMS

Apart from the system-imposed techniques, the group at left **must**, and the other two groups **may** use selectively precoordinated **indexing terms**

Precoordinated systems always use precoordinated terms: Elements **must** be precoordinated by the indexer at the input stage

- Synthetic classification systems
  - String indexing
  - Faceted classification systems

If in **paper format**, cannot be postcoordinated by the searcher; but **OPAC programs** may be designed to postcoordinate several precoordinated search terms, and/or may be designed to retrieve by a single facet or single element in a string, not necessarily the first facet or element.

Systems with limited precoordination: Selected indexing terms **may** be precoordinated, or the indexer may combine (precoordinate) several terms, depending upon the terms used and the "**game rules**" of the system

- Enumerative classification systems
- Alphabetical (word-based) systems
  - Subject heading systems
  - Descriptor systems

The searcher **may** combine (postcoordinate) any terms (controlled or uncontrolled, precoordinated or not, alphabetical or enumerative **if** the vocabulary is in an **electronic database** and **if** the program permits it. (Certain precomputer, paper-based "inverted" indexing systems also permitted it. They are no longer in use). Catalogs and bibliographies on cards or in printed form which trace subject terms at the bottom of each entry are **not** physically designed for postcoordination, although they do permit it, awkwardly.

The system is not precoordinated since computers treat all keywords as separate terms, but individual **keywords** may be precoordinated terms
|
Uncontrolled, that is, free-term, keyword, or derived indexing

Many searching programs permit postcoordination of keywords: Find term **x** and term **y**; or, Find term **x** and (if within **y** words) term **z**.

Figure 4.1. Information retrieval systems grouped on the basis of pre- rather than postcoordination.

searcher, or the indexing language itself? The answer is, all three. Figure 4.1 deals with this concept and lists various indexing systems on the basis of pre- or postcoordination. While reading the following sections you may find it useful to consult Figure 3.1, the section "Thumbnail Sketches of Major Indexing Systems" in Chapter 3, and Figure. 4.1.

Markers or Relators:
The Syntax of Information Retrieval Languages

The preceding section dealt with input (indexing) rules and standards. This section and the next one deal with methods and techniques of applying indexing languages to individual documents to make them effectively retrievable.

In Chapter 3, in "Syntactics," markers were mentioned that decree the relationship of the various semantic elements and give them added meaning. Markers also operate under a variety of names in information retrieval languages where they achieve dramatically different results, depending on the type of language, and in the MARC bibliographic format. For the sake of simplicity, this discussion uses the term "relators" generically for all of them. A relator:

- Indicates the relations between the semantic elements in an information retrieval statement;

- May determine the order of the semantic elements;

- Without itself being a semantic element, adds to the meaning of the statement, for example by preventing ambiguity; and

- In the form of MARC 21 codes, and especially of subfield codes, facilitates previously unachievable postcoordinated retrieval of individual language elements.

Subject headings may serve as an example of how this last point represents an important enrichment of retrieval techniques, although some grammatical problems remain to be worked out, and although few if any local programs are taking advantage of this enrichment as this is written. Subject headings list topics basically in alphabetical sequence, but permit further subdivision of most topics. The traditional paper-based relator indicates the sequence of subdivisions of any one heading but does not distinguish them by type:

```
Engineers—France. [geographic subdivision]

Librarians—Professional ethics. [topical subdivision]

Apples—South Carolina—Statistics.
   [geographic subdivision, further subdivided by form division]
```

As described in Chapter 2, Section "6XX Fields," the MARC subfield indicators, however, not only separate the sections of a precoordinated term or phrase but also specify the category of each subfield. For example, the first subfield indicator is always **$a**. In the MARC bibliographic format for subject headings, **$v** signifies a (form division) type-of-material subfield, **$x** signifies a general, that is topical (subject) subfield, **$y** a chronological (time period) subfield, and **$z** a geographical subfield:

```
$a Engineers $z France
$a Librarians $x Professional ethics
$a Apples $z South Carolina $v Statistics
$a Brewery workers $z Denmark $x Mortality
$a United States $x History $y Civil War, 1861-1865
   $x Artillery operations
$a Women costume designers $z California $z Los Angeles
   $v Biography
```

For printed or online display purposes the MARC program can convert all of these on command to the traditional "linear" paper-based format. But for searching purposes the program permits searching subject headings-plus-subdivisions not only in linear form as complete units, as in a paper-based file, but also searching subdivisions individually or in Boolean postcoordinated fashion, always provided the local program permits it. Among precoordinated controlled systems, so far only some faceted classification schemes and string indexing systems have attempted to come close to this capability.

In PRECIS, which is a string indexing system, the relators are called "role operators." They show relationship and regulate the order in which the language elements will appear (without the relators) in the printed PRECIS indexes that lead to the described document (Austin 1984 and 1998). In the following example, the relators/role operators are the parts in parentheses:

```
(0) Canada
(p) Chaplains
(1) Hospitals
(4) Training
```

The relators/role operators direct the program to list the document under the string *Canada. Hospitals. Chaplains. Training.* and to create four index entries:

```
Canada. Hospitals. Chaplains. Training.

Hospitals. Canada.
   Chaplains. Training.

Chaplains. Hospitals. Canada.
   Training.

Training. Chaplains. Hospitals. Canada.
```

Note that the relators help to clarify meaning. Other possible combinations could tend to be ambiguous or puzzling, such as *Chaplains. Canada. Training. Hospitals.*, which might mean "Chaplains for training hospitals in Canada," rather than the intended "Training of hospital chaplains in Canada."

In the UDC (1993), which is a synthetic classification scheme, punctuation and mathematical symbols are used as relators to clarify the meaning of a linguistic element, to dictate their order, and to distinguish otherwise identical numbers. For example, the number *51* means "Mathematics", *(51)* means "China", *(051)* means "In the form of a periodical", and *=51* means "In the Chinese language". A colon (:) between numbers means that both concepts are interrelated. Example:

```
Symbol for agriculture              63
Symbol for statistics               31
Therefore, Agricultural statistics  63:31
Statistics for agriculture in China 63:31(51)
```

Rules and Techniques for Pre- and Postcoordination

The preceding section dealt with the various roles of relators and their dramatically different effects when the indexer constructs a precoordinated indexing term or phrase according to the rules of the indexing language used. This section describes five semantic or syntactic techniques that the indexer has available for topics for which the controlled indexing language authorizes *no* unique subject label. Typically this involves works dealing with the interrelationship of several topics, with more than one topic, or with special aspects of a topic. In other words, works for which the indexer must either assign a not-quite-correct existing controlled indexing term, or must create, according to the rules of the language being used, one or more new indexing terms. In a sense this is the counterpart to "'Control' at the Searching (Retrieval) Stage." In one way or another, these five techniques combine or coordinate the necessary indexing/retrieval terms. Many reflect some of the principles discussed in Chapter 5, such as specificity of indexing; all use syntactic markers in input and/or output.

Semantic Precoordination

A single existing subject label (word or notation) in the authority list can express an interrelationship or special aspect. Precoordinated indexing terms are generally more specific than uncoordinated ones. Usually one cannot tell by just looking at the label whether an enumerative class notation is precoordinated or whether the words are subject headings or descriptors:

```
Subject heading:
    Music and society (for a work on the role of music
    in daily life today)

Descriptor:
    Educational economics (for the economic aspects of
    education)

DDC (an enumerative classification system):
    291.171 (for the role of organized religion in
    society)
```

```
LCC (an enumerative classification system):
    BF 56 (for the psychological aspects of economics)
```

Syntactic Precoordination Required

These precoordinated indexing systems require the indexer to combine index-ing terms according to specific guidelines:

```
Faceted classification system:

  The schedules of one example contain the separate symbols
    E to H: Libraries and special categories of users.
      Egg: Rural users
       Fv: Public Libraries


    D: Location
      D73: U.S.A.

  Accordingly, after subdividing each topic on the basis of
  that system's manual and schedules,
    FvEggD73: United States public libraries for rural users.


String indexing system:

  For a work on the uneasy relationship between the Sinhalese
  and the Tamils in Sri Lanka, the indexer analyzes the
  various elements according to precise rules, and the
  computer program combines them into the string
      Sri Lanka. Tamils. Relations with Sinhalese, 1948-1984.
```

Limited Syntactic Precoordination Permitted

The system does not permit precoordination of major terms with each other. It permits, but does not require, precoordination of a major term with a limiting auxil-iary to provide the desired precision of description:

```
Subject headings system:

  Some labels listed in the LCSH authority list are:
    Windmills          Law         Labor supply

  Among terms which may limit the scope of these labels are
      topical treatment terms like     History,
      geographical terms like          India,
      type-of-material terms like      Periodicals.
```

The indexer may combine these with a dash (or MARC relator),
for example

Windmills—History	$a Windmills $x History
Law—India	$a Law $z India
Law—Periodicals	$a Law $v Periodicals
(for a periodical in the field of law)	
Labor supply—History	$a Labor supply $xHistory

DDC (an enumerative classification system):

The schedules contain notations such as
070.4 (Journalism),
070.41 (Editing).

Elements which can limit the meaning (and which in the two
examples below use the first "zero" as relator) include
0207 (Humorous treatment) and
092 (Persons, including biographies).

The indexer can combine these into notations such as
070.40207 (a work ridiculing journalism) or
070.41092 (a biography of an editor).

Semantic Uncoupling

If it is linguistically impossible or awkward to combine alphabetical language elements, or if the controlled vocabulary does not permit the desired combined term, the indexer may (or must) select more than one authorized index term that in combination describes the special aspect or the interrelationship. To retrieve in OPACs documents on the intersection of such topics, Boolean searching is required.

Subject headings system:

For a work on nickel and chromium plating, the two labels:
1. Nickel plating.   2. Chromium plating.

For a work on social conflict as depicted in American
literature, the two labels:
1. Social conflict in literature. 2. American literature.

Both examples are from a controlled indexing vocabulary that did not authorize combining either of these pairs of terms. This can change at any time because it is a matter of scope (semantics) and controlled indexing vocabularies grow and change with changing needs. One problem with the semantic uncoupling technique is that a pair of subject headings typically does not explain the relationship between the pair, whereas a precoordinated term such as *Social conflict in American literature* usually does.

Semantic or Conceptual Analysis

This term is described in Chapter 5, Section "Aboutness and Conceptual Analysis," and should not be confused with "content analysis" or "analytics" as described in Chapter 6, Section "The Changing Range of Options." If the rules of the controlled indexing system demand semantic (that is, conceptual) analysis of a document's subject, separate indexing terms are assigned to every aspect of its subject. As with the preceding technique, if a document with all or most of these characteristics is desired, Boolean searching is required.

```
Descriptor system:
     A report on establishing a program for technology
     education in Oklahoma received the descriptors: Cur-
     riculum development; Industrial arts; Program descrip-
     tions; Program development; Program implementation;
     Secondary education; State programs; Technology.
```

In this example no descriptor covers the report's overall topic. The descriptor system is described in Chapter 6.

THE LEGACY OF PAPER-BASED RULES: DO THEY STILL SERVE A PURPOSE?

Most indexing languages, systems, and techniques mentioned in Chapter 3 and in this chapter were routine parts of bibliographic control before electronics and computers began to affect information retrieval thinking, and long before OPACs became standard equipment in libraries. For example, the techniques illustrated in the preceding subsection use controlled, and mostly precoordinated, terms in an attempt to circumvent the rigidity of linear shelving and filing. Are they still useful or needed in the more flexible electronic environment? Could not retrieval flexibility and multidimensional access be achieved equally well by postcoordinate natural language searching using keywords, Boolean formulae, and proximity operators? This would most likely save input cost and shift much of the effort to the searcher. Yet the basic approach to indexing languages, systems, and techniques has not changed, although some paper-based techniques and rules are being adjusted or augmented by techniques that computerization requires or permits, such as the revision of filing rules to more or less suit computer needs.

In general terms, among the reasons for keeping the existing principles and rules are:

- Paper-based files and printed lists ("hard copy") are being used, and will most likely continue to be used along with electronic files.

- Although many documents and document surrogates exist only online, for the foreseeable future most documents (such as books) and document surrogates (such as catalog cards or bibliographic descriptions) will continue to be shelved, respectively filed, as physical objects, that is, in linear "unidimensional" sequence. Rules and techniques that were designed (or turned out to be useful) for "multidimensional" access to these documents and document descriptions are as important now as ever.

- Multidimensional access is only one function of the retrieval process. Another function is display: Once retrieved, results must be displayed. Although electronics permits reformatting the retrieved document surrogates in many ways and in different sequences (provided the local system accommodates this), any one screen and its printout are unidimensional. Likely effects must be considered before changing or dropping one function because a change in one function may well affect the others.

- "Natural language" systems have, by definition, no record of hierarchical or other relationships. Loss of structure is acknowledged to be an obstacle not only to input (which is typically done by professionals) but especially to searching, which is most frequently done by others who are more likely to need "signposts" to clarify the vocabulary's structure.

- Existing paper-based rules and systems do not impede or prevent postcoordinate retrieval of keywords or natural language terms; they enrich it by furnishing another alternative.

- Most bibliographic and indexing programs include "default decisions" when several options exist, that is, decisions that the program makes automatically unless it is instructed otherwise. The default decision is the most likely alternative given a particular query, and searchers rely on it heavily. This means that each default decision must be carefully programmed and should not be affected adversely by changed rules.

- Syntax and relators contribute to meaning. The same words in different sequence can sometimes (not always) have different meanings: The subject heading string *Railroads—Study and teaching—France* retrieves works on how the topic of railroads is studied or taught in France. But *Railroads—France—Study and teaching* deals with the study or teaching of French railroads. This is true online and on paper, and postcoordinate searching by keywords would not aid in this type of distinction.

- No viable alternative to the set of paper-based principles and rules is on the horizon, nor has there been serious demand for one. A far more realistic and effective approach is the current (implicit or acknowledged) policy of adjustment and integration, rather than bibliographic anarchy.

- OPAC retrieval techniques depend on OPAC capabilities, and OPAC capabilities are being developed at least partly on the basis of bibliographic needs, and especially of bibliographers' increasing awareness of program shortcomings and capabilities. All these fields are complex, and OPAC capabilities especially are still in a state of flux; they are being explored and developed rapidly and on many fronts and in an atmosphere of an "expanding horizon" and of "increasing awareness of pitfalls and potentials." The variety of OPAC systems that are available "off-the-shelf" and can be customized gives the individual library many options but thereby also prevents the standardization that helps less-experienced searchers find their way. For a balanced, detailed, and informed description and discussion of the bibliographic and technical aspects and their interdependence, see Martha M. Yee and Sara Shatford Layne (1998). Much needs to be done; much can be done.

NONSUBJECT AND NONVERBAL INDEXING SYSTEMS

Most subject retrieval systems use words or notations to retrieve a document or a concept contained in a document. It is worth noting that other systems exist and are being developed that fall outside the scope of the present work. As of the date of this writing they are not used in OPACs and need not be subject-oriented but still fall in the category of unknown item indexing/searching systems. The most commonly used system is "citation indexing" (described in this section), which is based on association.

Nonverbal Indexing Systems

Nonverbal systems began to be developed from the 1980s on with the development of online retrieval. The rapidly growing number of nontextual databases is only beginning to be searched by nontextual means such as by color charts, matching images, geographic coordinates, or by musical themes. But because most search engines are text-based, a text description is usually added to nontextual data, so that searches can be initiated by text or by nonverbal means.

A nonverbal searching system can have advantages over a verbal system. For example, several well-developed nonverbal systems permit chemical structures searching. When the chemical structure's unique identifier (a registry number or systematic name) is not available, or for nonspecific or generic searches, the searcher can draw the structure on the screen using either the mouse or the keyboard for text input. "The advantage of this approach is that it is independent of any vagaries or artificialities of nomenclature, which, on occasion, can be rather arbitrary and are frequently inconsistent with names used in commerce. Graphical or topological searching provides the potential for effective searching for less-well-defined structures" (Maizell 1998, 212).

Some techniques used with verbal or numerical systems carry over to nonverbal systems, for example pre- and postcoordination, truncation, and controlled vocabulary, although they may be called by other names, and although the vocabulary may consist not of words but of chemical structures or standardized images. But, as of this writing, OPACs are not used to access nonverbal databases; there is no uniform standard as yet for nontextual searching techniques; and the entire area, including the technology, is still in a state of flux and exploration.

Citation Indexing

Because citation indexing is often used in lieu of, or (better) in addition to, subject searches, a brief general description is in order here. Citation indexing is not an indexing system as commonly understood, but a "bibliographic references" system that uses bibliographic citations (that is, document surrogates) to connect a document with subsequent documents that refer to, or cite from, the earlier document. It is based on the premise that, if an author refers to, or cites, another author's work, the two works have something in common, typically the subject. It depends completely on the writer's honesty in listing sources in a bibliography attached to the writing. The bibliography refers to items written earlier. It is a look backward. ("M" has cited "A" and "B" and "C," all of whom wrote before "M.") Citation indexing turns this concept around and lists, in addition, under "A" that "M" has subsequently cited "A's" work, under "B" that "M" has subsequently cited "B's" work, and under "C" that "M" has subsequently cited "C's" work. This is a look forward. Especially since the advent of computers, citation indexing is a viable technique for pursuing concepts through several generations of writers, both backward and forward. Ideally, it permits searchers to follow the development of a concept, its extension, its modification, and even its refutation.

Citation indexing is used extensively in the field of law. Lawyers must know how a statute or part of a code is applied and also which laws or prior cases were cited in a specific later case or administrative regulation. Its modern legal version began with *Shepard's Citations* in 1873, but its history in Talmudic law goes back to the twelfth century (Weinberg 1997). Its enormous expansion into other fields and to journal literature began with the advent of computers. In 1961 the Institute for Scientific Information (ISI), a commercial enterprise under Eugene Garfield, started the *Science Citation Index*, followed by the *Social Sciences Citation Index* in 1966 and the *Arts and Humanities Citation Index* in 1977. These multidisciplinary indexes are available on paper, CD-ROM, and the Internet and cover, among them, about 8,000 journals. They are also accessible in combined form online as the *Web of Science*.

Electronics and ingenuity enabled ISI to go way beyond the basic concept of citation indexing to create an increasing variety of additional products, for example several "Current Contents" editions that display the tables of contents from books, conference proceedings, and groups of journals in selected fields such as "Life sciences." Most are available in several formats. ISI also expanded beyond the original citation indexing concept by adding keyword access and access to abstracts. Libraries often use special ISI listings that indicate a journal's degree of use, as a basis for journal selection or retention. Academic institutions often use ISI products to judge a person's "productivity" as a factor in hiring and promotion. The suitability and fairness of both uses have been questioned more than once (Scales 1976), most recently by E. Szava-Kovats (1997).

Much has been written since the 1960s about citation indexing as such, and about ISI, whose extensive range of bibliographic products is listed at http://www.isinet .com on the Internet (accessed May 1, 2001).

RESEARCH IN
INFORMATION RETRIEVAL

Research literature must be read thoughtfully and with a grain of salt. Precise statistical studies based on shaky assumptions, or conclusions that go farther than the available evidence justifies, are not uncommon. In a painstakingly precise article, Thomas Mann (1997) demonstrates how a series of seemingly small errors and/or omissions by writers quoting and citing other writers and researchers, along with some editorializing, can lead to erroneous interpretation of research results and, in the cited case, probably to major, and potentially unfortunate, policy changes.

Controlled and Uncontrolled
Indexing Vocabularies

Since the 1960s, much research has been done to test whether controlled or uncontrolled indexing languages provide better retrieval results and, in the case of controlled vocabularies, whether alphabetical (word) systems or notational (classed) systems provide better results. One point that needed clarification was the definition of "better" retrieval results. In general, it is felt that a perfectly successful system retrieves all documents in a collection that provide the desired information (not only some of the documents) and provides only these documents (not also irrelevant ones). At first, researchers tended to think in either/or terms. A document either provided the desired information, or it did not; it either was or was not relevant. In the late 1960s researchers like Tefko Saracevic began to introduce finer measures of distinction, such as relevant, partly relevant, and not relevant. These finer distinctions were based on the mathematical fuzzy logic and fuzzy sets theory, which was first described in the mid-1960s by Lotfi Asker Zadeh. In information retrieval, fuzzy sets formulae are used to search, if necessary, less than exact matches with a search query, and also attempt to permit listing retrieved documents in probable order of relevance.

Shortly after the degrees of relevance began to be measured on a finer scale, researchers began to question the definition of relevance itself. Recent examples are studies by Rebecca Green (1995) and L. T. Su (1994) that tried to discern the many variables that can influence people's conception of relevance. Although quite a few researchers believe that variations in relevance assessments have no effect on measures of retrieval performance, Stephen P. Harter writes: "Variations in relevance assessments may [affect] the measurement of retrieval effectiveness" (1996, 37). Many writers agree with Saracevic, who writes even more bluntly: "Differences in human decision making have a large impact, if not even *the* [original emphasis] predominant impact, on how IR systems perform" (1991, 85).

The first major comparative experimental study of indexing systems, the so-called Cranfield I study, concluded in 1962 that the performance of an indexing system depended not on whether it uses a classed or alphabetical indexing vocabulary but on the power of the indexing language allied to the standard of indexing (Cleverdon 1962), still a commonly accepted conclusion. The study also introduced measurable concepts of retrieval performance in terms of precision (the number of relevant documents retrieved versus the total number of documents retrieved) and recall (the number of relevant documents retrieved versus the total number of relevant documents in the collection). Since that time it has been commonly accepted that these two measures have an inverse relationship: Steps taken to increase recall decrease precision, and vice versa.

Some researchers, including Elaine Svenonius (1986), question this theory with much justification, and Robert Fugman shows by means of examples like the following that, while often observed, the inverse relationship between precision and recall is not inevitable: "Several names may have been in use for a country or an industrial company in the course of time. When only one of these names is used as a search parameter, recall will be low. *Recall can be enhanced* through the inclusion of several of these names as alternative search parameters. But *by no means will precision decline simultaneously with the increase in recall*" (emphasis in original) (Fugman 1994, 154). Fugman even points out that, for example when searching for chemical compounds, it is perfectly possible to attain both 100 percent precision and 100 percent recall at the same time.

While researchers continue to investigate precision, recall, relevance, and related matters, studies by L. T. Su (1994) and others have shown that user satisfaction (which may or may not have much to do with the real effectiveness of a search) depends more on absolute recall than on precision. A small-scale study of Internet users suggests similar findings (Wolfram and Dimitroff 1997).

Partly because the Cranfield I project was criticized in reviews, the same researchers undertook a second experiment called, not surprisingly, Cranfield II. They concluded that natural language has a slight edge over controlled indexing vocabularies (Cleverdon 1966). Many writers in the field accepted this finding half-heartedly.

For many years conventional wisdom held that searching by notation, and free text searching, contribute to precision by virtue of being more specific and/or more current, and that controlled vocabulary serves primarily to promote recall by virtue of its classing action. These theories have by now probably been laid to rest. Karen Markey, Pauline Atherton, and Claudia Newton (1980) found that controlled vocabularies provide precision, and free text retrieval improves recall. Likewise, MaryEllen Sievert and Bert R. Boyce (1983) explained how, particularly in an online retrieval system, controlled indexing vocabulary becomes a precision tool rather than a broad recall tool.

Several very significant studies demonstrated that both free text and controlled vocabularies are needed for more complete results than either approach by itself could generate. Elaine Svenonius suggested that "free text and controlled vocabulary terms each contribute to precision and each to recall, but they do so in different ways, and it is the relative weight of the contributions that affects any given retrieval outcome" (1986, 335). Rolf G. Henzler (1978) and David Raitt (1980) illustrated with numerous examples that neither the free text by itself, nor the controlled alphabetical vocabulary by itself, leads to complete retrieval of all pertinent documents. Based on experimental results, Deborah Carrow and Joan Nugent (1977), Mary L. Calkins (1980), Ann H. Schabas (1982), Carol Tenopir (1985), and others found that controlled alphabetical and free text vocabulary searches each produces unique groups of documents, with some overlapping.

Researchers also investigated whether the addition of more content-bearing information to the basic bibliographic citation, such as the table of contents or an abstract, would improve results. Some of the research was inconclusive, but Martin Dillon and Patrick H. Wenzel (1990) found that, at least in a database that emphasized the physical sciences, the addition of such information tended to improve recall while precision suffers. Yee and Layne point out problems connected with such addition, which is likely to increase the amount of noise or false drops retrieved on any given search, especially as our databases get larger over time (1998, 132–40).

Classification Systems

The advent of OPACs revived an interest in classification as a searching tool. After almost a century of neglect, classification began to be investigated in the 1960s as a retrieval tool in the electronic environment.

By the end of the nineteenth century the classed catalog, in which the subject entries are listed in a separate, classed file, had been almost entirely replaced by the alphabetical subject headings in the dictionary catalog. But experienced searchers knew that the shelflist served as a substitute, albeit an imperfect one. Provided they could get access to the shelflist on cards (which was usually in the Technical Processing Department) they always searched it, along with the alphabetical subject headings in the public catalog, if they wanted to get a more complete listing of works on a topic.

Early in OPAC history Robert R. Freeman and Pauline Atherton (1968) studied the UDC as searching vocabulary in an electronic environment. They concluded that it could be used effectively as the indexing language in computer-based retrieval systems, but warned that the theory according to which UDC would develop in the future should take into account the requirements and capabilities of computer-based systems, and they called attention to the need for system designers to consider user needs and preferences. By 1993 a machine-readable version of the UDC, the UDC "Master Reference File," was completed, as were machine-readable versions of DDC and parts of LCC.

After a hiatus during which primarily alphabetical retrieval systems were investigated, online systems began to develop in the 1980s and 1990s the capacity to switch searchers from a word index, such as a subject heading or a keyword taken from a class schedule caption, to a classed sequence, enabling the searcher to browse in classed order. However, most substantial research and demonstration projects of the 1980s and 1990s were aimed at facilitating input rather than retrieval, that is, at helping the classifier rather than the searcher. For example, OCLC's *Scorpion* research project tested, in addition to several other features, feasibility and techniques of using tools like the DDC to perform automatic assignment of subject headings and class numbers for electronic items to save a human indexer's time. The techniques being investigated include comparing the terms in a document with terms in the DDC database, resulting in a ranked list of potential DDC numbers, which are then available to a human indexer for final choice. The researchers report that much work still remains to be done (Shafer 1997; Shafer et al. 1997).

In 1983 OCLC (a large utility that controls millions of bibliographic entries), the Council on Library Resources, and Forest Press (publisher of the DDC) sponsored the *Dewey Decimal Classification Online Project*, a thorough study of classification as a searching tool, under the direction of OCLC's Karen Markey. In this study bibliographic records with DDC numbers were enhanced automatically with subject terms associated with those numbers and taken from the DDC Schedules, captions, and Relative Index, and from the assigned subject headings. The DDC was found to be a major contributor of unique subject terms to the bibliographic database, that is, terms not available through subject headings or keywords taken from subject headings, and that the approach improved search performance. It was also found (not surprisingly) that some captions had to be reworded to improve their understandability to online catalog users (Markey and Demeyer 1986; Drabenstott et al. 1990). Meanwhile, many of the study's recommendations have been implemented. In 1984, a team led by Nancy J. Williamson of the University of Toronto began a series of studies designed to examine the suitability of the LCC for computerization, so that the schedules could be edited and used for assigning class numbers and for searching in an interactive online system. This project resulted in the conversion of LCC for online use.

The DDC Online Retrieval System (DORS) Project at the University of California, Los Angeles, was designed primarily for catalog users. It investigated searching by means of the DDC (Liu and Svenonius 1991). Among several helpful features the distinguishing one is an automatically generated alphabetical chain index that leads to the DDC notation. Chain indexes (more fully explained in Chapter 7) are not well known in North America. Unlike the better known combination alphabetical subject headings/classed notation, they are coordinated in specificity and meaning with the classification scheme because they are derived from it. Also, they are designed to lead to the desired specific notation as well as to the notation's broader hierarchical levels, which should help the searching process.

Searches Using
Combined Indexing Vocabularies

Even at the expense of spending more time and money in a search, and at the risk of receiving marginal material along with truly relevant items, it is generally acknowledged that a combined classed vocabulary/controlled alphabetical vocabulary/uncontrolled alphabetical vocabulary search produces the most complete file. Interestingly enough, most online databases created since the 1970s, both files of documents such as the ERIC database and OPACs like the University of Wisconsin-Madison's MadCat, were programmed to accept controlled and uncontrolled alphabetical subject vocabularies. This may have been an act of caution on the designers' part, or it may have been done merely because it is relatively easy to blend both systems in a computer program. In any case, by permitting access via both controlled and uncontrolled alphabetical indexing languages, the system designers anticipated at least some research results. As a result, the combined use of controlled and uncontrolled indexing terms in one search is fairly common, with keywords serving sometimes as access terms to controlled subject headings. However, in most systems access by class or call number has not nearly reached its potential. Controlled notational (classed) and controlled and uncontrolled alphabetical indexing vocabularies should be considered not only as alternatives, but as complementary. All have advantages in particular situations, and together they provide more comprehensive retrieval results than any one type of vocabulary by itself.

Future OPACs may well add or integrate into their subject retrieval capabilities a range of adaptations and amalgamations of other presently known techniques such as string indexing and/or faceting. Development of nonverbal indexing systems and their standardization and possible alignment with, or even integration into, the existing alphabetical and classed online retrieval techniques also deserves increased attention. Research and demonstration projects continue to be in order, although some might agree with Senator Simon Cameron, who is quoted as having said in 1861 (!): "I am tired of this thing called science. We have spent millions in that sort of thing for the last few years, and it is time it should be stopped." More research is needed, for example, on the permanent versus the temporary, elusive, shifting aspects of an individual searcher's relevance judgments.

Research on OPAC Searching

Some of the previously mentioned research took place without involving OPACs; other research involved them. For example, Cranfield I and II did not involve OPACs, but the DORS Project did. Along with OPACs came a shift in attitude on the part of the shakers and movers. Ann O'Brien describes it thus: "There was an implicit sense that serious [card] catalog users would familiarize themselves with the various constraints of the manual catalog and then benefit by their diligence. The perception now is that we cannot expect users to bring the same degree of application to a self contained, self service system, and most evaluations of such systems confirm this" (1994, 220).

Much OPAC research deals with basically abstract questions like recall, precision, and matching query vocabulary to controlled or uncontrolled indexing terms. Much is aimed at the development and refinement of algorithms to improve browsing and searching by controlling information overload and vocabulary differences. Another category deals more directly with OPACs and their capabilities, with command languages, possible options, screen configurations, and similar topics. Some research deals with bibliographic matters, such as how different types of indexing vocabularies, such as LCC, DDC, or Library of Congress Subject Headings (LCSH), can be used in or adapted to online use. Another type of research is on "catalog use," or "user studies," that is, users' searching behavior, reactions to (real or apparent) searching problems or success, users' backgrounds, use of types of information in the bibliographic citations, and similar matters. In addition, over the past forty years the interdisciplinary field of Human Computer Interaction (HCI) has developed with its own research agenda (Shackel 1997).

Since the 1930s, most user studies involving card catalogs have shown that the great majority of users did "known item" rather than "unknown item" searches. They searched for a name or title that they knew, rather than for a work whose existence they merely hoped for under a subject whose precise name they had to guess. Research studies involving OPACs, however, showed almost from the beginning that most user inquiries, successful or unsuccessful, were subject inquiries, that is, "unknown item" searches.

This may be due to the difference in media, to more sophisticated research design and interpretation, or to other factors. The typical information screen at the beginning of an OPAC search indicates more or less clearly that subject searches are possible and how to initiate them; such screens imply privacy for the searcher, but whether they are more conducive to conducting a subject search than, for example, signage in a library building that points to a "subject catalog" on cards is a matter of conjecture. Studies have shown that users of OPACs are actually more persistent than card catalog users, but that may be due to fascination with the new medium or to ease of exploration. The searcher need not move physically from one card tray to another (in large card catalogs sometimes over considerable distance), but ease of exploration may not necessarily lead to an increase in subject searches. On the other hand, keyword searching does seem to encourage exploration: The searcher need not know the exact form or specificity of a subject heading but can begin a topical search by entering one or more likely topical words, that is, keywords; however, most searchers do not know the negative aspects of this approach. Almost all OPACs support searching and scrolling by class number, giving searchers an additional subject approach that they did not have in the typical card catalog, but whether this added availability has contributed to more subject searches is questionable because studies have shown that users have not taken advantage of these features (Hsieh-Yee 2000).

An uncomfortably large number of OPAC-based studies in the 1980s showed that, although from 30 to 50 percent of subject searches failed to retrieve any records, those subject searches that were successful often led to an unmanageable mass of entries. Charles R. Hildreth (1989) and others attributed these failures to a variety of shortcomings in the first two generations of OPACs. In summary, the early OPACs did not provide enough help to the searcher: in translating search questions or keywords into indexing vocabulary, in tolerating misspellings and mistypings, in helping to refine search statements or to browse, in ranking large retrieval sets in order of relevance, in describing retrieved titles sufficiently to permit users to judge their usefulness. Such criticism, along with the increasing sophistication of computer languages and ever more exacting user demands, caused each new version of software and each generation of hardware to handle more, and increasingly difficult, options. It also led to research and demonstration projects like CHESHIRE and CHESHIRE II, which applied probabilistic theory, that is weighing, and refinements such as word stemming, to OPAC searching (Larson 1992; Larson et al. 1995).

Research on Internet Searching

Internet research and demonstration projects on bibliographic retrieval can be grouped into the same broad, not necessarily mutually exclusive, categories as OPAC research, with one additional category, studies on system capabilities of World Wide Web (WWW) search tools, also called "search engines," "WWW databases," topically organized "directories," "Internet indexes," "searchable subject trees," or "meta search engines." If done in-house by search engines they are rarely shared with the public because they touch on trade secrets. Other studies compare retrieval performance of selected groups of search engines, usually with sets of sample questions. Examples are reported by Nicholas G. Tomaiuolo and Joan G. Packer (1996) and Sarah J. Clarke and Peter Willett (1997).

With potentially simultaneous access to a wide range of independent databases on the Internet, the century-old desire to overcome vocabulary differences seems to have become a mandate but now involves more than just indexing languages (Zeng 1993). Research and demonstration projects that test how specific existing library and bibliographic standards like the *Anglo-American Cataloging Rules*, 2nd Edition (AACR2), DDC, LCC, UDC, and LCSH can be used, adapted, or improved for the Internet are ultimately efforts to make bibliographic control and retrieval at least as effective over a wide-ranging network of databases as it is in the individual library or information agency. In the background may also be the probably justified concern that "Internet-inspired classification schemes, paired with powerful search engines, have the potential to supplant library organizing techniques, or at least to provide parallel approaches that become the preferred access method for electronic data, leaving library classification to organize traditionally published materials" (Vizine-Goetz 1996, 1).

OCLC has undertaken for decades many research or demonstration projects, including projects that test whether and how cataloging standards can be used for or adapted to improve retrieval on the Internet. Much of its research deals with automated classification; with relevance ranking; with linking classed (DDC) and alphabetical terms to enrich searching capabilities in OPACs and on the Internet; and with enabling access to Internet resources. (Annual research summaries are available via http://www.oclc.org/research [accessed May 15, 2001]). For example, OCLC's *CORC* (Cooperative Online Research Catalog) project provides tools for the cooperative creation, maintenance, and use of metadata for Web resources (Hickey and Vizine-Goetz 1999). The *Scorpion* project explores the indexing and cataloging of electronic resources, primarily by automatic subject recognition based on the DDS (Shafer et al. 1997).

In the United Kingdom, the CATRIONA (*CAT*aloging and *R*etrieval of *I*nformation *O*ver *N*etworks *A*pplications) project is based on the assumption that Internet resources will be cataloged in a distributed fashion. Therefore, OPAC clients must be able to locate and search all of the individual Opacs that make up the distributed catalog. Under present conditions that is quite a tall order, but the project established that a distributed catalog of network resources integrated with standard Z39.50 library system OPAC interfaces is feasible at least on a basic level (Nicholson and Steele 1996; CATRIONA II 1999).

A major international project aiming to build large-scale information networks is "DESIRE: Development of a European Service for Information on Research and Education." Its second phase, DESIRE II, began in 1998. Its aims include developing a European network of cross-searchable services, including subject-based and regional exhaustive services. Automatic classification by embedded metadata, robot-gathered databases, and distributed Web indexing are some of the techniques being investigated. The detailed description is available at http://www.lub.lu.se/desire.

CONCLUSION

The semantic and syntactic aspects of indexing and retrieval languages, as well as the developing software and hardware, affect searching options. On the one hand, OPAC searchers have far more searching and display options available than the card catalog permitted. On the other hand these very options, along with sometimes puzzling instructions and the screen's spatial limitations, make the need for sophistication on the searcher's part more apparent than in the days of the card catalog. Bibliographic searching was never as easy as many people assumed; research and programming and hardware development (and a great deal of money) have made OPACs increasingly user-friendly but still puzzling enough for any but habitual users. An increasing range of options may result in over-refinement that goes beyond the "average user's" tolerance level. Standardization of onscreen symbols and of techniques would be a boon. In spite of this caution there can be no question that, on the whole, the computer has greatly enhanced our ability to control our literature bibliographically.

REFERENCES

Anderson, James D., and Frederick A. Rowley. 1991 [1992]. Building end-user thesauri from full-text. In *Advances in classification research, vol. 2. Proceedings of the 2nd ASIS SIG/CR Classification Research Workshop held at the 54th ASIS annual meeting, Washington, D.C., October 27–31, 1991*, 1–13. (ASIS Monograph Series). Washington, DC: Published by Learned Information for the American Society for Information Science.

Austin, Derek.1984. *PRECIS: A manual of concept analysis and subject indexing*. London: British Library.

———. 1998. Derek Austin: Developing PRECIS, Preserved Context Indexing System. *Cataloging & Classification Quarterly* 25 (2/3): 23–66.

Borgman, Christine L. 1996. Why are online catalogs *still* hard to use? *Journal of the American Society for Information Science* 47 (7): 493–503.

Calkins, Mary L. 1980. Free text or controlled vocabulary? A case history step by step analysis . . . plus other aspects of search strategy. *Database* 3: 53–67.

Carrow, Deborah, and Joan Nugent. 1977. Comparison of free-text and index search abilities in an operating information system. In *Information management in the 1980s: Proceedings of the American Society for Information Science, 40th annual meeting, September 26–October 1, 1977.* White Plains, NY: Knowledge Industry Publications.

CATRIONA II. 1999. CATRIONA II demonstrators: University management of electronic resources. Available: http://link.bubl.ac.uk/linksearch. (Accessed May 1, 2001).

Clarke, Sarah J., and Peter Willett. 1997. Estimating the recall performance of Web search engines. *Aslib Proceedings* 49 (7, July–August): 184–89.

Cleverdon, Cyril W. 1962. *Report on the testing and analysis of an investigation into the comparative efficiency of indexing systems.* Cranfield, England: College of Aeronautics.

———. 1966. *Factors determining the performance of indexing systems.* Cranfield, England: College of Aeronautics.

Cousins, Shirley Ann. 1992. Enhancing subject access to OPACs: Controlled vocabulary vs. natural language. *Journal of Documentation* 48 (3, September): 291–309.

DESIRE: Development of a European Service for Information on Research and Education. 1999. Available: http://www.lub.lu.se/desire. (Accessed May 10, 2001).

Dillon, Martin, and Patrick H. Wenzel. 1990. Retrieval effectiveness of enhanced bibliographic records. *Library High Tech* 8 (3): 43–46.

Drabenstott, Karen M., and Diane Vizine-Goetz. 1994. *Using subject headings for online retrieval: Theory, practice, and potential.* San Diego: Academic Press.

Drabenstott, Karen M., and Marjorie S. Weller. 1996. Failure analysis of subject searches in a test of a new design for subject access to online catalogs. *Journal of the American Society for Information Science* 47 (7): 519–37.

Drabenstott, Karen M., et al. 1990. Analysis of a bibliographic database enhanced with a library classification. *Library Resources & Technical Services* 34 (2, April): 179–98.

Dykstra, Mary. 1987. *PRECIS: A primer.* Revised reprint. Metuchen, NJ: Scarecrow Press.

Foskett, A. C. 1996. *The subject approach to information.* 5th ed. London: Library Association.

Freeman, Robert R., and Pauline Atherton. 1968. File organization and search strategy using the Universal Decimal Classification in mechanical retrieval systems. In *Mechanized information storage, retrieval and dissemination. Proceedings of the FID/FIP Joint Conference, Rome, June 14–17, 1967,* edited by Kjell Samuelson, 122–52. Amsterdam: North-Holland.

French, James C., et al. 1997. A classification approach to Boolean query reformulation. *Journal of the American Society for Information Science* 48 (8): 694–706.

Fugman, Robert. 1992. Illusory goals in information science research. In *Classification research for knowledge representation and organization. Proceedings of the 5th International Study Conference on Classification Research,* edited by N. J. Williamson and M. Hudon, 61–68. Amsterdam: Elsevier.

———. 1994. Galileo and the inverse precision/recall relationship; medieval attitudes in modern information science. *Knowledge Organization* 2 (3): 153–54.

———. 1995. The complementarity of natural and controlled languages in indexing. In *Subject indexing: Principles and practices in the 90's. Proceedings of the IFLA Satellite meeting held in Lisbon, Portugal, 17–18 August 1993*, edited by R. P. Holley, Dorothy McGarry, Donna Duncan, and Elaine Svenonius, 215–30. München: K. G. Saur.

Gauch, Susan. 1992. Intelligent information retrieval, an introduction. *Journal of the American Society for Information Science* 43 (2): 175–82.

Glassel, Aimée D., and Amy Tracy Wells. 1998. Scout Report Signpost: Design and development for access to cataloged Internet resources. *Journal of Internet Cataloging* 1 (3): 15–45.

Green, Rebecca. 1995. Topical relevance relationships: Why topic matching fails. *Journal of the American Society for Information Science* 46 (9): 646–53.

Harter, Stephen P. 1996. Variations in relevance assessments and measurement of retrieval effectiveness. *Journal of the American Society for Information Science* 47 (1): 37–49.

Henzler, Rolf G. 1978. Free or controlled vocabularies. *International Classification* 5 (1): 21–26.

Hickey, Thomas B, and Diane Vizine-Goetz. 1999. *The role of classification in CORC*. Manuscript of a paper published in the proceedings of the Online Information 1999 Conference, London, UK, December 1999. 6 pages. Available: http://www.oclc.org/oclc/research/. (Accessed May 15, 2001).

Hildreth, Charles R. 1989. OPAC research: Laying the groundwork for future OPAC design. In *The online catalogue: Development and direction,* edited Charles R. Hildreth, 1–24. London: Library Association.

Hsieh–Yee, Ingrid. 2000. Personal communication to John J. Boll. (Ms. Hsieh–Yee kindly reviewed an earlier draft of this section.)

Larson, Ray R. 1992. Evaluation of advanced retrieval techniques in an experimental online catalog. *Journal of the American Society for Information Science* 43 (1): 34–53.

Larson, Ray R., et al. 1995. Cheshire II: Design and evaluation of a next generation online catalog system. In *American Society for Information Science, Proceedings of the 58th annual meeting,* 215–25. Washington, DC: Published by Learned Information for the American Society for Information Science.

[LCSH]. 1998. *Library of Congress List of Subject Headings.* 19th ed. Prepared by the Cataloging Policy and Support Office, Library Services. Washington, DC: Library of Congress, Cataloging Distribution Service. 4v.

Liu Songqiao, and Elaine Svenonius. 1991. DORS: DDC online retrieval system. *Library Resources & Technical Services* 35 (4): 359–75.

Maizell, Robert E. 1998. *How to find chemical information: A guide for practicing chemists, educators, and students.* 3d ed. New York: John Wiley.

Mann, Thomas. 1997. "Cataloging must change!" and indexer consistency studies: Misreading the evidence at our peril. *Cataloging & Classification Quarterly* 23 (3/4): 3–45.

Markey, Karen, and Anh N. Demeyer. 1986. *Dewey Decimal Classification Online Project: evaluation of a library schedule and index integrated into the subject searching capabilities of an online catalog. Final report.* (Report number OCLC/OPR/RR–86–1). Dublin, OH: Online Computer Library Center.

Markey, Karen, Pauline Atherton, and Claudia Newton. 1980. An analysis of controlled vocabulary and free text search statements in online searches. *Online Review* 4 (September): 225–36.

Merrill, William Stetson. 1928. *Code for classifiers: Principles governing the consistent placing of books in a system of classification.* Chicago: American Library Association.

———. 1939. *Code for classifiers: Principles governing the consistent placing of books in a system of classification.* 2d ed. Chicago: American Library Association.

Morris, Anne. 1992. Overview of expert systems. In *The application of expert systems in libraries and information centers*, edited by Anne Morris, 1–33. London: Bowker–Sauer.

Nicholson, Dennis, and Mary Steele. 1996. CATRIONA: A distributed, locally-oriented, Z39.50 OPAC-based approach to cataloguing the Internet. *Cataloging & Classification Quarterly* 22 (3/4): 127–41.

[NISO]. National Information Standards Organization (U.S.). 1993. *Guidelines for the construction, format, and management of monolingual thesauri.* Approved August 30, 1993 by the American National Standards Institute. (ANSI/NISO Z39.19-1993. NISO Press.)

O'Brien, Ann. 1994. Online catalogs: Enhancements and developments. In *Annual review of information science and technology (ARIST),* 29: 219–42. Medford, NJ: Published for the American Society for Information Science (ASIS) by Learned Information.

Raitt, David. 1980. Aspects of searching via online systems using controlled and uncontrolled vocabularies. *International Association of Technological University Libraries, Proceedings* 12: 3–21.

Rowley, Jennifer. 1994. The controlled versus natural indexing languages debate revisited: A perspective on information and retrieval practice and research. *Journal of Information Science* 20 (2): 108–19.

Saracevic, Tefko. 1991. Individual differences in organizing, searching, and retrieving information. *Proceedings of the Annual Meeting of the American Society for Information Science* 28: 82–86.

Scales, P. A. 1976. Citation analyses as indicators of the use of serials: A comparison of ranked title lists produced by citation counting and from use data. *Journal of Documentation* 32 (1): 17–25.

Schabas, Ann H. 1982. Post coordinate retrieval. *Journal of the American Society for Information Science* 33 (January): 32–37.

Shackel, Brian. 1997. Human Computer Interaction—whence and whither? *Journal of the American Society for Information Science* 48 (11): 970–86.

Shafer, Keith. 1997. Scorpion helps catalog the Web. 3p. Available: http://orc.rsch.oclc.org:6109 /b–asis.html. (Accessed May 1, 2001).

Shafer, Keith, et al. 1997. Scorpion: Dewey database design. 8p. Available: http://orc.rsch.oclc .org:6109/b–asis.html. (Accessed May 7, 2001).

Shaw, Ralph R. 1961. *The state of the library art*, edited by Ralph R. Shaw. Volume 4, parts 1–5 (in one volume). New Brunswick, N J: Graduate School of Library Service, Rutgers–The State University. (Contents: *Notched cards*, by F. Reichman; *Feature cards (Peek–a–boo cards)*, by L. S. Thompson; *Punched cards*, by R. Blasingame Jr.; *Electronic searching*, by G. Jahoda; *Coding in yes-no form*, by D. J. Hickey.)

Sievert, MaryEllen, and Bert R. Boyce. 1983. Hedge trimming and the resurrection of the controlled vocabulary in online searching. *Online Review* 7 (December): 489–94.

Su, L. T. 1994. The relevance of recall and precision in user evaluation. *Journal of the American Society for Information Science* 45 (April): 207–17.

[SCM:C]. 1992– . *Subject cataloging manual: Classification.* 1st ed. Prepared by the Office for Subject Cataloging Policy, Library of Congress. Washington, DC: Cataloging Distribution Service, Library of Congress.

[SCM:SH]. 1991– . *Subject cataloging manual: Subject headings.* 1st. ed. Prepared by the Office for Subject Cataloging Policy, Library of Congress. Washington, DC: Cataloging Distribution Service, Library of Congress.

Svenonius, Elaine. 1986. Unanswered questions in the design of controlled vocabularies. *Journal of the American Society for Information Science* 37: 331–40.

Szava-Kovats, E. 1997. Non–indexed literature citedness. *International Information Communication & Education*, 16 (2): 203–9.

Tenopir, Carol. 1985. Full text database retrieval performance. *Online Review* 2 (April 1): 149–64.

Tenopir, Carol, and Pamela Cahn. 1994. Targets & freestyle: DIALOG and Mead join the relevance ranks. *Online Review* 18 (3): 31–47.

Tomaiuolo, Nicholas G., and Joan G. Packer. 1996. An analysis of Internet search engines: Assessment of over 200 search queries. *Computers in Libraries* 16 (6, June): 58–62.

[UDC]. 1993. *Universal decimal classification. International medium edition: English text.* 2d ed. BS 1000M. London: British Standards Institution.

Vizine-Goetz, Diane. 1996. Online classification: Implications for classifying and document[–like object] retrieval. [Electronic version of a paper published in] *Knowledge organization and change: Proceedings of the 4th international ISKO conference, 15–18 July 1996, Washington, D.C.* Frankfurt/Main: INDEKS Verlag. Available: http://orc.rsch.oclc.org:6109/dvgisko.htm. (Accessed May 1, 2001).

Weinberg, Bella Hass. 1997. The earliest Hebrew citation indexes. *Journal of the American Society for Information Science* 48 (4, April): 318–30.

Wolfram, Dietmar, and Alexandra Dimitroff. 1997. Preliminary findings on searcher performance and perception of performance in a hypertext bibliographic retrieval system. *Journal of the American Society for Information Science* 48 (12): 1142–45.

Woodward, J. 1996. Cataloging and classifying information resources on the Internet. *Annual Review of Information Science and Technology* 31: 189–219. Medford, NJ: Information Today, Inc., for American Society for Information Science.

Yee, Martha M., and Sara Shatford Layne. 1998. *Improving online public access catalogs.* Chicago: American Library Association. (For a brief history of OPACs (1980s–) and their immediate predecessors (1960s–), see pages 9–10 For the best contemporary "state-of-the–art" description of the indexing concepts and enabling technologies that bridged card catalogs and OPACs, see Shaw1961).

Zeng, Lei. 1993. Compatibility of indexing languages in an online access environment: A review of the approaches. In *Advances in classification research. Proceedings of the 3rd ASIS SIG/CR Classification research workshop held at the 55th ASIS annual meeting, Pittsburgh, PA, October 25, 1992,* edited by Raya Fidel, Barbara H. Kwasnik, Philip J. Smith, 3: 161–79. (ASIS Monograph Series.) Published by Learned Information for the American Society for Information Science.

5

Subject Indexing Process and Policy

INTRODUCTION

The subject retrieval function of an online catalog is dependent on two factors, as discussed in the previous chapters: controlled vocabulary and uncontrolled vocabulary. The former is typically applied by the cataloger who is creating the surrogate that will stand in the place of the actual item: the bibliographic record. This discussion deals mainly with human assignment of subject access controlled vocabulary, either subject headings or classification (although automatic indexing and classification for library catalogs are pursued experimentally).

The process of applying a controlled vocabulary is often referred to as "subject indexing" and is comparable in most aspects to other types of indexing. It involves three steps:

1. *Determining the aboutness* or subject content of an item,

2. *Conceptual analysis* to decide which of an item's aspects should be represented in the bibliographic record, and

3. *Translation* of the concepts or aspects into a controlled vocabulary, thus creating access points (International Organization for Standardization 1985).

All three of these processes should be governed by policies coming from an individual library or information agency, and from the standards such as subject headings lists and classification schemes that it uses. The individual library or information agency has the primary responsibility for serving its users and making its collection accessible. It must choose standards and systems that will allow it to fulfill this responsibility. The standards and systems make subject access achievable.

Few libraries can afford to develop their own unique standards and systems. The strictures of the chosen standards and systems are, then, the source of compromise between the needs of a given library's collections and users and the efficiencies of established means of subject access. For example, the *Dewey Decimal Classification*

(DDC) is a standard accepted by many libraries, but it is a general classification not designed to meet the particular needs of any specific user population. However, to create a classification is an immense task, and to use a unique classification would require a library to classify all of its own items with no assistance from being able to copy catalog records from other libraries and bibliographic databases. To be consistent in the use of DDC so that the system functions efficiently and to maintain compatibility with copy from other sources, a library must also follow the policies and procedures set out in the introduction to DDC. In this way the policies for classification stem from the standard that has been accepted. An individual library or information agency may choose to make exceptions to the policies and practices of a given standard. Such exceptions should be made judiciously because they will be expensive in terms of time. However, some local adaptations are necessary for significantly improved subject access in a particular context.

The object of subject indexing is to enable the user to retrieve those documents that pertain to the topic in which the user is interested (Cutter 1904, 12). This object has often been referred to as the "gathering" or "collocative" function of the catalog. The user's ability to retrieve these relevant documents is closely linked to the indexing process. The user, in a reversal of the indexing process, has to translate her or his needs into concepts, translate those concepts into indexing vocabulary, and then query the information system using this vocabulary to retrieve needed bibliographic items. Obviously, the indexing and user inquiry processes have to match in terms of the indexing labels and levels generated if the information retrieval system is to retrieve the information user's request. Although there are ways to facilitate this matching (described in Chapter 10), high-quality indexing is the most direct means of making appropriate links between a user and relevant documents.

From the perspective of the indexing process, the chances of a better match between indexing and user query processes depend on the following:

Indexing accuracy

Exhaustivity of indexing

Specificity of indexing

Indexing consistency

INDEXING ACCURACY

Indexing accuracy may be broken down into two aspects: the cataloger's ability to identify what concepts to represent and the cataloger's ability to translate those concepts into the controlled vocabulary. Although both of these aspects are difficult to achieve, the first is by far the more problematic. The identification of concepts within an item is a process that requires first the determination of its "aboutness."

Aboutness and Conceptual Analysis

M. E. Maron (1977) identified three different kinds of aboutness related to the indexing and retrieval process. The first is subjective aboutness (or S-about), which is the psychological concept, the individual's inner experience. S-about is, therefore, a very personal aspect of aboutness. The second is objective aboutness (or O-about), which is what the individual user will actually use to search. O-about is therefore an individual behavioral aspect of aboutness. The third is retrieval aboutness (or R-about), which is what groups of users who will find a document relevant will use in searching (e.g., a document is about cats if most of the users in a group who would find it relevant would seek the concept of cats in searching for it). R-about is therefore the most appropriate type of aboutness to use in a catalog because it is not limited to any one individual's conception. A cataloger who can be accurate in terms of identifying concepts to represent might well be defined as one who can achieve R-about or retrieval aboutness, because retrieval is the purpose of the process.

How can a cataloger determine the R-about of an item? Typically catalogers do not have time to read entire books or view full video recordings to determine what concepts to represent. Taking the case of a book, the cataloger will examine the title and table of contents, any illustrations, perhaps the publisher's "blurb" or the introduction, and often selected finer points such as section headings within chapters, bibliographic references, and the index. Occasionally the title alone will seem to be sufficient, such as *Principles of Sociology,* or *England 1870–1914,* or *Chemistry: An Introduction.* However, determining aboutness by a title is what Birger Hjørland (1992) refers to as a naïve approach to aboutness. Even seemingly straightforward titles may not be what they seem. Does *Principles of Sociology* need special subject treatment because it is a classic in its field published in the last century? Does *England 1870–1914* refer to political, economic, or social history, or all three? Does *Chemistry: An Introduction* include both organic and inorganic chemistry? Hanne Albrechtsen (1993) has suggested three approaches to determining aboutness: simplistic, seeking a direct reflection of the document; content-oriented, including what is implicit in the document as well as what is explicit; and requirements-oriented, based on predicted potential uses of the document. The simplistic approach presumes that there is an easily identifiable subject in any document. Superficial analysis by a cataloger or indexer would reflect a simplistic approach. Automatic indexing and retrieval (such as that used by most search engines on the World Wide Web) also depend on a simplistic approach because they are based on what words appear frequently and/or prominently in the text.

A more thorough examination by a human cataloger or indexer can result in a content-oriented approach. Teasing out what is implied about the subject as well as what is clearly stated adds depth to the analysis. However, the requirements-oriented approach includes not only the document itself but also its potential users. It is more like Maron's R-about in that it attempts to anticipate users' needs. It does not seek an ideally objective conception of the subject, but aims at making the representation as useful as possible. Hjørland (1992) describes this approach as pragmatic. The need to interpret the subject in relation to its intended audience begins the move from aboutness to conceptual analysis—choosing which elements of a subject should be represented in the catalog.

In these discussions of aboutness and conceptual analysis, there is a certain clash between the ideal of objectivity that catalogers frequently attempt to achieve and the ideal of serving the catalog's users, which can introduce intentional subjectivity such as "subject slanting" toward a specialized audience. How does this problem relate to accuracy? If one accepts a simplistic view of aboutness, then absolute accuracy is theoretically possible. There should be one objective interpretation of a given document. Elaine Svenonius and Dorothy McGarry (1993) analyzed the *Library of Congress Subject Headings* (LCSH) entries in a sample of 100 bibliographic records for scientific books to discover whether accuracy, including conceptual analysis, could be determined for purposes of quality control. They concluded that "objectivity in assessing subject heading assignment is feasible. However, some qualifications need to be made" (1993, 16). They found that most problems were with the application of the subject headings and only a few related to conceptual analysis. Svenonius and McGarry chose scientific topics to avoid problems of ambiguity, so their results in terms of conceptual analysis are limited. However, the study does suggest that a simplistic view may work effectively for a substantial number of documents in certain areas.

One of the major problems with a simplistic approach to conceptual analysis is the failure to represent implicit subjects. For example, most subject access in bibliographic records does not indicate the perspective of a work. One reason is that the perspective is often implicit rather than explicit. Whether a work is Marxist, psychoanalytic, feminist, poststructuralist, postcolonial, or some other identifiable approach is not always stated; it must be inferred from the text. Although it is more laborious to make such inferences, perspective is a factor of interest to many catalog searchers (Weinberg 1988). A balanced approach to aboutness and conceptual analysis, based on professional judgment, is probably the best way to optimize retrieval and catalogers' time. Certain aids can help create this type of accuracy, in particular scope notes and references that help to define and differentiate headings. These are discussed in the section, "Aids for Improving Consistency," in this chapter.

Accuracy in Application

The second aspect of accuracy, the translation of concepts into controlled vocabulary, is easier to assess. Svenonius and McGarry (1993) defined accuracy of application for LCSH as complying with the policies and procedures of the *Subject Cataloging Manual: Subject Headings* (SCM:SH), which documents how LCSH should be used. The technical aspects of applying subject headings include use of specific headings (in "Specificity of Indexing" in this chapter), avoidance of typographical errors, use of valid headings, avoidance of obsolete headings, and proper construction of subject heading strings (a main heading followed by subdivisions). Typographical errors may be inconsistencies in spacing, punctuation, capitalization, spelling, or coding. Lois Mai Chan and Diane Vizine-Goetz (1997) found similar types of errors as well as use of obsolete headings in a study of over 9,000 subject headings assigned by LC. They also identified patterns among the errors, suggesting that their control is manageable. Most such errors can be corrected without human intervention using machine-readable authority files and well-designed spelling error correction algorithms (O'Neill and Aluri 1980; O'Neill and Vizine-Goetz 1982).

The use of valid headings and avoidance of obsolete headings can be largely ensured by careful application of authority control. As discussed in Chapter 2, automated authority records are available for subject headings such as LCSH. Checking headings applied in bibliographic records against the authority records will create a high degree of accuracy for main headings. Some authority records exist for subject heading strings in LCSH, but because these strings can be built according to instructions in LCSH, many valid strings exist for which there are no authority records. Chan and Vizine-Goetz (1998), in another study, examined over 20,000 LCSH strings in existing bibliographic records and found that most of the strings were used only once. To create authority records for these strings would probably not be productive. However, for the frequently used strings it would be possible to generate a validation file (that is, an automated list of valid subject heading strings) automatically, based on the strings in a large and reliable database such as the Library of Congress's. Because construction of valid subject heading strings can be quite complex (as discussed in Chapter 6), accuracy could be significantly improved with some sort of automatic checking. However, even in this more technical aspect of accuracy, it is unlikely that automation can substitute completely for professional expertise.

This discussion of accuracy has focused primarily on subject headings, but it applies to other forms of controlled vocabulary as well. Conceptual analysis for classification is essentially the same as for subject headings and their assignment overlaps in terms of the subjects they represent. Classification numbers typically represent one or more topics included in subject headings for the same item (Xu and Lancaster 1998). Technical accuracy in classification has the same problems as in subject headings. Classification numbers can be invalid, obsolete, or improperly constructed. The existence of the MARC record for classification has the potential to provide the same assistance for classification as the authority records can for subject headings. Further, the electronic version of a classification can include numbers that have been correctly built, as *Dewey for Windows* already does increasingly for the *Dewey Decimal Classification* (DDC).

In all of these instances, accuracy must reflect not only the strictures of a particular standard such as LCSH or DDC, but also any local policies and procedures established by an individual library, information agency, or consortium. Without accuracy items will not be retrieved when they are wanted (lowering recall) and will be retrieved accidentally when they are not wanted (lowering precision). The scatter of some items being cataloged accurately and others inaccurately will mean that Cutter's gathering function, finding all that a library has on a given subject, will not be achieved. These poor results can come from either conceptual or technical inaccuracy. With accuracy in form and content of subject headings and classification, gathering of like materials together is more likely to be achieved.

EXHAUSTIVITY AND DEPTH OF INDEXING

In many instances, a bibliographic item may deal with a number of related but distinct concepts at the same time. Then the subject cataloger or indexer, having determined the item's aboutness, is faced with the problem of deciding how many of these concepts should be represented through the subject headings and classification number(s) assigned to the item. Exhaustivity is the number of concepts represented in the bibliographic record or the breadth of subject matter covered. Thus, exhaustivity is related to the conceptual analysis phase of indexing—to choosing what concepts will be represented. Depth is closely linked to exhaustivity. It is the number of headings that are assigned to a given document in subject indexing. Exhaustivity relates to the conceptual analysis phase of subject indexing and depth to the translation phase. Maron (1979) differentiated these two ideas by calling them *intensional depth* and *extensional depth*. When assessing what appears in a record, one is seeing the depth (extensional) rather than the exhaustivity. Hans Wellisch (1991) describes exhaustivity as the breadth rather than depth of indexing. However one looks at them, the two concepts are inextricably related and often considered interchangeable terms. In a practical sense they are.

The level of exhaustivity (or depth) is related to the detail of subject access. Are only concepts treated throughout the whole work represented or also concepts treated in just part of the work? If the latter, how much of the work? Half of the work? A chapter? A paragraph? Is a document about toy poodles, Pomeranians, pugs, and Pekinese given headings for all four or just one heading for toy dogs? Representation of more concepts is considered high exhaustivity and fewer concepts, lower exhaustivity. For example, records for two editions of C. G. Jung's work, *Synchronicity*, show different levels of exhaustivity. (Examples in this chapter are from the Library of Congress database via its *Z39.50 Gateway*, 1999.):

Record 1   650 ʙ0$aCoincidence$xPsychic aspects.

                   650 ʙ0$aAstrology.

Record 2   650 ʙ0$aCoincidence$xPsychic aspects.

                   650 ʙ0$aCausation.

                   600 10$aKepler, Johannes,$d1571-1630.

                   650 ʙ2$aOccultism.

                   650 ʙ2$aCoincidence$xPsychic aspects.

This example offers several interesting circumstances in relation to indexing quality. To begin with obvious exhaustivity factors, record 1 has only two headings, whereas record 2 has five. Two of the headings on record 2 are from the *Medical Subject Headings* of the National Library of Medicine (as indicated by the second indicator with a value of 2). Therefore, only three of the subject headings are LCSH headings. Nevertheless, record 2 represents more concepts than record 1. The heading common to the two records, *Coincidence—Psychic aspects* includes two concepts. Therefore, record 1 represents three concepts and record 2 represents four concepts in LCSH. Record 2 definitely has higher exhaustivity.

The tradeoff between high and low exhaustivity is that if a certain concept is not represented in the indexing, that item would not be retrieved through the missing concept, resulting in lower recall. If, on the other hand, every concept is represented, the user will be able to retrieve the document through any one or more of those concepts, with higher recall. However, if the retrieved document deals with those concepts only peripherally, the retrieval may be more frustrating than useful to the user due to lower precision of the search results. So if someone searches for works about Johannes Kepler and retrieves Jung's *Synchronicity,* it may not satisfy their information needs as it has relatively little information about Kepler in it. The Cranfield I experiments (Cleverdon 1962) discussed in Chapter 4 confirmed this logic with experimental findings that have been validated even by Cranfield's critics and by more recent researchers (e.g., Swanson 1965; Boyce and McLain 1989). If the user retrieves a number of such peripheral items, he or she may lose confidence in the indexing. Cyril Cleverdon (1965) maintained that there is an optimal level of exhaustivity of indexing, balancing recall and precision, beyond which retrieval effectiveness suffers (although Sparck Jones 1973 questioned the idea of an optimal level, suggesting that it depends as much on the searching as on the indexing).

Exhaustivity is sometimes equated with the number of subject headings assigned to an item. Measuring exhaustivity in these terms may be misleading because subject headings may duplicate each other conceptually even if they have been accurately assigned. They may provide different ways of representing the same concepts, and they may represent concepts through both subject headings and subdivisions. In the following example topics are repeated in different combinations so that there is not a one-to-one relationship between subject heading strings or their concepts:

```
245 10$aWomen's paid and unpaid labor :$bthe work
       transfer in health care and retailing /$cNona
       Y. Glazer.

650 ʙ0$aWomen$xEmployment$zUnited States.

650 ʙ0$aWomen$zUnited States$xEconomic conditions.

650 ʙ0$aCapitalism$zUnited States.

650 ʙ0$aSelf-service (Economics)$zUnited States.

650 ʙ0$aService industries$zUnited States.

650 ʙ0$aRetail trade$zUnited States.

650 ʙ0$aMedical care$zUnited States.

650 ʙ0$aHome care services$zUnited States.
```

Here a cataloger has made an effort to encompass the subject of the book even though LCSH does not have headings appropriate for it. Each subject heading may represent more than one concept, but due to the structure of LCSH those concepts may be repeated.

In measuring exhaustivity it is not enough to consider the topics represented. Form is another element that is often represented, as in the following example:

```
245 10$aBrutus, the wonder poodle /$cby Linda Gondosch ;
       illustrations by Penny Dann.

520    $aWhen Ryan's parents give him a toy poodle
       puppy, Ryan is disappointed that the dog is
       not bigger, but quickly learns that Brutus
       is the best ever.

650 ʙ1$aDogs$xFiction.

650 ʙ1$aPets$xFiction.

650 ʙ1$aSize$xFiction.
```

Here three different topics—*Dogs*, *Pets*, and *Size*—are represented plus the form of the work—*Fiction;* four concepts in three headings. (The level of specificity is low because the record uses LC's *Subject Headings for Children's Literature,* shown by the second indicator with a value of 1. See next section for a discussion of specificity.)

Library catalogs differ drastically from other online databases in relation to exhaustivity. The subject indexing in online catalogs is guided by the notion of summarization rather than exhaustive indexing; that is, assignment of only one subject heading that represents the total content of the bibliographic item is preferred to several subject headings representing parts of the item (Chan 1995, 161). Another way of thinking about exhaustivity is in terms of the level or unit of indexable matter (Milstead 1984, 93). Policy for subject access must define whether indexing will be limited to overall themes of the document in general or subthemes. Will each major section, each subsection, or even each paragraph be indexed? If the above document deals with the health and grooming of each type of dog (poodles, Pomeranians, pugs, and Pekinese), will there be separate descriptors for poodle health and poodle grooming, Pomeranian health and Pomeranian grooming, and so forth? Subject cataloging has traditionally followed certain guidelines for exhaustivity. The SCM:SH (Library of Congress. Cataloging Policy Support Office 1996, H180) governing LCSH indicates that 20 percent of an item must be about a given concept before a subject heading is applied. It also follows the "rule of three" dictating that up to three specific concepts in the same hierarchy may all be enumerated, but if there are four or more specific concepts in the same hierarchy the next broader concept should be represented. In the case of our example, four types of toy dogs are discussed in the document, so some broader term for toy dogs should be used instead of a heading for each specific type, according to LC policy. However, only two other topics, health and grooming, are included. Assuming that neither takes up less than 20 percent of the item, both should be represented in the subject headings.

In the example of Jung's *Synchronicity*, Kepler is discussed for about five pages of the total text of around 100 pages. Therefore, according to the SCM:SH there should be no heading for Kepler in the bibliographic records for this work. On the other hand, Jung includes an experiment in astrology to explore his idea of synchronicity. It takes up about 25 percent of the work. Therefore, there should be a subject heading for astrology. With these considerations, record 1 above seems a more accurate representation of the work than record 2. However, the subtitle of Jung's work is *An Acausal Connecting Principle*. The index has numerous entries for *causality* and *cause(s)*. Therefore, *Causation* seems an appropriate subject heading to represent this concept, but it is included in only one of the records. Neither of these records seems to be entirely satisfactory in terms of exhaustivity. Each leaves out a concept that according to the guidelines contained in the SCM:SH should be included, and record 2 includes a concept, Kepler, that is too peripheral for the summarizing level of exhaustivity set down in those guidelines.

The practice of summarization and the rule of three stem at least partly from the days of card catalogs when more subject headings increased the labor of filing and the physical space occupied by the catalog. Because these factors do not apply in the context of online catalogs, other criteria should be considered. It may be time to rethink the levels of exhaustivity in library catalogs. An example discussed in Chapter 2 is useful for this type of reconsideration:

```
245 00 $aTropical rainfall anomalies and climatic
       change / $cHermann Flohn (ed.).

505 ʰ0 $aTeleconnections of tropical rainfall anoma-
       lies and the southern oscillation / H. Behrend
       -- Teleconnections in the Caribbean and north-
       ern South America and the southern oscillation
       / C. Becker and H. Flohn -- Zonal surface winds
       and rainfall in the equatorial Pacific and
       Atlantic / H. Flohn -- Nauru rainfall,
       1893-1977 / H.-P. Junk -- Oceanic upwelling and
       air-sea-exchange of carbon dioxide and water
       vapor as a key for large-scale climatic change?
       / K.-H. Weber and H. Flohn.

650 ʰ0 $aRainfall anomalies $zTropics.

650 ʰ0 $aClimatic changes $zTropics.
```

If a user wanted a work discussing rainfall anomalies in the tropics in general, this book would be a disappointment. Each paper combines some anomaly or climatic change with some geographic area. No article deals with all anomalies in all of the tropics, nor do the articles as an aggregate have complete coverage. A higher level of exhaustivity could pinpoint the topics of each of the five papers in this book without misleading the user. Such a major change in policy would create anomalies in library catalogs, with some items having low and others high exhaustivity. However, the current situation in most online catalogs is that the higher exhaustivity is now being provided through keyword searching of notes such as this contents note. As we continue to explore the value of keyword searching, exhaustivity should be considered. Gunnar Knutson (1991) raised this issue in an experiment that added additional subject headings and/or contents notes to bibliographic records. The addition of more subject headings (presumably giving higher exhaustivity) resulted in more successful retrieval than the addition of contents notes. Research with this type of consideration will help guide our choices for future library cataloging.

SPECIFICITY OF INDEXING

Whereas exhaustivity is a factor of the conceptual analysis stage of subject indexing, specificity relates to the translation phase, and in particular, to the vocabulary and its use in translation. Specificity can be defined as the hierarchical level of subject representation. It is divided into three factors: the specificity and coextensiveness of the vocabulary, the specificity of its application, and the term specificity in the context of a given catalog.

Specificity and Coextensiveness of the Vocabulary

The specificity of the vocabulary is the level of detail of the terminology in a vocabulary in hierarchical terms. For example, a cataloger might want to represent toy poodles, but if the vocabulary includes no heading more specific than *Dogs* its level of specificity is too low to accommodate this topic. On the other hand, a highly specific vocabulary might represent even an individual toy poodle by name. LCSH falls mid-range on this topic. It has a heading *Poodles*, but is not so specific as to have a heading for toy poodles (even though it has one for *Standard poodle*).

Classifications as controlled vocabularies also have levels of specificity. For example, DDC has specific numbers for several breeds of dogs such as collies (*636.7374*), Afghan hounds (*636.7533*), and beagles (*636.7537*). It even has a number for poodles (*636.728*), but toy poodles are included in a general number for toy dogs (*636.76*). Therefore, DDC does not have a level of specificity sufficient to represent toy poodles by themselves. The *Library of Congress Classification* (LCC) is similar, having a number for poodles (*SF 429 P85*) and for toy dogs (*SF 429 T7*), but no number specifically for toy poodles. Generally, LCC is more specific in the area of dog breeds, having 131 entries under *SF 429 Dogs, By breed, A-Z*, whereas DDC has only 24 numbers in the range of *636.72-636.75 Specific breeds and groups of dogs,* and most of these numbers are for groups rather than specific breeds.

Specificity of the vocabulary then determines how detailed representation can be in hierarchical terms. A concept closely related to specificity of the vocabulary is coextensiveness. Coextensiveness is the match between the term available in the vocabulary and the concept represented in the document (Milstead 1984). The difference between specificity and coextensiveness is that specificity addresses only hierarchical detail, whereas coextensiveness is concerned with the inclusion of concepts in a vocabulary regardless of whether they are hierarchically related to a broader concept. For example, a book titled *Talking Back: Thinking Feminist, Thinking Black* is about African American women moving from silence to being able to voice their views. The concept of *voice* in the sense of being able to have one's say is not available in controlled vocabularies like LCSH and DDC. Therefore, it is not possible to represent this topic. There is also no more general concept that can be represented, so the problem is not lack of specificity, but lack of coextensiveness.

Doris Hargrett Clack (1978 and 1994) demonstrated the problems created by lack of a coextensive vocabulary in her two studies of subject headings for works on African American people and culture. The inability of LCSH to represent the topics of items in her studies was not always a lack of specificity. There were not necessarily general terms that could subsume the concepts in the items. There was often simply no way at all to represent the topics.

Poor coextensiveness can result in problems of both precision and recall. The following example illustrates this problem:

```
245 10$aIm/partial science :$bgender ideology in
    molecular biology /$cBonnie B. Spanier.

650 ʚ0$aMolecular biology.

650 ʚ0$aSexism in biology.

650 ʚ0$aFeminism.
```

Because perspective is not included in LCSH, this book, written as a feminist critique of the field of molecular biology, is open to misrepresentation. (Perspective can be included in subject standards, but it is not the policy in most commonly used subject heading lists or classifications). The subject cataloger has added the heading *Feminism* to try to bring out the perspective of the book. If a user uses a Boolean technique, *feminism* will be a helpful search term in combination with *biology* or *molecular biology*. However, the user searching for general works on feminism will also retrieve this book, which is not *about* feminism. Use of the heading *Feminism* in this manner lowers precision.

One way of increasing specificity is to add subdivisions to a subject heading. The Library of Congress typically does not try to add subdivisions to a heading on the basis of the size of the file of bibliographic records for greater specificity. However, it occasionally becomes a criterion, especially for chronological subdivisions.[1] For example, the subdivision – *History*, which is free-floating (that is, it may be added to many different headings) has long had subdivisions for centuries in the modern period. Thus, headings such as *Objectivity—History—17th century*, *Physics—History—18th century*, and *Furniture—History—19th century* can be created. In going farther back with these chronological subdivisions the Library of Congress needed to decide whether to treat each century separately or to use larger historical periods. The conclusion was to use spans of centuries because files would be large enough to warrant this level of specificity, but not so large that individual centuries would be required. Similarly, classification schemes will add more specific entries as the literature on a given topic grows. For example, the section in DDC for specific breeds and groups of dogs has twenty-four numbers in edition 21, but it had only eight numbers in edition 20 and four in the very brief 15th edition.

Specificity of Application

Specificity of application is the level of detail with which the vocabulary is applied. Common practice is that the most specific term available in the vocabulary that describes the document must be used and *not* any more general terms. So if the term *Toy poodles* is in the vocabulary it should be used for any document about toy poodles and other broader terms such as *Dogs*, *Poodles*, or *Toy dogs* should not. Or if, as in LCSH, LCC, and DDC there is no term for toy poodles, the next most specific term, *Poodles* or *Toy dogs* is used and more general terms such as *Dogs* are not used. The idea behind specificity of application is based on the syndetic structure of a subject heading list. If all books about any breed of dogs were listed under both their specific term (*Toy poodles*, *Pugs*, *Pomeranians*, *Pekinese*, etc.) and under *Dogs*, the file under *Dogs* would become unwieldy. Someone wanting a general book about dogs would also retrieve books about specific types of dogs, most of which would probably be irrelevant to the search. Therefore, under the general term *Dogs* there will be references to more specific terms including specific breeds. So a user searching *dogs* for a specific type of dog will be directed to search the narrower term. Such is the ideal situation.

The relative merits of this approach are questionable if users are sent all over the catalog. Bonnie Johnson and Kjestine Carey's study (1992) strongly suggests that users frequently do not choose the most specific heading. Further, if the references are not displayed in an online catalog or if there are not sufficient references the goal will not be accomplished. Mary Dabney Wilson (1998) gives the example of subject headings for individual corporate bodies that are not linked to LCSH headings for the type of institution. For example, the subject heading *Universities and colleges* does not have references to specific institutions of higher learning as narrower terms. Rather, it has a reference suggesting that the user see also "*names of individual institutions.*" Such a reference leaves it to users to think of specific institutions that might provide cases to satisfy their information needs and are likely to be represented in the catalog. On the other hand, making references from general terms to specific corporate bodies would add considerable labor to authority control and create long lists of references that might be tiresome or even confusing for users to work through. Another option would be to include the more general headings in the bibliographic records (as is already done with a few other types of topics such as biographies and archaeological sites). If the general headings were subdivided geographically or in some other appropriate way the problem of too many records under one heading and the resultant high recall might be avoided.

The problem of using a heading in a large number of bibliographic records in a catalog is that it becomes meaningless in differentiating between subjects, resulting in recall too high to be useful. If a very specific vocabulary is specifically applied it should lower the percentage of irrelevant documents retrieved when searched. In the same way, a general vocabulary will recall larger numbers of documents, and they are more likely to include those that are irrelevant (Wellisch 1991). This logical explanation has been documented at least since the Cranfield II studies (Cleverdon and Keen 1966).

Assignment of the most specific available classification number is as much the norm as assigning the most specific available subject heading. For example, the *Subject Cataloging Manual: Classification* (SCM:C) (Library of Congress. Office for Subject Cataloging Policy 1992, F10, 1), which governs LCC, and the introduction to DDC (1996, xxxvi–xxxvii) both mandate use of the most specific number available.

Term Specificity

How well a heading from a controlled vocabulary differentiates between topics in a particular catalog is referred to as "term specificity" (Sparck Jones 1972). Term specificity will vary from one catalog to another. For example, the term *Dogs* is likely to occur with more frequency in the catalog of a veterinary school library than in the catalog of a law library. Therefore, in the law library catalog it would have a high degree of term specificity because it would be useful in retrieving a small and precise set of documents. In the library of a veterinary school *Dogs* will not be a very specific term because there will be large numbers of works dealing with many different aspects of dogs. Searching *dogs* in such a catalog would result in enormous recall and very low precision. Therefore, the context of the catalog will affect the usefulness of assigning a given term. Term specificity should be a factor in deciding what vocabulary to choose for a particular catalog. The specificity of the vocabulary should be sufficient to gather like items in the collection and differentiate between dissimilar items in a manner useful to the users of that collection. However, because most libraries choose from a very small number of standards (typically LCSH, DDC, and LCC in North America), this tailoring to context is less likely to occur.

Summary of Specificity

To summarize this discussion of specificity one can say that specificity is first and foremost a quality of the vocabulary used for subject access. It is one type of coextensiveness, limited to the levels of hierarchy present in a vocabulary. Coextensiveness is the degree to which the concepts in the vocabulary accommodate the concepts to be represented in the catalog. How the vocabulary is applied—how concepts are translated using the vocabulary—obviously affects the effectiveness of the vocabulary. Specificity of application is a principle that comes from the mechanics of syndetic structure and authority control. If a vocabulary is to operate according to the ideal of gathering information through a hierarchical structure, then specificity of application is essential. The effect of specificity is also influenced by its contexts. Term specificity is the relative specificity of a vocabulary within a particular catalog or database. The ability of individual vocabulary terms to gather like items and to differentiate between unlike items will depend on the content of the catalog as a whole. These different views of specificity and coextensiveness all weave together to influence the levels of precision and recall in a given catalog.

INDEXING CONSISTENCY

A major goal of subject indexing is to gather items with similar subjects and differentiate them from items with different subjects. To achieve this gathering function implies that all items on the same subject will be consistently assigned the same terms. Consistency, then, requires that items on the same subject be conceptually analyzed and translated in the same way. To practice consistency, different indexers or the same indexer at different times must index similar items in the same manner. This inter-indexer or intra-indexer consistency is usually tested by comparing the same item indexed by different people or at different times. A long history of research has clearly established that indexing consistency is generally low. In reviewing fifty-seven studies, Karen Markey (1984) found a range of results, from a high of 82 percent consistency to a low of 4 percent consistency. Only eighteen of the studies Markey reviewed showed results over 50 percent. More recent studies have shown similar results (e.g., Chan 1989; Iivonen 1990). Janet McCue, Paul J. Weiss, and Marijo Wilson (1991) found that catalogers in a study at Cornell University editing cataloging copy made most changes to the topical subject headings fields of MARC records (650s), indicating that even when catalogers see the results of earlier work they are likely to make different judgments regarding representation of subjects. Markey also found a few studies of assigning classification numbers with consistency ranging from 34 to 80 percent.

Factors Affecting Consistency

Factors that influence indexing consistency have been identified in this research. Two factors in particular arise frequently:

Number of concepts represented

Size of the vocabulary used

It is useful to look at these factors individually. First, consistency diminishes as more concepts are represented. That is, the higher the exhaustivity, the lower the consistency and vice versa. Typically, indexers will choose the same first term for the major subject of a document, but consistency will decrease as they choose more terms. The suggestion here is that the core subject of a document will be agreed upon by most indexers, but its peripheral subjects are likely to be perceived differently. Second, as the size of the vocabulary grows consistency drops. That is, the more choices indexers have the less likely it is that they will choose the same terms. Larger, more complex vocabularies are also more likely to have high specificity, so there is at least some correlation between high specificity and low consistency.

An explanation of indexing inconsistency and its correlation with exhaustivity and specificity can be drawn from Zipf's "Law of Word Occurrences," which suggests that in any context in which language is used there is a core of terms that are used very frequently, a mid-range of terms used with moderate frequency, and a periphery of terms seldom used (Zunde and Dexter 1969b). The core is made up of relatively few terms and the periphery of an extremely large number. In the same manner, when indexers are reflecting a core of concepts or using a small core vocabulary they are likely to be more consistent than when they are concerned with a large periphery of concepts and terms. Lois Mai Chan (1989) contributes further to this notion in her study of consistency in assignment of LCSH headings. She found that although in a sample of 100 pairs of records only 15 percent had complete matches (six pairs matched because they had no subject headings and seven had only one subject heading), only 5 percent of the pairs were completely different. Chan's data suggest again that there is indeed some core that is fairly consistent. Mirja Iivonen tested different catalogers in different kinds of institutions in terms of both conceptual analysis and translation and found that:

> What is essential . . . is that, in spite of different wordings and explanations, each work has a core area, which is taken up by most of the indexers, but often with different terms and also by referring to different concepts. The area represented by the core terms in the indexing result can be referred to as indexing coherence. (1990, 19)

A further confirmation of the indexing coherence of core concepts is MaryEllen C. Sievert and Mark J. Andrews's (1991) study of *Information Science Abstracts.* That index designates major as opposed to minor descriptors. Sievert and Andrews found that consistency was higher among major descriptors, presumably the core concepts, than among minor descriptors. There is evidence in Mirja Iivonen and Katja Kivimäki's (1998) study of articles represented in both an English index and a Finnish index that the core concept even applies across languages. The example of Jung's *Synchronicity* shows the characteristic of a major concept and other peripheral concepts. In the LC database there are eleven bibliographic records that represent the text of Jung's *Synchronicity* itself or critical works about it. Of these eleven, ten include the heading *Coincidence.* Six use *Coincidence* without subdivision, five use *Coincidence—Psychic aspects* (one record includes both in a lapse of specificity of application). *Coincidence* is the core concept according to all but one of the LC catalogers who created these records over a number of years. The tally of headings in these records shows a roughly Zipfian distribution:

seven occurrences:

    — *Jung, C. G., (Carl Gustav), 1875–1961* (occurs in each record for a critical work)

six occurrences:

    — *Coincidence*

five occurrences:

    — *Coincidence–Psychic aspects*

three occurrences:

    — *Causation*

two occurrences:

    — *Astrology*

one occurrence:

— *Divination*

— *Jung, C. G., (Carl Gustav), 1875–1961–Views on coincidence*

— *Kepler, Johannes, 1571–1630* (+1 for book including a separate work on Kepler)

— *Occultism* (+1 coded as a *Medical Subject Heading*)

— *Parapsychology*

— *Personality*

— *Psychoanalysis and philosophy*

— *Psychoanalysis and religion*

— *Psychology, Religious*

— *Quantum theory*

— *Self*

— *Tao*

The core is clearly *Coincidence* with or without a subdivision. The periphery of headings with one occurrence each consists of twelve separate headings.

Other factors have also been found to affect indexing consistency, at least in some situations. Zunde and Dexter (1969a, summarized in Markey 1984) suggested twenty-five different factors divided into semantic (mainly attributes of the texts being indexed), pragmatic (characteristics of the indexers), and environmental (factors in the physical environment) categories. Susan Bonzi (1984) suspected that the discipline of the items being cataloged might affect consistency. She chose four disciplines, two concrete and two abstract, to test this hypothesis. However, she found that a more significant difference seemed to come from the methodologies used in the disciplines, with highly structured methodologies being more conducive to consistency. Annick Bertrand and Jean-Marie Cellier (1995) identified a number of factors that were linked to whether indexers were professionals or novices. Obviously, consistency is not a simple goal to attain, but it can be improved.

Aids for Improving Consistency

To aid consistency it is not always desirable to limit the size of the vocabulary or the number of concepts represented. High specificity and high exhaustivity may be needed to achieve other aspects of effective indexing. Certainly if consistency were the only goal it would be simple to have a vocabulary of one term that could express only one concept. If it were assigned to every item consistency would be perfect, but the indexing would be farcical. To assist in achieving some reasonable degree of consistency without resorting to such an extreme, various types of guidelines and instructions can be provided for both conceptual analysis and translation. The most obvious "guideline" is the use of a controlled vocabulary. It at least rules out use of synonyms. Further, a controlled vocabulary with a good syndetic structure (references between terms) to contextualize each term and scope notes to limit the terms will encourage consistency. For example, the following LCSH headings could be confusing without their scope notes (field 680 in MARC authority records):

```
150 ʬ0$aPay equity

680    $iHere are entered works on comparable pay for
       jobs that require comparable skills, responsi-
       bilities, effort, and working conditions. Works
       on equal pay for jobs that require identical
       skills, responsibilities, and effort are entered
       under$aEqual pay for equal work.


150 ʬ0$aEqual pay for equal work

680    $iHere are entered works on equal pay for jobs
       that require identical skills, responsibilities,
       and effort. Works on comparable pay for jobs
       that require comparable skills, responsi-
       bilities, effort, and working conditions are
       entered under$aPay equity.
```

Michèle Hudon (1998) is researching how to improve the effectiveness of this type of information with standardized definitions. Policies related to a particular institution or standard can also inform indexers' judgment for improved consistency. SCM:SH documents decisions of the Library of Congress in applying LCSH. For example, it indicates when LC contravenes the idea of specificity of application and its reasons for doing so. In cases such as subject headings for archaeological sites LC assigns a heading for the particular site, for its geographical place with a subdivision – *Antiquities*, for the people who historically lived at the site, and the heading *Excavations (Archaeology)* subdivided geographically (SCM:SH H1225). It is unlikely that consistency at this level of complexity could be maintained without a recorded policy. None of these means is foolproof, but each can contribute to more consistent indexing.

Searching Vocabulary

Of course one problem with the implications of inconsistency in indexing is the potential for inconsistency between subject indexing and user searching. Indeed, the same kinds of inconsistencies have been noted between users' vocabulary and the vocabulary in catalogs as between indexers. Allyson Carlyle (1989) used transaction logs (discussed further in Chapter 11) to compare users' input with LCSH. She found exact matches in terminology in only 50 percent of cases. In another transaction log analysis, Rhonda N. Hunter (1991) analyzed search failures, which she defined as searches that retrieved no records. Subject searches make up 53.8 percent of these failures (it is questionable whether all searches that retrieve no records are failures because there may be no relevant records in the database, in which case retrieval would be a failure).

The largest single cause of failure is from vocabulary errors, specifically use of an uncontrolled vocabulary term. Lourdes Y. Collantes (1995) asked users to name forty objects or stimuli and then compared the results among different users and with

LCSH. This study found great discrepancies similar to those found in the many inter-indexer and inter-cataloger consistency studies described previously in this chapter. Collantes concluded that naming is even more complex than expected because it is "both user-specific and object- or concept-specific" and it depends on stimuli both internal and external to the individual (1995, 131), suggesting that an enormous number of variables affect the information retrieval process. In spite of all of these variables, the existence of Zipfian patterns (see Nelson 1988) makes retrieval plausible in spite of inconsistencies.

To assist searchers in overcoming problems of inconsistency in catalogs, Iivonen (1990) suggests paying special attention to associative relationships in the catalog. Associative or affiliative relationships are the "*see also*" or "related term" (RT) references that are not hierarchical (as discussed in Chapters 3 and 6). Much of what Iivonen found in her study indicates that even though a core concept is generally identified by catalogers, it is not always consistently expressed. Different terms for expressing a concept are often linked by associative references such as "women RT feminism RT women's studies RT sex roles RT women's position" (Iivonen 1990, 20). If searchers follow the associative references they will more effectively gather similar items. It should be remembered that the use of associative references varies with individual vocabularies (LCSH uses relatively few compared to some thesauri), and too many of them can be as deleterious as too few—linking almost every term in the vocabulary to all of the others.

Consistency in Classification

Classification schemes have similar kinds of consistency problems. Typically they are organized by discipline so that inter- or multidisciplinary subjects are particularly difficult in terms of maintaining consistency. Bibliographic records with both DDC and LCC numbers often show a generally different interpretation of the subject between the two schemes. For example:

```
050  00$aTD224.S6$bR63 1994

082  00$a553.7/9/09757$220

100  1b$aRodriguez, J. Alberto.

245  10$aGround-water resources of Darlington, Dillon,
        Florence, Marion, and Marlboro Counties, South
        Carolina :$bwith an analysis of management
        alternatives for the city of Florence /$cby J.
        Alberto Rodr[i]guez, Roy Newcome, Jr., and
        Andrew Wachob.

650  b0$aWater-supply$zSouth Carolina.

650  b0$aGroundwater$zSouth Carolina.

650  b0$aGroundwater flow$zSouth Carolina$zFlorence
        Region$xComputer simulation.

651  b0$aMiddendorf Formation.
```

In this record the LCC number, *TD224.S6*, is in *Class T: Technology*, while the DDC number, *553.7909757* is in the *500*s, the sciences, and specifically the *550*s, the earth sciences. From the title and subject headings it appears that either interpretation is reasonable. In another example,

```
050 00$aTJ163.5.A37$bE53 1994

082 00$a333.79/6616/0954$220

245 00$aEnergy management and conservation in
       agricultural production and food processing/
       $cedited by S.R. Verma, J.P. Mittal, Surendra
       Singh.

650  0$aAgriculture$zIndia$xEnergy conservation.

650  0$aFood industry and trade$zIndia$xEnergy
       conservation.
```

the LCC number is again in technology, but the DDC number is in economics. From the title and subject headings, not only are these interpretations reasonable but the possibility of classifying this work with agriculture would also be plausible.

Consistency within a given classification scheme can be aided by scope notes such as

```
333.79 Energy — Class here power resources, production
of energy, interdisciplinary works on energy
```

and separate guidelines such as the DDC manual, which includes entries such as

```
300 vs. 600 — Social sciences vs. Technology
```

to help determine when to use which discipline. The SCM:C provides similar guidance (although it is not as complete a manual as others). For example, SCM:C includes an explanation of how to choose where to classify a work on foreign relations between two countries (F592, 2). It suggests that work on foreign relations between the United States and another country be classified with the other country. (This is an example of encouraging greater term specificity as, in libraries in the United States, the other country will differentiate more effectively.) Again, these devices will not create complete consistency but are likely to improve it.

Consistency and Theory

One of the assumptions we make about consistency is that because it enables gathering and reflects R-about (the concept a group of people would search to retrieve a given item they found relevant) it is essentially good and inconsistency is essentially bad. Given the powerful searching that can result from effectively gathered surrogates it is difficult to deny the "goodness" of consistency. To be able to retrieve all or most works on a given topic in one simple search is a worthy ideal that we should not give up. However, inconsistency may not be the evil implied in many discussions of the problem. Catalogers may be inconsistent in their representations of a given document, but users will be at least equally inconsistent in their searches. Just as terms assigned in a catalog reflect a Zipfian distribution, so do terms searched. Iivonen addresses the problem of trying to control for inconsistency in peripheral concepts:

> In many documents there are numerous peripheral themes, not all of which can be presented in indexing. Indexing can never repeat the content of the work completely; instead, indexing is always residual—some part of the work always remains untold. The indexer must select between numerous alternatives, when attention is paid to peripheral themes of the work. In this study, it emerged that the selection of peripheral themes presented in indexing is, at least partly, well considered and vindicative, including in many cases also the observation of the specific nature of one's own environment and "own users." (1990, 20)

Therefore, the representation of various peripheral concepts may assist retrieval for some subgroups of the heterogeneous community of users. Because not all concepts can be represented for any given item, representing some of these concepts will link some users to some items. They will not retrieve everything on a given topic, but will retrieve some, and most users probably neither need nor want everything.

CONCLUSION

Subject access in online catalogs is influenced by the policies and procedures of subject indexing. Accuracy requires that the conceptual analysis of an item reflect its content and that the concepts chosen be represented according to the policies of a given library and the standards it uses. The number of concepts chosen to be represented is a sign of the exhaustivity of the subject indexing. Higher exhaustivity represents more concepts. Library catalogs have traditionally practiced relatively low exhaustivity, choosing a policy of summarization over greater breadth or depth of representation. Different standards will have different levels of specificity. This specificity of vocabulary will affect what can be represented. To apply the vocabulary effectively the most specific terms that are appropriate to any given item should be used. This specificity of application ensures that the references in a catalog, going from broad to narrow, will lead searchers to relevant documents.

In the context of a particular catalog, a term's specificity will be relative to how often it appears. High term specificity means that the term appears relatively seldom in that catalog and, therefore, is very useful for differentiating between topics with some precision. The effectiveness of the catalog is also a matter of whether like items are gathered together. To achieve this object of the catalog, similar things must always be represented in the same way. Not surprisingly, this consistency is not attained in subject indexing.

Most documents seem to have a core topic that will be represented by most catalogers. However, how catalogers analyze and represent secondary or peripheral topics is likely to vary. Further, users' searching is not likely to be consistent with catalogers' representations. Consistency is inversely related to exhaustivity and specificity in that high exhaustivity or high specificity will foster low consistency. Other factors, such as the experience of the cataloger and the fullness of definition of the standard will also affect consistency.

All of these factors—accuracy, exhaustivity, specificity, and consistency— work together to make assignment of subject headings and classification numbers a complex operation. Policies and procedural documentation can help catalogers balance their perceptions of aboutness, their ability to use standards accurately, their practices of exhaustivity and specificity, and the resultant consistency, but informed professional practice (and a dash of serendipity) will also be required to achieve effective subject retrieval.

NOTE

1. Personal communication, Thompson Yee, Head, Cataloging Policy Support Office, Library of Congress, March 12, 1999.

REFERENCES

Albrechtsen, Hanne. 1993. Subject analysis and indexing: From automated indexing to domain analysis. *The Indexer* 18: 219–24.

Bertrand, Annick, and Jean-Marie Cellier. 1995. Psychological approach to indexing: Effects of the operator's expertise upon indexing behaviour. *Journal of Information Science* 21: 459–72.

Bonzi, Susan. 1984. Terminological consistency in abstract and concrete disciplines. *Journal of Documentation* 40: 247–63.

Boyce, Bert R., and John P. McLain. 1989. Entry point depth and online search using a controlled vocabulary. *Journal of the American Society for Information Science* 40: 273–76.

Carlyle, Allyson. 1989. Matching LCSH and user vocabulary in the library catalog. *Cataloging & Classification Quarterly* 10: 37–63.

Chan, Lois Mai. 1989. Inter-indexer consistency in subject cataloging. *Information Technology and Libraries* 8: 349–58.

———. 1995. *Library of Congress subject headings: Principles and application.* 3d ed. Englewood, CO: Libraries Unlimited.

Chan, Lois Mai, and Diane Vizine-Goetz. 1997. Errors and obsolete elements in assigned Library of Congress Subject Headings: Implications for subject cataloging and subject authority control. *Library Resources & Technical Services* 41: 295–322.

———. 1998. Toward a computer-generated subject validation file: Feasibility and usefulness. *Library Resources & Technical Services* 42: 45–60.

Clack, Doris Hargrett. 1978. The adequacy of Library of Congress Subject Headings for black literature resources. *Library Resources & Technical Services* 22: 137–44.

———. 1994. Subject access to African American studies resources in online catalogs: Issues and answers. *Cataloging & Classification Quarterly* 19: 49–66.

Cleverdon, Cyril W. 1962. Report on the testing and analysis of an investigation into the comparative efficiency of indexing systems. Cranfield, England.

———. 1965. The Cranfield hypotheses. *The Library Quarterly* 35: 121–24.

Cleverdon, Cyril, and Michael Keen. 1966. Factors determining the performance of indexing systems. Vol. 2. Cranfield, England.

Collantes, Lourdes Y. 1995. Degree of agreement in naming objects and concepts for information retrieval. *Journal of the American Society for Information Science* 46: 116–32.

Cutter, Charles A. 1904. *Rules for a dictionary catalog.* Washington, DC: Government Printing Office.

Decimal Classification. 1951. Standard 15th ed. Devised by Melvil Dewey. Lake Placid Club, NY: Forest Press.

Dewey Decimal Classification and Relative Index. 1989. Edition 20. Devised by Melvil Dewey, edited by John P. Comaromi et al. Albany, NY: Forest Press.

Dewey Decimal Classification and Relative Index. 1996. Edition 21. Devised by Melvil Dewey, edited by Joan S. Mitchell et al. Albany, NY: Forest Press.

Dewey for Windows. 1996. Version 1.0. Dublin, OH: OCLC Press.

Hjørland, Birger. 1992. The concept of "subject" in information science. *Journal of Documentation* 48: 172–200.

Hudon, Michèle. 1998. A preliminary investigation of the usefulness of semantic relations and of standardized definitions for the purpose of specifying meaning in a thesaurus. In *Structures and Relations in Knowledge Organization: Proceedings of the Fifth International ISKO Conference, 25–29 August 1998, Lille, France,* edited by Widad Mustafa el Hadi, Jacques Maniez, and Steven A. Pollitt, 139–45. Würzburg, Germany: Ergon Verlag.

Hunter, Rhonda N. 1991. Successes and failures of patrons searching the online catalog at a large academic library: A transaction log analysis. *RQ* 30: 395–402.

Iivonen, Mirja. 1990. Interindexer consistency and the indexing environment. *International Forum for Information and Documentation* 15: 16–21.

Iivonen, Mirja, and Katja Kivimäki. 1998. Common entities and missing properties: Similarities and differences in the indexing of concepts. *Knowledge Organization* 25: 90–102.

International Organization for Standardization. 1985. *Documentation—Methods for examining documents, determining their subjects, and selecting index terms.* (ISO 5963-1985 (E)). Geneva, Switzerland: International Organization for Standardization.

Johnson, Bonnie E., and Kjestine R. Carey. 1992. Broad and specific subject headings: Implications for users. *Technicalities* 12: 9–12.

Knutson, Gunnar. 1991. Subject enhancement: Report on an experiment. *College & Research Libraries* 51: 65–79.

Library of Congress. Cataloging Policy Support Office. 1996. *Subject Cataloging Manual: Subject Headings.* 5th ed. Washington, DC: Library of Congress, Cataloging Distribution Service.

Library of Congress. Office for Subject Cataloging Policy. 1992. *Subject cataloging manual: Classification.* 1st ed. Washington, DC: Cataloging Distribution Service.

Library of Congress. Subject Cataloging Division. 1982. *Class S: Agriculture*. 4th ed. Washington, DC: Library of Congress.

Library of Congress. 1999. *Z39.50 Gateway*. Available: http://lcweb.loc.gov/z3950/gateway .html. (Accessed March 2, 1999).

Markey, Karen. 1984. Interindexer consistency tests: A literature review and report of a test of consistency in indexing visual materials. *Library & Information Science Research* 6: 155–77.

Maron, M. E. 1977. On indexing, retrieval and the meaning of about. *Journal of the American Society for Information Science* 28: 38–43.

———. 1979. Depth of indexing. *Journal of the American Society for Information Science* 30: 224–28.

McCue, Janet, Paul J. Weiss, and Marijo Wilson. 1991. An analysis of cataloging copy: Library of Congress vs. selected RLIN members. *Library Resources & Technical Services* 35: 65–75.

Milstead, Jessica L. 1984. *Subject access systems: Alternatives in design*. Orlando, FL: Academic Press.

Nelson, Michael J. 1988. Correlation of term usage and term indexing frequencies. *Information Processing & Management* 24: 541–47.

O'Neill, Edward T., and Rao Aluri. 1980. *A method for correcting typographical errors in subject headings in OCLC records*. Columbus, OH: OCLC.

O'Neill, Edward T., and Diane Vizine-Goetz. 1982. Computer generation of a subject authority file. *Proceedings of the ASIS Annual Meeting* 18: 220–23.

Sievert, MaryEllen C., and Mark J. Andrews. 1991. Indexing consistency in Information Science Abstracts. *Journal of the American Society for Information Science* 42: 1–6.

Sparck Jones, Karen. 1972. A statistical interpretation of term specificity and its application in retrieval. *Journal of Documentation* 28: 11–21.

———. 1973. Does indexing exhaustivity matter? *Journal of the American Society for Information Science* 24: 313–16.

Svenonius, Elaine, and Dorothy McGarry. 1993. Objectivity in evaluating subject heading assignment. *Cataloging & Classification Quarterly* 16: 5–40.

Swanson, Don R. 1965. On indexing depth and retrieval effectiveness. In *Second Congress on the Information System Sciences*. Washington, DC: Spartan Books.

Weinberg, Bella Hass. 1988. Why indexing fails the researcher. *The Indexer* 16: 3–6.

Wellisch, Hans. 1991. *Indexing from A to Z*. Bronx, NY: H. W. Wilson.

Wilson, Mary Dabney. 1998. Specificity, syndetic structure, and subject access to works about individual corporate bodies. *Library Resources & Technical Services* 42: 272–81.

Xu, Hong, and F. W. Lancaster. 1998. Redundancy and uniqueness of subject access points in online catalogs. *Library Resources & Technical Services* 42: 61–66.

Zunde, Pranas, and Margaret E. Dexter. 1969a. Factors affecting indexing performance. In *Proceedings of the 32nd Annual Meeting of the American Society for Information Science*, 313–22. Westport, CT: Greenwood.

———. 1969b. Indexing consistency and quality. *American Documentation* 20: 259–67.

6

Subject Headings and Descriptors

INTRODUCTION

In the taxonomy of bibliographic indexing systems, subject heading systems are classed as controlled indexing vocabularies using words that may, but do not need to, be precoordinated and are intended to summarize the overall contents of a document with one or more authorized terms that are as specific as the topic they describe. Modifications of this basic concept are described later in this chapter.

Subject headings were invented in the nineteenth century as a reaction to, and improvement of, then-existing subject retrieval systems. The catalog itself had evolved over the centuries through several distinct but overlapping phases: first the inventory, that is, a list of books in shelf order, typical during the Middle Ages; second, the finding list, which began with the addition of author indexes, especially after the concept of personal authorship became common during the fifteenth century. Some libraries began having catalogs in very broad classed order with or without alphabetical author indexes; others had author catalogs in alphabetical order, usually without a title or subject index.

Prior to the early nineteenth century, more often than not a book was listed only once in a catalog. During the first half of the nineteenth century a growing number of librarians and bibliographers recognized the need for a multidimensional approach. Catalogs in which a work was listed more than once under different access points became more common. Often these catalogs were in classified order, typically with alphabetical author and title indexes and sometimes also a subject index. Many variations existed, one being the alphabetic-classed catalog, in which the classed groups were arranged in some kind of classed order but the groups were labeled not with notations but with subject words.

The development of improved and more detailed local classification schemes permitted nineteenth-century classed catalogs to be arranged in far more systematic order than classed catalogs of earlier centuries, so that related subjects were grouped near each other. This, along with the gradual introduction of publicly accessible catalogs in book and card formats, improved searching potential.

The prevailing attitude for much of the nineteenth century was that a book's subject matter could only be reflected and recorded by the terminology of the title page. By way of contrast, the Library of Congress (LC) *Subject Cataloging Manual: Subject Headings* (SCM:SH) states: "Assign headings based on an analysis of the work being cataloged. Subject headings do not need to be justified by descriptive cataloging notes" (SCM:SH, H180, Aug. 1996, 2). But even in the early nineteenth century the need for a topical as well as an alphabetical subject approach was felt. Hence, the title was often transcribed in "catchword title" form, that is, rephrased to be listed under the word in the title that best described its subject. This permitted in many cases works with different titles but on the same or related subjects to be listed together, like the sample catchword titles shown below. "Keywords" (described in Chapter 3) are direct descendants of catchword titles.

Painters, The lives of three Canadian

Painters, Wisconsin landscape

Painting as therapy

Painting, History of

Paintings, Oil and Watercolor, in the Evjue Gallery

The idea of describing a work's topic with standardized words independent of title page phraseology took hold only gradually. Andrea Crestadoro (1856) is usually given credit for advocating it in print, Ezra Abbott for being the first to use true subject headings in the high-exposure Harvard College catalog of 1861 (Hanson and Daily 1970, 4:266-67), and Charles Ammi Cutter (1876) for creating the first code of rules for a dictionary catalog, which included the first set of rules for subject headings. Cutter invented neither dictionary catalog nor subject headings, but selected from among a wide range of differing local practices those that seemed most effective to him, thereby creating a standard that is still felt today (Miksa 1983). The term "dictionary catalog" refers to multiple listings of a work under its author or authors, title, series name (if any), and subject heading or headings in one alphabetical sequence. Dictionary catalogs developed independently of, but approximately concurrently with, subject headings.

Once subject words had been freed from the phraseology of the title, catalogers had to create their own local lists of subject headings, for the sake of internal consistency. To facilitate standardization and consistency within and among libraries, an American Library Association (ALA) committee of which Cutter himself was a member compiled a composite listing of subject headings used in several large catalogs of the time. The ALA published it as *List of Subject Headings for Use in the Dictionary Catalogue* (American Library Association 1895). An approved list for all types of libraries, it was widely used. In 1897 the Library of Congress (LC) began publishing its own authority list, *Subject Headings Used in the Dictionary Catalogs of the Library of Congress* (Library of Congress 1897), which was partly based on the ALA list. After the ALA list had gone through several editions ALA decided to drop it in 1911, partly because by then LC subject headings had gained ascendancy especially in many large libraries. Also, LC had begun in 1901 to sell its catalog cards, on which LC subject headings were traced. Many libraries found this convenient, even with occasional editing. Later named *Library of Congress Subject Headings* (LCSH), the list has been updated in many editions. By now it is not only a virtually worldwide authority for subject headings in the English language but has also been translated into several other languages.

Because LCSH was even in its early days considered to be too comprehensive for small public libraries, with too many scientific, technical, and very specific terms, Minnie Earl Sears (1923) edited the *List of Subject Headings for Small Libraries,* which was based on subject headings used in nine "representative small libraries." This other well-known general subject headings authority list, later known as *Sears List of Subject Headings* (Sears 1997), has also gone through many editions. In addition to these lists many specialized subject heading lists or thesauri exist to serve the needs of information agencies and bibliographies that emphasize special topics such as medicine, architecture, or astronomy.

FOUR COMPONENTS

When considering subject heading systems it is important to distinguish among four components that, in spite of being independent, interact with each other:

- The terminology, that is, the vocabulary;

- The system-wide structure of this vocabulary, that is, the interrelationships between individual terms;

- The principles, policies, and methods inherent in any subject heading system, which cannot be changed without changing the nature of the system; and

- The subject heading policies and techniques that are not an inherent element of subject heading systems, and which can be changed at will.

Over the years none of these components has remained completely stable. The terminology has become far more specific, information professionals have become far more conscious of system structure, and the borderline between inherent and not inherent characteristics is subject to debate and is in some areas becoming increasingly hazy.

THE VOCABULARY

"Direct" and "Indirect" Subject Sequence

Created when the classed catalog was still common, when books were listed as parts of groups that were arranged in classed order, subject headings were designed to furnish a direct alphabetical approach to a topic and to works on that topic. In a classed listing, specific topics are grouped "indirectly" as subdivisions and subsubdivisions of broader topics, regardless of whether the topics are expressed in words or notations. Following is one version of an alphabetico-classed arrangement in which the topics are in classed order but are expressed by words rather than notations. (Note how much longer alphabetical labels are than numerical labels, shown in

Chapters 7 and 8; on the other hand, their meaning is transparent, unlike the meaning of, say, *876.345* or *TS4.R6*.)

Transportation

Transportation—Railroads

Transportation—Railroads—Electrification

Transportation—Railroads—Rapid transit systems

Transportation—Railroads—Rolling stock

Transportation—Railroads—Rolling stock—Locomotives

In an alphabetical listing of subject headings the same topics are typically listed directly under their own names.

Electrification of railroads

Railroad locomotives

Railroad rolling stock

Railroads

Rapid transit systems

Transportation

In a paper-based environment these were major differences because of the problem of "linearity" (described in Chapter 4). Subject headings were invented to help the searcher who was looking "directly" for a specific topic under its name. But (to mention only two points) what if the searcher thinks of a different name than the system provides, or cannot think of a topic's name? Both techniques have advantages and disadvantages. Standard arguments are that indirect (classed, grouped) listing of subjects permits extended searching of related concepts by grouping many (but not all) of them near each other but makes it difficult to find individual specific topics without using a guide to the classification scheme. Conversely, direct listing facilitates finding a specific topic because the searcher (so it is assumed) is likely to use the proper subject name but impedes searching for related topics because they are scattered by "the accident of the alphabet."

The question and problem of listing topics in classed (grouped) or alphabetical sequence carried over into formulating the subject headings themselves. Subject headings were invented to provide a "direct" approach to a topic. And yet . . .

Cutter's Pragmatic Solution

Charles Ammi Cutter dealt with, and thought of, subjects that reflected fairly broad concepts like *Agricultural chemistry; Missouri River; Survival*. The fact that books could be written on far more specific topics like *Radio isotopes in soil chemistry*; or *Survival after airplane accidents, shipwrecks, etc. in literature*; or *Engineering services marketing* to justify separate specific subject headings, or that LC adds now annually from 6,000 to 8,000 new subject headings, including headings with subdivisions, might well have astonished him, but would probably not have changed his basic guidelines.

Cutter's Rule 76 illustrates the conflict between his wish to use direct language in compound subject headings and his desire to group subject headings of related subjects together. Both techniques can be claimed to aid retrieval in a paper-based catalog. Using principles known in today's language as "literary warrant" as well as "user warrant" or "inquiry warrant," he instructs:

> 76. Enter a compound subject by its first word, inverting the phrase only when some other word is decidedly more significant or is often used alone with the same meaning as the whole name. [*Alimentary canal; Parliamentary practice; Solar system.* But: *History, Ancient; History, Mediaeval; History, Ecclesiastical*] (Cutter 1876, Rule 76).

Regarding subjects "whose names begin with an unimportant adjective or noun [such as] *Capture of property at sea*" Cutter writes: "If the subject be commonly recognized and the name accepted or likely to be accepted by usage, the entry must be made under it" (1876, 38). Cutter's solution was to decide partly on the basis of the type of compound term, but mostly on a case-by-case basis. He expected catalogers to use their judgment, especially in choice and form of a subject heading and, on the basis of usage: "Usage . . . is the supreme arbiter, — the usage, in the present case, not of the cataloguer but of the public in speaking of subjects" (Cutter 1876, 40). These guidelines, this pragmatic case-by-case approach caused inconsistencies, such as inconsistent phrasing of similar headings, which are still with us and which are inherent in the way concepts are grouped mentally and described by words. The only way to avoid them would have been to institute rigid syntactic rules like the ones mentioned in the next section.

Rigid Rules Instead of Pragmatism

Lack of rigid rules is bound to lead over time to inconsistencies. Several theoretical and practical systems were created that were based on far more rigid syntactical rules. Rigidity and definite standards have the advantage of predictability, which is as important in electronic as in paper-based retrieval. But they also have built-in problems and are not necessarily a "better" answer to more flexible systems, especially in an electronic environment.

An early advocate of virtually inviolate rules was J. Kaiser (1911), who advocated that in composite subjects that can be analyzed into a combination of a concrete and a process, the concrete should be cited first. Thus, "Heat treatment of aluminum" is entered as *Aluminum—Heat treatment*. If place is involved the place is interspersed between the concrete and the process, and double entry is made under place:

> *Aluminum—Great Britain, Sheffield—Heat treatment*; and
>
> *Great Britain, Sheffield—Aluminum—Heat treatment.*

Kaiser was a rather peripatetic special librarian, and his system influenced theoretical writers more than working librarians although, for example, the Library of the State Historical Society of Wisconsin followed for many years his principle of double entry for headings with geographic elements. A. C. Foskett (1996, 128–29) and John Metcalfe (1976, 175–83) provide summaries of Kaiser's system.

The PRECIS system (described briefly in the section "Markers or Relators . . ." in Chapter 4) is derived from, and closely linked to, classification concepts. It is noteworthy for its use of the principle of faceting, for its precise syntactic rules (in spite of a virtually uncontrolled vocabulary), and for its ability to synthesize a document's topic under various keywords. It was designed for generating a print catalog from a machine-readable file and was used extensively in the 1970s and 1980s, especially in Great Britain to produce its major current bibliography, the *British National Bibliography* (BNB). Although the technique seems to have good online potential, the vocabulary poses problems, and the system was apparently considered to be too labor-intensive to convert the program and technique to online use.

The National Library of Medicine (NLM) combined in the 1960s the medical subject headings used for cataloging and those used for journal indexing into the very effective *Medical Subject Headings* (MeSH), which are designed primarily for online use. The system has very precise and firm syntactic rules and rules of application. It is described at the end of this chapter.

"Direct" and "Indirect" Subject Headings and "Current Common Usage"

The notions of "user" and "usage" adjoin the question of "direct" versus "indirect," or "inverted" subject headings and have permeated subject heading work since the beginning. Two decades after Cutter first issued his *Rules*, the second edition of the ALA's *List of Subject Headings for Use in Dictionary Catalogs* (American Library Association 1898, iv) reflected the connection between the user and the form of subject headings. Half a century afterwards David Haykin, whose work served for decades as the closest equivalent to a subject cataloging manual, also expressed this principle: "The heading, in wording and structure, should be that which the reader will seek in the catalog, if we know or can presume what the reader will look under" (1951, 7). Another half century later, LC bases the establishment of new terms on literary warrant, that is, their most common use in the literature, and "to reflect current American usage for a concept" (SCM:SH, H187, Aug. 1996). This pragmatic approach is in many ways realistic and appropriate, but it has led over the decades to inconsistent phrasing of similar subject headings, as explained in the Preface to *Library of Congress Subject Headings*:

> Although the original intent was that subject headings would follow a [direct entry] plan instead of an alphabetic-classed plan, the [LCSH and other subject heading lists reflect] a reluctance to disperse related entries. Many headings were originally constructed in a manner which placed the name of a class first through the use of subdivisions, through inversion, or through parenthetical qualification. Examples of these are: *Photography— Studios and dark rooms; Geology, Stratigraphic—Cenozoic; Railroads— Tickets; Insurance, Fire; Art, Byzantine; Cookery (Fish); and Trials (Forgery)*. These headings and many similar ones continue to exist in the list today.(LCSH 1998, 1:viii-ix)

Assigning subject headings on the basis of their use is a very sensible principle. (Should users be expected to look under terms that they do not know or that are not used in the literature?) This principle is, however, more ambiguous and elusive than is apparent at first glance. The increasing specificity of subjects (*Monkeys as aids for the handicapped*; *Names carved on trees*), the continuing creation of interdisciplinary fields, and the different viewpoints with which topics can be written about or sought after are complicating factors. Library users, who are not one coherent and stable class, are another. (Chapter 9 discusses factors affecting user information needs and bibliographic searching habits and skills.) Also, many people use at different times different types of libraries—public, academic, research, or special—for casual, informational, or research purposes. All these points affect their needs, searching habits, and skills, and often choice of searching terminology.

There is ample evidence that since the 1980s LC has been moving toward a more systematic, although not rigid, structure of its subject headings.

THE SYSTEM STRUCTURE

Cutter's Syndetic Structure

Cutter is known for his strong advocacy of alphabetically arranged direct subject headings, which he called "specific" headings or entries. Less well known is the fact that he "advocated a syndetic approach, that is, one in which subjects are linked together in an underlying classification structure" (Foskett 1996, 123–24). For example, he wanted a "classed subject table" (Cutter 1876, 10) of the subject headings used in a dictionary catalog along with cross-references and even suggested a technique for compiling the table in a hierarchical arrangement. He recommended both *see and see also* cross-references, although for the latter he recommended only references among coordinate topics and downward references, from broader topic to narrower topic, with only occasional references from narrow to broader topic (Cutter 1876, rules 85–86).

Literature *see also* Poetry	but not	Poetry *see also* Literature
Poetry *see also* Epic poetry	but not	Epic poetry *see also* Poetry
Bamboo shoots *see also* Cookery (Bamboo shoots)		and the reverse
Cookery (Bamboo shoots) *see also* Bamboo shoots		

Until the arrival of bibliographic thesauri seventy-five years later, this practice was generally followed on the basis of the principle of specificity, under which works are entered under the most specific appropriate authorized heading in a hierarchy rather than under a more general heading. Searchers who looked under a broader heading (as many tend to do) would be helped by a "downward" reference but did not need an "upward" reference. A further assumption was that searchers who use a specific term are likely to think also of a broader term if needed, whereas searchers who start with a broader term are less likely to know how that concept is divided in the catalog being used. Thesauri, on the other hand, are designed on the principle that searchers and indexers need to be able to move in any direction—up, down, and across—within a network of conceptual relationships.

Loss and Rediscovery of Classification
in Subject Headings

Cutter's idea of needing an underlying hierarchical structure for an alphabetical subject headings vocabulary may have been self-evident to his contemporaries when classed catalogs were common, but it got lost over time with the gradual demise of the classed catalog itself. From the beginnings of alphabetical subject headings authority lists in the 1880s the compilers added new terms as needed for their collections and/or subjects. But they did so on an ad hoc basis, term by term. The concept of an overall, cohesive system structure was left to classification schemes, which had been the basis of the classed catalog. Subject headings were viewed as a new and different species that enabled searchers, and especially public library patrons, to access works on specific topics without having to know their place in a classified system.

To help searchers move among related concepts, or from unauthorized terms to authorized headings, the compilers gradually learned to insert *see* and *see also* references in their lists and in the card catalogs, but again on a case-by-case basis according to their judgment and without trying to create a coherent, overall syndetic alphabetical structure. It was no accident that LC's subject headings authority list, LCSH, was developed to complement, but independently of, LC's classification scheme, LCC. (LCSH 1998, 1: viii).

With the arrival of descriptors and thesauri in the 1950s and 1960s, information professionals began to be more conscious of overall structure even in alphabetical subject headings lists and also began to use explanatory terms such as *BT (broader term), RT (related term), NT (narrower term)*, and *USE*, instead of the less precise *see* and *see also* references. In her article with the telling title, "Cats: An Example of Concealed Classification in [Library of Congress] Subject Headings," Phyllis Richmond (1958) was probably the first to remind a new generation of librarians of the inevitable classified order in a list of alphabetical subject headings. She pointed out gaps and inconsistencies in that hidden classification.

Other writers have discussed or described class concepts in alphabetical lists since Richmond. In 1992 Roland Samleske found that in the young discipline of computer science "on the whole, information on computer software can be accessed effectively in terms of currency and completeness, but the procedure is time-consuming due to a large number of competing headings and an unclear hierarchical structure." He recommends eliminating headings that are not used in the discipline and creation of a clear hierarchical structure. Bella Hass Weinberg (1993) compared the implied tree structure of LC subject headings in the field of Judaica with corresponding LC classification classes. Like Richmond thirty-five years before, she points out inconsistencies and illogical relationships in the subject headings.

In the early 1980s LC began to take definite steps to develop and systematize the syndetic structure of its subject headings. Existing policies for hierarchical and associative references were more precisely defined, clarified, and codified. In 1986, with advice from ALA's Subject Analysis Committee, LC began to use thesaurus devices. Existing cross-references and tracings in its subject headings authority list were machine-converted automatically according to a formula: *see-also* became *NT*, *see* became *USE*, *x* became *USED FOR*, *xx* became *BROADER TERM*, and terms traced as both *see-also* and *xx* under an authorized term became *RELATED TERM*. (See the example *Cookery* in "Subject Headings Authority Lists" in Chapter 3).

LC was criticized at the time, partly because "multi-concept" or "cross-category" subject headings (*Flowers in literature*; *Television and children*; *Automobile driving on mountain roads*) do not fit easily into the "genus/species" hierarchical relationships that are expected of thesaurus structure (*Flowers / Roses / Tea roses*; *Literature / Fiction / Short stories*), but mostly for changing the existing terminology globally without editorial review of individual terms or of the overall structure. (LCSH contained more than 210,000 subject authority records at that time.) This clarified the meaning of the individual references but did not at that time improve the existing system structure.

To build up and regularize the overall syndetic structure LC codified, from 1983 on, a large number of specific rules. For example, when establishing a new subject heading the general policy is to establish also the next broader heading if it has not already been established, to permit a reference between these two hierarchical levels (SCM:SH, H370, Aug. 1996, 5). To control hierarchical links for "multi-concept" terms, the general policy is to link the topical terms following a subdivision, or in phrases the topical terms following *and* or *with*, and their next higher hierarchical level. LC's automated system generates the reciprocal *NT* references (SCM:SH, H370, Aug. 1996, 6–9).

```
Hydrogen as fuel
    BT Fuel
Education and crime
    BT Crime
[topical term] —Diagnostic use
    BT Diagnosis [or a more specific type of diagnosis,
                    if established for this topical term]
Church work with [group of people]
    BT [group of people]
```

If a new heading is a member of more than one hierarchy, LC policy is to link it to the next broader heading in *each* hierarchy" (SCM:SH, H 370, Aug. 1996, 5).

```
Women college administrators
    BT    College administrators
    BT    Women executives
    BT    Women in education
```

Related term references are made for new headings when terms are "mentally associated to such an extent that the link is made explicit in order to reveal alternative headings that might be of interest. . . . Frequently the concept represented by one of the headings is a necessary component in the definition of the other. For example, *Birds* is a necessary part of the definition of *Ornithology*" (SCM:SH, H370, Aug. 1999, 2).

```
Athletes                    Sports
    RT    Sports               RT    Athletes
```

These examples represent general rules only, without the exceptions made necessary by specific subjects such as biological names (H 1332) or the vagaries of language and the limitations of linearity. But they may give a hint that the creation and maintenance of a cohesive, effective, hierarchical, and associative alphabetical system that must employ very specific terminology and be effective online and in hard copy is an intellectually and administratively demanding task.

TYPES OF SUBJECT HEADINGS

Because LCSH has for many years been, in effect, the national and international standard for English-language subject headings, the following examples and policies are those of LC unless otherwise specified. In many respects they reflect Cutter. Lois Mai Chan (1995) provides an authoritative and detailed description and explanation of LC subject headings policies and practices. Subject catalogers, reference librarians, indexers, and anyone interested in designing online public access catalog (OPAC) programs would do well to study it thoroughly.

Form Headings; Subject Headings

In daily language the term "subject heading" is often used loosely and generically. Most "subject" headings are true subject headings, that is, intended to reflect what a work is about: *Butterflies; Migraine headache; Income tax evasion*. But works that are not limited to any particular subject or that deal with very broad subjects do not lend themselves to having true subject headings assigned. For these, "form" headings are used, which indicate what a work *is* rather than what it is *about*: *Almanacs; Devotional calendars; Library surveys; Encyclopedias and dictionaries; Yearbooks*. Collections *of* poetry are assigned the form heading *Poetry—Collections*. Musical compositions are assigned form headings that indicate the musical instruments used or the type of music, such as *Trios (Piano, flute, violin); Rock music*. If such works are limited to a topic, access is typically through a true subject heading subdivided by a "form division," such as *Banks and banking—Dictionaries* or a more precise "form heading" such as *Christian poetry*.

Many terms can be both subject headings and form headings: A collection *of* rock music and a work *about* rock music both receive the heading *Rock music*. The same is true for an almanac and a work about almanacs, for a collection of political plays and a work about them. Many form divisions can also be subject divisions. The form heading *Poetry—Collections* cited in the preceding paragraph for a collection of poetry becomes a subject heading if it is further divided by the form division *Bibliography* for a bibliography of poetry collections: *Poetry—Collections—Bibliography*. Such distinctions may seem unnecessarily fussy and legalistic, but with proper explanatory notes they aid searchers by establishing categories. They are especially needed in electronic displays, which still do not permit as quick and obvious an overview as the printed page or the card catalog.

Under an earlier policy LC used in many cases different forms for works *of* and works *about* a concept to help distinguish between the two. Many such distinctive headings are still in use. Some examples follow:

Form heading (works *of*)	Subject heading (works *about*)
Biography	Biography as a literary form
	Biography—History and criticism
Essays	Essay
Short stories	Short story
Symphonies	Symphony
Poetry—Collections	Poetry—Collections—Bibliography
	Poetry—History and criticism

Many such headings are gradually being revised. Under current policy, LC uses the same term for works *of* and works *about* something. Also, the MARC format coded form subdivisions and subject subdivisions alike as $x, so that searchers could not distinguish between the two. However, since 1999 the use of the MARC 6XX fields and of subfield $v for form subdivisions (which LC began using in February 1999) help to make the distinction in electronic searching: Works *of*, field 655, works *about*, field 650.

```
6XX $aPoetry $vCollections
6XX $aPoetry $xCollections $vBibliography
```

Searching under such ambiguous terms, in paper-based files or in OPACs that have *not* updated their existing records requires the searcher to examine each entry to further limit the results.

Categories of Subject Headings

Subject headings can be categorized in several ways. One way is to divide them into the following types (with numbers in the parentheses being their MARC21 bibliographic format tags as added entries):

personal names (600):
Wagner, Richard, 1813-1883; Cavanagh Family

corporate names (610):
Canadian Psychological Association

conference/meeting names (611):
Conference on Categorical Algebra

geographic names (651), including political jurisdictions, geographic regions, celestial bodies, natural features and man-made establishments "not capable of authorship":
Georgia; Bermuda Islands; Antarctica; Venus (Planet); Ohio River; Mississippi River Valley; Yellowstone National Park

names of selected works in the humanities, religion, or law which, because of their volume seem better accessible if recorded in standardized form:

titles in uniform title form (630)
Bible. N.T. Romans.

titles in name/title form (600, 610 or 611 with #t subfield element):
Shakespeare, William, 1564-1616. Hamlet.

the largest category is topical subjects headings which deal with abstract and concrete concepts and ideas, objects, situations, activities, processes and the like (650):
Economic forecasting; Arbors; Budget deficits; Enzymes; Organic compounds; Philosophy; Plant inspection

Syntax of LC Subject Headings

Library of Congress topical subject headings consist of one or more words depending on the concept being named; they can take the following forms:

Single-Concept Headings

1. Single or compound nouns or noun equivalents in singular or plural form:
   Discipline; Dogs; Poor; Running; Bioengineering; Electrometallurgy

2. Adjectival phrase headings:
   i. common adjective in the nominative or possessive case:
      Agricultural credit ; Extraterrestrial bases; King's peace
   ii. proper adjective in the nominative or possessive case:
      Brownian movements; Euclid's Elements
   iii. ethnic, national, or geographical adjective:
      Spanish literature; Jewish etiquette; Arctic raspberry
   iv. common noun used as an adjective in the nominative or possessive case:
      Electron microscopes; Children's art
   v. proper noun used as an adjective in the nominative or possessive case:
      Eisenstein series; Halley's comet
   vi. combination:
      Chemical fire engines; Chemical engineering laboratories

3. Nouns with parenthetical qualifiers (to distinguish between homographs, to avoid ambiguity, or to focus a term):

Darts (Clothing)	*Constructivism (Art)*
Darts (Game)	*Constructivism (Education)*
Darts (Musical group)	*Constructivism (Philosophy)*
	Constructivism (Psychology)

4. Prepositional phrase headings:

   Freedom of speech; Lacrosse for women; Photography of body builders; Counseling in secondary education

5. Inverted adjectival headings where the noun is brought into prominence:

   Art, Medieval; Chemistry, Organic

6. Inverted phrase headings:

   Debt, Imprisonment for; Plants, Protection of; Children's literature, Canadian

Multiple-Concepts Headings

1. Phrase headings (including complex phrases) that deal with interrelations between otherwise separate concepts:

   Education and the state; Literature and morals; Artists as authors; Personality tests for children; Indians of North America in literature; Infants switched at birth

2. Phrase headings for subjects that are often treated together in works:

   Weights and measures; Coal mines and mining; Good and evil

Subdivisions As a Delimiting Device

The main purpose of dash-subdivisions is to divide a topic into mutually exclusive subsections within the broader topic, so that the searcher, especially in paper-based files, need not go through a large group of citations, many of which are inapplicable to the search. There are four basic types of dash-subdivisions:

1. Form subdivisions that can be used with virtually any heading and that represent the bibliographic, literary, or artistic form in which the material on a subject is presented:

   Freedom of speech—Bibliography; Dogs—Periodicals; Library science—Encyclopedias; Budget deficits—Poetry

2. Time subdivisions, with the time periods depending on the topic:

   English literature—18th century; Greece—History— Geometric period ca. 900-700 B.C.; European fiction—Renaissance, 1450-1600

3. Geographic subdivisions that can be "direct" or "indirect" depending on the geographic area concerned:

   Music—British Columbia; Music—England—London

4. Topical subdivisions that describe a special focus of the main term:

    Churches—Heating and ventilation; Collective bargaining—Library employees; Power resources—Costs; Japanese language—Transliteration into English

5. Combinations of the above, which can get very complicated. They are discussed in "Subject Heading Strings with Geographic Terms" in this chapter.

RULES OF APPLICATION

The Changing Range of Options

Mindful of the subject heading principle to summarize a work's overall content, for much of the twentieth century LC and most other general libraries assigned a limited number of subject headings to most works. Several studies indicate that the average number of subject headings per book in major bibliographic databases (National Union Catalog, OCLC, MARC database, etc.) increased from 1.3 subject headings per book for the period 1950–1973 to 1.4 by 1980, rising to an average of 2 by 1989, with the latter figure breaking down to an average of 2.14 subject headings per title assigned by LC, and 1.9 subject headings by other libraries. (Shubert 1992, 77–78; Drabenstott and Vizine-Goetz 1994, 13). Libraries with special subject emphases (fine arts, library and information science, physics, etc.) often changed LC-supplied headings or added additional headings to the ones supplied with LC cards, to enrich subject access to their collections.

With regard to the number of subject headings assigned to a work the "rule of single entry" predominated for the first half of the twentieth century. But even at that time a range of options existed representing different levels of exhaustivity and depth, as discussed in Chapter 5:

One subject heading if it covers the work's topic "coextensively"	Two to four subject headings to cover a work's complex topic or topics between them "coextensively"	In addition to two to four subject headings to cover a work as a whole, analytical subject headings to cover a work's individual sections

"Coextensiveness" means matching of the subject term selected with the subject of the work with respect to topic, aspect, time, place, treatment, and format. The option used can vary from work to work and depends on the work's content, the vocabulary's ability to describe a complex subject with one or more subject headings, and the cataloging agency's policies. For example, collections of individual biographies tend to get analytical subject headings for each component biography, and before the creation of library systems and of centralized cataloging imposed a homogenized standard, small libraries doing their own cataloging tended to provide more subject headings and more analytics than large libraries did because they had to drain the most possible from their small collections.

From the 1960s on, LC policy moved away from the traditional *summarization* notion, and the proportion of works with more subject headings increased. Except for the use of analytical headings, LC's current policy declares a maximum of six subject headings as generally appropriate but permits up to ten subject headings per work, sometimes even more (SCM: SH, H180, Aug. 1996).

> After [determining a work's subject focus and identifying] how that basic subject is expressed [by LC's controlled subject headings vocabulary, assign] one or more subject headings that best *summarize the overall contents* of the work and provide *access to its most important topics.* LC practice [is to] assign headings only for topics that comprise *at least 20% of the work* [emphases added]. (SCM:SH, H180, Aug. 1996, 1).

With respect to specificity, LC's subject headings manual goes on to state,

> Assign headings that are as specific as the topics they cover. Specificity is not a property of a given subject heading; instead, it is a relative concept that reflects the relationship between a subject heading and the work to which it is applied. For example, a seemingly broad heading like *Psychology* is specific when it is assigned to an introductory textbook on psychology" (SCM:SH, H180, Aug. 1996, 2).

Cataloging or Indexing?

The distinction between "cataloging" and "indexing" has always been somewhat nebulous. Basically, cataloging describes a work as a whole entity, and subject cataloging and classification assign subject labels which, together, describe the work's overall topic. Indexing (except for periodical indexing, which works like cataloging) involves delving into a work, and subject indexing, like back-of-the-book subject indexing, analyzes an item at a much deeper level and provides access to many of the concepts contained within it, at a greater depth than even ten subject headings. In other words, although most articles in a periodical issue and many books are listed under only one or two subject headings, a back-of-the-book subject index contains hundreds of subject terms. The issue is further muddled by the recent tendency to use "indexing" to describe *any* kind of bibliographic access technique, and to use "descriptors" for any kind of subject indexing term.

The possibilities of electronic retrieval have encouraged some suggestions that LC index more deeply and exhaustively than heretofore. Because the space limitations of the card catalog or the book catalog are at present of little or no concern in OPACs, is there any reason to limit the depth of analysis, to restrict the number of subject headings assigned to a work, or to add to the bibliographic record more subject-rich fields like contents notes? Even the use of ten subject headings for a work (which, as of this writing, is very rare in practice) comes closer to subject indexing rather than subject cataloging. Subject indexing rather than subject cataloging a work is neither good nor bad in itself, but when some electronic systems balk at searching more than 1,000 records per topic (about the content of one card catalog tray), and when search failures can be due to lack of integrating the virtual bibliographic and authority files, other options may be more helpful.

Among the possibilities are greater use of scope notes for subject headings; enhanced user prompting; computer programming that can increase the number of subject access points by rotating the words and phrases following the comma in inverted headings into the entry-element position and by rotating subdivisions (of subject heading strings) into the entry-element position; making sure that the results of free text searches always include, as one option, the continuation of the search using controlled vocabulary; and using the concept of "major" and "minor" subject headings to describe a work or an aspect of it, just as some databases like ERIC and MeSH use major and minor descriptors. Martha M. Yee and Sara Shatford Layne (1998), and Karen Markey Drabenstott and Diane Vizine-Goetz (1994) describe many options.

Descriptors and Subject Headings

Although this chapter is primarily about subject headings and their use in OPACs, descriptors should also be kept in mind for purposes of comparison and because of their use in OPACs. The concept of descriptors was invented between 1947 and 1949, underwent a metamorphosis, and was reborn in essentially its present form in 1959 (Boll 1982), when computers and their predecessors were just beginning to be used for bibliographic retrieval.

Subject heading systems and descriptor systems have many similarities. For example, both are controlled alphabetical vocabulary systems that rely on using one specific label for a subject. Both systems rely on precoordinated terms to express complex topics if alphabetically possible, grammatically sensible, and if the combination of topics occurs often enough in a collection to make the precoordinated term a time-saver at the input and/or the retrieval stages. (See the examples of subject headings under "Rules and Techniques . . ." in Chapter 4.) Both systems rely on cross-references and hierarchy (a syndetic structure) to direct indexers and searchers from synonyms, other hierarchical levels, and variants of an authorized term to the authorized term and to related concepts.

The differences between the two systems are partly linguistic but lie mostly in their purpose and in the method with which the respective subject terms are used. Virtually no descriptors consist of strings of terms; multi-word descriptors are only in direct rather than inverted form. In indexing a document, descriptors are not limited to topics that constitute at least 20 percent of a work (in other words, they can be as index-like as seems appropriate); they are not limited by "coextensiveness" but can describe the same topic in a document on its specific as well as on a more general level. The same document could be described by one or two (or six, or ten) subject headings or by five to twenty descriptors. In addition to the typical (minor) descriptors, which are labels for concepts contained in a document, many descriptor systems use also major descriptors, which describe a work's overall topic or topics, thereby function more like subject headings. The ratio per work is usually one to two major and five to fifteen minor descriptors.

With respect to representing a document's content, subject heading systems are fundamentally designed to summarize the overall contents, but also to provide access to the document's other substantially treated topics; descriptor systems are fundamentally designed to handle individual concepts or aspects contained in a document, but many also employ major descriptors that cover the work's overall content. With respect to representing a document's content, both systems start from opposite sides but "sort of" meet in the middle. Differences between the systems are more pronounced with respect to "redundancy." Subject headings were developed to aid the patron who was looking for a specific subject. That was the basis of Cutter's often-quoted rule 161:

> Enter a work under its subject-heading, not under the heading of a class which includes that subject: Ex[ample]: Put Lady Cust's book on "The cat" under *Cat*, not under *Zoology* , or *Mammals*, or *Domestic animals*." (Cutter 1876, 66).

This concept of "coextensiveness" between document and indexing label (or group of labels) remains a cornerstone in subject heading theory. In a paper-based environment, space in a card catalog was at a premium. Topics are assigned *only* at the level at which they are treated in the indexed document. Searchers who look under a broader level are referred to the more specific level by cross-references. The result has been described as "Economy of input and redundancy in searching," but it also decreases the chances of long lists of overly specific documents under a broader heading. Conversely, descriptors were developed when masses of technical writing began to need control; when speed of input, and especially of searching, began to be more important; and when new technology began to facilitate postcoordinate combination of different terms. (For a contemporary description of these systems, see Shaw 1961.) This permitted the reverse policy of "redundancy of input and economy in searching."

Descriptor policy permits listing a topic under its specific name and, if needed, under a broader level. Because descriptors are primarily designed to record "concepts" or "aspects" contained in a document, such double listing is often inevitable and almost automatic. Presumably this increases the searcher's chances of finding the desired topic even when looking under an overly broad level, and postcoordination is designed to help focus the search. Descriptor systems rely on postcoordination, and this is where OPACs shine, hardware and software and searching skills permitting.

For example, an article with the title "Subject Analysis Tools Online: The Challenge Ahead" examines the limitations and potentials of the traditional subject language tools DDC, LCC, and LCSH and discusses their traditional functions and requirements for their becoming efficient online cataloging and retrieval tools, as the online catalog continues to be developed and refined. The actual descriptors assigned to this article in *Library and Information Science Abstracts (LISA)* are in the left column in the chart below; in the right column are LC subject headings that would be assigned to this article, but in three groups representing increasing levels of depth of analysis: Group 1, Traditional summarization of overall contents; Groups 1 and 2, Greater depth; Groups 1, 2, and 3, Current LC policy, summarization of overall contents, and access to its most important topics covering at least 20 percent of the work.

Descriptors from LISA abstract 91-4354	LC subject headings for the same article
Online catalogues	(1) Online catalogs—Subject access
Subject indexing	Subject cataloging
Information storage and retrieval	(2) Information retrieval
Information work	Information organization
Dewey Decimal Classification	(3) Classification, Dewey Decimal
Library of Congress Classification	Classification, Library of Congress
Classification	Subject headings, Library of Congress
Classification schemes	
General classification schemes	
Library of Congress Subject Headings	
Subject headings schemes	
Technical processes and services	

The wording differs because these are different controlled vocabularies. Note that only the first subject heading, but in this case no descriptor, comes even close to summarizing the article's overall topic, and that subject headings avoid listing the same topic under both a general and a specific term, whereas descriptors, by design, do it freely.

The two systems illustrate concepts described in Chapter 5, among them different levels of exhaustivity and depth. The differences between the two systems are, however, neither ironclad nor immutable. Even the essential differences between subject headings and descriptors are mere matters of degree and of policy, both of which can and have changed over time. Subject heading policies and terminology have undergone changes over the past century, and different organizations apply descriptors and subject headings, sometimes in somewhat different ways. Further changes are to be expected, possibly even to the extent that the two systems might ultimately blend.

POLICIES, CUSTOMS, CRITICISMS, SUGGESTIONS—AND OPACs

Criticism of Library of Congress cataloging policies was a rather popular professional spectator sport, especially during the 1970s and 1980s, although LC had tried for many decades, often on an informal basis, to take many of the needs and wishes of the library community into account. Driven partly by increasing recognition of its role as the standard setter and partly by the electronics-driven, increasing interdependence of national and other libraries, utilities, and online services, LC began in the late 1970s to coordinate its cataloging and bibliographic activities and decisions very closely with the library community. Since then, LC's policy changes are being made only after extensive consultation with, and sometimes only at the request of, the library community. Anyone who thinks that policy changes are easy nowadays, do not have wide-ranging implications, and simply require a dictum from LC's Director of Cataloging should read summaries of meetings of ALA's MARBI (Machine-Readable Bibliographic Information) or Subject Analysis Committee or of their various subcommittees; browse through the latest edition of LC's four-volume *Subject Cataloging Manual* or selected issues of LC's *Cataloging Service Bulletin*, such as the Winter 1997 issue; or read reports of OCLC's Office of Research, for a change of mind.

The following sections discuss a few of the issues and policies affecting the use of LC subject headings in OPACs. (For detailed description of factors affecting subject searching in OPACs and how searching can be improved, see Drabenstott and Vizine-Goetz 1994; Yee and Layne 1998).

Automatic Switching and End-User Thesauri

Two fairly common user traits that affect OPAC searching are that users are often unaware of a topic's different aspects and that they tend to begin a search on a different hierarchical level, usually broader, than the level desired. This is compounded by the fact that the user must enter a (usually unknown) search term and indicate a searching preference on an essentially blank screen, whereas in a printed list or a card catalog the user would get an idea of the words, sequence, and subdivisions even before asking the first question.

To circumvent differences between indexing terminology and searching terminology and to help searchers to find the appropriate level in a hierarchy, it would be helpful for OPACs to use either end-user thesauri and search trees (as described in Chapter 4) or to have automatic switching capability, like MeSH (described at the end of this chapter). LCSH does not have a formal end-user thesaurus but is, in effect, gradually integrating the equivalent into its subject authority structure. One method is to make certain that ultimately every term is part of the hierarchical structure. (In a few cases the nature of a term prevents this.) Another method, different from the traditional, selective cross-reference technique, is to require all catalogers, when establishing a new subject heading, to create references from *all other* equivalent terms and phrases found while conducting authority research for the new heading (SCM:SH, H373, Aug. 1996, 1–2).

```
Bobber fishing              USE   Bait fishing

British float fishing       USE   Bait fishing

Fishing with natural bait   USE   Bait fishing

Float fishing, British      USE   Bait fishing

Ledgering (Fishing)         USE   Bait fishing

Livebait fishing            USE   Bait fishing

Still fishing               USE   Bait fishing

Worm fishing                USE   Bait fishing

[Although the last reference is an upward rather than
an equivalent reference, it is made because it would
be impractical to make this a separate term.]
```

As another example, the same subject heading manual rule provides that, with some exceptions, new headings also be accessible through references under every "significant word in the file position, as long as the resulting combination of words represents an expression under which a catalog user *might logically be expected* to search" (emphasis added) (SCM:SH, H373, Aug. 1996, 1–2):

```
Driving, Truck       USE    Truck driving
                            [established heading]
Sources of light     USE    Light sources
                            [established heading]
```

These examples are transparent, visible cross-references; searchers who look up *Sources of light*: are referred to *Light sources*. Another possibility would have been to make the transfer automatic (automatic switching), so that the user who searches for *Bobber fishing* finds himself or herself looking at documents listed under *Bait fishing*, without knowing whether this is an error or not. A brief explanation or a *USE* reference is generally considered essential for such situations.

The Principles of the "Uniform Heading" and the "Unique Heading"

The following two principles are among the basic tenets of subject cataloging:

- **Uniform heading:** Collocating all material on a particular subject under only one uniform heading (with *USE* references from variants) to increase recall. (This avoids splitting the file on any one topic, thereby impeding searching.)

- **Unique heading:** Letting each unique heading represent only one subject (and distinguishing homographs by parenthetical qualifiers) to ensure precision and to minimize false hits in subject retrieval.

Most of the time LC and most other libraries follow both principles, which seem to be as important in OPACs as in paper-based files, but in a few cases LCSH violates one or the other when other considerations override them.

The principle of the uniform heading is overridden, for example, in situations in which it is felt that users will benefit from approaching a specific topic not only directly but also as part of a cluster at a more general, a "gathering" level. However, because this is a policy decision rather than an intrinsic element of the subject heading technique or vocabulary, decisions can and do change. For example, after extensive consultation with the profession, LC eliminated several such instances, such as the gathering level for North American Indian nations. For example, it no longer authorizes for a work about the pottery of one Indian nation double headings like *Comanche Indians—Pottery*, and *Indians of North America—Pottery* (*Cataloging Service Bulletin* 45, 80–81). But it has kept other instances of multiple-level entries, for example works about a type of building in a city (SCM:SH, H1334, Feb. 1999; SCM:SH, H1334.5, Aug. 1998).

```
(650)  Skyscrapers—New York (State)—New York.
(651)  New York (N.Y.)—Buildings, structures, etc.
```

Among other instances of still authorized double-level entries are battles that are listed under their own name and the name of the war of which they were a part, along with some other entries (SCM:SH, H1285, Aug. 1998). Needless to say, in each of these instances, works about the broader topic as such are also listed under it, so that two types of content are listed under the broader topic. This does not make for searching precision. Some way of either designing separate subject headings or using qualifiers or tags would seem advisable. In addition to the examples cited above and below are any topical headings if the work also discusses that topic extensively, for example *Art Deco* in the case of the work about New York skyscrapers.

The most multilevel and multi-aspect case is, perhaps, individual biographies (SCM:SH, H1330, Feb. 1999), which are listed under

(1) [The name of the person (or up to four persons)]

(2) [The class of persons]—*Biography*, such as *Football coaches—Biography; Italy—Kings and rulers—Biography.*

(2a) [Additional headings which specify sex or ethnic group], such as *Women architects; Afro-American lawyers.*

(3) [The person's association with a place or organization or event]—*Biography*, such as *Ohio—Biography; United States. Department of Agriculture—Officials and employees—Biography; World War, 1939-1945—Biography.*

Whether gathering levels are needed in OPACs is debatable; there is probably no one single overall answer. In a card catalog (where otherwise space considerations and the policy of "economy of input" prevailed) it was practical and helpful to find certain subjects listed under their specific heading *and* under a general gathering level heading, partly because of the tediousness of moving among many card catalog drawers to find more than one member of such a group and partly because it would have been otherwise difficult to obtain an overview of the group's members represented in the card catalog. In OPACs the system design may dictate the answer, for example whether the system permits double-posting names and works as subjects, that is, makes them searchable in subject indexes as well as in name-title indexes. (Yee and Layne 1998, 148).

One might also argue that even if the groups of headings cited above do represent different levels in their respective hierarchies they also represent different aspects of the topic at hand and are justified even in OPACs for linguistic reasons and because the limitations of linearity, although different, are just as pressing as in a card catalog. In either format the secondary headings are frequently the quickest means by which the searcher is able to find desired material efficiently.

Regardless of whether the principle of selective multilevel listing will be kept for OPACs, searchers should always be able to see where in the hierarchy they are searching. Whether searching under the more specific or the broader subject heading, a window listing automatically the headings on the next one or two higher and lower levels should be available, if possible coupled with a display function of the entries listed on these levels. Where appropriate, the basic level of such window listings should include individual names, such as:

> *Football coaches—Biography*:
>   NT [listing of individual names represented in the file]
>
> *Bridges—New York (State)*:
>   NT [listing of individual New York State bridges in the file]

This seems preferable to the technique that had to suffice in paper-based catalogs, that is, either assuming that the searcher knew the names of individual football coaches or merely pointing his or her nose in the right direction with a general reference: *See also names of individual football coaches.* When the system permits it, assigning the specific term during the cataloging process can generate automatically some of these listings or cross-references under the broader gathering level term. Online, authority control can permit this. When establishing subject authority records for individual cases, a 5XX reference should be added.

Precoordination, Postcoordination

Subject Heading Strings

Although many concepts can be expressed by one word, such as *Television, Students*, or *Cookery*, many other concepts represent combinations or refinements, such as *Television and children, Student assistance programs*, or *Cookery (Sausages)*. For such concepts the subject heading vocabulary usually precoordinates the indexing term. (The concept of pre- versus postcoordination is defined in Chapter 3. See also Figure 4.1.) Like all true subject heading systems, the LC subject heading system is basically a precoordinated indexing language designed to label a work's overall topic. This is especially obvious with many highly specialized subject headings.

To describe a bibliography of adult children of alcoholics in the United States, LCSH does *not* use the descriptor technique of employing a series of separate indexing terms of varying specificity, some of which may be precoordinated, but which, as a system, depends on postcoordination (such as *Alcoholics* and *Alcoholism* and *Addictions* and *Parent-child relationships* and *United States* and *Children* and *Adult children* and *Bibliographies*). Instead, LCSH, as a subject heading system, combines the pertinent concepts into a string that describes the work's overall topic according to definite rules: *Adult children of alcoholics—United States—Bibliography.* A history of seventeenth-century English clocks is described by the string *Clocks and watches—England—History—17th century.*

The use of subject strings results in classed subarrangements within a basically alphabetical system. The technique has been criticized as violating the principle of specific and direct entry,

> Automobiles—Motors—Crankshafts,   instead of
>   Crankshafts (Automobiles).

```
Insurance, Accidents,            instead of
    Accident insurance
```

but it also provides structure and thereby some degree of predictability. The need for subdivisions arose partly to improve searching speed and precision and partly to make subject searching possible at all. (A three-million-volume library had, perhaps, five million subject added entry cards, including probably seventy cards under *Clocks and watches* and at least 10,000 cards under *United States—History*. Few users would be willing to search through that many cards to find a work on a narrow subtopic unless the file were subdivided.) The limitations of linearity made the choice of the initial term and the method of subdivision of great importance in paper-based files. In an information retrieval environment, systems can be programmed to create additional entries for direct forms of inverted subject headings when no *see* reference exists for the direct form. Alphabetic-classed subjects are more difficult, but apparently not impossible, to handle (Drabenstott and Vizing-Goetz 1994, 10).

Subject Heading Strings from Different Angles

Subject heading strings increase specificity; that is, they describe a more specific or narrow subject concept than the initial term in the string by itself, even if precoordinated. The use of strings is, however, not carried to its ultimate conclusion, mainly for two reasons: Some works deal with topics that can be viewed from several perspectives, and some complex topics do not lend themselves to description in one subject heading string with any hope that a searcher could discern the meaning. Both situations require more than one subject heading string. For example, a work on the effect of municipally supplied water on early childhood mortality in urban Brazil could, theoretically, receive a string such as *Infants and children—Mortality—Effect of municipal water supply—Brazil*. The meaning is not really clear, and realigning the various units does not explain the topic any better. In a paper-based file that uses subject headings, this entry would only be filed under *Infants*, ignoring searchers interested in "Children" or the "Municipal water supply." Instead, LCSH dissects the work's subject matter into three strings:

```
1. Children—Brazil—Mortality; 2. Infants—Brazil—
Mortality; and 3. Municipal water supply—Brazil.
```

Note that descriptors (described earlier in this chapter and in Chapter 3), or faceted classification or the PRECIS technique (both described in Chapters 3 and 7) would handle such complicated subject relationships quite differently and, some people feel, more effectively. But when subject headings and subject heading techniques are employed, the skillful use of free text retrieval, truncation, and suitable postcoordinate Boolean searching techniques should retrieve a work like the one on the water supply from more query combinations than is possible in a paper-based file.

LC evidently feels that the technique of using multiple subject heading strings for complex topics is appropriate for online as well as on-paper use. For example, a recent decision changed the existing precoordinated string

```
[Class of persons or ethnic group]—Education—[Topic]
```

to two separate strings to be used for one work:

(1) *[Class of persons or ethnic group]— Education;* and
(2) *[Topic]—Study and teaching.* (CSB no. 75).

Example: A work on teaching dance to mentally handicapped children. Single heading used until 1996:

Mentally handicapped children—Education—Dance.

Multiple headings used since 1996:

(1) *Mentally handicapped children—Education;*
(2) *Dance—Study and teaching.*

This policy has the advantage of not only listing together, on the screen or on paper, works on mentally handicapped children, but also listing together works on teaching dance, while postcoordinate Boolean searching will retrieve the two concepts together, with or without their subdivisions, in OPACs if desired.

Another type of situation is the topic that can be viewed and searched with equal justification from opposite sides. For example, a work on the foreign relations between two countries receives *duplicate* subject headings, that is, two reciprocal subject headings, such as (SCM:SH, H2220, Aug. 1998):

(651) France—Foreign relations—Italy; and
(651) Italy—Foreign relations—France

Descriptor systems might well use, instead, three separate labels: *Foreign relations*; *France*; and *Italy*. Built-in switching has been described as the OPAC version of duplicate entry for subject headings and should handle such situations effectively.

Simplifying Subject Heading Strings

Because complex subject heading strings present both input and searching problems in both paper-based and electronic files, the length and complexity of subject heading strings has occupied librarians for some time. Before LC began issuing its *Subject Cataloging Manual,* even catalogers were sometimes confused about the sequence of subdivisions while, in Arnold Wajenberg's words, "no catalog user . . . would intuitively search under a [subject] heading such as *Tractors—Motors— Maintenance and repair—Study and teaching—Illinois—Champaign*" (Conway 1992, 17). Problems with long strings include, for example, the fact that many programs place a limit on the length of subject heading strings displayed in the inverted index. Some OPACs do not index subdivisions at all. On the one hand, truncation of long strings loses information for the searcher; on the other, users are more likely to input single terms or short strings than long precoordinated strings (Conway 1992, 47). A study by Lori Franz and others also showed that changing the order of subdivision will have little effect on end-user understanding, but as the number of words in a string increases, user understanding of the string decreases (1994).

Various methods of contracting or simplifying long subject heading strings are advocated, among them the removal of nontopical elements (format, chronological, etc.) from the string and placing them into fixed and/or variable fields in the MARC record, somewhat like the check tags in MeSH (which is described at the end of this chapter). In 1986 Pauline A. Cochrane made a detailed proposal to catalog and tag the subject string as a series of its constituent but independent parts (topical, chronological, geographic, etc.), which would be available for computer manipulation with varying display options for print or screen (Cochrane 1986, 62–68). Searching precision would then be improved not by subdivisions but by Boolean operations and by limiting a search.

In 1991 LC hosted an invitational conference, the Airlie Conference, much of which was devoted to strings and to bibliographic fields such as 007/00 (Category of Material), and 043 (Geographic area code). Among the problems considered were the likely effect of the loss of specificity to the basic subject, which results from separate coding of form, time, and so forth; and the technical difficulties of establishing the necessary linking mechanisms between, for example, the codes and natural language searching terms to permit effective searching, or between the basic subject in a subject heading string and the removed parts to minimize false drops when the separately coded factor (time, geographic area, etc.) does not apply to every subject string in a bibliographic record (Conway 1992).

Subject Heading Strings with Geographic Terms

Depending on the topic involved, subject headings that include geographic terms take two basic patterns:

(1) [Topic]—[Place]: *Labor supply—France,* and

(2) [Place]—[Topic]: *Iowa—History.*

Often, the topic demands more complicated versions. Examples of more complex strings are

(1a) [Topic]—[Place]–[Subtopic]–[Time]–[Form]:
Nobility—Great Britain—Costume—History—16th century—Pictorial works.

(2a) [Place]–[Topic]–[Time]–[Form]:
France–History–Revolution, 1789–1799—Periodicals.

For display on paper or on the screen, the order of sections in a subject string, especially with geographic terms, is usually important because it increases searching precision by clustering related subconcepts, and because citation order can affect the meaning. Although less important in those OPACs in which main heading and subdivision are equally accessible, the citation order can affect the meaning even there. For example, *Music—Argentina—History and criticism* means "History or criticism of Argentine music", whereas *Music—History and criticism—Argentina* means "History or criticism of [any kind of] music in Argentina". Sometimes, however, the sequence of sections in a subject string does *not* affect the meaning even in paper-based files: *Automobiles—Taxation* and *Taxation—Automobiles* both mean "Taxation of (or in connection with) automobiles".

After considerable investigation, and on the basis of recommendations made at the Airlie Conference, LC agreed in 1997 to basically one standard citation sequence, to facilitate string construction and consistency among catalogers, and to enable machine validation of subject headings: [Topic]—[Place]—[Time]—[Form], or [Topic]—[Subtopic]—[Place]—[Time]—[Form]. Exceptions are headings in special areas such as art, literature, and history. Strings beginning with a geographical term (items (2) and (2a) in the examples immediately above) are not affected (Conway 1992; Five year progress report . . . 1997, 48–49). Retrieval precision was aided when LC began to code form subfields as $v. Until 1999 form and topical subfields had been coded without distinction as $x.

Varying Terminology

Obsolete, Ambiguous, Synonymous Terms

If a concept or name is known by more than one expression, LCSH selects (with a few exceptions) one and refers from the others. It tends to use the current over the obsolete term, the latest over a former name, the common over the scientific name (if its meaning is precise and unambiguous), the English over the vernacular name (unless the concept is normally expressed in foreign terms), and the current over the obsolete spelling. If a choice must be made between a name, its acronym, or its abbreviation, LCSH authorizes the best known of these. A *USE* reference (formerly *see* reference) is made from the unauthorized form or forms to the authorized form. (OPAC studies indicate that users need more such references than currently exist.) The principles of the uniform heading and of the unique heading seem to make this policy as necessary in OPACs as in paper-based files, but in OPACs the references in these cases can be automatic so that the searcher who searches under an *un*authorized term will be switched automatically to the authorized term. To avoid confusion the resulting screen should carry a short note explaining the change in terminology. End-user dictionaries would be another possible solution.

Different Words or Spellings for the Same Concept

A person or an object can have several officially recognized names, and therefore be written about and searched, under different names: *Charlemagne* is also known as *Karl der Grosse*, and even by his Latin name, *Carolus Magnus*. The *Saint Gotthard Pass* is known in its location as *Passo del San Gottardo* and as *Sankt Gotthard Pass*.

The same things are sometimes spelled differently or called by different names in different countries with the same language: *Catalogues, Theatres, and Lifts* in England are *Catalogs, Theaters,* and *Elevators* in the United States, and a combination of the two in Canada. Which of these terms should be used as searching terms?

In card catalogs, *see* and *see-also* references were sometimes used for such cases, but many libraries did not use *see-also* references at all, for philosophical reasons, to save input time, or to keep the card catalog manageable in size. LC used relatively few *RT* and *USE* references in the past to emphasize hierarchy *(BT; NT)* and to reduce the size of its printed subject headings list (SCM:SH, H370, Aug. 1996, 10-11). Depending on the situation, OPACs that have the capability can either employ *USE* and *RT* references or switch automatically (with a brief explanation) from the searching term to the indexing term.

Changed Political Terminology

Political units sometimes receive new names as their governmental situation changes. *Ceylon* became *Sri Lanka, British Honduras* became *Belize, Canada (Province)* became *Canada, Pennsylvania (Colony)* became *Pennsylvania*. The more carefully administered card catalogs often had history cards at the beginning of the respective files to explain such situations, but to save input cost they became rare. OPACs could well revive modernized versions of history cards, especially as this information is usually already contained in the authority records. It could be displayed automatically in a window whenever a relevant name is called up and, because no longer limited by the 3-by-5-inch card format, could use tables or diagrams in addition to text to explain the sometimes rather complicated name and function relationships as needed.

Spoken or Manipulated Word Order?

As mentioned previously in this chapter, subject headings that consist of more than one word can exist in either spoken, "normal" word order, resulting in an alphabetical listing of topics, or in inverted or otherwise manipulated order, resulting in a categorized listing of topics (*Online catalogs* versus *Catalogs, On-line* or *Catalogs (Online),* or *Catalogs—Online*). In apparent conflict with the concept of user and usage, inverted headings have been used and fretted over since Cutter. LCSH has used subject headings in both spoken and manipulated order since its beginning. Since 1983, LC's policy, as described in LCSH is

> to use normal word order for topical headings except for headings with language, nationality, or ethnic adjectives, headings qualified by time period, such as *Art, Medieval*, headings qualified by artistic or musical style, headings with the adjective *Fossil*, and certain music headings (1998, 1: viii).

Exceptions exist to these groups. For example, topical headings qualified by nationality or ethnic groups are inverted unless the group is in the United States: *Cookery, Chinese*, but *Chinese American aged*. Parenthetical qualifiers, inverted headings, and hyphenated subdivisions are still being created, but are a distinct minority. However, in general, and in line with current LC policy (and in a reversal of Cutter's original rule) LC is moving toward almost exclusive use of spoken, normal word order and, moreover, toward increasing use of highly specific terms.

Some newly created or changed subject headings are the by-product of splitting concepts into more specific ones. For example, *Television credits* was split in 1997 into *Television actors and actresses—Credits* and *Television producers and directors—Credits*. Many seem to be part of the move to reduce the number of exceptional cases including filing sequence, such as eliminating in 1998 the hyphen in *Decision-making in animals* to read *Decision making in animals*. But the predominant trend toward spoken order and increasingly specific terms is represented by headings like the following new or converted ones: *Blue-chip stocks*; *Canine sports medicine*; *Charity sports events*; *Former Yugoslav republics*; *Gay clergy*; *Indians in the motion picture industry*; *Internet radio broadcasting*; *Late-term abortion*; *Lost films*; *Male child care workers*; *Presidential press secretaries*; *Proposal writing for grants*; *Wearable computers*. With the continuous growth of research library collections and the increasing specialization of writers and their works, the trend toward precise terminology will continue.

However, subject headings including LCSH are still a precoordinated indexing vocabulary, regardless of the vocabulary's phrasing: *Sports charity events* is as precoordinated a term as *Sports—Charity events*, and *Indians in the motion picture industry* is no less precoordinated than *Motion picture industry—Employees—Ethnic groups—Indians*. The difference lies in the structure of the file, direct or alphabetic-classed; it lies in the indexing philosophy brought to the selection of subject headings.

Note that many newly created headings in spoken order file alphabetically away from the main heading that would have been used in inverted phrasing or in a subject string, for example, *Stocks* versus *Blue-chip*; *Yugoslavia* versus *Former*, *Clergy* versus *Gay*. Direct subject headings favor the specialist who searches in a familiar field for a known specific topic. But direct subject headings conceal the framework within which they are placed. Not very many suburban public library patrons, college students, or faculty browsing outside their specialty are likely to search directly for *Lost films*, *Canine sports medicine*, or *Decision making in animals*, although *Presidential press secretaries* may be a more familiar term. The structure that helps locate other hierarchical levels (particularly in multihierarchy terms like *Canine sports medicine*) or related concepts, must be supplied by the thesaurus or other aids.

For OPAC searchers the increased use of very specific subject headings in spoken order seems to imply 1) a need for awareness of this policy; 2) that an alphabetical listing of subject headings in windows or side panels can be, but is not always, helpful; (3) the extensive use of *USE* references from alternative phrasings, or system ability to switch automatically; 4) that heavy use of keywords and Boolean searching may be useful; 5) an especially great need for seeing, either in an automatically opening window or by request, the hierarchy of the requested term once it is found (If a specific subject headings belongs to more than one hierarchy this requires structuring several hierarchies.); and 6) the need for a keyword search of subject headings that retrieves a KWIC or KWOC display.

Searchers in paper-based files have fewer aids available to them, such as KWIC displays or hierarchical outlines, and typically have no opportunity, or far fewer opportunities, to switch from one display sequence to another. But they do have the standard advantages of the paper-based product: an easier, more complete, and automatic overview of the total picture rather than a frame-by-frame approach and the ability to note from the beginning of the search the file's organization and the type of information available before having to frame a question. Other than that, they must rely on the standard thesaurus references imbedded among the bibliographic surrogates.

COMMENTS AND EXPECTATIONS

What Has Changed?

Most criticisms from library and information science writers over several decades about LCSH deal with the vocabulary and with the policies with which it is applied. Few deal with subject headings as such. Yet any attempt to adapt and, possibly, change LCSH and subject headings in general for the electronic environment must recognize and distinguish among the four components listed at the beginning of this chapter—vocabulary, the vocabulary's system-wide structure, inherent subject heading principles and policies, and noninherent policies and techniques—in relation to, and as increasingly affected by, the rapidly developing and expanding field of electronics and computer programming.

Technical limitations and characteristics have influenced bibliographic media in the past, do so now, and will in the future. Subject heading schemes were developed independently of classification schemes in the second half of the nineteenth century, following the extensive use of catchword titles in catalogs and bibliographies. Partly as a result of this compartmentalization, partly because the dictionary catalog could not easily integrate alphabetical and numerical sequences, and for other reasons, subject headings have been used in catalogs for subject retrieval, whereas class notations are primarily assigned to shelve the physical object, which makes it impossible to assign more than one notation per document. However, it is worth noting that in systems in which class notations are *not* intended to serve as location devices, more than one class notation can be assigned. Classed catalogs (described briefly in Chapter 7) are a case in point, and online demonstration projects have also used the technique of assigning more than one class notation as subject rather than location labels. Today, when Internet documents are not *shelved* by notation, and when OPACs have at least the potential of manipulating alphabetical and classed subject terms equally, class notations can be viewed and used as one of several subject access tools, and OPACs helped to make that practicable, a clear indication of how physical format and technology can affect abstract processes.

A basic question since the arrival of electronics has been whether the same subject retrieval vocabulary and set of policies is appropriate and effective online as well as on paper. On paper we deal with two different sequences of arranging subjects and their labels, alphabetical and numerical. The rules that are characteristic of each sequence dictate its arrangement. That is, the commonly accepted sequence of letters dictates the filing from A to Z, and the commonly accepted sequence of numbers dictates the filing (or shelving) from 0 to 9. The nature of letters and of numbers makes the two systems basically incompatible; that is, a number cannot be interfiled or intershelved in an alphabetical system (or vice versa) without an artificially created convention or without a supporting file such as an index.

In alphabetical systems decisions must be made regarding abbreviations (filed as written or as if spelled out?), filing sequences (multi-word terms filed word-for-word or letter-by-letter; punctuation of subject strings ignored or subarranged by category?), and similar decisions that may seem totally insignificant and arbitrary until one realizes that they can separate related topics by many pages in a thesaurus and by many frames in an OPAC. In other words, they affect ease of retrieval, including retrieval by subject. Depending on audience and type of search, such decisions result in a more or less user-friendly display. Many such decisions are really questions of direct versus categorized display. The question remains: Are rules designed for paper-based retrieval and for electronic retrieval identical, or even compatible?

In a paper-based environment, the inherent characteristics of each indexing system and language, along with its artificial conventions, and the resulting display are interdependent. Subjects, and document surrogates listed under these subjects, are displayed exactly in the order of subject headings and filing conventions that the indexer knows and intends. In a paper-based file the indexer controls the display. Except for real or assumed budget limitations, no other factors influence or dictate the filing or shelving sequence in a paper-based file.

In an electronic environment as now known, the indexer has far less control over the display, partly because bibliographic indexing and electronic retrieval follow different ground rules. Each tries to adjust to the other's purposes and limitations, but as this is written they are not yet a cohesive, always synergetic unit. Input and output are less cohesive than in a paper-based system because indexing is dictated by bibliographic and topical considerations; online retrieval is dictated by software and hardware capabilities and by the well-known limitations of screen display. This does not mean that bibliographic and electronic concerns are not interdependent. For example, an investigation of existing subject references in standard services demonstrated "how an emphasis on simplicity in programming over clarity of presentation can render references almost as unusable as if they were not displayed at all" (*Report to the ALCTS . . .* 1997, 2). Retrieval is no longer limited to the exact phrase of the indexing terms or subject heading string or even to controlled indexing terms but is far more fluid than in a paper-based environment. It provides more options but puts more responsibility on the searcher and programmer.

Adapting, Changing, Coordinating?

Most theorists favor gradual adaptation of LCSH vocabulary and policies to online needs, partly because a radical change would really be a change into the unknown, entail enormous cost and retraining of catalogers and searchers, and either lead to closing existing files (databases) or extensive changes and/or separate systems within one institution or network. Others view the requirements and potentials of the two types of catalogs as incompatible and favor radical changes for the sake of online needs. Arguments in favor of retaining subject heading principles and techniques mention, for example, that in addition to deep indexing the principle of retrieving works also on the basis of their overall content is as valid today as ever; that precoordinated subject strings are needed to fulfill the precision objective of the subject catalog to help those users who cannot imagine how to narrow a search; and that at present no postcoordinate indexing system can provide, or is designed to provide, by itself, the organized precision of a precoordinate one. Among the believers in gradual adaptation are the authors of this book.

Proposals range from radical change to adjustment. One radical suggestion was to adapt PRECIS (described in Chapters 4 and 7), a precoordinate system with precise syntactic rules and the great advantage of synthesizing under every heading a document's content. Another was to use descriptors, a postcoordinate system with limited use of precoordinate terms. Moderate proposals include Mary Dykstra's suggestion for keeping subject heading principles but keeping the currently used LCSH headings as the basis for creating a clearly organized "truly precoordinate and analytico synthetic system" on the basis of precise syntactic rules that recognize the different roles of verbs and of nouns serving as objects, agents, properties, and so forth (Conway 1992, 41). The need for a logical syndetic structure, clear rules of synthesis, and well-defined, consistent facets is also stressed by Chan (1995, 401–5). With respect to terminological problems, Hope Olson suggests "pushing at the boundaries of LCSH" (Olson 1996, 11).

Actual LC policy, or at least the effect of LC policy, seems to be along moderate lines: retention of basic subject heading principles and techniques, accompanied by a series of gradual changes to accommodate online needs without ignoring the needs of paper-based files on cards or on the printed page. See, for example, the justification for using the direct form of subject headings for American ethnic groups such as Afro-American artists, Afro-American dentists, and Afro-American teachers: "This enables American library users to find all topics related to a specific American ethnic group filed together *in the subject catalog or on the screen*" (emphasis added) (SCM:SH, H351, Feb. 1998, 1). Until such time as LC and the profession may introduce basic changes, this is a wise cautionary policy, especially since the politically correct professional mindset for some time has been "gung ho" in favor of online retrieval without consideration of paper-based file needs which, after all, continue to exist.

Subject Labels in Classed and/or Alphabetical Sequence

The previously mentioned "fluidity" of electronic retrieval, which permits the searcher to construct search phrases different from, or in addition to, the assigned precise subject indexing terms or subject heading strings, may be one reason that faceted indexing seems to be emerging as one of the most effective online indexing techniques, as Marcia Bates notes (Conway 1992, 97). More than one writer suggests systems that, in one way or another, reflect the idea of constructing indexing labels by means of clearly defined facets, independent but linked by precise syntactic rules, which are available for computer retrieval manipulation in any desired order, hierarchical, alphabetical, by format, time period covered, date of publication, or other factors, although as of this writing in many online systems only potentially.

In this connection, linking LC subject headings and LC class notations has occupied information scientists for many years. (Micco 1997; Cochrane 1986). The Library of Congress and the Online Computer Library Center (OCLC) have for some time attempted to link the use of class notations and subject headings, but in many instances this is not possible, partly because there are often no exact equivalents. Although the classification systems involved are divided by discipline and the subject heading systems are not, the vocabulary of both systems can express, at least theoretically, the broadest and the most specific topics with identical specificity. Is the duplication of subject labels expressed in words and in notations still valid and useful in an electronic environment? The important point is, of course, not the fact of double-labeling in itself but the resulting ability to present and to access every topic, and works on every topic, in different contexts and from different vantage points.

Thesauri do that. Although never easy, it is easier to group concepts into facets and hierarchies, and then assign to each concept an alphabetical and a notational label while the system and its vocabulary are being created, than to try to do it retroactively. Thesauri like the *Thesaurus of ERIC Descriptors* (ERIC 1995) and the *Art and Architecture Thesaurus* (1994) are cases-in-point. Each covers only a broad field of interest rather than the world of knowledge and is therefore less difficult to construct than a general thesaurus would be. A model worth examining carefully is the National Medical Library's online subject heading system, MeSH, and its thesaurus, which is being used effectively in the field of medicine and health care, viewed broadly. Because it deals with one broad area of application much of its vocabulary does not apply to most other broad areas such as the humanities. But its technical aspects, such as integration of every subject into two coordinated structures, syntax, use of precoordination and postcoordination, methods of delimiting subjects, use of subject heading as well as descriptor techniques, and method of indicating different areas and fields to which a specific concept applies might be adaptable to a general indexing language.

It is not our purpose to advocate one system or another, but merely to raise some questions (which is easier than providing an answer!). The one thing of which we can be certain is that more change, incremental or profound, will continue to come and that the decision will need to be made whether to strive toward a system that can accommodate both electronic and paper retrieval or one that can provide only electronic retrieval. It behooves us as a profession to try to direct future changes into the channels that are most effective and usable for the variety of needs of the several intended audiences.

MEDICAL SUBJECT HEADINGS (MeSH)

Since transforming its medical subject headings in the 1960s for online use, the National Library of Medicine (NLM) uses its classification system, in NLM's own words, "for shelf arrangement of books." This makes shelf browsing still possible, but for online subject retrieval NLM uses its far more flexible and finely tuned medical subject headings system, MeSH. The following sections are limited to a selective description of the MeSH thesaurus, vocabulary, and methods of application. Among features deserving of more attention are the various online capabilities that enable and enrich MeSH performance. Two of these are the system's incorporation of what is, in effect, an end-user dictionary and its ability to display a list of related descriptors at several hierarchical levels when a term is entered. The discussion is intended to illustrate the following:

- The use of separate labels for bibliographic and call number functions permits flexibility in bibliographic retrieval.

- Subject labels can be alphabetical or notational terms with the same degree of specificity. The degree of specificity can be increased through postcoordination.

- Subject labels can be built into a hierarchically and laterally coordinated structure that uses both alphabetical and notational labels, and therefore display possibilities, and that permits easy switching among these structures.

- Different aspects of one topic can be listed together clearly and synoptically regardless of whether the search begins with an alphabetical or a notational term.

- An online system with simple, clear, and inviolate hierarchical and syntactic rules is possible and effective.

- A system that uses precoordinated terms and postcoordinate retrieval not as an exception but as a basic technique can be very flexible and can achieve very high specificity.

- The history of a subject label, such as changes in scope or wording, can be shown with a minimum of verbiage but precisely and clearly.

- It is possible to integrate automatic switching from previously used to currently used terminology.

- It is possible to combine subject heading techniques and descriptor techniques online effectively.

All these features are important for effective subject retrieval, and especially for narrowing down a search to the desired aspect and degree of specificity. (Narrowing down a subject search in a large file that uses detailed subject labels is in many systems a rather time-consuming and unsatisfactory part of online searching.) Ability to pinpoint is especially important in medical research and diagnosis; the MeSH vocabulary and syntactic input as well as retrieval rules are designed to achieve high precision.

The Vocabulary

The NLM subject headings, unlike LC subject headings, underwent in the 1950s and 1960s major conceptual scrutiny from two perspectives that at that time were quite revolutionary: computerization and using the same subject indexing vocabulary both for cataloging of books and for indexing journals. (Conventional wisdom had been that periodical articles dealt with more specific topics than books and therefore required a much more specific indexing vocabulary. This was probably correct for general, but not specialized, periodicals and books as long as only one or two subject headings were assigned to one book.) Since the 1960s the MeSH vocabulary, policies of application, and online and paper bibliographic products have been continuously adjusted in the light of experience.

The MeSH vocabulary includes more than 19,000 main subject headings and eighty-two topical subheadings or qualifiers. Each subject heading or qualifier is listed in the NLM thesaurus with the categories of topics with which it may be used and with a scope note or explanatory annotation. As of 1999 MeSH no longer uses form, geographic, or language subheadings but, instead uses other techniques. MeSH uses also "publication types" headings that correspond to LC's "form" headings such as *Reviews; Clinical trials*, which may, like many LCSH form headings, also be topical headings. But MeSH uses devices that distinguish clearly between identical terms as topical headings, topical subheadings, and "publication type" headings. MeSH also uses "check tags," which are required whenever applicable and which specify the kind of study, the type of study, and the source of support. Examples are *Animal; Human; Female; Support, Non-U.S. Government; Case Report; Comparative Study*. The program also permits limiting searches by other criteria such as language, type (such as "book"), medium (map; computer), location (such as "Internet"), and other criteria.

Application

Medical subject headings are used in *Index Medicus* (NLM's major paper index to journal literature); MEDLINE (the online version of *Index Medicus*); LOCATOR *plus* (until 1998 CATLINE, the online version of NLM's printed, now discontinued, *Current Catalog of Medical Literature*); and many specialized databases, catalogs, indexing services, and bibliographies. MEDLINE is now available in three files: *Internet Grateful Med* (which allows tailoring the search); *PubMed* (the most user-friendly); and *MEDLINEplus* (emphasizing consumer health). To save printing space and cost, documents are listed in the printed *Index Medicus* only under the "major descriptors" that reflect a document's overall, predominant topic or topics. Marked with an asterisk (*), they fulfill the traditional role of subject headings. In the online products, documents are listed under these as well as under "specialized descriptors" (formerly called "minor descriptors"), which fulfill the traditional deep analysis role of descriptors.

The vocabulary is applied according to NLM's own strict syntactic rules. The method of application is a blend of subject heading format and descriptor technique (described in Chapter 3 and previously in this chapter in "Descriptors and Subject Headings"), with emphasis on the latter. (This mixture may explain why the explanatory literature uses both terms, sometimes in the same paragraph.) Following subject heading usage, some subject headings are inverted, and subject headings can be delimited by topical subheadings or qualifiers, although no strings with more than two elements are permitted. If more than one qualifier is needed, or if the subject heading is both a major (*) and a specialized heading for a particular document, the subject heading is repeated, thereby avoiding the problem of sequence of subheadings. Following is an example of the same subject heading used with three different subheadings for *one* document, indicating that the article is mainly about the prevention and control of coronary disease but also contains information on the epidemiology and metabolism.

```
Coronary Disease / ep [Epidemiology]
Coronary Disease / me [Metabolism]
*Coronary Disease / pc [Prevention & Control]
```

Following the descriptor technique, the subject labels are designed primarily to describe elements and concepts in the document rather than the whole document. On the average from twelve to twenty-five "subject headings" are used per document, including usually three to four major descriptors. The rest are specialized descriptors, publication type headings, geographic descriptors, and the required check tags such as *Adult; Human; Middle age.* By way of illustration, following is the list of subject labels used for an article on the use of vitamins and trace minerals with antioxidant properties to prevent eye disease:

```
Adult                    Cohort Studies
Age Factors              Diet
Aged                     Human
*Antioxidants / tu       *Macular Degeneration / pc
   [Therapeutic Use]        [Prevention & Control]
```

*Cataract / pc	Macular Degeneration / pp
[Prevention & Control]	[Physiopathology]
Cataract / pp	Middle Age
[Physiopathology]	*Vitamins / tu [Therapeutic Use]

The MeSH Thesaurus

The MeSH thesaurus appears in a printed and an online version and records each subject label in alphabetical and notational form and sequence along with detailed rules of application. The printed format seems to be more helpful and quicker for an initial general overview of terms and categories than the online format. The thesaurus consists of the *Tree Structure,* the *Alphabetic List,* the *Annotated Alphabetic List,* and the *Permuted Medical Subject Headings.* Online, the system permits seamless switching from one list to the other, a virtual integration of all three structures, but they are described separately here because they exist separately in print and to illustrate their different structures.

The *Tree Structure* is divided into fifteen categories, each with an identifying letter:

Anatomy	[A]
Organisms	[B]
Diseases	[C]
Chemicals and Drugs	[D]
Analytical, Diagnostic and Therapeutiques Technics and Equipment	[E]
Psychiatry and Psychology	[F]
Biological Sciences	[G]
Physical Sciences	[H]
Anthropology, Education, Sociology and Social Phenomena	[I]
Technology and Food and Beverages	[J]
Humanities	[K]
Information Science	[L]
Persons	[M]
Health Care	[N]
Geographic Locations	[Z]

Each category is divided into subcategories. Each subcategory is identified by an alphanumeric symbol that indicates the category to which it belongs and its location within that category. Category "E", for example, is divided into:

Diagnosis	[E01] +
Therapeutics	[E02] +
Anesthesia and Analgesia	[E03] +
Surgical Procedures, Operative	[E04] +

```
Investigative Techniques          [E05] +
Dentistry                         [E06] +
Equipment and Supplies            [E07] +
```

The plus sign (+) following the alphanumeric symbols indicates that the subcategory can be further subdivided topically. Subcategory E02, for example, is further subdivided into fifty sub-subcategories in alphabetical order, many of which are further subdivided hierarchically. Following is a selective list. (If applicable, the use of a term in different categories or subcategories is indicated. Example: "Drainage — Postural".)

```
THERAPEUTICS                      [E02]
   ACUPUNCTURE                    [E02.030] +
   ALTERNATIVE MEDICINE           [E02.040] +
   BED REST                       [E02.075]
   BIOLOGICAL THERAPY             [E02.095] +

 . . . . . . . . . . . .

   DIET THERAPY                   [E02.293] +
      DIABETIC DIET               [E02.293.257]
      DIET, FAT-RESTRICTED        [E02.293.275]
      DIET, PROTEIN-RESTRICTED    [E02.203.330]

 . . . . . .

   DRAINAGE                       [E02.306] +
      POSTURAL         [E02.306.221] [E02.780.221]
                       [E02.880.150]
                [E02.306.221 is part of Therapeutics;
                E02.780.221 is part of Physical Therapy;
                E02.880.150 is part of Respiratory
                Therapy.]

 . . . . . . .

   DRUG THERAPY                   [E02.319]

 . . . . . . . . . . . .

   THERAPY, COMPUTER-ASSISTED     [E02.950] +
```

The printed *Alphabetic List* is issued with the January issue of *Index Medicus* and in Book 1 of the annual *Cumulated Index Medicus*. Its first section records every subject heading and topical subdivision and the notational equivalent or equivalents in one alphabetical sequence, regardless of which hierarchy or hierarchies it belongs to or its level in it. It also records the year of adoption and years of earlier terms, and it records and traces cross references.

Diet Fads

    E02.40.287   I03.287

    X Food Fads

[This subject heading is part of two hierarchies: E02.40 (Alternative Medicine) and I03 (Human Activities). The year of adoption is not recorded. A see-reference was made to it reading *Food Fads* see *Diet Fads*.]

Diet, Sodium-Restricted

    E02.293.510

    80; was DIET, SALT-FREE 1963-79

    X   Diet, Low-Salt

    X   Diet, Low-Sodium

    XR Sodium Chloride

[This term was adopted in 1980, to replace the term *Diet, Salt-Free* which had been used from 1963 to 1979. Two see-references are made to it from *Diet, Low-Salt* and *Diet, Low-Sodium*, as well as a *consider-also* reference: *Sodium Chloride* consider also *Diet, Sodium-Restricted*.]

Diet Therapy

    E02.293 +

[The first heading at left is a subject heading. The slash and small initial letters in the second heading indicate that it is a topical subdivision.

/diet therapy

    75; used with Category C & F3 1975 forward

It was adopted in 1975 and may be used with categories C (Diseases) and F3 (Mental Disorder)]

Dietary Oils see Dietary Fats, Unsaturated

The second section of the printed *Alphabetic List,* titled "Categories and Subcategories," records, within each category, the various subcategories in alphabetical order, with subdivisions and with their notations in one or more hierarchies.

```
E02  PROCEDURES AND TECHNIQUES - THERAPEUTIC
Therapeutics              E02
  Acupuncture             E02.30         E02.40.25
    Acupuncture Anesthesia E02.30.70     E02.40.25      E03.155.43
    Acupuncture Therapy    E02.30.100    E02.40.25
      Acupuncture Analgesia E02.30.100.48 E02.40.25     E03.91.48
. . . . . . . . . . .
  Alternative Medicine    E02.40
. . . . . . . . . . .
    Anthroposophy         E02.40.60
. . . . . . . . . . .
    Music Therapy         E02.40.580    E02.831.440    F04.754.549
```

The *Annotated Alphabetic List* (available only as a separately published print publication) is adapted to the needs of catalogers, indexers, and online searchers. It contains more information on each subject heading and subheading than does the *Alphabetic List* and contains a list of the required check tags that are not available in the *Alphabetic List*. The individual terms in the *Annotated Alphabetic List* are also available online with even more complete explanatory information than in the printed version.

Following is an example of a scope note in the printed *Alphabetic List:*

```
/biosynthesis
    66; used with Category D 1966-89; D8-9, D12-13, &
    D24 1990 forward
```

Following is the scope note for the same term in the printed *Annotated Alphabetic List:*

```
/biosynthesis
    subhead only; includes "formation" & "production"
    of substances by living tissue or organisms; see
    MeSH scope note in Introduction; indexing policy:
    Manual 19.8.9. DF /biosyn or B1
    66; used with Category D 1966-89; D8-9, D12-13 &
    D24 1990 forward
    search policy: Online Manual; use main heading /B1
    or /B1 (SH) or SUBS Apply B1
```

Permuted Medical Subject Headings is derived from major and minor descriptors, cross-references, citation type, check tag, and geographic descriptors. It lists for each significant term used in MeSH headings all headings that include that term. It does the same for selected roots, such as *-lysis-* or *-angio-* (*Angiocardiography; Chalangiography*). This arrangement

- Overcomes the problem associated with inverted and phrase headings where the user is typically uncertain about the form of the authorized heading and, therefore, under which term to search;

- Enables searchers who approach this term through the keyword approach to become aware of the nature of information being recalled; and

- By displaying all the headings that contain a given significant word or word root, displays the range of its use and facilitates ways of narrowing down a search.

```
CHEMICAL
  BLOOD CHEMICAL ANALYSIS
  BURNS, CHEMICAL
  CHEMICAL ACTIONS
  CHEMICAL ACTIONS AND USES
  CHEMICAL & PHARMACOLOGICAL PHENOMENA
    . . . . . . . . . . .
```

```
DEPRESSION, CHEMICAL
DICTIONARIES, CHEMICAL
HYPOPHYSECTOMY, CHEMICAL
MODELS, CHEMICAL
MULTIPLE CHEMICAL SENSITIVITY
RIOT CONTROL AGENTS, CHEMICAL
```

Among them, the *Alphabetical List,* the *Tree Structure,* and *Permuted MeSH,"* online or on paper

- Permit access to a topic from any level, that is, permit easy vertical moves, thereby broadening or narrowing a search;

- Show the various contexts of a term, exhibit clearly the various hierarchies that contain different aspects of a term, show a term's range of use, and permit easy lateral moves;

- Show (individually) a subject in different context; and

- Permit switching to the other lists, although not with equal ease.

MeSH Online

The greatest advantage of the online version of MeSH, if used with an appropriate program, is the great variety of searching and display possibilities and the enormous versatility. For example, one can search under DIET THERAPY in the *Tree Structure* to retrieve articles on diet therapy, or select more specific concepts related to diet therapy, such as *fat-restricted diet*, *protein-restricted diet*, *reducing diet*, and *sodium-restricted diet*. From the tree the searcher can switch to each term's scope note, and back. Although subject headings may consist of only two elements, subject searches can combine many aspects and can also be limited by many aspects, and citations can be displayed in a great variety of sequences and in varying degrees of completeness. Many possibilities exist. MeSH is available online to the public at http://www.nlm.nih.gov free of charge.

CONCLUSION

The Library of Congress subject headings list is the major means of providing subject headings for bibliographic records in OPACs. The LC subject headings and subject heading policies are subject to criticism, but LC is reacting positively and is adjusting its vocabulary and policies gradually to the demands of online retrieval without destroying their effectiveness in paper-based retrieval. A basic question is whether LC (and, therefore, most other North American and many other general libraries) will maintain this subject policy. At this stage of developments it seems to be the more cautious and responsible policy for a general national library, which LC is in effect, although not in name.

The Library of Congress has substantially increased the number of subject headings typically assigned to a work. In this connection it may well be worthwhile to investigate the use of "major" and "minor" subject headings, with the former corresponding to the traditional "overall" subject headings approach to a work and the latter leaning toward an indexing approach. The National Library of Medicine and several descriptor systems make this distinction. This would make a useful distinction between paper and online use, and online it would permit recall by a work's general topic without destroying access by its more specific topics. If the local library's online program permits access from any part of a subject heading string, that capacity, along with the use of keywords, multiplies the number of potential subject access points.

Most policy matters, such as whether to assign subject headings to individual works of fiction, can be adjusted without destroying inherent subject heading or descriptor techniques. But a major, long-term controlled study of the size and caliber of the Cranfield studies (Cleverdon 1962; 1966) would be useful to investigate the relative merits of the standard subject headings strings approach, a limited subject strings approach like NLM's, the descriptor approach, or, what is the most likely development, a combination of these.

Several thesauri, most of all the MeSH thesaurus, show that subject terms can be structured into an alphabetically and hierarchically coordinated system. Whether it is possible to coordinate two essentially independent general retrieval vocabularies like LCC and LCSH at this late stage is a matter of opinion. Even though LC went to great trouble and expense to superimpose for online searching a hierarchical code structure on LCC, it does not make lateral moves easy, and there are too many non-matches between individual LCSH and LCC terms to make switching from one vocabulary to the other really reliable. Some classificationists believe that the creation of a tightly organized syndetic alphabetical and classed structure for LCSH within itself, like NLM's MeSH, would be more feasible and more beneficial than trying to coordinate LC subject headings with the LC classification system.

Whatever degree of change in subject headings is involved, Marcia Bates makes the important point that the range of design possibilities available to information retrieval system developers has grown so enormously that subject access for OPACs must be designed with a full cognizance of automation possibilities: "Significant cost savings and improved access may possibly arise only from a review that takes a whole system viewpoint" (Conway 1992, 93).

REFERENCES

American Library Association. 1895. *List of subject headings for use in dictionary catalogs.* Prepared by a committee of the American Library Association. Boston: Library Bureau.

———. 1989 *List of subject headings for use in dictionary catalogs.* 2d ed., rev. Prepared by a committee of the American Library Association. Boston: Published for the A.L.A. Publishing Section by the Library Bureau.

Art and Architecture Thesaurus. 2d ed. 1994. Toni Peterson, director. New York: Oxford University Press.

Boll, John J. 1982. From subject headings to descriptors: The hidden trend in Library of Congress subject headings. *Cataloging & Classification Quarterly* 1(2/3): 3–28.

Cataloging Service Bulletin 75 (Winter): 45.

Chan, Lois Mai. 1995. *Library of Congress Subject Headings: Principles and Application.* 3d ed. Englewood, CO: Libraries Unlimited.

Cleverdon, Cyril W. 1962. *Report on the testing and analysis of an investigation into the comparative efficiency of indexing systems.* Cranfield, England: College of Aeronautics.

———. 1966. *Factors determining the performance of indexing systems.* Cranfield, England: College of Aeronautics.

Cochrane, Pauline Atherton. 1986. *Improving LCSH for use in Online Catalogs: Exercises for self-help with a selection of background readings.* Littleton, CO: Libraries Unlimited.

Conway, Martha O'Hara, ed. 1992. *The future of subdivisions in the Library of Congress Subject Headings System: Report from the Subject Subdivisions Conference sponsored by the Library of Congress, May 9–12, 1991* [the "Airlie" Conference], edited by Martha O'Hara Conway. Washington, DC: Cataloging Distribution Service, Library of Congress.

Crestadoro, Andrea. 1856. *The art of making catalogues.* London: British Museum (Ann Arbor, MI: University Microfilms, 1968).

Cutter, Charles Ammi. 1876. *Public libraries in the United States of America; their history, condition and management. Special report, part 2: Rules for a dictionary catalogue.* Washington, DC: Government Printing Office.

Drabenstott, Karen Markey, and Diane Vizine-Goetz. 1994. *Using subject headings for online retrieval: Theory, practice, and potential.* San Diego: Academic Press.

[ERIC]. 1995. *Thesaurus of ERIC descriptors.* Phoenix: Oryx Press.

Five-year progress report on Subject Subdivisions Conference recommendations, December 1996. 1997. *Cataloging Service Bulletin* 75 (Winter): 47–53.

Foskett, A. C. 1996. *The subject approach to information.* 5th ed. London: Library Association Publishing.

Franz, Lori, John Powell, Suzann Jude, and Karen M. Drabenstott. 1994. End-user understanding of subdivided subject headings. *Library Resources & Technical Services* 38 (3): 213–26.

Hanson, Eugene R., and Jay E. Daily. 1970. Catalogs and cataloging. In *Encyclopedia of library and information science,* edited by Allen Kent and Harold Lancour, 4:242–305. New York: Marcel Dekker.

Haykin, David Judson. 1951. *The Library of Congress subject headings: A practical guide.* Washington, DC: Government Printing Office.

Index medicus. 1960– . Washington, DC: National Library of Medicine.

Kaiser, J. 1911. *Systematic indexing.* London: Pitman.

Library of Congress. 1897. *Subject headings used in the dictionary catalogs of the Library of Congress.* 1st ed. Washington, DC: U.S. Library of Congress, Subject Cataloging Division.

[LCSH]. 1998. *Library of Congress subject headings.* 21st. ed. 1998. Prepared by the Cataloging Policy and Support Office, Library Services. Washington, DC: Library of Congress, Cataloging Distribution Service. 4v.

[MeSH]. 1960– . *Medical Subject Headings. Alphabetic list.* With each January issue of *Index Medicus; Annotated alphabetic list.* [Annual]. Bethesda, MD: National Library of Medicine; *Permuted medical subject headings.* [annual]. Bethesda, MD: National Library of Medicine; *Tree Structure.* [Annual]. Bethesda, MD: National Library of Medicine. [All also available online. MeSH is available online to the public free of charge: http://www.nlm.nih.gov.] (Accessed May 6, 2001).

Metcalfe, John 1976. *Information retrieval, British & American, 1876–1976.* Metuchen, NJ: Scarecrow Press.

Micco, Mary. 1997. Mary Micco discusses LC's role in Internet subject retrieval. *LC Cataloging Newsline; Online Newsletter of the Cataloging Directorate, Library of Congress* 5 (12, December). Available: http://lcweb.loc.gov/catdir/locn. (Accessed May 9, 2001).

Miksa, Francis. 1983. *The subject in the dictionary catalog from Cutter to the present.* Chicago: American Library Association. (Shows that subject cataloging has undergone significant changes since Cutter.)

Olson, Hope A. 1996. Between control and chaos: An ethical perspective on authority control. In *Authority control in the 21st century: An invitational conference, March 31–April 1, 1996. Proceedings.* Available: http://www.oclc.org/oclc/man/authconf/holson.htm. (Accessed May 11, 2001).

Report to the ALCTS/CCS Subject Analysis Committee [by the] Subcommittee on Subject Relationships/Reference Structures, June 1997. Available: www.ala.org/alcts /organization/ccs/index.html. (Revised May 10, 1999). (Accessed May 11, 2001).

Richmond, Phyllis. 1958. Cats: An example of concealed classification in subject headings. *Library Resources & Technical Services* 3 (Spring): 102–12.

Samleske, Roland. 1992. Computer science terminology and the Library of Congress subject headings: the case of software. *Technicalities* 12 (2, February): 11–13.

[SCM:SH]. 1996. *Subject cataloging manual: Subject headings.* 5th ed. Prepared by the Cataloging Policy and Support Office, Library of Congress. Washington, DC: Library of Congress, Cataloging Distribution Service.

Sears, Minnie Earl. 1923. *List of subject headings for small libraries.* New York: H. W. Wilson Co.

———. 1997. *Sears List of subject headings.* 16th ed. Edited by Joseph Miller. New York: H. W. Wilson.

Shaw, Ralph R., ed. 1961. *The state of the library art.* Volume 4, parts 1–5 (in one volume). New Brunswick, NJ: Graduate School of Library Service, Rutgers—The State University. (Contents: *Notched cards,* by F. Reichman; *Feature cards (Peek-a-boo cards),* by L. S. Thompson; *Punched cards,* by R. Blasingame Jr.; *Electronic searching,* by G. Jahoda; *Coding in yes-no form,* by D. J. Hickey.)

Shubert, Steven B. 1992. Critical views of LCSH—ten years later; A bibliographic essay. *Cataloging & Classification Quarterly* 15 (2): 37–91.

Weinberg, Bella Hass. 1993. The hidden classification in Library of Congress subject headings for Judaica. *Library Resources & Technical Services* 37 (October): 369–79.

Yee, Martha M., and Sara Shatford Layne. 1998. *Improving online public access catalogs.* Chicago: American Library Association.

7

Bibliographic Classification

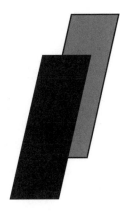

INTRODUCTION

This chapter examines the nature and use of classification in information retrieval, that is, bibliographic classification, with emphasis on classification thinking for online public access catalogs (OPACs). Classification is the systematic arrangement of objects or concepts in groups or classes according to their similarities and differences or their relation to a set of criteria. The types and arrangement of classes depend on what is being classified, for what purpose, and by whom. For example, languages may be classified genetically (on the basis of shared ancestry) or typologically (on the basis of vocabulary and structure). Drugs may be classified by chemical group (such as alkaloids), pharmacologically (that is, by the way they work in the body), and according to their therapeutic use. Chemists and physicians tend to view them in different groupings. Also, classification systems are not immutable. Over time, advances in knowledge and changes in attitudes tend to result in refinement, rearrangement, and even discarding of existing classes or parts of classes.

Bibliographic classification is designed to arrange documents and document descriptions in one or all fields of knowledge systematically and to group like concepts together and related concepts near each other in a manner that places the whole before its parts, so that an orderly progression is achieved. The groups are usually called "classes," and the symbols used to describe a class are often called "class numbers" or "classification numbers." Because these symbols can be letters or numbers or combinations of letters and numbers (but not words), they are preferably called the "notation."

In information retrieval, notations and subject headings are labels that describe the subject matter of documents. Each notation is part of an orderly structure called a classification scheme or system. Many such schemes exist. Some are special, that is, devoted to a specific subject such as medicine, ignoring all other subjects (like law), or considering them only in relation to their own topic, such as the patient's legal right to privacy. Other classification schemes are general and cover all fields of knowledge. Each scheme has a different breakdown and amount of detail.

The essential difference between a classed arrangement and an alphabetical subject heading arrangement (both of which may deal with the same field or with all fields) is the order in which the subjects (and, therefore, works on those subjects) are listed and arranged. In a list of subject headings, or in a bibliography arranged alphabetically by subject headings, subjects and works about them are listed in alphabetical order, by spelling. In a classed scheme, the same subjects and the same works are listed in groups, subgroups, and sub-subgroups—that is, in hierarchies—by likeness and relatedness rather than by spelling.

Once the creator of a classification scheme has arranged the groups and subgroups, notations are assigned. Notations are advantageous because they keep the groups in classed order, since they are assigned after the groups are formed, and they are usually shorter than words.

Books with the same class notation are subarranged by an alphanumeric book number (also called Cutter number), which is not part of the classification system and is commonly based on the author's name. The resulting unique combination is the "call number," that is, the number by which a book can be retrieved (called) from the shelves. Some libraries use the first few letters of the author's name instead of an alphanumeric book number.

Even in an alphabetical arrangement, subjects that are conceptually related can be listed near each other in two ways: 1) by happenstance, by what may be called "the accident of the alphabet," such as *Diet* and *Dietitian* or *Magnetic Pole* and *Magnetism*; or 2) by manipulating the alphabetical label so as to achieve a classed arrangement or subarrangement, such as *Librarians—Biography*; *Librarians—Education*; *Librarians—Japan*; *Art—History*; *Art, Medieval*. (See "Syntax of Subject Headings" in Chapter 6 for other examples.) But the predominant alphabetical sequence is by spelling rather than by meaning. The different arrangements of the same subjects— alphabetical or classed—affect information retrieval.

CLASSIFICATION CONVENTIONS

Until late in the nineteenth century the typical class notation tied a book to a specific location as if it had been chained. The typical book number meant, for example, "This book is in Alcove 7 (which contains natural history) in the second bookcase (which contains biology), third shelf, on which it is the fifth book: VII 2.3.5." This fixed location shelving system used very broad classes, and new books were simply added at the end of each broad class. Needless to say, the system caused problems. From the 1850s to the 1870s several well-known American librarians suggested other systems, which Melvil Dewey between 1873 and 1876 blended together with his own ideas into a totally new system of *relative* rather than *fixed* location, far more precise than the former shelving method (Wiegand 1996). This is the *Dewey Decimal Classification* (DDC), the basis of most currently used bibliographic or shelving class systems.

Classification conventions that resulted in rules on how a scheme should be structured and applied have existed for over a century. Over the years these conventions have been refined and formalized, so that one can now speak of classification theory and principles. The word "theory" in this context does not imply the existence of knowledge based on hypotheses and subsequent search for evidence. Rather, it refers to a body of knowledge that, on the basis of observation and experience, 1) suggests the criteria by which the comparative usefulness of different classifications may be measured; 2) shows how to ensure that the various criteria are satisfied to the maximum possible extent; and 3) recognizes that the criteria have different degrees of importance in different situations, some of which are mutually incompatible. It is important to realize that two basic sets of classification theories and principles exist, for enumerative classification schemes and for synthetic classification schemes. For both sets, which are described later in this chapter, formal classification principles were mostly evolved between 1925 and 1980. A third set of principles for classification in online catalogs is waiting to be developed. Because OPACs and other electronic retrieval systems tend to amalgamate the various alphabetical and classed retrieval systems, it is likely that these principles will also be an amalgamation, will be closely linked to software and hardware standards and to retrieval options, and will separate subject and shelving functions.

THE USES OF BIBLIOGRAPHIC CLASSIFICATION

Bibliographic classification as now practiced has three uses:

- In the physical arrangement of documents on shelves or in files,

- In the arrangement of document surrogates (bibliographic descriptions, or "entries") that represent documents to form paper-based catalogs, indexes, and bibliographies, and

- In computer information retrieval systems in which the classification notations and the document surrogates are in machine-readable form and can be readily manipulated like alphabetical terms (keywords, descriptors, subject headings).

Before describing these purposes in detail, it is necessary to describe the components of classification systems and the types of classification schemes that exist.

COMPONENTS OF BIBLIOGRAPHIC CLASSIFICATION SCHEMES

A bibliographic classification scheme involves the following:

- A verbal description, topic by topic, of the things and concepts that can be represented in or by the scheme.

- An arrangement of these verbal descriptions in classed or logical order that is intended to permit a meaningful arrangement of topics and that will be convenient to users.

- A notation that appears alongside each verbal description, which is used to represent it and which shows the order. The entire group of verbal descriptions and notations form the schedules.

- References within the schedules to guide the classifier and the searcher to different aspects of a desired topic or to other related topics (like the related term references in alphabetical lists).

- An alphabetical index of terms used in the schedules, and of synonyms of those terms, that leads to the notations.

- Instructions for use. General instructions (with examples) are usually to be found at the beginning of the scheme, and instructions relating to particular parts of the schedules are, or should be, given in the parts to which they relate.

- An organization that will ensure that the classification scheme is maintained, that is, revised and republished. This is external to the scheme, but an important factor in evaluating its comparative usefulness.

CLASSIFICATION AND DIVISION

One way of viewing the basic process of classification, and therefore the way in which schedules of terms are derived, is to consider the logically opposite process of division. A group of abstract concepts (such as *Emotions),* or of objects (such as *Furniture),* or of activities (such as *Gardening)* can be divided into smaller groups. These smaller groups can each be divided into yet smaller groups, and the process can be repeated until eventually it is no longer desirable or necessary for the given purpose.

For example, taking *Animals* as the broadest group permits dividing the group into smaller groups:

```
Animals
    Invertebrates
    Vertebrates
```

Each group may be further subdivided, thus:

```
Vertebrates
    Cold-blooded vertebrates
    Warm-blooded vertebrates
```

Yet further subdivision is possible:

```
Warm-blooded vertebrates
    Birds
    Mammals
```

If the process of division is continued, eventually a stage is reached at which further division is impossible; at that point, individual terms or items have been reached.

The results of the process of division are diagrammed in Figure 7.1. This is a selective presentation, and the various groups have not been broken down as far as is possible, but it allows definition of some terms.

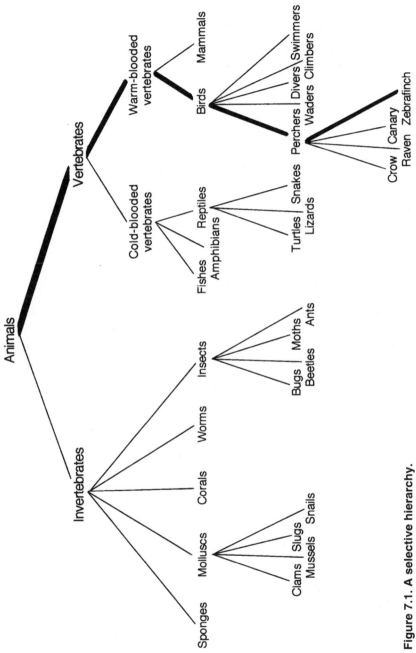

Figure 7.1. A selective hierarchy.

HIERARCHIES AND
CHARACTERISTICS OF DIVISION

Figure 7.1 represents a "hierarchy." If it is turned upside down, so that *Animals* appears at the bottom, it somewhat resembles a tree, which gives rise to the alternate name for hierarchies, "tree structures." Each word or phrase in the diagram can be referred to as a "term." The heavy line represents an example of a "chain," a succession of divisions subordinate one to another, obtained by moving down the hierarchy (or up the tree). Each term in that chain belongs to a different hierarchical level.

In the hierarchy the groups *Perchers, Climbers, Swimmers, Divers,* and *Waders* all belong to the larger group, *Birds.* The smaller groups can be grouped together into a larger group by what they have in common (in this instance, their birdlike nature). Conversely, the larger group, *Birds,* can be divided into the smaller groups by a more precise characteristic, such as *Swimming birds.* The principle on which a large group is divided into smaller groups is referred to as the "characteristic of division." In Figure 7.1, the characteristic of division used for birds is what birds predominantly or characteristically do. In engineering, the characteristic of division is typically the fields to which engineering is applied: chemical, civil (roads, bridges, buildings, etc.), electrical, geological, and mechanical.

Common characteristics of division are 1) class to class member, or genus to species, as *Primates* to *Apes*; 2) the whole to its parts, as *Nervous system* to *Spinal cord*; 3) continuous process, as in *Textiles, Carding, Spinning, Weaving, Finishing;* 4) increasing complexity, as in *Music for Duets, for Trios, for Quartets*; 5) chronological, as in the history of a country; and 6) by space or area, as the geography of a continent to the geography of a country in that continent. With the best of intentions, however, and in spite of much logic, every classification scheme also contains a considerable number of arbitrary and sometimes even ludicrous groupings.

The same characteristic of division may be used more than once. For example, in a scheme devoted to the anatomy of birds, the characteristic of division might be body parts, producing an array with notations for body parts such as *Head, Body, Wings,* and *Legs.* The same characteristic could then be applied to each of these parts, such as *Head,* to produce a lower level array including notations for head parts such as *Eyes, Beak,* or *Nostrils;* the same or a different characteristic might be used to further subdivide that array. For example, the *Head* part might be subdivided by the characteristic of *Disease.* In this way, numerous arrays of notations can be made up at several different hierarchical levels.

Hierarchies exist not only in classed vocabularies that use notations but also in alphabetical schemes, as described more fully in Chapter 6. Gorillas are a genus of the biological family of apes, regardless of whether their label is the word *Gorilla* or the notation *Sh.* Although a list of subject headings in alphabetical order does not make hierarchies obvious, they exist in every field, as information scientists have gradually rediscovered.

Natural and Artificial Classification

Classification creates groups and subgroups, whenever possible, on the basis of selecting one kind of similarity or dissimilarity. It is possible to distinguish between natural classifications—those based on supposedly inherent qualities of the things classified, as are found in botany and astronomy—and artificial classifications, which involve the point of view of the classifier and which have as a result different arrangements from natural classifications. An example is the label *Fishing and whaling industry* where, although fishes and whales are biologically different kinds of animals, they have the artificial or viewpoint similarities of being harvested or hunted in similar ways. Similarly, birds can be classed artificially as *Cage birds,* or *Game birds,* or *Agricultural pests,* not on the basis of what they do but on the basis of how humans view them.

Almost all subjects can be divided in more than one way. For example, the subject *Weaving of textiles* can be further subdivided by material, by manufacturing process, by color, by destined usage, and so forth. Each possibility represents a different characteristic of division.

In bibliographical classifications, which are intended to assist in the retrieval of documents and more particularly in the retrieval of the information contained in those documents, it is sometimes necessary to use not only logical divisions but also other, sometimes overlapping, characteristics of division based on what kinds of writings exist in the respective fields. For example, a classification for documents relating to birds may have groups for their body parts such as wings, claws, feathers, and beaks in addition to, or rather than, groups for their actions such as perchers, waders, and swimmers. The DDC contains places for *Sanitary and municipal engineering, Aerospace engineering,* and *Military and nautical engineering,* each of which contains elements of the standard engineering subdivisions *Chemical, Civil, Electrical, Geological,* and *Mechanical engineering.* Such overlapping characteristics of division make for difficult classification decisions and double searching. The greater the care that is taken when considering the characteristics of division, both in relation to choosing them when the classification is devised and to their application when the resulting classification scheme is applied to documents, the more likely the classification is to be successful as a means of providing access to bibliographical records.

The amount of literature in a given subject may also influence a bibliographic classification scheme. In general, the more literature that exists in a field, the more subdivisions its classification will require, for intellectual as well as practical reasons: intellectual so that different subconcepts are listed separately, and practical so that each subgroup is small enough to permit effective browsing.

Appearance of a new subject that does not fit easily into an existing schematic structure may throw an existing scheme into disarray or may at least cause questions as to where to fit it into the scheme. Examples are the appearance of computers in the 1950s and of microcomputers in the 1980s.

Characteristics of Division, Facets, and Arrays

When a characteristic of division is applied to a group such as birds, the smaller groups that result on the next lower hierarchical level may collectively be referred to as an "array." Although the term has other meanings in other contexts, in information retrieval an array may be defined as the set of subgroups that results when a characteristic of division is applied to a level in a hierarchy. Every subgroup should exclude all of the others, and the whole array should be exhaustive of the contents of the class. This is best achieved by using only one characteristic of division for any one hierarchical level; otherwise, concepts may overlap and confusion may result.

For example, two characteristics of division commonly applied in classifying people and information about them are their age groups (children, adolescents, adults, the elderly) or their sex (male, female). In the DDC, through Edition 20, published in 1989, these were applied simultaneously to the second level of the hierarchy for *Education*, so that in the same array there was a subdivision for *Education of women* and one for *Education of adults.* (One must remember that this arrangement was produced 130 years ago when women's education was considered revolutionary, or at least progressive, and something to be highlighted!) As long as class numbers are used as shelving numbers (call numbers), only one number may be assigned to a document, and the problem for the classifier and the searcher in cases like this is where to classify or to search for a work on the education of adult women.

Similar problems are visible in any classification scheme, especially enumerative ones, and are caused at least partly by the way literature tends to be written in any field. To continue the education example from the DDC, in the 21st edition, published in 1996, the first array divides the topic *Education* partly by educational level (*Elementary, Secondary, Higher*) and partly by topics such as *Activities, Philosophy, Curriculum,* and *People.* The problem again is where to place, and search for, topics like *Curricula for secondary schools.* To cite two examples from the Library of Congress classification (LCC): The topic *Economic history and conditions* is listed twice, once as *HC,* where it is subdivided by region or country, and once as *HD,* where it is subdivided by topic, such as *Production,* or *Land use.* The problem here is where to class a work on, for example, *Economics of land use in Peru.* In the section on *Hunting* one finds on the same hierarchical level *Deer hunting* (*SK301*) and *Hunting in the United States* (*SK361*). Here the problem is where to place a work on *Deer hunting in the United States.* Typical solutions to such problems are described later on in this chapter, Section "Some Solutions to the Compound Topics Problem."

In many instances, the division of a field into conflicting arrays in an enumerative scheme is understandable because different books written on one topic break it up in different, and often conflicting, ways. This would explain dividing, in an enumerative scheme, *on the same hierarchical level, Birds* by natural division into, for example, *Perchers,* on the one hand, and on the other hand also by artificial division into *Cage birds,* or *Game birds.* Because the two groups of classes overlap, the notation for *Game birds* includes some perchers, but not all, and the notation for *Perchers* includes some cage birds, but not all. It would explain in another hierarchical scheme dividing architecture on the same hierarchical level by material (such as *Buildings made of concrete*) and by function (such as *Department stores*). Again, because the two groups overlap, where should one place, or search for, *Department stores built of concrete?*

In enumerative schemes different hierarchical levels may well, and meaningfully, be divided by different characteristics of division. Indeed, this is essential to create logically arranged topical relationships. An example is dividing *Architecture* by building purpose (*Public structures, Residential buildings,* etc.), creating for each category a second more specific subarray again based on purpose (*Farm houses, Apartment houses, Motels*) and then creating within each subarray a sub-subarray by geographic location.

Partly to circumvent the rigidity and linearity of enumerative systems, partly to disassociate subject retrieval from shelving, as well as for other reasons, synthetic, or faceted, classification systems were invented during the early part of the twentieth century. Their structure and rules require their characteristics of division, called "facets" to be, in effect, separate hierarchies independent of each other. Individual facets are often referred to by the name of the characteristic of division used to produce them; thus, the facet created by using a parts characteristic of division will be referred to as the "parts" facet. In a properly designed faceted classification system, facets cannot have conflicting arrays because they are "mutually exclusive and collectively exhaustive." This simplifies the classifier's and the searcher's work. Faceted systems are described later in this chapter, Section "Synthetic Classification."

Progress Toward Flexibility

It would be wrong to give the impression that there is a complete separation of the two kinds of bibliographic classification, enumerative and synthetic. They do have a common basis. For example, both involve hierarchies, and the factors described in the section "Components of Bibliographic Classification Schemes" in this chapter apply to both kinds. Most classifications in use involve a greater or lesser amount of synthesis. In the case of the basically enumerative DDC, the amount of synthesis permitted is limited but increasing. Synthetic, and especially faceted, schemes, on the other hand, usually do rely on a designated sequence of facets in the notation. This imposes a certain rigidity on the notation, similar to the rigidity of enumerative schemes, and impedes searching for the last few facets of a faceted notation in a paper-based file.

To permit flexible, multiple approaches to a topic, librarians, long before the invention of faceted schemes, invented a catalog format, the "classed catalog," described in the Section "The Classed Catalog" later in this chapter. To facilitate access by all facets in a faceted notation as used in a paper-based file, British librarians invented during the first half of the twentieth century chain indexing and string indexing (both also described later in this chapter; respectively, in Section "The Principle of Inversion" and in Section "PRECIS"). If librarians and programmers are on their toes, recognize the potential, and are willing to invest the necessary intellectual effort and financial means, it is quite likely that computerization will blur even further the distinction between enumerative and synthetic classification schemes; will even amalgamate classed and alphabetical searching into a cohesive structure; and will achieve total flexibility by permitting subject searches from every element and every concept, which is expressed in a subject label such as a notation. Several experiments along these lines are under way.

Although the differences between enumerative and synthetic classification schemes are not absolute and ironclad, and although there are indications that computerization may lead to further blurring of distinctions between the two systems, for the sake of clarity the following sections emphasize the characteristically different aspects of each rather than their similarities.

ENUMERATIVE SCHEMES

In an enumerative classification scheme, every topic that can be classified by the scheme is represented—enumerated—by one notation in the schedule. Topics that are not enumerated separately must be subsumed under the closest broader topic. For example, if a scheme has no notation for *Sled dog races*, books on that topic would be classed with books on *Dog races*. And if the scheme had no notation for that topic, either, the book could be classed with works on *Races and racing*. Conversely, in a collection or bibliography or database that concentrates on dogs, even more precise classes than *Sled dog races* would be needed and enumerated, perhaps with separate notations for each breed of dog used, for the different types of sled dog races, for codes of pertinent racing rules, and so forth.

Linearity

Although refinement solves the problem of classing narrow compound topics precisely in an enumerative classification scheme, it also exacerbates another problem that exists to some extent even when classes are broad: the limitations imposed by linearity. Discussed in Chapter 4, linearity describes the fact that documents, or paper-based document surrogates (that is, bibliographic entries on catalog cards or on the printed page) can be shelved or filed in order by only one characteristic of division. Therefore, documents that deal with the interrelationship of two subjects can be listed or shelved by only one of these two subjects, with the other subject as a subdivision of the first one. For example, the DDC has a spot for *Social behavior of animals* (see *591.56* in Figure 7.2) and a spot for *Lions* (see *599.757* in Figure 7.2). Works on the social behavior of lions can be listed on paper, or shelved, at least theoretically, under number *599.757* with the animal, in a subsection *Social behavior (599.757 156)* or under number *591.56* with the action, without specific reference to lions. Shelving, or listing on paper some works under one notation and others under the other, would not solve this problem, because this would split the collection between the two locations and destroy the very purpose of classification.

To understand the dilemma, one must realize that to achieve consistent groupings every type of classification, like every other type of information retrieval method, is based on its own sets of principles and objectives, which result in specific rules. (One might think of them as game rules.) Although they might be regarded as part of the problem, the rules are actually a necessary solution and result in an orderly arrangement that places like works together and related works near each other. Arguments and doubts do arise because "relatedness" is a matter of opinion, depends on the classifier's and searcher's professional background and point of view, and is apt to change with time. For example, for its 21st edition the DDC's *zoology* section was completely restructured on the basis of how zoologists study animals and, secondarily, to make the numbers shorter than in earlier editions. This edition places animal behavior in general in one place, next to other works on animals in general (see *590* to *591.59* in Figure 7.2) and places works on the behavior of specific genera, species, and so forth with the animal (see *597.951 56, 599.353 156,* and *599.757 156* in Figure 7.2). This seems logical but, because of the nature of enumerative systems, is still subject to the limitations of linearity.

Although all classification schemes are designed to bring like things together, to bring related things near one another, and to separate both from unrelated things, enumerative classifications are specifically designed to concentrate on the major, overall topic of the work being classified and to pay less attention to its minor topics. (It must be remembered that today's enumerative classifications were invented more than 130 years ago, when books tended to be written about more general topics.) The system of emphasizing the overall topic works well unless a work deals with a highly compound topic such as *Diseases / of the digestive organs / of lizards / caused by parasites / in Grant County, Wisconsin*. Then the question arises, which is the major topic, the disease, the organ, the animal, the causative agent, or the location? In Figure 7.2 this topic could, at least theoretically, be placed in *571.910 977 577* or *571.999 179* or *573.339* or *597.95*. (To take us back to the topics of Chapter 6: Would the same or different problems arise if we dealt with indexing labels that are not also shelving labels, or with labels like descriptors?) If the long DDC numbers seem unreal, remember that, first, most of these are very specialized topics, suitable for a special library or a medical bibliography, but not likely to be in a general public library. Second, long numbers do not bother the computer, as one can observe at any supermarket checkout point.

Changing the order in which topics are aligned in an enumerative classification does not solve the problem of linearity. In Figure 7.2 the general life sciences processes are listed first (see *570* to *572.419 757*), followed by biological systems (see *573.1* to *573.6*), and then followed by zoölogy (see *590* to *599.757 159*). To find "everything" on, for example, *lions* one must look in even this highly selective list in more than ten places. But in this list material on *parasitic diseases* is listed together (see *571.999*).

Figure 7.3 (page 166) is a partial revision of Figure 7.2, showing two of many other possible characteristics of division. Like Figure 7.2, Figure 7.3 shows that searching for broad topics in a detailed enumerative classification scheme may require looking in many locations, regardless of how the broad topic is broken down. Although the breakdown in Version A of Figure 7.3 places material on *Mice* or *Lions* together, it requires looking in many places for material on topics such as *Diseases of the circulatory systems*, or *Diseases caused by parasites*. In addition, although the breakdown in Version B places material on *Diseases of the circulatory system* together, it requires searching many places for topics like *Lions, Diseases of lions*, or *Diseases caused by parasites*. Other possible breakdowns would have similar results. This is typical of enumerative schemes: Linearity causes the subtopic at the lower hierarchical level to get scattered, especially when the scheme is refined. Nevertheless, only one of several possible characteristics of division can be used to shelve documents.

Another problem is that linearity also makes it difficult to recognize, in a shelf or paper-based search, the extent of an array or the next broader or narrower hierarchical level of a subject, although effective searching often requires it. The shelf browser would be aided by the titles on the spines and the paper file user would be aided by the bibliographic description (the document surrogate). However, it is virtually impossible for either to get, for example, a helpful idea of how many classes of animals are involved and how these classes are broken down. Only a sophisticated user will be able to narrow down a search (for example, from *Insects* to *Beetles*) or to broaden it (for example, from *Legs* to *Motor organs*) to get a quick overview of the available resources from which a choice can be made.

With proper programming and appropriate other devices, computer-based classification can show and indeed already has shown, hierarchical as well as lateral relationships and permit access even by a subsumed topic. This capability is important because users often begin a subject search with a term broader than actually available and have no other way of knowing how a classification scheme breaks a topic down.

570	Life sciences, Biology
571.633	Cell anatomy
571.633 1	Cell anatomy in animals
571.633 179	Cell anatomy in reptiles
571.633 179 5	Cell anatomy in lizards
571.633 19	Cell anatomy in mammals
571.633 193 53	Cell anatomy in common mice
571.633 197 57	Cell anatomy in lions
571.9	Diseases (Pathology)
571.91	Diseases of animals
571.910 967	Diseases of animals in Central Africa
571.910 977 577	Diseases of animals in Grant County, Wisconsin
571.917 9	Diseases of reptiles
571.917 95	Diseases of lizards
571.919	Diseases of mammals
571.919 353	Diseases of common mice
571.919 757	Diseases of lions
571.956	Diseases caused by air pollution (Can be sub-arranged by animal or plant, like 571.999)
571.999	Diseases caused by parasites
571.999 179	Parasitic diseases of reptiles
571.999 179 5	Parasitic diseases of lizards
571.999 19	Parasitic diseases of mammals
571.999 193 53	Parasitic diseases of common mice
571.999 197 57	Parasitic diseases of lions
571.999 24	Parasitic diseases of liliopsida plants
571.999 244	Parasitic diseases of orchids
571.999 25	Parasitic diseases of conifers
571.999 252	Parasitic diseases of spruces
572.4	Metabolism (The chemical changes creating energy in living cells)
572.417 9	Metabolism in reptiles
572.417 95	Metabolism in lizards
572.419	Metabolism in mammals
572.419 353	Metabolism in common mice
572.419 757	Metabolism in lions
573.1	Circulatory systems, circulatory organs, circulation (Biology) (Can be sub-arranged by organ, pathology, and animal, like 573.3)
573.117 9	Circulatory system in reptiles
573.117 95	Circulatory system in lizards
573.119	Circulatory system in mammals
573.119 353	Circulatory system in common mice
573.119 757	Circulatory system in lions
573.139	Diseases of the circulatory system in animals
573.139 179	Diseases of the circulatory system in reptiles
573.139 179 5	Diseases of the circulatory system in lizards
573.139 19	Diseases of the circulatory system in mammals
573.139 193 53	Diseases of the circulatory system in common mice
573.139 197 57	Diseases of the circulatory system in lions
573.2	Respiratory system [in animals], respiration, respiratory organs (Can be sub-arranged like 573.3, by organ, pathology, and animal.)

Figure 7.2. Selective enumerative classification for biology/zoology: skeleton outline of DDC classes 570 to 599.

573.3	Digestive system [in animals], digestion, digestive organs
573.319	Digestive system in mammals
573.319 353	Digestive system in common mice
573.319 757	Digestive system in lions
573.339	Diseases of the digestive system [in animals]
573.339 19	Diseases of the digestive system in mammals
573.339 193 53	Diseases of the digestive system in common mice
573.339 197 57	Diseases of the digestive system in lions
573.35	Mouth and esophagus (May not be divided by animal. See text)
573.356	Teeth (Can be sub-arranged by pathology and animal, like 573.36)
573.36	Stomach
573.361 79	Reptile stomachs
573.361 795	Lizard stomachs
573.361 9	Stomachs in mammals
573.361 935 3	Stomach in common mice
573.361 975 7	Stomach in lions
573.363 9	Stomach diseases
573.363 917 9	Stomach diseases in reptiles
573.363 917 95	Stomach diseases in lizards
573.363 919	Stomach diseases in mammals
573.363 919 353	Stomach diseases in common mice
573.363 919 757	Stomach diseases in lions
573.37	Intestine (Can be sub-arranged by pathology and animal, like 573.36)
573.6	Reproductive system in animals, reproduction (Biology)
	(Can be sub-arranged like 573.3, by organ, pathology, and animal.)
590	Zoölogy
591.5	Animal behavior, animal psychology
591.56	Social behavior of animals
591.59	Communication among animals
591.967	Animals in Central Africa
591.977 577	Animals in Grant County, Wisconsin
592	Invertebrates (Zoölogy)
594	Mollusks
597	Cold blooded vertebrates, Fishes
597.8	Amphibians
597.9	Reptiles
597.95	Lizards
597.950 977 577	Lizards in Grant County, Wisconsin
597.951 56	Social behavior among lizards
597.951 59	Communication among lizards
598	Birds
599	Mammals
599.353	Common mice
599.353 097 757 7	Common mice in Grant County, Wisconsin
599.353 156	Social behavior of common mice
599.353 159	Communication among common mice
599.757	Lions
599.757 096 7	Lions in Central Africa
599.757 156	Social behavior among lions
599.757 159	Communication among lions

Version A	Version B
Mice	Diseases
In Grant County, Wisconsin	Of the circulatory system
Social behavior	Caused by parasites
Communication	In mice
Cell anatomy	In lions
Circulatory system	Caused by air pollution
Digestive system	In mice
Metabolism	In lions
Diseases	Of the digestive system
Of the circulatory system	Caused by parasites
Of the digestive system	In mice
Caused by air pollution	In lions
Caused by parasites	Caused by air pollution
Lions	In mice
In Central Africa	In lions
Social behavior	Of the reproductive system
Communication	Caused by parasites
Cell anatomy	In mice
Circulatory system	In lions
Digestive system	Caused by air pollution
Metabolism	In mice
Diseases	In lions
Of the circulatory system	etc.
Of the digestive system	
Caused by air pollution	
Caused by parasites	
etc.	

Figure 7.3. Two alternatives for arranging the subject matter in Figure 7.2. (class numbers omitted).

Some Solutions to the Compound Topics Problem

Several solutions to the problem of compound topics are possible in an enumerative scheme. One is to have definite rules such as, "Class by the emphasis of the work: if it emphasizes the disease, class with diseases; if it emphasizes the animal, class with the animal." The result is that the classifier sometimes must make rather arbitrary decisions, and in any case the shelf browser—if well enough informed to know both notations—must search both of them to get all likely material on the desired topic.

Another possible rule is, "If there is conflict between a topic and a time period, class with the topic: When the scheme has spots for 'Laws of the USA', and another one for 'Nineteenth century laws', class a book on Nineteenth century US laws with 'Laws of the USA'." Another typical rule, more automatic and less opinion-based than the previous two examples, is, "Class with the number coming first (or last) in the schedules." Such rules help the classifier and result in consistent decisions but, again, are not of much help to the shelf browser who is not likely to be aware of the rules or to know both numbers.

Another possible solution is for the designer of the scheme to refine it so that specific notations exist for even highly compound subjects. Note that, in an enumerative scheme, compound things and concepts *(Effect of climate on building design; Cataloging of microforms; Truss bridges built of wood)* can be expressed only as either a broad topic *(Building design; Cataloging; Truss bridges)* or a subdivision of only one of the broader terms *(Climate* or *Building design; Cataloging* or *Microforms; Truss bridges* or *Wood)*. If some works on the specific topic were listed under one broad term and some under the other, the topic would again be divided haphazardly, destroying the purpose of classification. If all works on the specific topic were listed under both broad terms, the paper-based files (so the reasoning has gone) would become too unwieldy, especially in large libraries with millions of catalog cards. Therefore, the compound thing or concept is classed in only one of two possible locations, and people who look for it in a paper-based file or who shelf browse for it in the other location are out of luck.

Because enumerative schemes often use topical subdivisions such as

Cataloging

— of books

— of serials

— of microforms

— of computer programs,

they actually often join two or more different concepts. This often requires subject-specific rules. To create a cohesive, logical structure, these rules should be based on objectives. For example, in the 21st edition of the DDC (1996), one objective is to list general biological topics (such as *cells, diseases, metabolism, circulation*) as part of *biology,* first in general and then within each of these topics as manifested in specific animals. (See *571.633* to *571.633 197 57,* and *572.4* to *572.419 757* in Figure 7.2, for example.) But works dealing with the animals as such, including their behavior, are listed under *zoölogy* (See *590* to *599.757 159* in Figure 7.2.) This is a very reasonable distribution of topics, based on expert opinion, but it does not solve the problem of linearity. Faceted classification systems avoid much of this rigidity, and one of the computer's great advantages is that it makes it possible to avoid this rigidity altogether; it increases the number of listing and access options, provided the program permits it and the component parts of the notations are identified sufficiently.

Disciplines in Enumerative Schemes

Enumerative bibliographic classifications are based on the assumption that all knowledge can be divided into one cohesive but rigid structure. However, because any subject can be viewed, and therefore grouped, as part of at least two entirely different structures, the schedule designer faces the problem of which of these structures to use. For example, the subject of *marriage* can be viewed either as a cohesive entity as a "concrete" subject or distributed according to aspect, that is, according to the emphasis of the work being classed. If the latter, the ethical aspects of marriage are classed with other works on ethics, the religious aspects with other works on religion, the sociological aspects of marriage with sociology, to name some possibilities. For retrieval purposes (on the shelves, in the card catalog, or online) is it more helpful to group everything on marriage together, or to group everything on, say, law together, including marriage laws?

Bibliographic classification systems, and especially enumerative classifications, structure the world of knowledge into disciplines, traditional broad areas of teaching that were customary when the respective scheme was invented. These are disciplines like the social sciences, technology, literature, or philosophy. As a result, works on any concrete subject (like *Horses*, *Elections*, *Paper*, *Parent-child relationships*) are distributed among many places, depending on the discipline, aspect, or viewpoint involved. Works on *angels* may be found in the

> Discipline of religion, section Christian doctrine, for works on their role according to Christian belief;
>
> Discipline of religion, section Mohammedan doctrine, for works on their role according to Muslim belief;
>
> Discipline of religion, section Jewish theology, for works on their role according to Jewish belief; and
>
> Discipline of art, for works on, or of, pictorial representations (paintings, statues, etc.) of angels.

Some of the places where books on *rabbits* may be found are

On breeding of rabbits:	In the discipline of agriculture and related products, section on animal husbandry
On commercial hunting of rabbits:	In the discipline of agriculture and related technologies, section on hunting, fishing, conservation
On hunting rabbits as a sport:	In the discipline of recreational and performing arts, section on fishing, hunting, shooting
On anatomy of rabbits:	In the discipline of biology, section on physiology
On rabbits as agricultural pests:	In the discipline of agriculture and related technologies, section on animal pests
On fossil remains of rabbits:	In the discipline of paleontology, section on paleozoology
On rabbits as food:	In the discipline of technology (applied sciences), section on home economics

Different classification schemes divide knowledge in different ways, but these examples show how a concrete subject like angels or rabbits tends to be distributed among disciplines under the currently used system. Grouping resources by discipline separates materials on a concrete subject. However, grouping resources by concrete subjects would separate resources in a discipline. Because classification is traditionally used not only as a filing device in the paper-based shelflist but also as a shelving device for the actual documents, either system would cause problems in shelf browsing or in searching a paper-based shelflist. Grouping everything on fossils together will disadvantage the person who wants broad coverage of rabbits, including their early ancestors; grouping everything on rabbits together will disadvantage the person who wants broad coverage of paleozoology. The result will be the same: People looking for a group that happens to be torn apart by the classification scheme must look in several places. This is akin to the problem of inverted subject headings (that is, classed subarrangements) in the otherwise alphabetically sequenced subject heading file, described in Chapter 6. Both represent fairly rigid structures that are not well positioned to answer questions outside their respective structures.

Looking at the doughnut rather than the hole, one realizes that about half the time users are likely to find the grouping that suits their purpose. But a 50 percent success rate is not something to crow about. Therefore, information scientists have sought other means to counteract the problem of linearity and to improve the success rate. Synthetic classification is one of them. Its principles can be, and have been, applied successfully to an electronic environment. With appropriate OPAC menus, which are largely still on the wish list, and which offer searchers clear choices among the different disciplines, users should be in a much better position than they can be in a paper-based file to narrow down their search to the desired aspect of a concrete subject.

SYNTHETIC CLASSIFICATION

The second type of classification scheme, synthetic classification, works like building blocks. It is especially suited to fields and situations (such as highly specialized bibliographies or documentation centers) in which many of the topics involve compounds of more than one concept or thing. Synthetic classifications combine, or synthesize, the symbols for different concepts to create compound notations for compound concepts or things. For convenience, "notation" is used in this chapter to refer to the entire set of symbols associated with a combined (synthesized) topic, and "symbol" refers to the symbols used for any one part (facet) of this combined topic. The most highly developed kind of synthetic classification is called "faceted classification."

Origins of Faceted Classification

The basic concept of faceted classification goes back more than 300 years, to people like Cyprian Kinner (d. 1649), George Dalgarno (1626?–1687), and John Wilkins (1614–1672) (Schulte-Albert 1974). However, these concepts were not developed, were not practically used, and were forgotten. The less precise concept of synthesis—the building of notations out of component parts to represent complex or very specific subjects—was invented in the late nineteenth century by two Belgians,

Paul Otlet and Henri LaFontaine, who have not received full credit for this then-revolutionary aspect of their classification scheme, the *Universal Decimal Classification* (UDC). In the 1920s, the Indian librarian S. R. Ranganathan, inspired by concepts of his British teacher W. C. Berwick Sayers (Palmer 1955), reinvented the basic concept independently and formulated it into a series of new classification principles. With these he created the first, and so far only, general faceted classification scheme. It uses five facets, and is called the "colon classification" because the various symbols that make up the notation are separated by colons (Ranganathan 1933).

The Classification Research Group (an independent group of mostly British librarians and classificationists) had great influence on the development of classification theory, especially during its early years, the 1950s to 1970s. Its members experimented with Ranganathan's principles, developed them further, and created individually several major special faceted schemes. British classificationists are also responsible for developing derivatives of faceted classification such as chain indexing and the subsequently described string indexing system. Most U.S. information scientists were more interested at that time in working with alphabetical retrieval vocabularies. More recently, faceted classification has again become of interest to North American information scientists in connection with its use in OPACs and with interdisciplinary topics (Chan 1990, 9; Liu 1990; ASIS 1991; Beghtol 1998a; 1998b).

In its ideal version the major characteristics of faceted classification are

- Separate and independent hierarchies for every facet and every subfacet;

- Strict adherence to the use of a single characteristic of division in each facet or subfacet;

- System-wide rules for combining the facets into a sequence that results in the compound notation;

- Labels that clearly distinguish each facet; and

- Most important, an alphabetical index that permits access to each part of a compound notation (even the facets that are subsumed under the first facet), as well as to the total notation.

Most faceted classifications are special, that is, intended to be used in connection with the literature of a particular discipline or broad area of study, such as library science or engineering. Their designers view the broad area of study from several angles (like the facets in a diamond), making each angle into a facet. Each facet has its own hierarchy with its own characteristics of division and its own symbols. The typical faceted classification is, therefore, multihierarchical or polyhierarchical. However, this is not so true, or so obvious, in ordinary synthetic classifications generally, because in some the hierarchies are not easily distinguished by recognizable symbols.

In a faceted classification the symbols of the various facets are combined according to specific rules to form the notation for the works being classified. In architecture, for example, there may be a *Materials* facet, a *Structures* facet, an *Architectural styles* facet, and a *Location* facet (as shown in Figure 7.4), along with several other appropriate facets, not shown. To build a notation, for example, for "Apartment houses built of reinforced concrete in Milan, Italy, in Neo-Renaissance style" the classifier using this particular imaginary scheme finds the symbol for *Apartment houses* in the structures facet (*T21*) and the symbol for *Reinforced concrete* in the materials facet (*M31*) along with symbols *S32* and *L364*, and puts the four together according to precise guidelines, that is, synthesizes them to form the notational symbol for *Apartment houses built of reinforced concrete in Neo-Renaissance style in Milan, Italy.* According to the guidelines used, this might be *L364M31S32T21*, or some other combination. Note that each facet has its own distinct symbols (mnemonic if possible) so that the experienced user can recognize the basic structure of a notation. The more facets, the more precise the description and the longer the notation. The long, detailed notations characteristic of faceted schemes used to be considered a disadvantage for human users but are no obstacle to a computer.

L	**Location Facet**	**S**	**Architectural Style Facet**
L1	Place	S1	Architectural styles
L10	United States	S10	Romanesque
L17	Wisconsin	S12	Neo-Romanesque
L173	Dane County	S20	Gothic
L1736	Madison	S22	Neo-Gothic
L20	Canada	S30	Renaissance
L26	British Columbia	S32	Neo-Renaissance
L264	Vancouver	S40	Baroque
L30	Europe	S50	Empire
L36	Italy	S60	Cape Cod
L364	Milan	S70	Ante-Bellum Plantation
L37	Spain	S80	Bauhaus

M	**Materials Facet**	**T**	**Structures Facet**
M1	Construction material	T1	Structures
M10	Stone	T10	Office buildings
M20	Wood	T20	Residential buildings
M21	Laminated wood	T21	Apartment houses
M30	Concrete	T22	Single family dwellings
M31	Reinforced concrete	T23	Duplexes
M40	Metal	T24	Town houses
M41	Steel	T30	Bridges
M42	Iron	T31	Suspension bridges
M50	Glass	T32	Arch bridges
M53	Plain glass	T33	Cantilever bridges
M54	Frosted glass	T34	Truss bridges

Figure 7.4. Skeleton section from an imaginary faceted classification scheme on architecture. As described in the text, it is *not* well designed and violates a basic principle of faceted schemes.

The number and the kinds of facets vary with the subject and the intended use. From 1970 to 1993 the *Library and Information Science Abstracts* (LISA) scheme used, for example, the Classification Research Group's *Classification of Library and Information Science* (1971), which contains six facets, such as *Type of user* and *Type of library resources*. This permits synthesizing topics such as *Use of maps* (Type of library resources facet) *by adolescents* (Type of user facet) *in public libraries* (Type of library facet). All LISA facets are broken down into several subfacets, each with its own hierarchy. LISA, incidentally, has since 1993 used a very broad class system that is more suitable for a selection tool like LISA instead of this excellent, minutely structured system. This illustrates that not only the facets, subfacets, and terminology, but also the precision of a classification system must be attuned to its purpose as well as to its subject.

Well-designed faceted schemes avoid the occasional overlap of classes and the occasional conflict in characteristics of division that are inevitable in many enumerative classification schemes. Figure 7.4 illustrates a poorly designed faceted scheme. Note, for example, that it violates a basic principle of faceted schemes: The structures facet contains two different, potentially overlapping, characteristics of division: *Residential buildings* is divided by type of building, whereas *bridges* is divided by means of construction. It would have been better to label this facet *Structures and construction* with two subfacets: *Structures*, and *Construction techniques*. Or, a separate *Construction* facet could have been created.

The Principle of Inversion; Chain Indexes

Although the Principle of Inversion does not have to be employed with a faceted classification (Mills 1967, 20), the two are often used together. The principle was developed in connection with paper-based files but contains aspects that seem also to be useful for OPACs. It determines the order of the terms in the schedule and the sequence in which the symbols for the various facets are combined into the notation for the topic as a whole. The purpose is to arrange document surrogates in a card index or printed bibliography (or on the screen) in a manner believed to be most helpful for listing and retrieving bibliographic citations in the subject area of that classification scheme.

The technique is to list topics (that is, facets) in the schedule in increasing order of significance as determined by the designers of the system and to combine them in reverse (inverted) order into a notation, so that in a sequential listing of documents, such as in a paper-based file or on the screen, the most significant topics would be listed first. The revolutionary innovation of this approach can be appreciated if one remembers that most "standard" classification schemes, enumerative as well as synthetic, are based on "logical" concepts, that is, on how the different parts of a particular topic fit together rather than on the basis of how effectively its parts, or combinations of parts, can be found in a file.

The imaginary (and highly selective) skeleton scheme for architecture shown in Figure 7.4 was designed with the idea that the structures facet (*T*) is the most important one, (this idea is, of course, debatable) and, if it is used, every other facet should be subsumed under it. Therefore, it was made the last facet, leading to the following kinds of faceted notations. Note that only those facets are used that are needed to describe the document being classified.

L36	Italy
L364	Milan, Italy
M31	Reinforced concrete
M31L364	Reinforced concrete (buildings) / in Milan, Italy
S32	Neo-Renaissance style
S32L364	Neo-Renaissance style / in Milan, Italy
T21	Apartment houses
T21L364	Apartment houses / in Milan, Italy
T21M31	Apartment houses / built of reinforced concrete
T21M31L364	Apartment houses / built of reinforced concrete / in Milan
T21S32	Apartment houses / in Neo-Renaissance style
T21S32L364	Apartment houses / in Neo-Renaissance style/ in Milan
T21S32M31L364	Apartment houses / in Neo-Renaissance style / built of reinforced concrete / in Milan, Italy

Because the documents are listed in classed, that is, notational, order, an alphabetical index is needed to find document descriptions at the desired notation. For this purpose faceted schemes are frequently used together with an alphabetical chain index. That system was developed by Ranganathan as a method of providing a multiple access alphabetical index to a classified card catalog (Svenonius et al. 1992, 352–53). Chain indexing requires one single bibliographic description (document surrogate) listed under the document's class notation in the classed file. From this notation are derived in semiautomatic fashion alphabetical index entries that lead to the document's class notation as well as to successively more general levels of the document's compound topic.

Continuing the example from Figure 7.4, *Apartment houses built of reinforced concrete in Neo-Renaissance style in Milan, Italy*, the document surrogate is fully described according to the principle of inversion under the faceted notation

T21S32M31L364

In words, this translates as

Apartment houses / Neo-Renaissance style / Reinforced concrete / Milan

C. David Batty (1970) and Thomas D. Wilson (1971) describe the chain indexing technique that also uses the principle of inversion. The first chain index entry lists in reverse order the words that describe the combined notation. This index entry is co-extensive in meaning with the meaning of the combined notation. According to the "game rules" of chain indexing, alphabetical index access is furnished not only to this specific level but also to successively broader hierarchical levels. This permits alphabetical access to every subsumed facet and thereby avoids the limitations of linearity.

```
Milan, Italy. Reinforced concrete. Neo-Renaissance style. Apartment houses
                                                           T21S32M31L364

Reinforced concrete. Neo-Renaissance style. Apartment houses
                                                           T21S32M31

Neo-Renaissance style. Apartment houses                    T21S32

Apartment houses                                           T21
```

In the index these entries would of course be listed in alphabetical order along with other index entries. The combination of listing documents in the classed file under one facet sequence (surrounded by documents with the same primary subject) while accessing them through the alphabetical index through the reverse facet sequence makes them accessible through every indexed facet while preserving the principle of "economy of input," which was very important in a paper-based file and is still of use in the computer age. It means that every access phrase is used only once. In the example there is no index entry for the sequence *Apartment houses / Neo-Renaissance style / Reinforced concrete / Milan, Italy*. That sequence is available through the classed file, as previously explained.

This system is difficult to imagine for those of us brought up professionally on alphabetical subject headings and on classification systems that use one notation to express a subject and location. But its basic ideas make eminent sense for a classed subject file, either paper-based or electronic. Because many users tend to begin their search using far broader subject terms than the topic they are actually seeking, chain indexing may be one of several useful devices to help users find the appropriate level of specificity even in an electronic environment. Fortunately the 153 field of the *MARC Format for Classification Data* permits this because it is designed to record captions for all superordinate levels of the notation's hierarchy.

In the 1990s several notable researchers showed interest in chain indexing as an online retrieval device. As an example, Elaine Svenonius designed with collaborators the experimental DDC Online Retrieval System (DORS), one of the few electronic systems so far designed for OPAC users rather than for classifiers. It generates a chain index, using not a faceted classification but the enumerative DDC. Their conclusion was, in general, favorable providing certain anomalies in the DDC schedules were corrected (Svenonius et al. 1992; Liu and Svenonius 1991). Elaine Broadbent experimented with several indexes, including a chain index for the extremely enumerative LCC (Broadbent 1995). These researchers found the technique promising, that the chain should be as short as possible, and that inconsistencies in the schedules require human intervention for chain indexing to work effectively.

Advantages of Faceted Classification

Faceted classification schemes have advantages over traditional enumerative schemes, which should not be overlooked even in today's electronic environment. It is noteworthy that the editors of the DDC are attempting to introduce gradually more faceted features into that enumerative scheme (Classification Editorial Policy

Committee 1996, 1: xiv), and the editors of the already synthetic Universal Classification (UDC) are planning to increase its faceted features, too (McIlwaine 1994, 31).

A relatively minor advantage is that the schedule of a faceted scheme takes up much less space than the schedule of an enumerative scheme with the same degree of specificity. To achieve with an enumerative scheme the same degree of specificity possible with the faceted scheme illustrated in Figure 7.4 could require even in this highly selective scheme up to 20,736 lines rather than the 48 lines actually used. This is because, in an enumerative scheme of equal specificity, the schedule would have to list under every structure every architectural style, and again under every architectural style every type of material, and so forth, unless the schedule used space-saving devices like the "divide like" device. Even with such devices, 48 lines would not suffice.

A second, and much more important, advantage is that faceted schemes permit, and even encourage, far more specific classification than do most enumerative schemes. Referring to Figure 7.2 and the "game rules" mentioned in connection with it, the three-element combination *Parasite induced / diseases of the circulatory system / of lions,* for example, would not be permitted. Only two elements can be combined in this example under the DDC 21 "game rules": *Parasite induced diseases of lions (571.999 197 57)* or *Diseases of the circulatory system of lions (573.139 197 57)*. In a fully developed faceted system it should be possible to classify even more precise combinations of facets, such as *Effects of drought / caused by deforestation / on the frequency / of parasite induced diseases / of the circulatory system / of lions / in Kenya.*

A third advantage of faceted classification is that, even before the advent of the computer, it not only permitted but actually encouraged the previously discussed chain indexing technique, which provides indexing access to every facet of the combined notation.

Another advantage is that faceting and chain indexing can both be used in an electronic environment provided the classification schemes used are edited in a more consistent manner. The MARC capabilities permit it, and both DDC and LCC are now available in electronic format. Furthermore, with suitable programming, it is possible to provide at the stroke of a key classified as well as alphabetical displays of relevant documents (Anderson 1991, 5).

Last but not least, because a well-developed faceted scheme has definite rules about the concepts that should be described in a notation (that is, the building blocks) and about the sequence in which facets should be combined in that scheme, it requires less judgment and fewer judgmental decisions in individual cases when compound topics must be classified. (See "Some Solutions to the Compound Topics Problem" in this chapter.)

Of course, it is possible to ask whether it is necessary to classify works so precisely. The answer may well be that it is not, at least not for arranging books in a general library. For such libraries, enumerative classifications are generally considered sufficient for shelving purposes. Conversely, if the classification is to form the basis of a successful information retrieval system in a special library or in a bibliography or documentation system that controls the literature of a special field for research purposes, it is vital that each of the various elements of that subject be recorded and searchable. Considering the highly specific articles, and even books, written today, it is ineffective to classify into a broad class a document that deals with a highly specific subject. The specific document would be "lost" among many other documents dealing with other aspects of the same broad class. Even an OPAC cannot make a class more specific than the classification system used permits, unless in postcoordinate searching the class number is combined with other terms such as keywords.

Faceted classification does present the danger of developing nonexistent subjects, such as *Nutritional organs of freshwater whales.* Classifiers must obviously know their subjects. However, this danger may also be an advantage, as the structure of a faceted classification may allow the accurate classification of topics that did not exist at the time the scheme was created, without any revision or amendment whatsoever. One well-known faceted scheme for the packaging industry had the terms *extrusion* and *paper,* although the extrusion of paper was regarded as impossible until twelve months after the scheme was published.

THE CLASSIFICATION SYSTEM

Structure, Hospitality, and Expressiveness

The principles on which a bibliographic classification system for machine-readable bibliographic records is designed need not be identical to the principles used in designing a classification for shelving documents and for filing paper-based bibliographic entries. However, regardless of environment, the classification system should be logically and consistently structured, without exceptions. There is a tendency to believe (erroneously) that the computer can do almost everything automatically and that class structure, therefore, does not matter. But even when used electronically, a classification system is only as good as its internal logic and consistency. Even the best notation is not much good for retrieval if the classification system does not provide clear, unambiguous locations and relationships and permit the logical insertion of new topics. If the hierarchy is not automatically and consistently visible it must be built in artificially, which is in effect what the MARC Format for Classification Data does.

The order in which class symbols (that is, topics) are listed in the classification schedule or are combined in a faceted notation dictates the order of the documents and document surrogates arranged by that classification. Space limitations and the limitations of linearity made order extremely important in paper-based systems and in arranging the physical documents. Order is less significant in machine retrieval with all of its inherent flexibility than it is for shelving or for filing paper copy. But it is still subject to the restraints of the classification system and the computer program employed.

"Hospitality" refers to the classification scheme's capacity to assimilate change, that is, its capacity to continue to reflect the appropriate order of terms and relationships after deletions, additions, and changes are made over time to the topics in the schedules. This is important to human searching, but especially also to OPAC use if the classification scheme is to permit scrolling and hierarchical searching via the notation (that is, the broadening or narrowing of a search between a general topic and its parts). The big problem with providing for hospitality, on paper or online, is that "new subjects can develop in two dimensions: hierarchically and collaterally, that is, some being subdivisions of existing subjects, and some being coordinate with existing ones. In Ranganathan's words, a good notation must provide both hospitality in chain and hospitality in array" (Liu 1990, 15). Hospitality is, however, usually achieved at the expense of expressiveness. (Liu provides some good examples.)

An "expressive notation" is one in which the symbols reflect not only the order of the terms in the schedules but also their hierarchical relationships. For example, if a group of items or concepts is given the symbol *5* and the group is divided into smaller groups, and each smaller group is given a notation that begins with the number symbol *5* (*51, 52, 53,* etc.) then the notation is expressive. The symbol for each of the smaller groups represents not only the smaller group but also the smaller group's inclusion in the larger group. If the notation does not permit hierarchical searches by its structure, information scientists can build it in artificially. Although expressivity is useful for hierarchical machine searches, it is not essential because "there are many ways in which the computer can easily accomplish these operations in a consistent and reliable manner" without it (Liu 1990, 16).

In recent decades classificationists have tended to feel that hospitality is more important than expressiveness. That seems especially true for electronic use of classification schemes. "Present day notations, especially those used in modern special classification schemes, have tended to be non expressive, faceted, and brief" (Liu 1990, 16).

Schedules and Index

In schedules as well as indexes, typography and layout are important factors on the printed page and on the screen. If these are clear, and if indentions and differing kinds and sizes of typefaces indicate the hierarchy clearly, then it becomes much easier to locate relevant numbers and terms in the schedules.

Wherever necessary to avoid ambiguity and to ensure uniformity of classification, schedules should contain notes clarifying the meaning and scope of the notations. Cross-references to related notations in other parts of the schedules are also essential, to guide the classifier as well as the searcher. If searching by classification numbers is developed to its full potential in OPACs, the schedules and indexes should be designed for and be helpful not only to catalogers and indexers but also to searchers. Only in recent years have attempts been made to do online what more imaginative catalogers have done, individually and on a much more limited basis, for decades with subject headings in public card catalogs: rephrasing instructions meant for catalogers into language that is meaningful to patrons as searchers. This is now called "end-user language." For example, the following statement, taken from the LCC "K" schedule is, of course, meant for classifiers:

```
KJC 4432 Feudal law
         Class here general and comparative works on
         feudal law. For feudal law of an individual
         country see the subclass for the country.
```

For searchers this should be rephrased something like this:

```
KJC 4432 Feudal law
         Here are found general and comparative works on
         feudal law. For feudal law of an individual
         country or jurisdiction see the name of the
         country or jurisdiction subdivided by Feudal
         law, such as: Tuscany—Feudal law.
```

In fairness it must be pointed out that creating end-user language online is fraught with far more problems and ramifications than when creating it in a paper-based card catalog.

The Notation

Although the structure of the classification system is perhaps the most important factor in its effectiveness, unless the notation is appropriate to the classification's purpose, the classification cannot be used to its full potential, especially in an electronic environment. During the design of the schedules, consideration must be given to the notation that is to be used. The two most common U.S. classifications, the DDC and the LCC, were designed long before OPACs were even a gleam in librarians' eyes, so neither their structure nor their notation were designed for efficient electronic retrieval. As illustrated in Chapter 8, the DDC has several features that make it quite suitable for electronic retrieval. But its editors, and especially the LCC editors, had to go to great lengths and expense to counteract shortcomings of notations and structure in their respective systems to make them more suitable for sophisticated online retrieval.

Definition and Purpose

The notation of a bibliographical classification scheme is the symbol associated with each term that describes a subject concept and appears alongside it in the schedules. The notation's purpose in a paper or electronic environment is

- To represent and stand for the subjects that appear in the schedules;

- To represent the classed order (order by likeness) of those subjects (That is usually the order that the system designer deemed to be desirable for bibliographic retrieval purposes.);

- To show the relationships between topics by showing their relative positions in the hierarchies and, where the classification is explicitly polyhierarchical in nature, by distinguishing between the different hierarchies; and

- To represent the subject or topic of each individual book or document as fully as possible or as fully as is desirable.

The wording of the last reason emphasizes that there is a difference between what is desirable and what is possible. It also implies that the fullness or specificity desirable for a document may vary in the context of various collections and, depending on the subject's relative importance in a particular collection, even within a collection.

Symbols and Bases

The symbol for a particular topic consists of a sequence ("string" in computer jargon) of characters taken from the set used for the notation generally. The number of different characters used in a character set for the notation is called its "base." A notation of arabic numerals has the base ten; a notation based on the letters of the English alphabet has the base twenty six; a notation using both has a base of 36. The base is even larger if other symbols are used (such as *, #, /). A notation that consists of only one kind of character, such as letters *or* numbers, is called "pure." A notation with a mixture of different kinds of characters is called "mixed."

Because a pure notation conveys order clearly to humans, a pure notation has in the past been regarded as having some advantage over a mixed one, and the use of characters other than letters and numbers (such as * # / -) has been considered as something to be avoided because there is no universally accepted order for such characters. Mixed notations have frequently been used because they have a larger database than either of the pure notations, with the LCC being the outstanding example. Mixed notations are particularly suitable for faceted classifications because they can be quite expressive.

Integer, Decimal, Radix Fraction Notation

The normal sequence of numbers is the sequence in which we count: 1, 2, 3 . . . 9, 10, 11 . . . 27 . . . 34 . . . 98, 100, 101, 103 . . . 910 . . . 920, 1000, . . . and so forth. When numbers are used in this way in a notation, it is called an "integral notation," because the numbers have their normal values as integers. Another system exists also, in which an imaginary point is placed in front of each number, which is then regarded as a decimal number. This alters the relative positions and the overall order considerably. All the numbers beginning with 1 precede all those beginning with 2; long and short numbers are intermixed. Thus the order of the numbers in the earlier example becomes

1, 10, 100, 1000, 101, 103, 11

2, 27

3, 34

9, 910, 920, 98

This system has major advantages in facilitating both hospitality and expressiveness. Because of the imaginary decimal point, it is referred to as a "decimal system." The principle can also be applied to letter notations. Because there cannot be decimal letters, the expression "radix fraction" notation is sometimes used for such letter systems.

The Qualities of Notation

Suitable qualities of notation read by humans are usually stated to be

Brevity,

Simplicity,

Expressiveness,

Hospitality, and

Mnemonic capability.

Brief notations are important to humans but only of slight importance to machines. They are easier for humans to remember and to enter into the computer, and they take up less storage space. Simplicity is also of great importance to humans, because simple notations are easier to remember and to enter into the machine as searching devices. Simplicity is not important for machines. Expressiveness, as described in "Structure, Hospitality, and Expressiveness" in this chapter, is very important for humans and useful, but not essential, for machines because "there are many ways in which the computer can easily accomplish these operations in a consistent and reliable manner" without it (Liu 1990, 16). Hospitality, also described in that section, is important in connection with the system's structure and the individual notation. Mnemonic capability—memory-aiding devices, such as using notations beginning with *M* for music—is helpful for experienced and inexperienced humans, but not for machines.

Of the five notational qualities originally listed as important for humans, only one seems to be also important for electronic retrieval: hospitality. To it, Liu adds four more that are important for OPACs. In addition to being hospitable, the notation should be

- synthetic, that is, composed of sections each of which stands for a specific part or aspect or topic of the combined notation: The computer can decompose and manipulate the notation to provide access through any one of its sections;

- easily generated and manipulated by the computer, to save the time and avoid the possible errors from assigning notations manually;

- capable of being used to generate a hierarchical display and to broaden and narrow searches;

- flexible, that is, it should allow for alternate arrangements of a compound or synthetic number so that a multi-topical book can be classified and accessed in more than one place. (Liu 1990, 17)

Hospitality and Multidisciplinary Topics

Hospitality, as previously defined, refers to the classification system's capacity to change with the field it represents. Essential elements of hospitality are the system's ability to absorb and integrate new concepts logically and the notation's ability to express them. Both are relatively easy as long as the new concepts fit into the existing classification structure. Multidisciplinary topics, however, usually do not, for largely historical reasons.

Bibliographic classification systems developed over time as part of their contemporary culture and philosophical outlook. Major developmental stages were set by the medieval university's academic disciplines, the *trivium* (the three "lower" liberal arts: grammar, logic, and rhetoric) and the *quadrivium* (the four "higher" liberal arts: arithmetic, music, geometry, and astronomy), and in the seventeenth century by Sir Francis Bacon's philosophy. This developed into bibliographic classification systems based on academic disciplines. The resulting scattering of "concrete" subjects among various disciplines is described in "Disciplines in Enumerative Schemes" in this chapter.

Alphabetical subject heading vocabularies are typically not divided by discipline although they have hierarchies, acknowledged or implicit. Most, like the *Library of Congress Subject Headings* (LCSH) are not divided at all. Others, like the *Thesaurus of ERIC Descriptors* or the *Art and Architecture Thesaurus,* are divided into categories not based on disciplines.

Because bibliographic classification traditionally includes shelving, that is, placement of the actual documents, books on "concrete" subjects like "the blind" or "gold" have always been difficult to place if they dealt with the respective subject from all possible angles, involving several disciplines. Multidisciplinary or interdisciplinary subjects are a different and more pressing problem because not just an occasional work but the entire, newly developed topic straddles more than one discipline and/or is marginalized in the classification scheme's structure. Topics like *Biotechnology, Space medicine, Ethnobotany, Women's studies,* and *Computers,* cannot be integrated effectively into a disciplinary structure.

The definition of what constitutes a "discipline" changes over time. Even the need to use disciplines at all is being challenged. Although no consensus has been reached on how to replace or modify them, it is recognized that disciplines, as presently constituted, do not fulfill the traditional desiderata of being mutually exclusive (that is, do not overlap) and jointly exhaustive (that is, account for all possibilities), and that these qualities are, in any case, unrealistic. As of this writing there is no commonly agreed-upon answer to how multidisciplinary topics or marginalized fields can best be handled in a discipline-based classification system, and opinion is divided as to whether a completely new classification system is an option. There does seem to be agreement that, *if* a new system is adapted or adopted (which is not likely soon), it should be freely faceted, loosely structured, and flexible, so that it can support multiple perspectives and hospitality is more important than the traditionally desired (but not always achieved) mutual exclusivity and joint exhaustivity of disciplines (Beghtol 1998a and 1998b; Williamson 1998).

Using a less radical approach, an example of how a marginalized field can be integrated into the existing structure of DDC is Hope Olson's ongoing project to create links between terms in a major special vocabulary (in this case the feminist vocabulary of *A Women's Thesaurus*) and numbers in the DDC (Olson 1998; Olson and Ward 1998).

Other suggested solutions include assigning a single notation for a multidisciplinary topic in existing general class systems, using the classed catalog format (manual or electronic, described below) to permit multiple classification coordinated with multiple alphabetical access, using the *Universal Decimal Classification* (UDC), or developing a new system based on some principle other than academic fields. One interesting suggestion is to use the 2d edition (in progress) of the *Bliss Bibliographic Classification* (BBC). This is a fully faceted system organized on the basis of the traditional disciplines, but contains as one of its major units a *Phenomena* class designed for multidisciplinary treatment of topics.

Just as the invention of hierarchical classification many centuries ago and the more recent invention of synthetic classification systems required an imaginative wrench away from then-traditional thinking, the OPAC-aided use of classification for retrieval is encouraging our generation to re-evaluate the usefulness of bibliographic classification systems based on academic disciplines and on the limitations of linear shelving.

PURPOSES OF CLASSIFICATION

With the desirable qualities of classification systems and the two types of systems in mind, it is useful to review and expand the three purposes of classification: 1) the physical arrangement of documents on shelves, that is, shelf classification; 2) the arrangement of document surrogates (variously called "bibliographic records," "document descriptions," "bibliographic entries," or "entries") in catalogs, indexes, and bibliographies that are paper-based, that is, on cards or on the printed page; and 3) the arrangement of computer-based information retrieval systems, in which the class notations, and often also the documents, are in machine-readable form.

Subject Notation and Call Numbers

The original purpose of library classification was the arrangement of books on the shelves of a library in a sequence according to their subject, so that users might find together on the shelves items that they might wish to use at the same time to meet the same "want." Although it is essentially impossible to achieve an ideal shelf arrangement because of the variety of wants of different inquirers and because shelf arrangement can only be linear, the designers of classification systems try to create systems that meet the needs of most of their patrons most of the time. That is a major reason why general classification systems are updated continuously to stay "alive" and why many special classification systems exist for special libraries or bibliographic services that concentrate on one topic to the exclusion of most others. Detailed and up-to-date shelf classification, however, serves little purpose unless a precise alphabetical index to the notations exists and unless readers have direct, personal access to the shelves.

We are used to thinking of the call number as the notation that describes both a work's primary subject and its physical location. This is a practical and effective system for most general libraries. But other systems do exist. The notation that places a document into an intellectual class structure need not also indicate its physical location. That is, the class notation (used for bibliographic access and retrieval) need not be the same as the call number that locates the physical object. The one can be highly specific and/or analytical and/or synthetic, the other more general or based, perhaps, on the type of document or the size of a book, to indicate its location. Shelving by size results in substantial space-saving, which can be a major advantage in large libraries. It also prevents shelf browsing, a usually enjoyable and often helpful activity. Academic faculties especially tend to be emotionally in favor of shelf browsing—usually without knowing its considerable disadvantages (Boll 1985, 21–31)—but shelf browsing is less necessary in the electronic age, provided a helpful, precise, bibliographic classification system is used and the program permits access by multiple approaches and permits multiple configurations.

Differentiating between the bibliographic retrieval notation (the subject notation) and the shelving notation (the call number) is not a new idea. In classed catalogs (described in the next section) and in OPACs and other electronic files, it permits assigning more than one bibliographic retrieval notation to a document. Although not yet commonly accepted, the idea is being reintroduced in connection with OPACs (Koh 1995, 197; Goldberg 1996, 41) and should be seriously considered at a time when alphabetical as well as notational authority lists have become increasingly specific and encourage analysis along with the traditional emphasis on overall content.

Classification in Paper-Based Files

In most North American libraries the second use of classification has been to list bibliographic entries by call number in classed order, that is, shelving order, in the shelflist. The shelflist is useful for inventory purposes and for monitoring collection growth, but if it goes no farther than duplicating the arrangements of the document surrogates and of the actual documents, and is accessible (on paper or in electronic format) only to the staff, its role as a bibliographic retrieval tool is limited. As discussed in previous chapters, listing the same work in an alphabetical sequence and in a classed sequence places it in different contexts and enhances retrieval. Therefore, the shelflist is at least a bibliographic enhancement of the alphabetical catalog and should be so used. The capability exists, both on paper and online.

The main difference between classing books and classing the entries that describe them is that a book can be shelved in only one place but can be represented by more than one bibliographic entry in the paper-based list, one under each subject notation that describes the book. This is especially beneficial in the case of enumerative classification schemes because it counteracts the limitations of linearity. In an alphabetical subject file more than one alphabetical subject heading can be used; in a classed file more than one class notation can be used for the same purpose. The classed catalog, described below, is an example. A recent online variant of the traditional classed catalog technique is the assignment of multiple DDC class numbers in the OCLC NetFirst database (Vizine-Goetz 1996b).

The Classed Catalog

Multiple listing of a work under several class notations avoids the limitations of linearity. So do alphabetical indexes to a classed file of entries, a combination represented by catalogs in classed format. Figure 7.5 (page 184) shows a schematic excerpt of a hypothetical paper-based classed catalog. Note that it has two separate alphabetical sections: an alphabetical index to the class notations under which the documents are fully listed and an alphabetical section under which the same documents are listed under author, title, and series. (In this selective example the document descriptions refer to one book that is listed under two class notations in the classed subject catalog. Comparison with Figure 7.2 will explain why the work on "parasite-caused diseases of the circulatory system of reptiles" could—had to—be listed under two numbers in a classed file using DDC21.)

Primitive versions of classed catalogs existed during the Middle Ages and even earlier. They used few and very broad classes and were more like shelflists, but with little systematic order. Author indexes to the classed listing were introduced around 1500 but were rare, and multiple listings (rather than one main listing with an index) began in the eighteenth century. In the early part of the nineteenth century, the classed catalog became very popular and developed into a sophisticated device with systematic classification schemes, subject indexes, and author listings or indexes. Different variations existed. During the last quarter of the nineteenth century, alphabetical subject headings began to replace the classed catalog, so now few librarians can even envision what it can do. But in recent decades interest in the classed catalog has been rekindled by researchers who recognize the great potential of classed catalog capabilities in an online environment even if its physical features and format are not imitated slavishly (Chan 1990; Liu 1990; Vizine-Goetz 1996b). Several subject

Excerpt from the **alphabetical subject index** which leads from the words which describe a subject.to the class number under which that subject is listed in the classed file. In this seletive example, the references below lead to two class (*subject*) numbers which were assigned to one document. These differ from the call (*location*) number (not shown).

Excerpt from the **classed file (or, classed subject catalog), that is, subjects listed in numerical order**. Under each number more than one document can be listed. Full bibliographic description is given for each document under its class numbers, as well as the call number which indicates the document's location.

All entries below refer to the same document, listed under two subject numbers

Excerpt from the **alphabetical author-title-series file.** For each document full bibliographic description is given under each applicable name or title, as well as its subject (class) number(s) and the call number. Users need go from this file to the classed file *only* if they want to learn what other documents are available under these subject (class) numbers.

Circulatory system	000	Allen, Mary
Reptiles	....	....
Diseases 573.139 179	100	Bellini, Max
Circulatory system	....	....
Reptiles	200	Gonzales, Andrea
Diseases 573.139 179	....	Investigation into reptile ...
Diseases	300	(Full bibliographic description is
Circulatory system	....	given.) 571.999 179
Reptiles 573.139 179	571.999 179	573.139 179
Parasitic	(With full bibliographic	(Also call number)
Reptiles 571.999 179	description of the document	....
Reptiles	which, in this case, is also	Hausdorfer, James
Circulatory	listed under 573.139 179. The	....
system 573.139 179	call number (not shown) is also	Investigation into reptile ..., by
Parasitic 571.999 179	given)	Andrea Gonzales.
Parasitic diseases	....	(Full bibliographic description is
Reptiles 571.999 179	573.999 179	given.) 571.999 179
Reptiles	(With full bibliographic	573.139 179
Circulatory system	description of the document	(Also call number)
Diseases 573.139 179	which, in this case, is also	....
Diseases	listed under 571.999 179. The	Polanski, Morton
Circulatory	call number (not shown) is also	....
system 573.139 179	given)	Zander, Robin
Parasitic 571.999 179	....	....
	600	
	....	
	700	
	....	
	900	

Figure 7.5. Excerpt from a hypothetical classed catalog using the DDC, an enumerative classification. In this example the subject index, the classed file, and the author/title/series file all refer to one book dealing with parasite-caused diseases of the circulatory system of reptiles, listed under two pertinent class numbers.

bibliographies and announcement media, including some major ones like *Physics Abstracts*, are issued in a paper-based classed version in addition to their electronic formats.

Classification and OPACs

Exciting possibilities exist in the use of library classification to retrieve machine-readable bibliographic records. Classification used in computerized files potentially permits, for example, the added dimensions of truncation, hierarchical searches, searching by other than the first element in a combined or faceted notation, and searching even enumerative notations by attributes other than subject (such as: Within this span of numbers search only textbooks) provided the scheme is precise enough or can be manipulated to permit such questions. Although many programs permit access by known class notation, the full potential of hierarchical searches, of "exploding" or "imploding" notations, has not yet been reached in automated catalogs, although it has been reached by several databases (for example, the National Agricultural Library's *Agricola,* the National Library of Medicine's MEDLINE, and *Geo Ref).*

The MARC format permits searching by elements other than the first one in both subject headings and class notations, but so far few, if any, OPAC programs have been designed to take advantage of this potential. Many OPAC programs permit truncating words, but if truncation is to be successful in class notations the classification system and the individual class notation must be designed to permit it, or it must be superimposed on the schedules. (This is discussed in more detail in Chapter 8.) Linking the shelflist to the classification schedule also presents problems that need solutions.

As described in Chapter 4, Section "Searches Using Combined Indexing Vocabularies," research has shown that, even at the risk of receiving marginal along with truly relevant items, a combined classed vocabulary/controlled alphabetical vocabulary/uncontrolled alphabetical vocabulary provides the most complete retrieval results. If as complete a list of records as possible is desired, all of these approaches must be used. The classed catalog, chain indexing, and string indexing came close to that capability. Most programs cannot match it yet. Virtually all permit searching by subject heading or keyword; many permit access via a known call number, some even by the initial part of a call number; and some permit scrolling the shelflist up and down; but few if any permit broadening or narrowing down a search by means of class numbers. "Very few [OPACs] have incorporated effectively either the syndetic structure of LCSH or the structure of classification schemes to allow users to browse up and down the hierarchical relationships, which, because they aren't being displayed to users, are thereby concealed in our subject heading and classification systems" (Yee and Layne 1998, 141).

Few, if any, programs permit search phrases consisting of class notations or that combine subject headings, keywords, *and* class notation. If an OPAC searcher wants, for example, works on architecture in Wisconsin it would be helpful to use a search phrase such as FIND [class notation for Wisconsin architecture] OR [subject heading for Wisconsin architecture] OR [keywords Wisconsin OR Architecture]. If one wanted to find works on architecture in Wisconsin prior to, or apart from, the influence of Frank Lloyd Wright (who is generally associated with this topic), a search phrase such as the following would be helpful: FIND [class notation for Wisconsin architecture] OR [subject heading for Wisconsin architecture] OR [keywords Wisconsin AND Architecture] BUT NOT ([class notation for Frank Lloyd Wright] OR [subject heading for Wright]).

From the 1960s on the use of classification as an online retrieval tool began to have strong advocates, such as Pauline Cochrane (1982a, 1982b), Phyllis Richmond (1983), Karen Markey (1986), and Carol Mandel (1986, 10–12), but as late as 1991 its use was "still a matter for discussion and experimentation" (Liu and Svenonius 1991, 359), possibly because the various techniques that can make its online use effective were just beginning to be invented. Interest in classification as an online access device to bibliographic records has continued to grow since then, and both DDC and LCC are now available in electronic formats that can be used for cataloging and retrieval purposes.

Since the 1960s many research and demonstration projects have studied the possible adaptation of paper-based retrieval techniques to computer use: descriptors, subject headings, class notations, faceted classification, the classed catalog, chain indexing, and others. Many of these adaptations are by now routine features of OPACs; others are still being investigated or adapted, often in combination with each other. (This, incidentally, illustrates one reason why today's professional should have basic knowledge of paper-based techniques that may, or may not, be adaptable to online use. Another reason is that members of any profession should have at least a basic knowledge of their profession's history, of what was attempted, achieved, or failed, and why, so that they can learn from past experience.)

Even in an electronic environment order and linearity, and at least some of the traditional principles of classification, cannot be ignored in at least two important situations:

- When the program permits default arrangements, that is, listing notations or documents in a predesignated order unless the user inputs contrary instructions. That order should obviously be meaningful and logical rather than haphazard.

- When the searcher wishes to browse either the schedule or the catalog in numerical order it is as important as ever for the order to follow—to cite only one example—the traditional classification rule, "The whole should be listed before its parts," unless there is a compelling reason not to do so.

Classification on the Internet

The following two statements represent a fairly common point of view of information professionals, although not necessarily of the general public:

[A]s is abundantly evident from the Internet experience, retrieval of masses of data can be useless if it cannot be displayed in some logical fashion in the context of related and peripheral information. (Williamson 1998, 117)

[A]nyone who has surfed the Internet realizes the crying need for better organization of this amorphous, ever shifting, ever changing universe of unsorted information. Clumsy search engines such as Yahoo!, Infoseek, and AltaVista are the equivalent of seventeenth century efforts to guide library users by dividing library collections into the disciplines of theology, medicine, philosophy, and history. (Maxwell 1998, 195)

The Internet's many advantages are counterbalanced by at least three factors:

1. Frequent changes and short lifespans of many Internet components.

2. Its inability to provide an overview of, let alone topical approach to, its search engines and Web sites. Occasional articles online and in print provide selective listings. Printed (!) directories and guides, limited by subject or type, are usually the best and most comprehensive sources to learn what is available in their respective areas on the Internet. Examples are *U.S. Government on the Web* (Hernon et al.1998) and *Directory of Library Technical Services Homepages* (Stewart 1997). One online list of search engines, comprehensive but unstructured and nonevaluative, is *Search Engine Colossus: International Directory of Search Engines* (http://www.searchenginecolossus.com/) (Accessed May 12, 2001). It is keyed to advertisers' needs and permits call-up alphabetically by country or by broad category such as "Academic," "Music," or "Youth."

3. Widely varying classification (and therefore retrieval requirements and capabilities) of two groups of Web sites.

One of the groups of Web sites is the popular search engines such as AltaVista, HotBot, Webcrawler, or Yahoo!, most of which are essentially commercial services aimed at a broad audience. Their sources and classification system are therefore selective and typically divided into broad categories and subcategories based on popular interest rather than on an attempt to cover the world of knowledge comprehensively; categories such as "Business," "Sport," "Investing," "Computers," "Education." In this respect they might be compared to the *Reader Interest Classification,* which some libraries use for current or popular books. At this stage in its development, classification in these popular search engines may serve as a compass but is nowhere near precise enough, or flexible enough, to lead to specific works in multimillion-volume collections or to answer specific reference questions as precisely and reliably as a library catalog or as a well-trained reference librarian.

One criticism of these popular search engines is their violation and/or simplistic use of tried-and-true classification techniques, such as their mixed, not mutually exclusive, and therefore confusing, use on the same hierarchical level of disciplines (like *Humanities)*, concrete subjects (like *Shopping*) and bibliographic form or purpose (like *Reference*). On the other hand, the use of the topical rather than the discipline approach for "the ordinary, non-academic person looking for information to satisfy his day-to-day needs and interests [is helpful] as long as it is followed consistently on the same hierarchical level" (Van der Walt 1998, 383). In spite of their shortcomings, and in spite of sometimes strange answers to queries, most popular search engines are powerful and can develop into effective tools.

The second group of Web sites uses standard bibliographic techniques, including detailed classed and/or alphabetical retrieval vocabularies. It includes an occasional search engine. *Beyond Bookmarks: Schemes for Organizing the Web* (http://www.public.iastate.edu/~CYBERSTACKS/CTW.htm) "is a clearinghouse of World Wide Web sites that have applied or adopted standard classification schemes or controlled vocabularies to organize or provide enhanced access to Internet resources" (*Beyond bookmarks* 1999). It lists more than ninety sites, mostly bibliographic in nature, but many more online library catalogs, thesauri, and bibliographies belong to this category.

An interesting Internet resource is the *Internet Scout Project*, designed to advance resource discovery on the Internet and to demonstrate how these resources can be controlled bibliographically by using traditional cataloging principles and existing taxonomies such as LCC and LCSH, with appropriate adjustments and in concert with the emerging metadata standard known as the *Dublin Core* (Glassel and Wells 1998). Between 1996 and 2000 the project issued the *Scout Report Signpost* which listed more than 11,500 evaluative annotations of journals, projects, demonstrations, lectures, conferences, and other resources in many fields, arranged by very broad LCC classes.

In 2001 *Signpost* was replaced by *The Scout Report Archives*, arranged by CYRUS (Classify Your Resources Using Scout) classification. CYRUS is a far more specific classification, but not as specific as either DDC or LCC. Interestingly, it uses words instead of notations, resembling somewhat an improved alphabetic-classed system. The *Scout* annotations, always noted for clarity, are enriched in the *Archives* with appropriate LCSH tracings and multiple CYRUS and LCC class "notations." Multiple subject access means and use of words, rather than notations, are designed to facilitate public access. The project is an illustration of what can be done effectively on the Internet. It is accessible at http://scout.cs.wisc.edu/archives (Accessed May 12, 2001).

ALPHABETICAL INDEXES TO CLASSED FILES

Indexes for Enumerative Schemes

OPAC programs permit searching under subject headings and/or under keywords but, as of this writing, few permit access to a class notation by its descriptive term. Yet this access is essential for both electronic and paper-based bibliographic files. In the latter the document description, or one copy of the document description, is filed under one or more pertinent subject notations. An alphabetical index leads to these notations. Index access should be under terms that are likely to be thought of:

```
Anatomy, Humans     611
Human anatomy       611
```

Because the subject exists in the context of other subjects and tends to be divided among different disciplines, qualifying phrases or precise use of indentions in the index or other devices appropriate to the screen should help users decide which of several possible notations to search in the classed documents file:

```
Anatomy                      571.3
                                (Meaning: The basic, general, notation)

    domestic animals         636.089 1
                                (Meaning: Anatomy of domestic animals)

    drawings

        animals              743.6

        humans               743.49
                                (Meaning: Anatomical drawings of humans)

    humans                   611 (Meaning: Human anatomy)

    microorganisms           571.633 29
```

Clarity is even more important in OPACs than it is in paper files because the screen carries less information than the printed page, and switching screen displays can lead to unexpected results. Any lack of clarity, any ambiguity, wastes the searchers' time or even may mislead them.

Two Methods of Providing Index Access to Classed Files

Both methods described below try to improve recall by permitting access to subjects in a classed as well as in an alphabetical context. In a paper-based environment this twofold subject access is typically achieved by listing documents in classed order while providing word access to the notations through an alphabetical index. However, the two most common general classification vocabularies, DDC and LCC, are not integrated with the most common subject heading vocabulary, LCSH, because each was developed independently and by a separate staff. As mentioned briefly in Chapter 6, Sections "Subject Labels in Classed and/or Alphabetical Sequence," and "Summary," the terminology, scope, and meaning of individual concepts are often not identical. This impedes subject retrieval.

The two methods described below achieve twofold coordinated subject access by integrating the alphabetical and the classed subject terminology. In the health sciences field, *Medical Subject Headings* (MeSH) has this kind of coordination, and in the realm of OPACs several projects, including OCLC's "ExTended Concept Trees" project, attempt to move in the same direction (Vizine-Goetz 1996a).

The "Multiple Listing" Method

In card catalogs and printed bibliographies in which subjects are arranged in classed order, the multiple listing method is one possibility. With it, the document description (the bibliographic entry) is listed under more than one class notation, just as in a card catalog, which uses alphabetical subject headings, the entry is listed under more than one subject heading. This method can be used when the class notation is not also used as a shelving device, or when only one of the several class notations is so used. As mentioned previously, it is especially useful for enumerative schemes where the notation often cannot express as many subject interrelationships as is possible with faceted schemes. It was typically used with classed card catalogs. The alphabetical subject index refers to every notation under which a document is described.

If the paper-based system uses faceted classification along with the multiple listing method, the document would have to be listed under every combination of facets that describe it. Using the example in Figure 7.4, this would require listing a work on *Apartment houses (T21) built in Milan, Italy (L364) in Neo-Renaissance style (S32) of reinforced concrete (M31)* under up to 24 notational combinations along with an alphabetical index reference from each of them. Some possible notational combinations are

    T21S32M31L364

    T21M31S32L364

    S32M31T21L364

Although a large number of notational listings is theoretically possible under this system, space and money considerations caused the document description to be listed usually under no more than three or four combinations in a paper-based file, along with the few corresponding index entries. This forfeited much of the advantage of faceted classification. To take full advantage of the benefits of faceted classification, access must be possible to every facet of a combined notation and to the combined notation itself.

In its NetFirst database OCLC has adapted to OPACs the concept of classifying documents under more than one notation (Vizine-Goetz 1996b). It uses the DDC, an essentially enumerative system, effectively. Needless to say, the methods of accessing the notations via their alphabetical names are entirely different from those suitable for a paper-based system and require carefully constructed internal supporting systems.

The "Single Listing, Multiple Indexing" Method

The second method of arranging bibliographic entries in paper-based files in which subjects are arranged in classed order is to list a document only under the one class notation that best describes its topic. The alphabetical subject index provides access to that notation. This method is necessary if the class notation is also the location device.

In paper-based files this method is especially useful if used with a faceted classification constructed according to the principle of inversion, and with an alphabetical chain index, both described previously in this chapter. The combination of these two methods is efficient: It leads to every facet of the combined notation as well as to the combined notation, and it is economical of space, which is very important in a paper-based file. It was used for many years in the printed *British National Bibliography* (BNB) and several other national bibliographies. However, its ease of application depends on the classification system it indexes. Inconsistencies in the classification system—some of which are described in Chapter 8—create difficulties in the chain index that make it difficult to automate it. When production of the BNB was about to be automated in 1971, Derek Austin developed string indexing, a system of indexing which, in addition to other advantages, did not depend on a classification system. In the meantime the development of OPACs and the automation of LCC, DDC, and UDC have caused the editors of all three systems to move increasingly toward eradicating inconsistencies. None has reached the goal so far.

PRECIS, a String Indexing System

An indexing technique of great interest for OPACs is the string indexing system known as PRECIS (PREserved Context Indexing System), invented by Derek Austin (1984 and 1998; Foskett 1996, 132–39) (and explained in Chapter 4, Section "Markers or Relators" and Chapter 6, Section "Rigid Rules Instead of Pragmatism"). Although it can be used manually and for back-of-the-book indexes, it was designed primarily for computers. It provides access to a multiconcept topic by each of its elements and, unlike in chain indexing, each index entry is a brief synthesis of the indexed document's content; that is, each index entry is coextensive with the document's topic. Also, unlike chain indexing, PRECIS is independent of any classification system and therefore can (but does not have to) be used in conjunction with any classification.

The indexer writes down the document's subject as a string of terms that form, in effect, an abstract of the document according to a prescribed linguistic formula. Each concept in this string is then tagged with a symbol recognizable to the computer program. (These are the only intellectual parts of the work: summarizing content and assigning correct tags.) The computer then shunts the different sections of the string so that, in the printout resulting from this program, each becomes an access point.

Using as example the string *Parasite caused diseases of the circulatory system of lions*, the computer program will shunt this into the following index entries, most of which consist of two lines, called the "lead and qualifier line" and the "display line." Note that the PRECIS program is designed to rephrase parts of the string as needed:

```
Parasite-caused diseases.
   Circulatory system. Lions.

Circulatory system. Parasite-caused diseases.
   Lions.

Lions. Parasite caused diseases of circulatory system.
```

First adopted in 1971, PRECIS was designed with the production of printed indexes in mind. Although it is being used for this purpose in only a few cases as of this writing (Austin 1998), its flexibility and its ability to access a multi-topical work from every angle while furnishing a synthesis of the content make it a good candidate for OPACs. Some conceptual adaptation and much technical inventiveness will undoubtedly be necessary, but it should even be possible to combine the concepts and techniques developed for PRECIS with those developed for chain indexing. Among classificationists there is definite interest in using or adapting PRECIS for online subject retrieval (Cousins 1992; Godert 1991).

LIBRARY POLICIES AND THE UNDERUSE OF CLASSIFICATION

Before considering the many functions and abilities expected of OPACs in connection with classed access, it may be instructive to consider the other side of this coin: Should librarians, indexers, catalogers, and administrators, do anything to support, or even permit, the desired functions to be attainable, let alone effective? Indeed, they should.

For example, they should remember that classification not only serves as a location tool but has also a bibliographic function. Disregard of this function may explain the all-too-common, unfortunate "underuse" (to coin a term) of classification. Especially since the 1960s, quite a few libraries, especially some large ones, have followed an administrative policy which, for the sake of economy of input, requires processing shortcuts that tend to make effective integration of new resources into a local collection difficult, and that thereby hamper online retrieval effectiveness. In these libraries the purpose of classification has been reduced to devising call numbers that serve essentially as parking devices, that is, are primarily intended to allow individual volumes to be found on the shelves and only secondarily to permit some collocation of related material (Dahlberg 1977; Comaromi 1981; Hill 1984).

The fact that many academic libraries use the Library of Congress classification does not help. It was not designed to be a generally applicable system but rather to reflect the holdings of one library that emphasizes the social sciences. From the beginning, it was not always logical in its breakdown. For example, it arranges many specific topics alphabetically rather than in classed order, that is, by spelling rather than by meaning. As the system grew and accepted new topics, it became increasingly less logical.

Ignorance of classification's bibliographic function, or a tendency to treat it lightly, causes too many libraries to destroy available classification information. To cite one example: After explaining how LCC and DDC sometimes complement each other in dividing subjects, Chan points out, "In databases which carry both DDC and LCC numbers . . . searchers have a wide choice of search parameters. They may use [both schemes] complementary to each other. . . . Having both DDC numbers and LCC numbers in your bibliographic records is equivalent to having two classified catalogs in one. It is, therefore, regrettable that, when loading MARC records into the online catalog, some libraries strip the records of the class numbers not used for local shelving purposes. Users are being deprived of very useful access points" (Chan 1990, 15, 19).

Oblivious to the individual library's responsibility as part of a maturing bibliographic structure in this day of OPACs, multimillion-member utilities, and the Internet, some libraries went during the "conversion" process from card files to online use beyond stripping supplied access points that were not needed locally. Too often, speed was more important than precision, economical input more important than thoroughness, so that too often fields that permitted either quality were ignored or filled in with the default value instead of the value that would have made the particular bibliographic record more flexibly accessible.

As long as open stack access and shelf browsing are permitted, and especially when OPACs will routinely permit "shelf browsing" and hierarchical searching on the screen, it is essential that works be classed accurately, precisely, and into cohesive groups and that those readers, for example, who wish to search exhaustively be made aware of the several notations that may have been assigned over the decades to the same concept. It is essential that not only researchers but every librarian who does or teaches OPAC searching view class notations not merely as shelving, but as bibliographic tools. To enable OPACs to do the many things we ask of them, it is essential that every applicable field in the MARC record, fixed or variable, be filled out conscientiously and accurately.

A WISHLIST FOR CLASSED ACCESS IN OPACs, WITH EMPHASIS ON SEARCHING RATHER THAN INPUT

Except for the first two categories, "General" and "Searching and display," this wishlist focuses on OPAC capabilities connected with classification. Many concepts in it apply also to alphabetical subject terms. The list is based on ideas expressed by several writers in the field over the years, and on personal preferences. It is couched in general terms and is by no means complete or intended to be balanced, but it should help to focus thinking. Specific problems, suggested solutions, alternatives, technical limitations, and research results are in the literature. Among well-known reports are those by Karen Markey and Anh Demeyer (1986), Mia Massicotte (1988), Karen M. Drabenstott and Diane Vizine-Goetz (1994), Gertrude Koh (1995), and Martha M. Yee and Sara Shatford Layne (1998).

We are asking infinitely more of the OPAC than we ever imagined asking of the paper-based catalog, whether on cards or in book form. Many of the following abilities are already being applied, although no OPAC or program so far is designed to handle the total combination. Whether that combination is desirable is another matter. Whether the enormous effort, expense, and funds needed to achieve all that writers and practitioners in the field want is helpful or justified is, ultimately, a political and administrative decision. Technically it does seem to be feasible.

General

The overarching need is for clear, brief instructions in nonprofessional language, with options clearly indicated, if necessary by a succession of screens. Example: Terms like *Backup* can be ambiguous: *Backup* to the preceding screen or the preceding search phrase? Many programs do not indicate clearly (or at all when using an unfamiliar computer) how one can "get out" of a screen or search procedure or how decisions can be reversed. Explanation balloons that arise as the cursor sweeps over a term, and especially over an icon, should be standard, with clear indication how the balloons can be inactivated or activated.

Searching and Display

- Several searching complexity levels should be available, from "standard" with automatic defaults and clear listing at every step of selected choices to "special" (that is, advanced). Ability to switch from one "default" level to another, especially when switching from searching to display, is important.

- Except at the "standard" level, the user should be able to enter the system at any point and to skip any unneeded steps. Regardless of where begun, searches should be capable of being limited: by format, date, language, country of publication, or other factors.

- The system must permit several searching techniques such as command, menu, and relevance ranking, and permit switching from one to the other at any stage in a search. The display screen should indicate the searching and/or display standard used.

- The search instructions should indicate clearly whether a precoordinated set of terms is required, permitted, or not available. For example, "Search [space available for name of a topic, which can be a number]; followed by Search [space available for name of a second topic]" does not make it clear whether the second subject *must* or *may* be added, or can be ignored. That applies also to the limitations.

Classification Schedule (Notation) Versus Shelflist (Call Number)

The classification schedule represents the class system used, such as LCC, and follows its sequence and guidelines. The shelflist represents the works in an institution classed and arranged in "shelving sequence" by call numbers, on the basis of the classification schedule.

- The system should permit searching (and for authorized persons input) in the schedules as well as in the shelflist. Switching back and forth among the classification schedule and the institution's shelflist should be possible at any stage of a search. It should always be transparent to the nonprofessional searcher what the difference between the two is, and whether a search phrase or screen involves a notation or a call number.

- A search for a notation that is not available in the schedule, or a call number that is not available in the shelflist, should show the nearest available notations surrounding the desired notation, with the option of showing also the next higher and lower hierarchical levels, and with an explanation of why the answer differs from the search phrase.

- Access by a range of numbers should be possible in either the shelflist or the classification schedule. When displaying one number or a range of numbers, especially in the schedule, the captions and explanatory terms associated with that number or range of numbers must be shown with each number to make it meaningful.

- There should be two separate sets of phrasings for captions or notes in the schedules or for notes in the index, one for catalogers, the other for searchers. The default would be the searching phrases.

- Access to either the classification schedule or the shelflist should be by a number or by alphabetical terms such as subject headings, or keywords from the caption, notes, index, or other terms used for the number in the schedules.

- Whenever a class or call number is shown, the searcher should be able to call up a window showing that number and its broader and narrower hierarchical levels, all with captions. There should be an option to display the previously mentioned hierarchical levels either as notations with captions or verbally as a chain index.

- When searching the shelflist, display of document surrogates within one class (broad or narrow) should be possible by shelflist order, in chronological order, by date of publications, by relevance ranking, or other pertinent factors.

- Searching should be possible that combines one or more subject headings or key terms and one or more class notations, using Boolean formulae such as Search ([subject heading X] or [subject heading Y]) but not [class Z].

- During Boolean searches that employ keywords from different parts of the schedules, display of the classification numbers associated with these keywords should be possible, along with their scope notes and the number of bibliographic records associated with each number in the shelflist and with the combination requested. (Given the awkwardness with which most present classification schemes accommodate interdisciplinary topics, this is especially important for interdisciplinary topics, such as *City planning,* or *The influence of religion on art.*) Note that this disregards the shelving function but emphasizes the bibliographic function of a class number.)

- It should be possible to show in a window the history of the use of any number shown on the screen, indicating when the respective classification authority (such as DDC, LCC) made a change, and when the local library instituted it. Ultimately this could even be built automatically into the schedule, with notes like: "Number X: Not used by LCC after 1971." "Not used by this library after 1973. New number is ..." (for concepts and numbers that have undergone a series of changes over the years it is probably best to record under each number only the immediate past and following concept or number lest the note get too complicated).

Scrolling

- Once access has been gained to a notation in the schedules, the searcher should be able to scroll up or down the notations in the schedule. Captions and notes should be shown along with the notation. For any single notation, switching to the shelflist should be possible, indicating whether it was used in the shelflist and, if used, how many works are listed under it, with brief author, title, and date of publication.

- Once access has been gained to a call number in the shelflist, it should be possible to scroll up or down the call numbers. Every call number should also show on one or two lines the author's surname or full name, the brief book title, and the date of publication.

- It should be possible to switch from the brief bibliographic information indicated above to full bibliographic description, and back, possibly using windows, as well as to switch from scrolling in the schedules to scrolling in the shelflist, and vice versa.

- Scrolling the shelflist should permit the option of scrolling the combined shelflist of a library with several departments or branches, or of limiting the search by location (that is, by department or branch), by size, or other factors. In a library system with central cataloging, scrolling the combined system shelflist should be possible.

Hierarchical and Lateral Movement

- The searcher should be able to enter the system from the beginning, that is, with an overview of the main classes, with the further ability to narrow down each class and each number or group of numbers to either the next more specific level or to a summary of the level that is suitable for the limited space on a screen display. Each number or group of numbers should be accompanied by a caption and/or notes. It should be possible to go up and down that hierarchy.

- An expert system would be useful that automatically shows for a synthesized call number (from the shelflist) in a window, if asked, both hierarchies so that by switching from the shelflist to the classification outline the search may be adjusted as needed. (For example, the number for *Butterflies in Dane County, Wisconsin*: Show one hierarchy for *Butterflies* and another one for *Dane County;* or the number for *Afro-American conductors*: Show one hierarchy for *Conductors* and another one for *Afro-Americans.*) LCSH does this for newly established subject headings, and MARC coding permits it for subject headings as well as class numbers.

- The searcher should be able to access a topic either as a "concrete topic" (such as *Salmon*) or by discipline (such as *Zoology*) with the further ability to move the search from the concrete topic to the appropriate discipline (such as from *Salmon* to *Zoological aspects of salmon*), or from the discipline to the desired concrete topic (such as from *Zoology* to, again, *Zoological aspects of salmon*).

- If the search begins with a word (*Salmon, Fishes, Zoology*) rather than with a request for an overview of the classification schedules, the system should provide an overview of both the subject headings and the class notations associated with the requested term, and permit searching options. This is in line with the "integrated approach" that Koh (1995) advocates and that seems to be the most helpful feature for indexing systems without truly integrated alphabetical and notational structure.

ONLINE SEARCHING BY CLASS NUMBER

Chapter 10 provides an overview of searching in OPACs. This section discusses some aspects of OPAC searching by class number.

Command Approach

Although at present OPACs differ greatly in their capabilities, most permit searching through at least two types of approach: the command approach and the menu approach. The command approach is typically used if the searcher seeks a known author, title, subject, or series, or wishes to try the keyword approach. Keywords used in Boolean formulae can be helpful for searching complicated topics like *Effect of fertilizer runoff on algae production*, which the searcher may not be able to search by known subject heading or class notation. At present, many forms of command exist that are not particularly user friendly. Committee Z39 (On Library Work, Documentation and Related Publishing Practices) of the National Information Standards Organization has developed a standard for a common command language which is, unfortunately, largely ignored (NISO 1992).

If the program and database permit it, the command approach can also be used to search for a known class number in the schedule or a call number in the shelflist. Although progress in developing classed access in OPACs has been impressive, most OPACs that permit classed access have not reached their full potential, which includes, for example, the ability to search in either the class schedule or the shelflist, with the ability to switch back and forth and simultaneously see the desired notation's hierarchy. Nevertheless, experienced OPAC searchers may find the existing limited classed searching ability helpful even for "unknown items" searching. If the searched OPAC has truncated searching ability and scrolling ability, searchers who know the basics of the classification used, or who have access to its index and schedule, can enter the online shelflist at or near the desired notation and browse.

Menu Approach

For less-experienced users, or for experienced users who wish to explore various aspects of one subject, the menu approach may be better. Menus present to the user a series of options on the screen. The user can select an option and then narrow it down further, screen by screen, as needed. Each screenful of options presented in menu form is an array, just as the result of a step in the division process in bibliographic classification is an array. The arrays in the menu must be organized in a hierarchy, like a classification scheme, so that the user is shown an appropriate succession of menus and can move up and down the hierarchy.

Unfortunately, OPAC menus sometimes present unnecessary difficulties to the searcher who is not a frequent user. Options often are insufficiently explained and many databases and programs differ technically far more than their differences in content and purpose justify. There is great need for technical standardization, for example with respect to clarity of screen layout, instructions on how to get on, stay on, and move from one search to the next. All this imposes the obligation on the library to supply the user friendliness toward which the systems are striving.

In addition to the new problems created by computer-based information retrieval there is a carryover of some old problems. Some are due to known user habits of requesting information (Koh 1995, 199–201). For example, users may approach a topic indirectly, by searching a broader concept than the one actually desired, because they have no way of knowing how precisely subjects are broken up by the classification scheme, and because the concept of "disciplines" is essentially foreign to many people. Therefore, they cannot know that a "concrete" topic like *Salmon* can be distributed among several places in the classification scheme, depending on whether the zoological aspects, the economic aspects, the gastronomic aspects, or the artistic representations of salmon are desired.

Users are likely to seek a topic under its concrete aspects, such as *Salmon*. Menus must therefore permit this approach and then lead the user to the particular discipline desired, such as zoological aspects of salmon. Because some users are also likely to approach the same topic initially by discipline ("I have a zoological question"), menus must permit this approach as well, then lead the user to the specific concrete topic desired, such as *Salmon,* within the appropriate discipline. Also, many users do not distinguish clearly in their minds between subject headings (with their characteristics), keywords (with their different characteristics), and class notations (with their quite different characteristics). At the beginning of a search the various retrieval options should be presented in a way that helps users to decide which technique to use for a given request.

Another point concerns the limited size of the screen, which often does not permit listing in one array all options that are appropriate to a particular menu stage. In such cases, the screen must cluster the options into groups that can then be further subdivided as needed.

Some Possible Sets of Menus

Some of the menus illustrated in Figures 7.6 through 7.10 represent presently used types. However, because the use of menus for OPAC searching by class or call number is still in a fluid state of development, these menus, as a set, are not copied from a presently used system but point to what may well be feasible in the near future.

The first screen might look like Figure 7.6. Users who are interested in a biological topic would select line 5 and would find, after some further screens designed to narrow down the topic to biology, a screen such as that shown in Figure 7.7 (page 200). The instructions at the bottom of these figures are only representative of a number of choices that might be made available and shown on the screen, such as the opportunity to go back to the previous display, which will often be the next broader array, or to another type of display, such as by subject heading.

Figures 7.6 and 7.7 show that even the classed menu approach is not designed for ignoramuses. Like information retrieval in general, it demands a general cultural background. This has always been true, but the computer tends to show this more clearly, more brutally, than paper-based systems did in the past.

1	Logic, Mathematics, Statistics,
2	Psychology, Knowledge and its communication; Electronic science and technology
3	Chemistry, Physics, Applied chemical and physical sciences
4	Astronomy, Earth sciences and their application, including Geology and Geography
5	Biology, Zoology, Agriculture, Food technology, Ecology
6	Human sciences: Anthropology, Medicine, Education, Sports and Recreation
7	Social, Historical, Political and Military sciences and technologies
8	Economics, Industry, Technology and Engineering
9	The Humanities: Language, Literature, Fine arts, Philosophy, Religion, Popular culture, Folklore

CLICK THE LINE NUMBER THAT BEST

REPRESENTS YOUR DESIRED TOPIC

Figure 7.6. Possible menu of disciplines. The instructions at the foot of this and the following figures are only representative of the number of choices that might be made available.

By the time the user has reached the level of specificity shown in Figure 7.7, the system would refer internally to the appropriate notations, or ranges of notations, so that users could call them up and view the entries listed under them. This is where the problem caused by relocations of individual notations begins. For example, between the 20th and the 21st editions of the DDC (published in 1989 and 1996, respectively), programmers and catalogers would have had to change, for example, the original internal reference in Figure 7.7 *Maturation of animals* (not shown, but option 2 in Figure 7.7) from 591.3 to 571.871 if the DDC were used. Relocations, deletions, and especially additions, are equally frequent in LCC as, indeed, they must be in any living bibliographic classification that tries to keep up with developing knowledge.

Users who have called up the display in Figure 7.7 and who are interested in the zoological aspects of salmon would then select line 13 and, after some further screens designed to narrow down *Coldblooded vertebrates* to *Fishes*, would call up a screen such as that shown in Figure 7.8 (page 201). Note that this menu deals primarily with the zoological aspects of fishes and other cold-blooded vertebrates. This menu will lead to further menus since, for example, in line 4 the subsection *Toleostei (fully-boned fishes)* includes at least five genera and forty species of fishes. Once the searcher has reached the most precise menu available in a particular series of menus, that menu will carry a comment to that effect. The searcher will then need to enter a new command (such as DIS(play)) to get a listing of the actual entries available in this class.

ZOOLOGY; ANIMALS

1	Natural history of animals
2	Genetics, evolution, maturation
3	Physical adaptation, behavior
4	Pathology of animals
5	Animal ecology, geogreaphic area, environment
6	Invertebrates
7	Worms
8	Marine and seashore invertebrates
9	Mollusks
10	Other invertebrates, including insects
11	Vertebrates
12	Chordates
13	Coldblooded vertebrates, including fishes and reptiles
14	Mammals, including primates and forebears of humans

CLICK THE LINE NUMBER THAT BEST
REPRESENTS YOUR DESIRED TOPIC

Figure 7.7. Discipline of zoology as it might be shown in a menu.
In Figures 7.7 through 7.10 the system would refer internally to the appropriate
notations, or ranges of notations, so that searchers could call them up and view
the entries listed under them.

Selection of line 9 in Figure 7.8 leads to the same menu that the user would call
up by beginning the inquiry with a concrete topic: *Salmon,* or *Fishes,* rather than with
the broad discipline of *Zoology.* This menu is illustrated in Figure 7.9 (page 202). If
menus are based on a classification scheme, then Figures 7.6 to 7.8 represent, in effect, the schedules, and Figure 7.9 represents the index to the schedules. Selection of
line 7 in Figure 7.9 should call up the menu represented by Figure 7.8. Selection of
line 8 in Figure 7.9 should lead to a menu that explains how the concrete topic *Fishing
industry* is distributed among the various disciplines. Figure 7.10 (page 203) illustrates this.

COLDBLOODED VERTEBRATES; FISHES

ZOOLOGICAL ASPECTS

1   Fishes in general

     Species of fishes

2   Agnatha (Jawless fishes) including hagfishes and lampreys

3   Selachii, holocephali, sarcopterygii, including cartilaginous fishes, sharks, rays

4   Actinopterygii (Ray finned fishes) including bowfins, ganoids, lungfishes,

              toleostei (fully boned fishes) such as carp, catfishes, and eels

5   Protacanthopterygii, salmoniformes, including trout and salmon

6   Scopelomorpha, perciformes

7   Amphibians, including frogs, salamanders, toads

8   Reptiles, including alligators, crocodiles, lizards, snakes, turtles

OTHER THAN ZOOLOGICAL ASPECTS

9   of fishes

10   of amphibians

11   of reptiles

CLICK THE LINE NUMBER THAT BEST REPRESENTS YOUR DESIRED TOPIC

DISPLAY IN NUMERICAL ORDER   O

DISPLAY IN ALPHABETICAL ORDER BY CAPTION & INDEX TERMS   O

Figure 7.8. Menu illustrating a further subdivision of the discipline zoology, with reference to other disciplines.

	FISHES AND FISHING
1	Fishes (All aspects)
2	Artistic aspects (drawings, etc.)
3	Culture and conservation
4	Economic aspects
5	As a natural resource
6	Paleozoological aspects
7	Zoological aspects
8	Fishing industry
9	Fishing as a sport

CLICK THE LINE NUMBER THAT BEST
REPRESENTS YOUR DESIRED TOPIC

DISPLAY IN NUMERICAL ORDER   O

DISPLAY IN ALPHABETICAL ORDER
        BY CAPTION & INDEX TERMS   O

Figure 7.9. Sample of a menu showing the distribution of a concrete topic (*Fishes*) among various disciplines, with references to related topics.

	FISHING INDUSTRY
1	All aspects
2	Economic and commercial aspects
3	Government control
4	Administrative aspects
5	Legal aspects
6	Labor, equipment, technology
7	The product

CLICK THE LINE NUMBER THAT BEST
REPRESENTS YOUR DESIRED TOPIC

DISPLAY IN NUMERICAL ORDER   O

DISPLAY IN ALPHABETICAL ORDER

    BY CAPTION & INDEX TERMS   O

Figure 7.10. Distribution of a concrete topic among disciplines. Line 7 leads again to Figure 7.9.

Menu Shortcuts and Alternatives

Although menus seem essential for the inexperienced user and are often helpful to the experienced user, the slowness of going through a long succession of menus to identify a topic is exasperating for the experienced user who has a precise question in mind. If the system does not permit the command approach, or if the experienced user chooses not to use it, the system should permit shortcuts. Among possibilities are use of function keys, or of "pop-up" menus that show in a hierarchical display the titles or summaries of the various menu levels to permit any level to be selected directly.

The risk, particularly with menus based on inquiry warrant, is that menus might become self-perpetuating: They provide a procrustean bed, an unchanging framework, even when users' approaches tend to change over time. Eventually, the design of menus may become completely dynamic and independent of human menu designers. The way in which one user after the other arrives at a definition of his or her need may be allowed to affect the system, so that the system "learns" to cope with, and adjust to, the needs of subsequent inquirers. This, however, requires the creation of knowledge-based (intelligent) systems. How soon such systems will be able to cope reliably with general, as opposed to specialized, inquiries is arguable. In the future, technology warrant may even cause menus to be supplemented or even superseded by other types of linkages growing out of mark-up languages like HTML and SGML or XML. It is difficult to even imagine what some of the economically viable possibilities will be.

REFERENCES

Anderson, James D. 1991. Ad hoc: user-determined classified displays based on faceted indexing. In *Proceedings of the 1st ASIS/SIG/CR Classification Research Workshop held at the 53rd ASIS annual meeting, Toronto, Ontario, Canada, November 4, 1990, 1–7.* (ASIS monograph series). Published by Learned Information, Inc. for the American Society for Information Science.

ASIS. 1991. 53rd annual meeting. *Proceedings of the 1st ASIS/SIG/CR Classification Research Workshop held at the 53rd ASIS annual meeting, Toronto, Ontario, Canada, November 4, 1990.* Published by Learned Information, Inc. for the American Society for Information Science.

Austin, Derek. 1998. Derek Austin: Developing PRECIS, Preserved Context Index System. *Cataloging & Classification Quarterly* 25 (2/3): 23–66.

Austin, Derek, with assistance from Mary Dykstra. 1984. *A manual of concept analysis and subject indexing.* 2d ed. London: The British Library.

Batty, C. David. 1970. Chain indexing. In *Encyclopedia of library and information science, 4:* 423–34. New York: Dekker.

Beghtol, Clare. 1998a. General classification systems: Structural principles for multidisciplinary specification. In*Structures and relations in knowledge organization. Proceedings of the Fifth International ISKO Conference, 25–29 August 1998, Lille, France,* edited by Widad Mustafa el Hadi, Jacques Maniez, and Steven A. Pollitt, 89–96. (Advances in knowledge organization, vol. 6). Würzburg: Ergon-Verlag.

———. 1998b. Knowledge domains: Multidisciplinarity and bibliographic classification systems. *Knowledge organization* 25 (12): 1–12.

Beyond bookmaks: Schemes for organizing the Web. 1999. [Compiled and maintained by Gerry McKiernan, Iowa State University Library. Available: http://www.public .iastate.edu/~CYBERSTACKS/CTW.htm. (Accessed May 11, 2001).

Boll, John J. 1985. *Shelf browsing, open access and storage capacity in research libraries.* (Occasional papers, no. 169). Urbana-Champaign: University of Illinois Graduate School of Library and Information Science.

Broadbent, Elaine. 1995. Classification access in the online catalog. *Cataloging & Classification Quarterly* 21 (2): 119–42.

Chan, Lois Mai. 1990. The Library of Congress classification system in an online environment. *Cataloging & Classification Quarterly* 11 (1): 6–25.

Classification Editorial Policy Committee. 1996. Preface by the Decimal Classification Editorial Policy Committee. In *Dewey decimal classification and relative index devised by Melvil Dewey.* Edition 21, 1: xiii–xv. Albany, NY: Forest Press.

Cochrane, Pauline Atherton. 1982a. Classification as an online subject access tool: Challenge and opportunity. In *Subject access: Report of a meeting sponsored by the Council on Library Resources, Dublin, Ohio, 1982,* edited by Keith W. Russell. Washington, DC: Council on Library Resources.

―――. 1982b. Classification as a user's tool in online public access catalogs. In *Proceedings of the 4th International Study Conference on Classification Research, 1982.* Frankfurt: Indeks-Verlag.

Comaromi, John P. 1981. *Book numbers: A historical study and practical guide to their use.* Littleton, CO: Libraries Unlimited.

Comaromi, John P., and Margaret J. Warren. 1982. *Manual on the use of Dewey decimal classification.* 19th ed. Albany, NY: Forest Press.

Cousins, Shirley Anne. 1992. Enhancing subject access to OPACs: Controlled vocabulary vs. natural language. *Journal of Documentation* 48 (3, September): 291–309.

Dahlberg, Ingetraut. 1977. Major developments in classification. *Advances in Librarianship* 7: 41–103.

[DDC]. 1996. *Dewey decimal classification and relative index devised by Melvil Dewey.* Edition 21. Albany, NY: Forest Press. 4 vols.

Drabenstott, Karen M., and Diane Vizine-Goetz. 1994. *Using subject headings for online retrieval: Theory, practice, and potential.* San Diego: Academic Press.

Foskett, A. C. 1996. *The subject approach to information.* 5th ed. London: Library Association Publishing.

Glassel, Aimée, and Amy Tracy Wells. 1998. Scout Report Signpost: Design and development for access to cataloged Internet resources. *Journal of Internet Cataloging* 1 (3): 15–45.

Godert, Winfried. 1991. Facet classification in online retrieval. *International Classification.* 18 (2): 98–109.

Goldberg, Jolande E. 1996. Library of Congress classification: Shelving device for collections or organization of knowledge fields? *Advances in Knowledge Organization* 5: 33–42.

Hernon, Peter, et al. 1998. *U.S. Government on the Web: Getting the information you need.* Englewood, CO: Libraries Unlimited.

Hill, Janet Swan. 1984. Online classification number access: Some practical considerations. *Journal of Academic Librarianship* 10 (March): 16–22.

Koh, Gertrude S. 1995. Options in classification available through modern technology. *Cataloging & Classification Quarterly* 19 (3/4): 195–211.

Liu, Songqiao. 1990. Online classification notation: Proposal for a flexible faceted notation system (FFNS). *International Classification* 17 (1): 14–20.

Liu, Songqiao, and Elaine Svenonius. 1991. DORS: DDC Online Retrieval System. *Library Resources and Technical Services* 35 (4, October): 359–75.

Mandel, Carol A. 1986. *Classification schedules as subject enhancement in online catalogs: A review of a conference sponsored by Forest Press, the OCLC Online Computer Library Center, and the Council on Library Resources.* Washington, DC: Council on Library Resources.

Markey, Karen. 1986. Subject searching in library catalogs. In *Improving LCSH for use in online catalogs*, edited by Pauline A. Cochrane, 243–56. Littleton,CO: Libraries Unlimited.

Markey, Karen, and Anh Demeyer. 1986. *Dewey Decimal Classification Online Project: Evaluation of a library schedule and index integrated into the suject searching capabilities of an online catalog.* (OCLC Research report series OCLC/OPR/RR-86/1). Dublin, OH: OCLC.

Massicotte, Mia. 1988. Improved browsable displays for online subject access. *Information Technology and Libraries* 7 (4, December): 373–80.

Maxwell, Margaret F. 1998. Margaret F. Maxwell: Bequest of joy, a life with books. *Cataloging & Classification Quarterly* 25 (2/3): 191–97.

McIlwaine, I. C. 1994. UDC: The present state and future developments. *International Cataloguing and Bibliographic Control* 23 (2, April/June): 29–33.

Mills, J. 1967. *A modern outline of library classification.* London: Chapman & Hall.

NISO. 1992. *Common command language for online interactive information retrieval.* Developed by the National Information Standards Organization; approved August 6, 1992 by the American National Standards Institute. (ANSI/NISO Z39.58-1902). Bethesda, MD: NISO Press.

Olson, Hope A. 1998. Mapping beyond Dewey's boundaries: Constructing classificatory space for marginalized knowledge domains. *Library Trends* 47 (2, Fall): 233–54.

Olson, Hope A., and Dennis B. Ward. 1998. Charting a journey across knowledge domains: Feminism in the Dewey Decimal Classification. In *Structures and relations in knowledge organization. Proceedings of the Fifth International ISKO Conference, 25–29 August 1998, Lille, France,* edited by Widad Mustafa el Hadi, Jacques Maniez, and Steven A. Pollitt, 238–44. (Advances in knowledge organization, vol. 6). Würzburg: Ergon-Verlag.

Palmer, Bernard I. 1955. The colon classification. In *An introduction to library classification,* edited by W. C. Berwick Sayers, 161–71. London: Grafton.

Ranganathan, S. R. 1933. *Colon classification.* Madras, India: Madras Library Association; New York: H. W. Wilson.

Richmond, Phyllis R. 1983. Futuristic aspects of subject access. *Library* Resources *and Technical* Services 27 (January–March): 89–93.

Schulte-Albert, Hans G.1974. Cyprian Kinner and the idea of a faceted classification. *Libri* 24: 324–37.

Stewart, Barbara. 1997. *Directory of library technical services homepages.* New York: Neal-Schuman.

Svenonius, Elaine, et al. 1992. Automation of chain indexing.In *Classification Research for Knowledge Representation and Organization. Proceedings of the 5th International Study Conference on Classification Research, Toronto, Canada, June 24–28, 1991,* edited by Nancy J. Williamson and Michèle Hudon, 351–64. Amsterdam, Holland: Elsevier.

Van der Walt, Martin. 1998. The structure of classification schemes used in Internet search engines. In *Structures and relations in knowledge organization. Proceedings of the Fifth International ISKO Conference, 25–29 August 1998, Lille, France,* edited by Widad Mustafa el Hadi, Jacques Maniez, and Steven A. Pollitt, 379–87. (Advances in knowledge organization, vol. 6). Würzburg: Ergon-Verlag.

Vizine-Goetz, Diane. 1996a. Classification research at OCLC. Available: http://www.oclc.org /oclc/research/publications/review96/. (Accessed May 10, 2001). 6p.

———. 1996b. Online classification: Implications for classifying and document[-like object] retrieval. *Knowledge organization and change: Proceedings of the 4th International ISKO Conference, 15–18 July 1996, Washington, D.C.* Frankfurt/Main: INDEKS Verlag.

Wiegand, Wayne A. 1996. *Irrepressible reformer: A biography of Melvil Dewey.* Chicago: American Library Association.

Williamson, Nancy. 1998. An interdisciplinary world and discipline based classification. In *Structures and relations in knowledge organization. Proceedings of the Fifth International ISKO Conference, 25–29 August 1998, Lille, France,* edited by Widad Mustafa el Hadi, Jacques Maniez, and Steven A. Pollitt, 116–24. (Advances in knowledge organization, vol. 6). Würzburg: Ergon-Verlag.

Wilson, Thomas D. 1971. *An introduction to chain indexing.* Hamden, CT: Linnet Books.

Yee, Martha M., and Sara Shatford Layne. 1998 *Improving online public access catalogs.* Chicago: American Library Association.

8

Online Catalogs and the Dewey Decimal and Library of Congress Classifications

INTRODUCTION

This chapter provides a brief introduction to the *Dewey Decimal Classification* (DDC) and the *Library of Congress Classification* (LCC) and examines their suitability for retrieving subject information through online public access catalogs (OPACs). It should be read with Chapters 3 and 7 in mind, because it is based on many of the points raised in those chapters. The DDC and the LCC are discussed here because they are the most frequently used classification schemes, with consideration of the LCC mostly limited to North America. The *Universal Decimal Classification* (UDC) is fairly common in countries other than the United States.

Almost all MARC records contain LCC notations and Library of Congress (LC) subject headings. Many also contain DDC notations. These subject labels, along with the keywords contained in the title, contents note, subject headings, and other parts of the MARC record, can be used for retrieving the record through the subject or subjects it represents.

In the 1950s and 1960s, many writers and researchers tended to think of subject retrieval either only in terms of alphabetically arranged files accessible through alphabetical terms (subject headings, descriptors, keywords) or only in terms of a classed file, accessible through class numbers. More recent thinking and research recognizes (or, more correctly, has begun to confirm the old assumption) that each method has its strengths and weaknesses, and that when as complete as possible a collection of documents on a topic is desired, a combination of all three methods—controlled alphabetical terms, controlled class notations, and uncontrolled keywords—is stronger than any single method.

THREE SUBJECT RETRIEVAL METHODS

Simply put, the document groupings that result from the various file arrangements can be summarized as follows: In a classed file a document is seen within the context of a larger group of related documents; in an alphabetical file a document is seen under its own subject, independent of any context. With respect to keywords, a few paper-based files or indexes used to be arranged by keywords; in electronic systems that use keywords, regardless of the order in which documents are assembled, a document is accessible by most of the words used to describe it.

To illustrate the effect of classed versus alphabetical groupings, for example, in the DDC, the symbol for library science is *020* and the symbol for the American Library Association, the chief professional organization in this field, is *020.62273*. In other words, material on these closely related topics is shelved closely together or is listed closely together in a classed file and can thus be found together. However, when the topics are listed in an alphabetical file they are listed under the respective terms *Library science* and *American Library Association.* Because of what might be called "the accident of the alphabet" they are thus widely separated by unrelated subjects ranging from *Animals* to *Law reform.*

Conversely, material on the topic of library buildings can be found listed under the one alphabetical term *Library buildings.* But when one looks for it in a classed file that is arranged by disciplines, it is widely separated: For example, in the DDC the architectural aspects of library buildings are found with *Architecture* under *727.8*; the construction aspects are with *Technology* under *690.78*; and the functional planning (the efficiency) aspects are with *Library science* under 022.3. Exactly the same situation exists in LCC.

This situation may seem irrational, but it is based on two reasonable rules that help to make each of these systems work economically for the indexer as well as for the searcher: 1) List each topic only under the most specific authorized subject heading that describes it and 2) classify each work, also as specifically as feasible, in the discipline to which it pertains. One effect of these rules is that persons who are searching for a specific topic do not need to go through a large group of more or less suitable entries to find their specific topic. As Carol A. Mandel pointed out with respect to library classification: "A classification number may sometimes provide the most precise access point, as in cases where only a specific aspect of a subject is wanted (e.g., frogs from a culinary aspect)" (1986, 11). On the other hand, another effect of these rules is that searchers who wish to do an exhaustive search for a topic, for example for a term paper or a dissertation, must employ both types of files. In the past, the linearity of paper-based methods coupled with the need for economy made it necessary to arrange a file in only one sequence, either alphabetical or classed. The computer, if properly programmed, permits using both sequences.

Computers also encourage a third helpful approach, by keyword, that is, by uncontrolled terms. Because most users (and librarians) cannot be expected to carry thousands of class numbers and authorized subject headings in their heads, this is an important initial access technique, a starting point that can lead to clusters of relevant documents under the various controlled headings. Keywords should, however, be used with caution because they tend to result in "overload," that is, too many documents, including a high proportion of "false drops" (irrelevant documents).

There is little doubt that efficient subject retrieval systems of the future will employ all three methods—the classed approach, controlled alphabetical vocabulary, and uncontrolled keywords—all in a wide variety of capabilities depending on the individual OPAC, and most likely fine-tuned by relevance ranking. One of the problems to be faced is the optimum interrelationship among these methods within one system, and especially the problem of adjusting relevance ranking to the varying moods and demands of the individual searcher.

LCC AND DDC AS RETRIEVAL TOOLS IN OPACs

The traditional general professional opinion, expressed also in the first edition of this work, held that DDC's characteristics make it very well suited to being a subject retrieval tool for OPACs but that LCC's characteristics make it a very poor subject retrieval tool for OPACs. To some extent this generalization is still true, but the creation of the MARC Format for Classification Data (MARC 21 cf) and the editorial work that preceded the creation of electronic versions of both classification schemes have now made it possible for both to be used as effective subject retrieval devices. Also, the editors of both schemes have begun to introduce editorial policies and features that make the schemes better suited to electronic retrieval. In addition, the 1980s and 1990s have seen much research and experimentation that is likely to enable both systems to reach optimum performance. Both systems, as well as the computer programs, still have a long way to go, and a great deal of money and effort must be spent before OPACs will have reached the flexibility, the multidimensional approaches, and the different levels of approaches (ranging from simple to expert) of which the electronic format is capable. It may even be hoped that ultimately a series of nationally or internationally accepted operational and performance standards can be achieved.

SOME PROBLEMS WORTH NOTING

The development of OPACs brought some problems to light that had not existed when paper formats were used, that had not been recognized as problems because the public did not have access to the paper-based classification schedules, or of which the profession had simply been unaware up to then. A few of these problems are described in the following sections to illustrate why much editorial work is necessary before a paper-based classification schedule can be transferred to an effective electronic format.

Problems with Notations and Index Terms As Retrieval Devices

Figure 8.1 (page 212) uses LCC to illustrate a problem that is common to all classification schedules, whether enumerative or faceted: Many notations and many descriptive captions are insufficient by themselves to serve as effective retrieval devices. The scope of a notation like *TH 6493* and of a term like *Tubs* in Figure 8.1 can only be understood if it is read in the context of the hierarchy, in this case:

```
    Building construction (and in particular construction of)
       Plumbing and pipe fitting (which includes plumbing of)
          Bathrooms and similar rooms (and in particular of)
                Tubs (that is, bathtubs).
```

In other words, the concept is bathtubs as part of buildings' plumbing construction.

```
TH                  Building construction
TH 6101-6887           Plumbing and pipe fitting
TH 6485-6512              Plumbing of special rooms and areas
TH 6485-6500                Bathrooms. Toilet rooms. Lavoratories
TH 6491-6496                  Baths
TH 6491                         General works
TH 6492                         Shower baths. Sprays
TH 6493                         Tubs
TH 6494                         Foot baths
TH 6495                         Sitz baths
TH 6496                         Bidets
```

Figure 8.1. Selection from the LCC schedule for *T (Technology)*.

Likewise, the scope of a span of notations like *TH 6491-6496* in Figure 8.1 can only be understood if the caption, notation, or method of presentation on the screen makes it clear that this group of numbers refers to the various fixtures that are called *baths,* and the activity of baths in the sense of bathing is classed elsewhere, including *RA 780* for the hygienic aspects (that is, bathing for the sake of cleanliness) and *RM 819 to 822.W2* for the medical aspects (that is, bathing as part of a cure). As shown, the captions do not provide this kind of help to the searcher. As long as only catalogers, who are familiar with the idea that a concrete topic like *baths* can be distributed among different disciplines, used the schedule, this mattered very little. But when classification schedules become searching tools for nonprofessionals it matters very much.

Similarly, to the reader of the index to the LCC, the scope of the term *Tubs* is not obvious if the index entry merely indicates

```
    Tubs      TH 6493
```

because the term by itself has several meanings such as buttertubs, washtubs, bathtubs, or in slang even slow-moving boats.

Problems of this nature were recognized in the 1980s (Markey and Demeyer 1986), if not earlier. Since that time the questions of end-user language and of rephrasing captions and notes in the schedules and terms in the index for users as well as for indexers have become the subject of study and efforts to correct the problems (Mitchell 1995; Vizine-Goetz 1996).

Browsing Problems

Regardless of the classification scheme a library employs, users have shelf browsed for generations with no, or only very limited, understanding of the meaning of specific notations. They could move with fair success along the shelves and inspect works with numbers and titles such as

```
515.25      Equations and functions
515.3       Differential calculus and equations
515.3077
515.4       Integral calculus and equations
515.4076
515.52      Eulerian integrals
```

without having to know that the *077* in *515.3077* meant "A programmed text in differential calculus," or that the *076* in *515.4076* meant "A workbook with problems in integral calculus." The titles on the book spines usually explained the books' topics. OPAC users meet essentially the same situation if their OPAC program permits scrolling bibliographic entries in classed sequence.

The initial listing of bibliographic entries in shelflist order should use one to two lines per entry so that a fair number can fit onto a screen; it should be sufficient to provide basic information that permits the scanner to either ignore the work or study the entry more closely. It should consist of the call number, brief author and title, and the date of publication. Provided the title is not too brief, this is about as helpful as shelf browsing: On the one hand the scroller cannot examine the book immediately, but on the other hand, he or she is able to scroll books even if they are not on the shelf because they are in use or shelved separately because of size or rarity. Following are two such entries, less than ideal, taken from two different OPACs. The programmers evidently either were unaware of the many past studies indicating what parts of the description are most essential, or decided to ignore them.

```
659.2972 J716   Public relations for the design pro
N510 A37        Museums and money, the impact of fun
```

To learn whether the works are up-to-date (one was published in 1946), were written by known persons, were published by reputable publishers, or that the "fun" in museums actually means "funding," further search steps are necessary.

To search an OPAC as efficiently and as effectively as its program permits, OPAC searchers must be far more sophisticated than shelf browsers, even if the program will lead them automatically to some answers. To mention truncation as one example, OPAC users must know at least what truncation is and what it is supposed to achieve. They must either know, or the system must tell them, where and how it can be applied, and what to do when it does not bring desired results. For example, to truncate a notation like *83?34* to retrieve all types of German-language literature of the Reformation period, the searcher must either know the structure of DDC's literature section or be instructed by the computer how to truncate this particular type of notation, or the notation must have a built-in device that causes truncation to occur at the correct spot in the notation. Although the computer can be programmed to do much of the work, probably via menus or directives, OPAC users must clearly be better informed about classification principles and searching techniques than casual shelf browsers to take full advantage of OPAC capabilities.

To mention another example: in databases or union catalogs that are accessible by both DDC and LCC (at present hardly any, but potentially all of them), users must either know, or be told, that these two classification systems divide the discipline of literature quite differently. Browsing a *Literature* shelflist in DDC order or in LCC order will show the same holdings in different groupings and answer different questions.

COMPONENTS OF
ONLINE CLASSED RETRIEVAL SYSTEMS

Ignoring, for purposes of this chapter, requirements of subject heading and keyword access, a system that permits sophisticated access by classification requires three to four basic units, as shown in Figure 8.2. A file of document surrogates (entries), the classification schedules as authority, and an index to the class notations are essential. A machine-readable file of the actual documents is highly desirable (and essential if keyword searching of the actual documents is desired in addition to keyword searching of the subject headings, classification captions, and titles). Users should be able to enter the system with a known class notation or with an alphabetical term that describes the concept represented by a class notation.

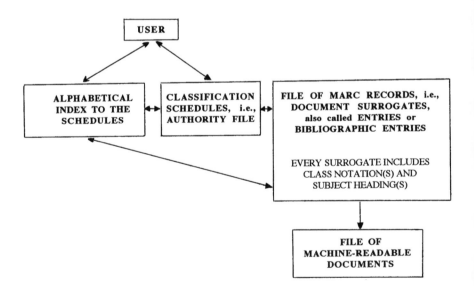

Figure 8.2. Online classed retrieval components.

DESIRABLE FEATURES OF
ONLINE CLASSED RETRIEVAL SYSTEMS

Chapter 7 includes a section, "A Wish List for Classed Access in OPACs, With Emphasis on Searching Rather Than Input," as well as a discussion of factors that affect classed retrieval in automated files. Many of the listed factors and capabilities depend on the computer program and on hardware. Others depend on the classification system and its notation, and these are among the concerns of this chapter. The DDC and LCC are examined in the light of the following points:

- Structure of the classification system:

  — Is the structure logical and, equally important, consistent?

  — Does it permit browsing by means of backward and forward scrolling?

  — Does it permit hierarchical searching?

  — Does it permit multiple subject notations to be assigned to one document, either individually or synthetically?

  — Is it hospitable hierarchically as well as collaterally? That is, does it permit meaningful insertion of new subjects as subdivisions of existing ones and as coordinates of existing ones?

  — Does it accommodate interdisciplinary subjects meaningfully?

- Qualities and structure of the notation: Is it suitable for bibliographic functions? Specifically:

  — Does it show the relationships between topics by showing their relative positions in the hierarchies?

  — Does it permit synthesis, and does it distinguish between the different hierarchies in a synthesized notation?

  — Does it permit left, internal, and right truncation?

  — Does it permit hierarchical searching?

  — Does it permit meaningful insertion in the schedule of new subjects as subdivisions of existing ones and as coordinates of existing ones?

  — Does it permit meaningful insertion in the schedule of interdisciplinary subjects?

- Format and wording of schedule and index:

  — Is the wording suitable for input as well as for searching?

  — Do schedule and index refer to related aspects or to a subject in other disciplines?

CHARACTERISTICS OF THE DDC

The DDC was first published by Melvil Dewey in 1876. It is now in its 21st edition. It is basically a theoretical scheme, designed to contain room for all knowledge, without attention to the subject emphases of the holdings of any one library. Although its use in North American libraries, especially academic libraries, decreased during the 1960s and 1970s, it is the most widely used library classification system in the world. It is used in more than 135 countries and has been translated into more than thirty languages, from German to Gujarati. In the United States, 95% of all public and school libraries, 25% of all college and university libraries, and 20% of special libraries use the DDC (DDC 1996, 1: xxxi).

To permit evaluation of the DDC as a retrieval tool in OPACs, it is first necessary to describe its major characteristics and, subsequently, problems that do, or may, arise from these characteristics or from exceptions to the standard DDC patterns.

System Structure

The DDC uses a pure notation based on numbers. Its structure is basically hierarchical, which aids its use as a retrieval device in electronic tools. The difficulties that exceptions to the generally hierarchical structure cause in OPAC use are described subsequently in this chapter in the section "The DDC and OPACs."

The DDC is divided into ten main classes:

000-099	Generalities, including Knowledge, Library science, Bibliographies
100-199	Philosophy; Psychology
200-299	Religion
300-399	Social sciences, Statistics, Customs, Etiquette, Folklore
400-499	Language
500-599	Natural sciences and Mathematics
600-699	Technology (Applied sciences), Manufacture
700-799	The Arts; Recreation and Performing arts
800-899	Literature and Rhetoric
900-999	History, Biography, Geography

Further subdivisions are also in groups of ten, for example:

300-309	Social sciences in general
310-319	Statistics
320-329	Political science
330-339	Economics
340-349	Law
350-359	Public administration and Military science
360-369	Social problems and services, Association

```
370-379   Education
380-389   Commerce, Communications, Transportation
390-399   Customs, Etiquette, Folklore
```

Still further subdivisions are in groups of one, for example:

```
370         Education
371           Schools and activities; Special education
372           Elementary education
373           Secondary education
374           Adult education
375           Curricula
[376 and 377 are left vacant in DDC 21 for future use]
378           Higher education
379           Public policy issues in education
```

Notational Structure

The DDC notation is, in general, "expressive," that is, it indicates, at least to the initiated, which notation (and therefore which concept) is a subdivision of which other concept: *378.11* is a subdivision of *378.1,* which is a subdivision of *378,* which is, in turn, a subdivision of *370-379,* which is a subdivision of *300-399.*

Decimal Numbers

Numbers divided beyond three figures become decimal numbers. This permits, at least theoretically, virtually infinite subdivision of any topic as the need arises.

```
378       Higher education
378.1       Organization and activities in higher education
378.11        Personnel management
378.111         Administrators
378.12        Faculty and teaching
378.124         Personal and professional qualifications
```

Figure 8.3 (page 218) shows selectively the resulting arrays as part of a hierarchical diagram.

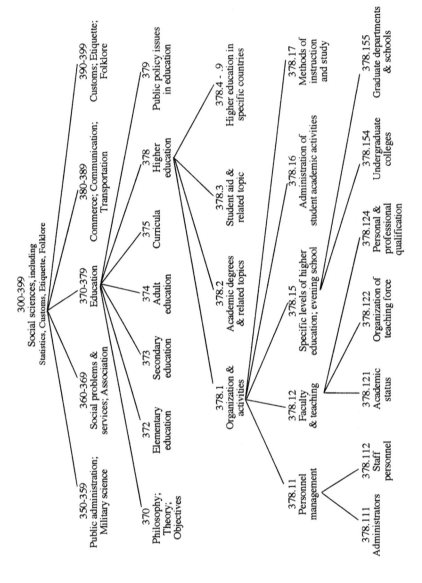

Figure 8.3. A highly selective table showing different levels in the DDC hierarchy of the social sciences (300-399).

Ability to Truncate and to Search Hierarchically

The truncation technique is commonly found in alphabetical retrieval systems. The truncation symbol is often "?" or "*" and, depending on the computer program, can stand for one or more characters. The DDC's hierarchical structure and expressive, decimal notation also permit effective truncation wherever these three features are consistent.

Right truncation (that is, truncating the right side of a notation) applied to an expressive notation allows a search to be extended or broadened. Using Figure 8.3 as an example, a shelflist search that began with the notation for *Administrators in institutions of higher education* (*378.111*) can be broadened by means of right truncation to *378.11?*, which would retrieve items with numbers *378.111* and *378.112*. Further right truncation will broaden the search to *378.1?*, asking, in effect, "What do you have in all arrays grouped under *378.1?* This means retrieval of works listed under

378.11, 378.111, 378.112

378.12, 378.121, 378.122, 378.124

378.15, 378.154, 378.155

378.16, and

378.17

but not works listed under 378.2, 378.3, etc. The search could be further expanded by truncating to *378?* and further to *37?*. Although *37?* would retrieve everything cataloged on Education, and *3?* would retrieve everything cataloged on the Social sciences, the field covered by them is so broad that such coverage would be rarely needed. Also, the quantity of material on such broad subjects suggests a need for some way of preventing extremely broad searches from being performed, possibly by limiting the number of items that can be retrieved in response to a truncated notation search, or by discouraging such a search by indicating the quantity of entries involved.

Assuming that the classification system and notation as well as the computer program permit hierarchical searching also, note that the search results will differ if the hierarchical searching technique is employed rather than the right truncation technique. Again using Figure 8.3 as an example, a search that starts with *378.111* and includes the directive, "Search the next higher level" results in retrieval of items listed under *378.11* but omits items listed under *378.111* and *378.112*. The directive, "Search the next higher level to *378.11*" results in a list of items classed under *378.1*, and the directive "Search under the next lower level to *378.11*" retrieves items listed under *378.111* and *378.112*.

Another difference between the truncating and hierarchical searching techniques is that, by definition, the former operates only "upward," that is, from a level to higher, that is, broader, levels of the classification system. Hierarchical searches, on the other hand, can be executed "upward" or "downward," that is, from a level to either broader or more specific levels, provided they exist.

The two techniques can cause dramatically different results. Depending on what is wanted, one or the other may be more helpful. The differences between the techniques are the same whether the shelflist or the classification schedule are searched. The one will result in a listing of documents, the other in a listing of class notations and their captions.

Standard Divisions: Form of Presentation, Geographical, and Time

The DDC permits addition to the number that expresses a document's topic of nontopical standard numbers that express the form in which the topic was presented, the geographical area to which it is limited, or other factors.

For example, *06* added to a topical number always means *An organization in that field;* adding -*0207* always means *Humorous treatment of the topic.* Adding -*0977583* to a topical number always means *That topic in Madison, Wisconsin,* -*097758* always means *In South Central Wisconsin,* -*09775* always means *In Wisconsin,* -*0977* always means *In North Central United States,* -*0973* always means *In the United States,* and so forth. In paper-based systems, the use of consistent numbers with the same meaning throughout the schedules is a mnemonic or memory aiding device. In automated systems it is potentially even more important and permits truncation and hierarchical searching. (The key terms in this connection are "consistent numbers" and "the same meaning.")

If the OPAC program and the notation's structure permit internal truncation, consistently applied standard subdivisions permit broadening a topical search while retaining limitations such as, "In country X" or "In the form of". Figure 8.4 illustrates this point. (It also contains exceptions to the standard patterns, described subsequently in this chapter in the section "Inconsistent Symbols and Meanings in DDC and OPACs.") Figure 8.4 is a different selective breakdown of DDC class 370 than that shown in Figure 8.3. In Figure 8.4 the notation for *Statistics of undergraduate colleges* is *378.154 021*, where *021* represents *Statistics.* If the user wants to broaden that topic without eliminating its statistics aspect, middle truncation, to *378.15?021*, will expand the topic to *378.154 021, 378.154 302 1* and *378.155 021.* Truncation to *378.?021* leads to topics *378.002 1, 378.013 021, 378.040 21, 378.154 021, 378.154 302 1,* and *378.155 021.*

If the OPAC program and the notation's structure permit right truncation, the searcher can broaden the geographical aspects of a topical question when using the DDC. Using Figure 8.4 again as an example, if the searcher wishes information on *Secondary education in Madison and Dane County, Wisconsin (373.775 83)* but does not find enough under this number, truncating to *373.775 8?* will broaden the search to *373.775 82 (Dodge County)* and *373.775 83 (Dane County).* Further right truncation to *373.775?* will expand the search to include, in addition, whole sections of the state (*373.775 3* and *373.775 8*). Still further right truncation to *373.77?* includes the states of *Wisconsin (373.775 3)* and *Missouri (373.778).* By now the search seems to be fairly far removed from the original search question, but additional right truncation to *373.7?* leads to *Secondary education in the USA (373.73)* as well as the totally unrelated *373.71 (Secondary education in Canada), 373.714 (Secondary education in Quebec),* and *373.72 (Secondary education in Mexico).* From a reference point of view, when using the right truncation technique, the most likely sources could be listed under *373.775 83 (Madison), 373.775 (Wisconsin),* and *373.73 (Secondary education in USA).* But it takes reference knowledge, including knowledge of classification policies and of a classification system, to decide whether truncation or hierarchical searching (or neither) is likely to answer a specific question efficiently. Either can be very effective.

370	Education (General)
370.21	Statistics [of education]
370.72	Research [on education]
372	Elementary education
373	Secondary education
373.020 7	Humorous treatment
373.021	Statistics [of secondary education]
373.021 8	Standards [in secondary education]
373.021 84	in Europe
373.021 842	in England
373.072	Research [on secondary education]
373.7	in North America [i.e. Sec. ed. in North Am]
373.71	in Canada
373.714	in Quebec
373.72	in Mexico
373.73	in USA [ie. Secondary educ. in USA]
373.775	in Wisconsin
373.775 3	in Wis. North eastern counties
373.775 8	in Wis. South central counties
373.775 82	in Dodge county
373.775 83	in Dane Co. incl. Madison
373.778	in Missouri
378	Higher education
378.002 1	Statistics [of higher education]
378.002 18	Standards [in higher education]
378.013	Professional education
378.013 021	Statistics [i.e., Statistics of prof. ed.]
378.04	Private colleges and universities
378.040 21	Statistics
378.1	Organization & activities in higher education
378.11	Personnel management [in higher education]
378.110 207	Humorous treatment [of pers. mgmt.in h. ed]
378.110 942	in England
378.110 973	in USA [ie.Pers mgmt in higher ed. in USA]
378.110 977	in North Central USA
378.110 977 5	in Wisconsin
378.110 977 58	in Wis. South Central counties
378.110 977 583	in Madison
378.15	Specific levels of higher education; evening school
378.154	Undergraduate colleges
378.154 021	Statistics
378.154 3	Junior colleges
378.154 302 1	Statistics
378.155	Graduate colleges and schools
378.155 021	Statistics
378.2	Academic degrees
378.73	in USA [ie., higher education in USA]
378.775	in Wisconsin

Figure 8.4. Selected DDC 370-379 (Education) numbers with selected form and geographic divisions. (The space following every third figure after the decimal point is a convention to make it easier for humans to read these numbers. It has no classification significance. Underlining in this figure is to clarify the meaning.)

For example, if the computer program and the notation permit left truncation, it would be possible to enter *?0942* to retrieve information about books that deal with a large range of subjects relative to Britain. Although this particular example may be unlikely because an excessive quantity of material might be retrieved, left truncation could be of use to the person interested in some less well-known or smaller part of the world, such as Angelina County in Texas. It would be interesting and useful, for example, to be able to check the OPAC of a national library and to retrieve all cataloged information about one particular region regardless of the subject.

The effectiveness of truncation and hierarchical searching is closely tied to the topic of the search as well as to a classification's structure and notational patterns. To cite two examples, in Figure 8.4, as previously mentioned, right truncation of *373.7?* for material on secondary education in a Wisconsin county leads to one possible source (*373.73*) and three unlikely ones (*373.71, 373.714,* and *373.72*). However, for a question on climate or commerce or any other topic that touches the entire North American continent, it would have led to three, rather than one, likely sources. Going back to Figure 7.2 (pages 164 and 165), in a search for all kinds of fishes, right truncation of *597?* will lead to the fishes but, because of the DDC's structure, will also retrieve cataloged items on amphibians (597.8) and reptiles (597.9). If such inconsistencies are to be avoided, the retrieval system must superimpose on the classification scheme other devices such as tags that label different sections of a notation or different parts of the schedule as, indeed, has been done.

Truncation and hierarchical searching usually broaden recall (that is, retrieve more items), albeit often at the expense of decreasing precision: Casting a wider net increases the chances of obtaining relevant documents that might otherwise have been missed; but it is also likely to increase the proportion of irrelevant documents obtained. In spite of acknowledged limitations, the overall assessment of truncation and hierarchical searching as retrieval devices is positive.

Standard Notational Patterns in Literature, Linguistics, History, and Geography

If consistently used, standard notational patterns permit truncation and in some cases hierarchical searching. Using *Literature* and *History* as examples, the following charts illustrate standard DDC notational patterns for the respective topics.

DDC literature symbols are composed of the following elements. The number for *Discipline of literature* remains, of course, the same, the numbers for the literary genre are consistent, while the numbers for the language and the period of creation vary with the literature.

Discipline of literature	Language of writing	Literary genre	Period of creation	Examples
8	2	1	.7	English poetry of the early nineteenth century: 821.7
8	3	2	.6	German drama of the classical period (1750-1830): 832.6
8	91.44	3	71	Bengali fiction of today: 891.44371

Internal truncation thus permits queries like the following:

```
83?4    for all types of German language literature of
        the Reformation period.
```

Internal and right truncation permits, for example,

```
8?1?    for all poetry in the collection, regardless
        of language or time period
```

The DDC history symbols are composed of the following elements:

Discipline of history	Continent	Country or place*	Historical period	Examples
9	4	4	.082	History of France during the Fourth Republic, 1945–1958: 944.082
9	4	4.36	082	History of Paris during the Fourth Republic, 1945–1958: 944.36082
9	4	9.4	06	History of Switzerland during the nineteenth century: 949.406
9	4	9.47	06	History of the Swiss alpine regions during the nineteenth century: 949.4706

* Subdivided as needed by smaller geographical units.

The historical time periods of a country and of its subdivisions are the same. Internal truncation thus permits queries like the following:

```
944?082     for the history of the various regions,
            towns, etc. of France during the Fourth
            Republic
```

SCROLLING AND HIERARCHICAL SEARCHING WITH NOTATIONS

Scrolling (also called "linear scrolling") the shelflist is the ability to read call numbers and the corresponding brief document descriptions in the order in which works are arranged on the shelves, as if standing in front of the shelves, that is, in "shelflist order," but without the restrictions of size or rarity that often result in rare and outsized books being shelved apart from regular books. Scrolling should permit looking at these call numbers in ascending and descending order (forward and backward scrolling). If, in addition to the shelflist (with call numbers), a classification's schedule (with class notations) is online, linking schedule and shelflist provides benefits. The schedule provides the structure, cross-references, scope notes, and directives that the shelflist is not equipped to furnish. Scrolling the schedules can enrich a search regardless of whether a notation has been used in a particular library.

Technically, the linkage is difficult to achieve. A system's ability to scroll notations and call numbers effectively depends on the software, the hardware, the classification systems structure—especially the structure of fairly narrow concepts—and the notation. Consistent structure and an expressive notation may help OPAC searchers to make their search effective and keep it within predictable, defined limits. Scrolling permits browsing and is for many users comfortable, but it can also be time-consuming before a desired specific subclass is reached. The menu approach, that is, hierarchical searching, usually provides a better initial overview and is probably best used at the beginning of a classed search, followed by scrolling once the desired specific array has been reached.

Hierarchical searching is the ability to move from one level of specificity of a given topic to the next broader (more general) level and/or to the next narrower (more specific) level. In this chapter "Hierarchical searching" means "Hierarchical searching by class number or by call number." Like scrolling, effective hierarchical searching depends on the software, the hardware, the classification system's structure, and the notation. Hierarchical searching of alphabetical terms such as subject headings is equally possible, provided the alphabetical system's structure is logical and, especially, consistent.

Although this chapter deals with classification, the presently envisaged ideal OPAC subject retrieval system integrates, or at least coordinates, retrieval vocabularies, both terms and structures. That is, it reaches a notation via a subject heading or a keyword taken from subject headings, class number captions or index terms; it uses the notation itself as a scrolling device; it uses notation or subject heading as an indicator of subject scope, subject hierarchies, and interrelationships; and it is a retrieval device either by itself or through the use of Boolean formulae, which combine a notation with another notation, subject headings, keywords, names, or other terms.

THE DDC AND OPACs

General Comments

The following subsections deal with the use of DDC as a searching and retrieval tool in OPACs. The ways in which the MARC program may alleviate or overcome some of DDC's and LCC's shortcomings as OPAC retrieval tools are discussed in a separate section at the end of this chapter.

Like any classification scheme, the DDC has advantages and disadvantages when examined with automation in mind. The following discussion attempts to describe its positive as well as negative characteristics for OPACs. In spite of its many excellent features, the DDC has disadvantages (Dahlberg 1977; Hill 1984; Maltby 1984). It is old, having been created more than a century ago, and then for a library which, by today's standards, would be regarded as very small. This makes it all the more remarkable that it has held up so well and is very effective in today's and, from all appearances, tomorrow's world.

Originally designed for filing bibliographic entries (document surrogates) in paper-based files, the DDC was developed for use by humans, primarily in shelf arrangement and to some extent in classed catalogs, not for use in a computer. Inconsistencies mattered less because humans are flexible. A classification scheme that is to be used as a retrieval device in an OPAC should be consistent in structure and notation, although inconsistencies can sometimes be circumvented by sophisticated algorithms or retrieval programs or tags that identify the various sections of a classification scheme and/or the component parts of a notation.

Although the DDC is in some respects a remarkably consistent scheme—far more so than the LCC—and its editors have been moving in recent editions toward increasing consistency, it still contains many inconsistencies that make the creation of menus, the display of arrays, browsing by means of scrolling, and the use of truncation not only less than automatic but often difficult to achieve. Also, although it has in several places a structure resembling the more versatile and precisely structured faceted classification schemes, and although its editors have introduced elements of faceting in a few selected instances, it is overwhelmingly enumerative, with the typical limitations of enumerative schemes.

The basic problem DDC shares with LCC and other classification schemes designed in pre-electronic days is the need to serve two masters of different abilities and limitations: Humans, who are flexible but have a limited attention span, ability to absorb, and patience; and computers, which are much less flexible but have an unflagging attention span, patience, and the ability to absorb. For example, long or complicated numbers are a problem for humans but not for computers; identical numbers (or words) with two different meanings are a problem for computers but much less so for humans.

Nevertheless, the DDC has a great deal in its favor as a bibliographic online organizing and retrieval device. Its flaws are the exception rather than the rule. They are far outweighed by its advantages. It is basically well designed, with a hierarchical structure and expressive notation that permit arrays; hierarchical searches; and right, internal, and left truncation. It is maintained and continuously developed by the Forest Press, whose parent organization, OCLC (Online Computer Library Center) is not known for betting on losing horses. It is a living scheme, which, within limits, keeps pace with progress, creating with each edition new class categories or adapting existing ones as needed. There is considerable quality control in the revision and updating of the scheme, based partly on advice and reactions from practicing librarians. Continuous efforts are also being made to make the scheme more international and more faceted. Last, but not least, from the early days of online retrieval, the DDC has also had strong advocates among researchers and experts in the field, and OCLC is conducting a continuous series of research projects intended to explore and improve DDC's usefulness online without neglecting its traditional roles.

DDC Structure and OPACs

■ The DDC obeys many logical principles of a well-designed classification scheme, for example, that the whole of a subject should precede its parts. But because it was created more than 100 years ago, its basic structure reflects the knowledge, attitudes, emphases, and political situation of that time. One example is the topic of Psychology (150-159), which is still placed in the middle of Philosophy (100-149, 160-169) instead of with Medicine and health (610-619), to which it belongs according to current thought. The use of arrays and scrolling is not aided by this structure.

- Because the DDC was created before many of today's scientific and technical achievements and before many of today's social concepts were developed, the scheme originally devoted proportionally far less space and detail to the social, pure, and applied sciences (300s, 500s, and 600s) than today's state of knowledge requires. However, new fields can be, and are being, inserted, thanks to the DDC's hospitality.

- The scheme's decimal notation permits the addition and insertion of new concepts as needed. The scheme is hospitable but, like all classification schemes, especially enumerative ones, makes it difficult to insert interdisciplinary fields without contortions or arbitrary decisions. This does not facilitate hierarchical searching.

- Because of the limited notational base of ten, the numbers resulting from inserting new concepts are often quite long (*581.760 73 Aquatic gardens*), which may be a problem for humans but not for computers. The notational base, however, also causes some new topics to be inserted in ways that cause problems in logical relationships and, therefore, online classed searching ability.

- The DDC is at least comparatively familiar to many librarians and information specialists and, to a lesser degree, to the public. Its decimal notation makes it relatively easy to be directed to specific topics, to see them in relation to related topics, and to remember favorite topics for future use.

The DDC Notation and OPACs

- The DDC notation has a numerical base of ten. Therefore, if the notation were to be truly expressive, each topic could be divided into no more than ten subgroups. Unfortunately, nature does not work that way. Among the more obvious areas where the subject has broken the bounds of ten are:

  — Life sciences, Biology (570-599): Conceptually, Plants (580-589) and Animals (590-599) are subdivisions of Life sciences, Biology, but the notations do not read that way.

  — Chemical engineering and related [manufacturing] technologies (660-689): Conceptually, this is one broad unit, subdivided into different types of manufacture, but the notations do not express, for example, that 685.22 (Manufacture of leather clothing and accessories) is a subdivision of 660.

Although such situations cause problems when the actual numbers are used to produce arrays, the problems usually can be solved through the use of menus or other devices.

- The DDC has, with some exceptions, an expressive notation in decimal form. The three factors—logic, expressive notation, and decimal numbers—facilitate hierarchical search and permit truncation.

- The DDC uses standard subdivisions, whereby to each subject, broad or specific (*Social sciences, Education, Secondary education, Teaching French in secondary schools*), can be added generally consistent symbols that indicate the format in which the subject is being treated or the geographic area with which it is concerned.

- The DDC uses mnemonics even in some of its topical numbers, particularly in *Literature (800-899)* and *Geography, Biography*, and *History (900-999)*. Although this is helpful for humans it is less so in an electronic environment partly because computers do not seem to need mnemonics as such and partly because the searching approach to a number is often through the words (subject headings, captions, keywords) that express that number's meaning.

Scrolling, Displays, Multiple Subjects, and OPACs

Although one can always quarrel with the logic of any classification scheme, the DDC is generally considered to be reasonably logical and effective for a general library in its grouping of related concepts and in its separation of unrelated ones. However, although it breaks down each major topic reasonably, the relationships among the major topics themselves are often tenuous. This is true for any classification scheme. For example, although the concepts of *Education* (370-379) and *Commerce* (380-389) (see Figure 8.3) are broken down more or less reasonably, there is little obvious logical connection between the last notations in the 370-379 group and the first few notations in the 380-389 group: *379.986 (Public education policy issues in Novaya Zemlya)* and *380.1 (Commerce)* are hardly logically connected. Scrolling of class notations or of entries in call number order should, therefore, be limited to searches within any one major topic, such as *Education*.

In the desired displays of hierarchical arrays, the standard divisions mentioned in connection with Figure 8.4 may cloud the overall picture for the person who is trying to learn where in this network the desired topic is located. In other words, for the person who sees a screen array resembling Figure 8.3, a clearer picture of the classification scheme may evolve if the display excludes, at least in some subjects, those notations and, therefore, arrays that indicate forms of presentation or geographic location. (Samples of such notations are shown in Figure 8.4.) In subjects in which the geographical aspects are major elements, such as history, geography, or trade and industrial laws in various countries, such arrays should, of course, be kept.

The reader may by now suspect that decisions such as how much scrolling is helpful or what should be included in an array are not always automatic or easy but often require judgment and individual decisions. The rest of this discussion should confirm that impression.

Like any enumerative scheme, the DDC suffers from the inability to assign a class number that truly reflects works relating to more than one field, such as "Effect of gasoline prices on automobile travel." By tradition and policy, if only one call number is assigned to such a work as a shelf location number, the work is classed under the topic affected, in the above case under *388.342 (Automobile travel)*. If the searcher looks, however, under *338.2328 (Prices in the oil and gas industry)* for such a topic, or scrolls looking for it, the work will not be found, in spite of the DDC's basically logical structure. This is *not* a flaw in the DDC but rather in the policies with which enumerative classification schemes are applied. The solutions to this problem depend on the total configuration of an OPAC's retrieval possibilities. Possible solutions range from multiple classification (assigning both class numbers, which would then be no longer shelf location numbers but retrieval numbers), to reliance on subject headings, to reliance on keywords in the title or subject headings or class number captions.

DDC Inconsistencies and OPACs

In an online system that permits broadening and narrowing a topical search by moving up and down the hierarchy and permits broadening a topical search through truncation, two of the most important features are a consistently logical structure and a consistently expressive notation. This requires that topics at any one level in the consistently logical hierarchy have a notation that has at least one more symbol at the end than the notation for the topic at the immediately more general level, as shown in Figure 8.5 (taken from DDC, 21st edition, 1996).

Although overall the DDC does quite well with respect to both logical structure and expressive notation, there are still quite a few exceptions that make truncation and hierarchical display based solely on the notation less than automatic and affect hierarchical online searches negatively. Three types of structural inconsistencies (missing links, unsought links, false links) and two types of notational inconsistencies (inconsistent symbols and inconsistent meanings) in the DDC are described in the following subsections. The same types (and others) are found in many other classification schemes.

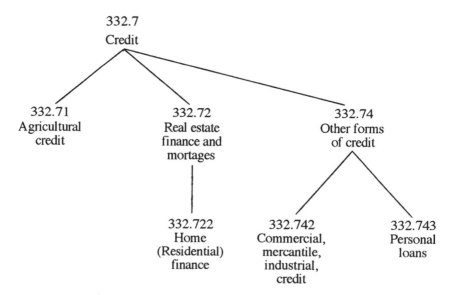

Figure 8.5. Example of an expressive notation that permits an automatic move to the next broader array by truncating the last figure on the right.

OPACs and Missing Links in DDC

In some places in the schedules, a step in the logical hierarchy was originally left out. It is difficult, especially in an online catalog, to do a classed search from a specific concept to the next broader one if that concept has no notational symbol. In the language of faceted classification specialists, this is the problem of the "missing link." Figures 8.6 and 8.7 show one of many examples of how the DDC editors have tried to solve this problem.

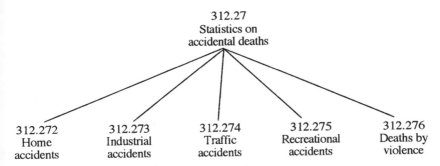

Figure 8.6. Breakdown of *312.27* in DDC, 16th edition, 1958.

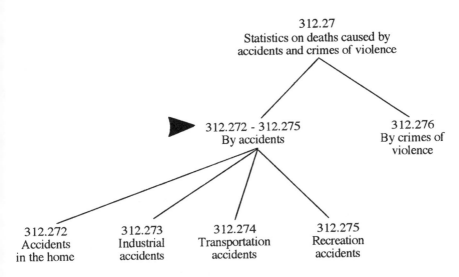

Figure 8.7. The more logical breakdown of 312.27 in DDC, 17th edition, 1965. The symbol ▶ indicates a new level of centered heading with its range of numbers.

In the 16th edition of the DDC (1958), the concept *Statistics on deaths caused by accidents and crimes of violence* was broken down directly into five subcategories, as shown in Figure 8.6: one category for *Crimes of violence* and four for specific types of accidents. There was no middle-level category for *Statistics on deaths caused by accidents*. With the 17th edition (1965), the editors wished to introduce a more logical theoretical structure. To do this, they had to add a new hierarchical level for *Statistics on deaths caused by accidents*, to balance *Statistics on deaths caused by crimes of violence*. But they also did not want to disturb the meanings of the existing numbers, possibly to save libraries, in this particular situation, from having to reclassify works already in their collection. They invented the concept of "centered headings" with a range of numbers and marked with the symbol ▶ in the margin (> since DDC, 20th edition, 1989).

This creates a logical structure, as shown in Figure 8.7, and permits effective display of arrays, but it does not permit right truncation to reach the next broader level. For example, dropping the second *3* in *312.273* (Figure 8.7) will not lead to the next broader array, but will cause a move to the second broader array. Also, because they are technically difficult to use in spite of their logic, the centered headings notations are never assigned and therefore cannot be used in recall. It would be far better if the notation were consistently expressive, rather than only most of the time. (Figure 8.5 illustrates an expressive notation, taken from DDC, 21st edition, 1996.)

OPACs and Unsought Links in DDC

"Unsought links" is also a term used by faceted classification specialists. These links occur when the notational chain involves a link whose terms should be ignored in the compilation of an alphabetical index because the terms do not lead to a recognizable or useful concept. One example is notations with captions for which no single natural language term exists. Such notations are often created for the sake of a logical hierarchical structure and are, therefore, useful for displaying arrays and for hierarchical searches, but the caption is not useful as a retrieval device. Notation *179* and its caption, in Figure 8.8, is an example: *Other ethical norms* is not a suitable index term, nor can that concept be described by other terms that are likely indexing terms.

Another example of an unsought link is the notation that has a caption consisting of two terms, each of which has its own notation. See, for example, notation *312.27* and its two subdivisions in Figure 8.7.

OPACs and False Links in DDC

False links can cause misleading hierarchical searches if the notation is used as the basis for arrays and truncation. A false link occurs when the notation indicates that one topic is subordinate to another when, in fact, this is not the case. Use of the notation to produce an array thus results in wrong answers, as shown in Figures 8.9 and 8.10. In Figure 8.9, the notation for *Portugal (946.9)* makes it appear to be a subdivision of *Spain (946)*. Use of the notation as a searching device for the query "Produce the array of *946, Spain*" shows Portugal erroneously as a region of Spain (DDC 1996). Likewise, in Figure 8.10 (page 232), use of the notation *597 (Fishes)* as a searching device for the query, "Produce the array for *597*" shows amphibians (*597.8*) and reptiles (*597.9*) as types of fishes. In both Figures 8.9 and 8.10, the indentions of the captions show correct relationships; the notations do not.

```
170        Ethics (Moral philosophy)
...
177             Ethics of social relations
177.1              Courtesy, politeness, hospitality
177.2              Conversation, gossip
177.3              Truthfulness, lying, slander, flattery
...
178             Ethics of consumption
178.1              Consumption of alcoholic beverages
178.7              Consumption of tobacco
...
179             Other ethical norms
179.1              Respect for life and nature
179.2              Treatment of children
179.3              Treatment of animals
...
179.6              Courage and cowardice
```

Figure 8.8. Number *179* illustrates a notation that is useful for arrays but whose caption does not furnish a helpful index term.

```
946        Iberian Peninsula and adjacent islands; Spain
           [This notation is used for works on Spain.]

946.1        Northwestern Spain, Galicia
946.2        Western Spain; León region
946.3        Castile

...

946.9      Portugal [Portugal is a separate country]
```

Figure 8.9. Example of a false link. *946.9* classes *Portugal* as a subdivision of *Spain* (*946*), which might surprise the Portuguese and makes hierarchical searching of the two notations problematical.

```
597              Cold-blooded vertebrates; Fishes
                 [This notation is used for works on Fishes.]

597.2               Agnatha (Jawless fishes)
597.3 - 597.7       [Specific kinds of fishes]
597.3                  Selachii, Holocephali, Saropteriygii
...
597.783                Tunas
597.8            Amphibia
597.9            Reptilia
```

Figure 8.10. Notationally, *597.8* and *597.9* are subdivisions of *597*, making *amphibia* and *reptilia* subdivisions of *fishes*. Because all three are on the same hierarchical level, the notations represent false links. That *597* has a double meaning and also stands for the next higher level (*Cold-blooded vertebrates*) of all three classes is another impediment to hierarchical searching by notation.

Although missing links, unsought links, and false links are problems, they can be ameliorated by various means such as menus, improved terminology in captions, tagging, or careful use of terms in the index, always with not only the input stage but also the output stage in mind: the cataloger/indexer as well as the end-user.

OPACs and Inconsistent Symbols and Meanings in DDC

In a faceted scheme, the notations for different facets use unique symbols. The operations facet may use symbols beginning with *A*, such as *A17*; the materials facet may use symbols beginning with *B*, such as *B17*. When these symbols are combined into one notation, they keep their uniqueness. Because this is impossible in an enumerative classification with a base of ten, identical DDC symbols sometimes carry different meanings. Moreover, to keep relationships logical, the standard subdivisions mentioned in connection with Figure 8.4 vary in length even for the same topic.

For example, although the symbol group *0941* always means *in Britain*, and *021* always means *statistical form of presentation*, other combinations may have the same meanings:

```
372.941 (instead of 372.0941): Elementary education in Britain
335.00941 (instead of 335.0941): Socialism in Britain
338.43000941 (instead of 338.430941): Prices for secondary
  industries in Britain
666.321 (instead of 666.3021): Statistics on pottery
629.450021 (instead of 629.45021): Statistics on manned space
  flight
```

Conversely, the symbols *-41* and *-21* do not uniquely and invariably represent *Britain* and *Statistics.*

```
629.41:   Space flight
631.41:   Soil chemistry
635.921:  Plant diseases caused by environmental factors
821:      English poetry
```

Overcoming DDC Inconsistencies

The previous subsections of this chapter may well have created the impression that the DDC is not particularly useful for automated retrieval. It was, after all, created for human use at a time when inconsistencies mattered less because humans are flexible, and it does have the inherent limitations of a basically hierarchical system. However, this very hierarchical structure, combined with an expressive notation, actually melds well with the flexibility that electronics permit.

In addition to the reasons cited earlier for using DDC as a searching tool in an OPAC environment, one of the most encouraging factors is the imaginative research program that Forest Press classificationists and OCLC researchers are conducting to not only increase DDC's usefulness online but also to link it to other indexing vocabularies: "In 1996 five areas of classification research were identified and targeted for focus: (1) Developing customizable views of the DDC; (2) Enhancing links to other thesauri; (3) Improving links to DDC editions in other languages; (4) Transforming the captions into end user language; (5) Decomposing numbers and using component parts for improved access" (Vizine-Goetz 1996, 1).

One research project reported is the "OCLC NetFirst browsing capability," which uses the structure of DDC but not its class numbers to provide end-user access to the complete NetFirst database. Access is by words that represent concepts from the first, second, and third DDC summaries and permit (at this early stage still rudimentary) hierarchical searches. The point is that topics are accessed and found in classed rather than in alphabetical subject heading order, enabling users to retrieve relevant items that might not be as easily discovered using traditional keyword searching capabilities. Figure 8.11 (page 234) lists the first-level search terms on NetFirst that correspond to the ten main classes in the first DDC summary. Once a main class (or first-level search term), such as *Health, Home, Technology*, has been selected, a subsection (or second-level search term), such as *Health and Medicine*, can be chosen, followed by a further sub-subsection, as shown in Figure 8.12 (page 235).

Other research and demonstration projects reported include a project to provide multilingual access to a set of records, the mapping of LC subject headings to DDC numbers in the DDC 1996 database, linking the DDC with still other subject access systems, and using various techniques to browse by DDC class. Some projects have cutesy names, but that should not detract from their significance as important steps toward making DDC more effective in an electronic environment and toward linking different indexing languages and vocabularies to advance subject retrieval.

NetFirst First Level Browse Categories	Corresponding DDC Classes
Arts, Recreation, Sports	700-799
Books, Computers, Internet	000-099
Economics, Education, Society	300-399
Genealogy, Geography, History	900-999
Health, Home, Technology	600-699
Language & Linguistics	400-499
Literature	800-899
Philosophy, Psychology, Paranormal	100-199
Religion	200-299
Sciences & Mathematics	500-599

Figure 8.11. First level search terms on NetFirst. In spite of somewhat different terminology, these correspond to the ten main classes in the first DDC summary. Although listed in roughly alphabetical order they lead to classed groups of subjects which can be further broken down in classed order. *Source:* Adapted from Vizine-Goetz 1996, 2.

An important tool to help overcome many inconsistencies in any classification system, including the DDC, is the *MARC 21 Format for Classification Data*, (MARC 21 cf) described in Chapter 2, and, with respect to its searching potential, at the end of this chapter. In effect, it superimposes a consistent structure on the classification system itself. As of this writing, it is used primarily for input rather than both input and retrieval. Needed is not only development of techniques but especially a willingness on the part of library science and information professionals to use the full range of retrieval possibilities once they are truly integrated: controlled alphabetical, controlled classed, and uncontrolled vocabularies. Just as important is a willingness on the part of library administrators to accept the undoubtedly greater expense of inputting original classification numbers and subject headings conscientiously and fully.

The most correct DDC standard form divisions or geographical qualifiers, the most precise class notations, are not useful searching devices unless they are put into the system precisely and correctly by staff well trained in coding as well as in cataloging. Once budgets are no longer divided on the basis of "input expenses" (technical services) versus "retrieval expenses" (public services), once it is realized that now more than ever optimum retrieval is only possible with precise bibliographic input, these ongoing expenses may be easier to accept and to justify. They should not be an insurmountable obstacle to a profession that has become used during the past forty years to spending millions of dollars on special projects: in the 1960s and 1970s by converting many academic libraries from DDC to LCC; in the 1970s and 1980s by

NetFirst: Second-Level Browse Catalogies, Subcategory Illustrated:	Corresponding DDC Classes
Health, Home, Technology	
Agriculture, Gardening, Pets	630-639
Building Construction	690-699
Business and Management	650-659
Chemical Engineering	660-699
Engineering	620-629
Home, Family, Food	640-649
Health and Medicine	610-619
Manufacturing (by Product	660-669
Manufacturing (by Material)	670-689
Technology	600-699

Figure 8.12. *Health and Medicine* **as an example of second-level search terms on NetFirst.** Searchers who selected *Health, Home, Technology* from the listing in Figure 8.11 will see the above display. If interested in health concerns for travelers they can search under *Health and Medicine* (*610-619*) and refine further to the most specific sublevel *Travel and Tourism* (*613.68; 616.9802*). *Source:* Adapted from Vizine-Goetz 1996, 2.

converting retrospectively to the MARC bibliographic format; in the 1980s by "retrospective conversion" to AACR2 entry heading style; and since the 1970s by purchasing ever newer and more powerful, but short lived, computers and computer programs.

RELOCATIONS: A PROBLEM FOR ANY LIVING CLASSIFICATION SCHEME

For users of any living classification scheme—enumerative like DDC or LCC, or synthetic like UDC or the Colon Classification—a big obstacle to consistent retrieval is that, over the years, the locations and notations for many concepts were changed (although Dewey promised—optimistically and naively—in the second edition of the DDC that, once a notational symbol had been used for a topic, it would always represent that topic and, conversely, the topic would be represented only by that notational symbol). This principle of the "integrity of numbers" had great appeal, partly because it was made at a time when librarians who used the then-customary "fixed location" method of shelf-bound classification had to reclassify their collections from time to time to accommodate growth.

Integrity of numbers has two effects. First, once a work has been given a symbol, that symbol will not have to be changed, because it will continue to appear in later editions of the classification scheme and will, therefore, be used for new books on the same subject. Second, patrons who search for a topic will find both old and new material on that topic in one place. The problem with this principle is that knowledge does not stand still. As fields of learning develop and change, the classification schemes representing these fields must change. There is a need for notational hospitality: insertion of new concepts, deletion of outdated concepts, realignments, and divisions. Therefore, notational symbols may have to be changed if new topics are to have a logical home and if a helpful and current arrangement of the schedules, of the books on the shelves, and of the entries in a classed file is to be achieved. New discoveries, inventions, and changing relationships within agriculture, or astronomy and astrophysics, or sociology, or pharmacology, are examples of how much topics and relationships can change in the course of a few decades.

Under pressure for more standardization for the sake of effective electronic retrieval, DDC has also changed in recent years many synthesized numbers that include form or other divisions to create more uniformity. For the same reason, and after much soul searching, LC began in the late 1990s to standardize some of the many "tables" it uses to complete notations. Primarily for the same reason efforts were stepped up in the 1990s to update the UDC (1993) and make it more consistently faceted.

The introduction of a new class number means either that a new concept is introduced or that a concept that formerly formed part of another notation now has a new, separate spot. As a corollary, when the notational symbols are changed in new editions of a classification schedule, old and new books on a topic will not necessarily be shelved together or listed together in a classed arrangement.

Most numerical changes between DDC editions involve only single numbers, such as moving *Manufacture of sweaters* from *687.38* in DDC's 18th edition (DDC 1971) to *687.146* in the 19th edition (1979). There were 341 relocations in the 19th edition of DDC, and approximately 900 relocations and about 400 "reductions" (shifting a topic to a number shorter than the old one, but not otherwise differing from it) in the 20th edition (1989). LCC also adds and deletes numbers frequently, although less obviously. For example, in 1987 LCC introduced 3,698 new class numbers and deleted 452 class numbers. In 1988, it introduced 3,872 new class numbers and deleted 457 existing class numbers. Occasionally, DDC changes whole sections from one DDC edition to the next to reflect basic changes, or basic expert approaches, in a topic. (For some editions DDC referred to basically changed sections as *Phoenix* schedules.) For example, in the 21st edition (1996) the *570-599* section (*Life sciences; Biology*) was entirely restructured, and *370-379* (*Education*) was extensively revised. LCC has made few basic changes to whole sections in the past, although increasing use of class numbers for retrieval purposes may make them more desirable.

The relocations of individual topics, the introduction of new notations, and the deletion of old notations have a profoundly negative effect on the thoroughness of subject searches, both manual and automated. Because libraries cannot reclassify substantial portions of their holdings whenever a new DDC edition is published or whenever a new quarterly issue of *LC Classification Additions and Changes* appears, they either reclassify very selectively or not at all. Although most patrons are not aware of it, this means that a searcher who finds a suitable class symbol has a fair chance of finding only recent material, or only older material, or only part of the topic that is being searched. This is not conducive to thorough, or especially to historical, research.

Especially invidious are partial relocations, that is, changes in which the notation remains but part of its meaning has been altered, so that the user who looks at the shelves, or at the entries in a classed file, does not realize that the total number of entries under one class number really represents two different subject concepts. Figure 8.13 (page 238) illustrates how DDC numbers *792.7, 792.8, 792.82, 793.3,* and *793.32* remained as notations but with a scope that changed considerably among the 19th, 20th, and 21st editions. For example, *792.8* took on a much wider meaning in the 20th edition and then a somewhat more restricted meaning in the 21st; *793.3* took on a different meaning in the 20th edition; the topic of *793.32* in the 19th edition was moved elsewhere in the 20th and again elsewhere in the 21st; *792.324* from the 19th edition was split into two other numbers for the 20th. Users are typically unaware of such changes, and their search results therefore are often less effective than they could be.

Figure 8.14 (page 239) illustrates various levels of full and partial relocations in LCC. As in DDC, hundreds of such relocations occur every year as, indeed, they must in any living classification scheme. Many are minor, such as the first example in which the part of the notation standing for *James Ward* was changed from *W3* to *W33*. Many LCC numbers changed meaning to permit more precise breakdown of a topic, as in the examples for *HD 1529* and *HD 9707*. Some changes, however, are more basic and represent a change in approach to a topic. One such example is the topic *Computer stores,* which was moved from *HF 5468.2* (part of *Business*) to *HD 9696.2* (part of *Special industries and trades*). Another is the topic of *Tax evasion,* which was moved from *HJ 2348.5* (part of *Taxation*) and split between the legal and criminal aspects of tax evasion, *K 4486* and *HV 6341-6344*.

The LCC policy change that involved undoubtedly the largest number of volumes is in the field of literature. For many decades LC, with few exceptions, had grouped fiction written or translated into English into one collection arranged alphabetically by author in two groups: under notations *PZ 3* for fiction writers who began publishing prior to 1951 and *PZ 4* for fiction writers publishing after 1951. It was, in effect, an international fiction browsing collection in English, in two groups, each of which was arranged alphabetically by author. Nonfiction literary works, such as poetry, and fiction written in a foreign language, were classed with the literature of the respective language, such as *PC 1001-1977* for *Italian literature*, *PE* for *English literature*, or *PL 1001-3207* for *Chinese literature*. In 1980, LC abandoned the concept of the *PZ 3-4* browsing collection of fiction written or translated into English and began classing all fiction with the respective literature classes, an arrangement more suitable to a research library. (Large academic libraries that did not want to go to the expense of reclassing and reshelving tens of thousands of volumes had to split their fiction collection, which did not help shelf browsing.)

Users doing a subject search must be unusually sophisticated and alert to recognize such scope changes in a class notation. The problem has existed for more than a century. Online catalogs are likely to show it more clearly but can, if properly programmed, also provide the necessary linking between old and new notations. (The potential exists in the MARC program.) This will involve an enormous amount of historical research, and will probably be economically feasible only if the linking is done once and for all by the organization responsible for the classification scheme, on the basis of its schedules, rather than individually by each library on the basis of its own classifications decisions (which are hard to trace in any case). This means that the wording linking old and new notations must be cautious, because a library may or may not have reclassified its older works or may or may not have used the new notation for newer works. For example:

```
134      (Hypnotism) changed in 1965 to 154.7.
         Works published after 1965 are likely to be
         classed 154.7.

154.7    (Hypnotism): Prior to 1965 classed as 134.
         Works published prior to 1965 are likely to be
         classed 134.
```

Situations in which a concept is transferred from one notation to more than one new notation are even more tricky. For example, *656 (Transportation and railroading)* became the range of *385-388* in the 15th edition of DDC (1951). LCC notation *HJ 2348.5* represents such a split, which distributed the original concept among two disciplines, as shown in Figure 8.14.

Constant Class Notation	DDC 19th Edition	DDC 20th Edition	DDC 21st Edition
792.7	- - - - - - - - - - -	Tap dancing	Variety shows and theatrical dancing
792.78	- - - - - - - - - - -	- - - - - - - - - - -	Theatrical dancing; Tap dancing
792.8	Ballet	Ballet, ballet dancing; Comprehensive works on dancing; Modern dance; Theatrical dancing	Ballet; Comprehensive works on dancing; Modern dance
792.82	Ballet dancing	Choreography	Choreography
793.3	Dancing; Comprehensive works on dancing	Social, folk, national dancing	Social, folk, national dancing
793.32	Theatrical dancing	Clog dancing	Clog dancing
792.324	Tap and clog dancing	- - - - - - - - - - -	- - - - - - - - - - -

Figure 8.13. Examples of full and partial relocations in DDC over three editions. Most notations in this example continued to exist, but their meanings changed.

Constant Class Number	LCC 1989	LCC 1998
	English philosophy	English philosophy
B 1674.W3	Ward, James	--------------
B 1677.W33	--------------	Ward, James
	LCC 1980	**LCC 1982**
	Agricultural laborers	Agricultural laborers
HD 1529	Canada	Canada: General works
HD 1530	--------------	By region or province, A-Z
HD 1531	Other American regions or countries, A-Z	Other American regions or countries, A-Z
	LCC 1980	**LCC 1983**
HD 9707	Optical goods	Optical goods: General works
HD 9707.5	--------------	Special equipment, A-Z
		.S73-734 Stereoscopes
	LCC 1991	**LCC 1998**
	Commerce: Business	
HF 5468	Branch stores. Chain stores	--------------
HF 5468.2	Computer stores	--------------
		Economics: Special industries & trades
HD 9696.2	--------------	Computer stores
	LCC 1991	**LCC 1997**
	Revenue. Taxation.	
HJ 2348.5	Tax evasion: General works	--------------
HJ 2348.6	US: General works	--------------
HJ 2348.63	US: By state, A-W	--------------
HJ 2348.7	Other countries, A-Z	--------------
K 4486	--------------	Tax evasion: Law
HV 6341-6344	--------------	Tax evasion: Criminology

Figure 8.14. Various levels of full and partial relocations in LCC.

SUBJECT NOTATIONS
AND LOCATION NOTATIONS

From an administrative viewpoint it is desirable to have notations which, once assigned to a document, need not change as the scheme itself changes. It is very time-consuming and expensive to change existing notations manually on large numbers of paper-based records and on the physical documents themselves. So far as the internal operations of OPACs are concerned, this point is less significant. Although it will always be necessary to add or change notations by hand on paper-based documents and bibliographic records, notations in electronic documents and in electronic bibliographic records can be changed globally, that is, simultaneously, without inspecting them individually—at least in some situations, and subject to the restraints of the classification scheme, the computer program employed, and the computer itself. Within the foreseeable future the most likely situation for libraries will be that class notations can be changed globally in the OPAC in at least some cases but must in all cases be changed by hand on the actual physical documents.

Global changes are feasible when a relocation does not involve a change in scope and is not part of a revision of a whole field. However, when one existing group is to be reclassified into two or more different groups, global reclassification is usually impossible, even in OPACs. It will usually be necessary to inspect every document individually to decide to which of the two or more new classes it belongs. In the future it may be possible to make even such changes globally, especially in electronic documents, based on word frequency counts in the various documents and/or on association of clusters of subject headings with the older class notation, but these techniques need more development, and considerable skepticism exists about their validity.

Regardless of whether global changes are possible electronically, it is more economical if corresponding changes do not need to be made on the physical documents themselves. This implies that it may be desirable for documents to have two notational symbols: one describing the document's subject, used for electronic display and retrieval of the bibliographic record and updated as the classification scheme changes; and another, permanent one, a *call number*, for shelving or filing and for retrieving the document itself. This is not a new concept, although it is seldom put into practice in North America. One rare exception is technical reports in microform, which are numbered, and typically shelved, in sequential issuing order regardless of subject. In "Subject Notation and Call Numbers" in Chapter 7 this idea was mentioned in connection with saving space. Here, it is mentioned in connection with keeping the classification system up-to-date. However, it does not avoid the necessity of examining at least the bibliographic record, and usually also the physical document, whenever global changes are not feasible.

CHARACTERISTICS OF THE LCC

The LCC began to be developed some twenty years after the DDC was introduced to the public in 1876; most of its schedules were developed between 1898 and 1910. Unlike the DDC, it was not designed as a theoretical scheme suitable for all general libraries but rather as an in-house scheme designed to reflect the emphases and purposes of the Library of Congress. As a result, it devotes proportionally greater space to the social sciences, especially history, political science, and law, and relatively little space to philosophy, religion, and the humanities. It also breaks down some subjects in ways more attuned to its own mission than to the needs of a publicly accessible open-stacks library. The Librarian of Congress was rather astonished when, soon after the scheme began to be developed, other libraries began to express an interest in it (Miksa 1984, 39).

Like the DDC, the LCC is an enumerative scheme but, unlike the DDC, LCC has no synthetic features whatsoever. It is probably the most enumerative general scheme ever published. Its enumerativeness and detail are shown by the fact that all of its printed schedules together take up about 3 1/2 *feet* of shelf space, whereas the four volumes of DDC's 21st edition (1996), including over 300 pages of a classification manual, take up only 6 1/2 *inches.* Also, unlike the DDC, the LCC notation is basically nonexpressive.

System Structure

The LCC uses a mixed notation of letters and numbers, and is divided into the following twenty-one classes.

A	General works
B	Philosophy; Religion
C	History: Auxiliary sciences
D	History: General and Old World
E-F	History: America
G	Geography; Anthropology; Folklore, etc.
H	Social sciences
J	Political science
K	Law
L	Education
M	Music
N	Fine arts
P	Philology and literature
Q	Science
R	Medicine
S	Agriculture
T	Technology
U	Military science
V	Naval science
Z	Bibliography; Library science

Each class, with the exception of classes *E, F,* and *Z,* is divided by a second, and sometimes also by a third, letter into subclasses. Class *Q,* for example, is divided into:

Q	Science (General)
QA	Mathematics
QB	Astronomy
QC	Physics
QD	Chemistry
QE	Geology
QH	Natural history (General), Biology (General)
QK	Botany
QL	Zoology
QM	Human anatomy
QP	Physiology
QR	Microbiology

Typically, the second letter indicates a subdivision of the main topic. For example, *QC* (*Physics*) is a subdivision of *Q* (*Science*), and the notation is to that extent expressive. But there are exceptions. For example, *HC* and *HD*, representing different aspects of *Economic history and conditions,* are conceptually part of *Economics,* which is, however, also represented by a two-figure notation, *HB.*

Although each schedule (letter) of LCC is structured on the basis of the subject concerned, a general arrangement pattern of seven categories does exist within each schedule. The first six categories deal with aspects of the topic as a whole: the physical format in which it is being treated—such as serials, collections of articles, or dictionaries—or the manner in which the topic is discussed—the philosophy of the topic, the study and teaching of the topic, general works on the topic, laws and regulations on the topic, or juvenile works on the topic. The seventh category consists of topical subdivisions, such as *The brain* as a subsection of the section *The nervous system,* which is, in turn, a subsection of *Human anatomy.* Many topical subdivisions are themselves subdivided by their own seven categories.

Notational Structure

Further Subdivision by Sequential Cardinal Numbers

Within each subclass notations are numbered by sequential cardinal, rather than decimal, numbers from 1 to approximately 9999. The subclass *QC* (*Physics*), for example (which does not go as high as approximately 9999), consists of the following major divisions:

QC 1-75	Physics in general
QC 81-114	Weights and measures
QC 120-168.85	Descriptive and experimental mechanics

QC 170-197	Atomic physics. Constitution and properties of matter
QC 221-246	Acoustics. Sound
QC 251-338.5	Heat
QC 350-467	Optics. Light
QC 474-496.9	Radiation physics (General)
QC 501-766	Electricity and magnetism
QC 770-798	Nuclear and particle physics. Atomic energy. Radioactivity
QC 801-809	Geophysics. Cosmic physics
QC 811-849	Geomagnetism
QC 851-999	Meteorology, Climatology.

QC 811-QC 849 (*Geomagnetism*), for example, is divided as shown in Figure 8.15 (pages 244-45). When the notational base gets squeezed over the years by insertion of too many new topics, the system sometimes employs decimal numbers, but not in a hierarchical sense. In other words, in Figure 8.15, *QC 815.2* is not viewed notationally or conceptually as a subdivision of *QC 815*. Sometimes the decimal numbers happen to be in a location where they could have hierarchical value, as with *QC 825* and *QC 825.1-QC 825.7*, but this is purely accidental, and *QC 825.75 is* conceptually hardly a subdivision of *QC 825.7*. LCC's notation reflects order but is basically non-expressive.

Further Alphabetical Subdivision

In the 1870s Charles Ammi Cutter developed an alphanumeric system to arrange books within one class alphabetically by main entry heading, that is, usually by author. Libraries that classify by DDC use these Cutter numbers, or an adaptation called Cutter-Sanborn numbers, each of which has its own authority list or authority table. (Cutter 1901; Sanborn 1896). The Cutter and Cutter-Sanborn numbers are preceded by a real or imaginary period and are therefore read as decimal numbers, so that, for example *.R59* precedes *.R6*. Frequently referred to as "author numbers," they are followed in libraries that class by DDC by one or more letters, which stand for the work's title and are called the workmark. LCC does not use workmarks but uses other devices for subarranging works by one author within one class.

The Library of Congress adapted the system but uses its own "Cutter" tables. Typical LCC call numbers consist of a class number followed by a "Cutter" number for the main entry heading and by the year of publication, such as *BF 1597* (class number) *.F76* (Cutter number) *1881* (year of publication) for a work by Thomas Frost on magicians. Unlike libraries using the DDC, LCC uses its Cutter numbers not only for author sequence within one class but quite frequently also for further subdivision of the class. Although such subdivision is part of the class number, it does not follow classification principles but is subject to "the accident of the alphabet." These Cutter numbers are followed by a second Cutter number, which usually stands for the main entry heading, resulting in "double Cutter numbers." In some cases even the second part of a double Cutter number is, instead, part of the classification system and stands

GEOMAGNETISM

Cf. QC 750+, Magnetism; QE 501.4.P35, Paleomagnetism

QC 811	Periodicals, societies, congresses, serial collections, yearbooks
.15	Collected works (Nonserial)
813	History
814	Early works through 1800
	General works, treatises, and textbooks
815	1801-1969
.2	1970-
.5	Juvenile works
.7	Addresses, essays, lectures
816	Special aspects of the subject as a whole
	Observatories
818.A2	General works
818.A5-Z	By region or country, A-Z
819	Instruments and apparatus, including magnetometer
820	Technique. Instruction for observers
820.6	Data processing
821	Handbooks, tables, formulas, etc.
822	Maps and mapping, including construction, use, and interpretation of maps
	Magnetic surveys: Geographic areas are not subdivided by country
825	General works
.1	North America
.2	Mexico, Central America, and West Indies
.3	South America
.4	Europe
.5	Asia
.6	Africa
.7	Australia
.75	New Zealand

Figure 8.15. Detailed breakdown of *Geomagnetism* (*QC 811-QC 849*).

.8	Arctic regions
.9	Antarctica
826.A-Z	Oceanic areas, A-Z
	Geomagnetic field (Analysis and theory)
827	General works
828	Secular variation
830.A-Z	Magnetic observations. By name of issuing observatory, A-Z
831	Diurnal variation
833	Other periodic variations
835	Magnetic disturbances, including magnetic storms
	Geomagnetism and related aspects
836	Sunspot periods
837	Eclipses
839	Meteorological phenomena
841	Geological structure
843	Earthquakes
845	Earth currents
849	Deviation of the magnetic compass and other magnetic instruments.
	Magnetism of ships and aircraft.
	Cf. TL 589.2.C6, Aeronautical instruments
	Cf. VK 577, Nautical instruments

for still further subdivision of the class number. Because LC has a long-standing policy against more than two Cutter numbers (except for maps in Class G), the author's name is not represented in a double Cutter call number in which both Cutter numbers stand for the class.

Alphabetical subdivision in LCC may be by topic, geography, language or nationality, or other attributes. Figure 8.16 illustrates subdivision by geography and by topic. The two examples below the horizontal line in Figure 8.16 are complete call numbers using double Cutter numbers. In the last example both Cutter numbers are part of the class number; in the next to the last example the second Cutter number represents the main entry heading and is, therefore, not part of the class number.

LB 2802	(Administration of institutions of higher education in individual U.S. cities) is subdivided alphabetically by city. Therefore:
	LB 2802 .C5 ... in Cincinnati, Ohio
	LB 2802. D3 ... in Dallas, Texas
BF 575	(Special forms of emotion) is subdivided alphabetically by emotion. Examples:
	BF 575 .A5 Anger
	BF 575 .B3 Bashfulness
	BF 575 .H4 Helplessness
	and so on through Narcissism, Repentance, Stress, etc.
QD 181	(Individual inorganic chemical elements) is subdivided alphabetically by the chemical element's name. Examples:
	QD 181 .A6 Argon
	QD 181 .C5 Chlorine
	QD 181 .H4 Helium
	QD 181 .K6 Krypton
	QD 181 .Z7 Zirconium
JN 5985	(Political parties in the Netherlands) is subdivided by party name. Examples:
	JN 5985 .C3 The (Dutch) Catholic Party
	JN 5985 .N3 The (Dutch) National Socialist Party

JN 5985 .N3 J6 1968	*Het national-socialisme in Nederland: voorgeschiedenis ontstaan en ontwikkeling,* by A. A. Jonge. 1968.
D 639 .P7 C24 1996	*Propaganda and censorship during Canada's great war,* by Jeff Keshen. 1996.

Figure 8.16. Examples of LCC topical and geographic subarrangement in alphabetical rather than classed order.

In Figure 8.16, above the horizontal line are class notations to which second Cutter numbers would be added for the main entry heading, plus the number for the year of publication. Below the horizontal line are complete call numbers using double Cutter numbers. In *JN 5985 .N3 J6 1968*, the *N3* is part of the classification and stands for the (Dutch) National Socialist Party; the second Cutter number, *J6*, represents the author, *Jonge*. In *D 639 .P7 C24 1996*, both Cutter numbers are part of the class notation: *P7* stands for *Propaganda* and *C24* represents the geographic subdivision, *Canada*. LCC does not add a third Cutter number for the main entry heading, except for maps.

Tables

To save space in the printed LCC schedules for recurring patterns of subdivisions LCC makes extensive use of tables. Some tables are applicable to only a small section of a class, others to an entire class, and still others generally throughout the system. These tables subdivide a subject topically (that is, by subject), by geographic area, by time period, by form, or by type of material. Some tables subarrange works by and about individual authors or artists. The notations in different tables are applied differently: Some are appended to a base number, others are added mathematically to a base number. For input purposes knowledge of how to apply these tables is essential. An excellent, detailed description and instructions for their use appear in Lois Mai Chan (1999). This chapter focuses on whether they influence OPAC ability to, for example, search hierarchically by LCC call number.

Notations in LCC tables are generally of two types: Cutter numbers, which are intended to subarrange works alphabetically by topic, form, geographic area, and so forth; and arabic numbers, which are designed to subarrange works within a topic in designated subgroups. Figure 8.17 (page 248) shows selected examples of Cutter numbers and arabic numbers taken from applicable tables.

Hospitality

The LCC scheme is hospitable; that is, it permits insertion of new topics by means of gaps in the lettering and in the numbering. In the main classes, letters *I, O, X,* and *Y* have not been used, and gaps are also left in many subclasses. For example, *TB, TL,* and *TM* are blank. Also, the use of further subdivision of subclasses through a third letter could be expanded. Gaps also exist in the numerical sequences, and nonhierarchical decimal numbers are used when needed, as illustrated in Figure 8.15.

Since the Middle Ages, librarians have sometimes provided for expansion by means of gaps in sequential numbering or lettering, usually finding themselves out of room after some time. But, the gaps, along with LC's not always logical structure and nonhierarchical notation, can come in handy. For example, between 1950 and the 1980s, *HD 9696* (*Electronic industries*) was created between *HD 9695* (*Electrical machinery and supplies*) and *HD 9697* (*Electrical industries*) with a potentially unlimited number of specific subtopics (from *Audio equipment industry—HD 9696. A923* to *Vacuum tubes—HD 9696 .V33*) without disturbing any adjoining numbers. As the Classification Committee of the American Library Association's Resources and Technical Services Division reported approvingly in 1964: "LCC has the advantage of not being logical in exposition, as a rule, and while it is practically impossible

BF 1434	(Occult sciences in specific areas) uses appended Cutter numbers (taken from the "Regions and Countries Table") to subdivide alphabetically by region or country.
BF 1434.G8	Occult sciences in Greece
BF 1434 .I74	Occult sciences in Islamic countries

PN 5201-5220	(Journalism in Germany) uses numbers taken from the applicable table and added mathematically to *PN 5200* for further subdivision. In the table 8 is the number for *20th century journalism*, and *14. T4* is the number for television journalism.
PN 5208	(20th century journalism in Germany)
PN 5214 .T4	(Television journalism in Germany)

Biographies of individuals are assigned a class number usually based on the person's specialty, to which a Cutter number is appended based on the person's name. In one of several applicable tables an alphanumeric symbol is added to the resulting number to indicate the type of biographical material. Examples: *A3* (Autobiography, diaries, etc.); *A4* (Letters), both subarranged by date; *A6-Z* (Biography and criticism), subarranged by author.

Z 720 .M67 A3 1970	Mohberg, Nora Fladeboe. *After you, Andrew*. [an autobiography by a librarian].
Z720 .H26 $35	Scott, Edith. *J. C. M. Hanson and his contribution to twentieth-century cataloging*. [A biography of Hanson by Scott]

Figure 8.17. Examples of three different types of LCC tables that use Cutter numbers and/or arabic numbers. Other techniques of applying tables to a basic number, or span of numbers, exist.

to memorize, it is easy to expand without upsetting existing classified books. The advantage of nonlogical classification is apparent in dealing with rapidly advancing subjects" (Statement on types . . . 1965).

LCC AND OPACs

General Comments

The following subsections deal with the use of LCC as a searching and retrieval tool in OPACs. The ways in which the MARC 21 classification format may alleviate or overcome some of LCC's and DDC's shortcomings as OPAC retrieval tools are discussed in a separate section at the end of this chapter.

Like all major library classification schemes currently in use, LCC was designed before electronics were even a gleam in any librarian's eyes. It was designed for shelving purposes in a closed-stacks library, to be used in conjunction with the then recently invented subject headings. It is designed for a library with an experienced reference staff (another then recent invention), not for public use. As other libraries began to use it and opened their own stacks to the public, LCC began to be used as a shelf browsing tool. As its shelflist became available on microcards it was increasingly used as a searching tool. Now, in an OPAC environment, its original purpose as a shelving tool has become secondary and its usefulness as an online searching tool has come to the fore.

- LCC is often criticized as a searching tool, and LC policy toward it has frequently come under attack over the years. However, when it is used by a skilled and imaginative professional in conjunction with subject headings, it can be a very effective retrieval tool, as Thomas Mann has illustrated (1991, 1993). Chan (1986, 1990, 10–22) described and illustrated several types of situations in which LCC is uniquely effective, sometimes because of its very specificity.

- The LCC notation can be found in almost all MARC records and is at least somewhat familiar to many patrons of academic libraries. They therefore tend not to be in awe of it, although they typically do not know it well enough to take real advantage of it or to circumvent its pitfalls. This may be one reason why people whose research interest seems to involve only very few highly specific LCC notations support it strongly.

- Although the following subsections list many LCC characteristics that impede its effective use in OPACs, one must not forget that it is maintained by a well-funded, leading organization, the Library of Congress. It is therefore a live scheme which, within limits, keeps pace with progress, adding new topics and changing others as needed.

- Although many of the ideas that LCC introduced (Miksa 1984) early in its development make it extremely difficult to use for real information retrieval in a computer, other than just for browsing in the shelflist, since the late 1980s LC's Cataloging Directorate and its Cataloging Policy and Support Office have taken a series of steps to make LCC a far more effective online tool. These include converting to the *MARC 21 Format for Classification Data*, working toward standardizing patterns and tables, and beginning to introduce LC subject headings into class number captions. The situation is very fluid. Also, in effect, the *MARC 21 Format for Classification Data*—if used—potentially acts as a superimposed structure that provides the consistency that most existing library classification systems lack. (The *MARC 21 Format for Classification Data* is discussed separately in "MARC Format for Classification Data" and "MARC Format for Classification Data: Searching Capabilities" in this chapter. For a more complete discussion of *MARC 21,* see Chapter 2.)

Much remains to be done in this gradual conversion of a nineteenth-century shelving system to a twenty-first-century online topical retrieval tool. The process is not without controversy; some writers (who tend not to have administrative or fiscal responsibility for LC, with its nationwide and international scope) would prefer a radical break with the traditional retrieval systems and question whether the step-by-step approach, which is characteristic of LC, will lead to the desired result.

LCC Structure and OPACs

Synthesis

LCC is a highly enumerative scheme without synthetic features. (The tables do not represent synthesis but merely mean that more than one section of a class can be subdivided in the same way.) Neither enumeration nor lack of synthetic capability helps or hinders recall by notation, or scrolling, but neither is helpful to hierarchical searching. Neither prevents assigning multiple class notations to a document to express subject interrelationships.

Hospitality, But Problematical Logic

LCC is very hospitable, both hierarchically and laterally, although the insertions may not always be in an entirely logical place. Occasional lack of logic makes scrolling and especially hierarchical searching less effective and reliable than desirable. Also, LCC's hospitality does not help any more than hospitality in any other enumerative classification system when new interdisciplinary subjects must be inserted. Subjects like *Hydrophonic agriculture in space*, *Micro surgery*, and *Electronic advertising* must still be inserted with one or the other parent topic or in a quite unrelated place. Hierarchical searching by class notation from or to the parent topics may prove difficult.

Logically, theoretically, and by definition, classification involves hierarchy. To permit hierarchical searches, from broad aspects of a topic to more specific concepts and vice versa, the whole must precede its parts, and the parts must progress in some standard, logical sequence, either sequential or by inherent logic. Unfortunately, LCC contains quite a few examples where a whole topic and its parts are not listed together, thus impeding online scrolling and, especially, hierarchical searching.

For example, LCC's emphasis on the geographical/political approach—which is quite defensible considering its role—causes topics like geography, travel, ethnology, social life, and customs to be split into those subjects in general and the same subjects as applied to a specific country:

Geography and travel in general: *G - GF*;

Geography and description of individual countries: *D - F*

Ethnology in general: *GN 301 - GN 673*; individual ethnic groups: *D - F*

Manners and customs in general: *GT*; of specific countries: *D - F*

Historical geography in general: *G 141*; of individual countries: *D - F*

Another example of topics that are classed in a way that makes hierarchical topical searches difficult if not impossible is "Artistic aspects of photography." *Photography* as such is classed in *TR 640-688*, as part of *Technology*. On the one hand, if the subject matter of a photograph is emphasized rather than the artistic aspects, LCC understandably groups the photographs with the subject: photographs of natural history topics with *Natural history* (*QH 46*), photographs of modern Greece with the *History of Greece* (*DF 719*). Yet even the artistic aspects of photography are classed in *TR 640-688* as part of *Technology* rather than as part of *Art* (*N72 .P5*), and are therefore outside the *Art* hierarchy.

Sometimes LCC uses ranges of numbers and alphabetical subdivisions to collect otherwise unrelated subjects on the basis of a superficial likeness. Although this permits scrolling within the range and the alphabetical subdivisions, it impedes scrolling and hierarchical searches of the topic concerned. Examples are "Caricatures of things, people, etc." and "Special subjects" as represented in the visual arts in general. (*Special* means "individual" or "specific.") In both cases the subjects themselves are classed throughout the schedules, from *A* to *Z*, but caricatures of the same subjects are gathered together under *NC 1763* (*A-Z*) as part of *Drawings, Design, and Illustrations*, and the same subjects as depicted in the *Visual arts in general*, are gathered together as part of *Art* under *N 8217-N 8266*. Examples of the effect of this are shown in Figure 8.18.

A subject	Notation for the subject itself (A-Z)	Notation for a caricature of that subject (NC 1763)	Notation for that subject as depicted in the visual arts (N 8217-N 8266)
(1)	(2)	(3)	(4)
Circus	GV 1800-1831	NC 1763 .C46	N 8217 .C3
Dentistry	RK 1-715	NC 1763 .D3	N 8217 .D6
Fishing	SH 401-691	NC 1763 .F5	N 8250
Industry	HD 2321-4730.9	NC 1763 .I48	N 8218
Law. Lawyers	K	NC 1763 .L3	N 8219 .L3
Money	HG 201-1496	NC 1763 .M55	N 8215 .M56
Sex roles	HQ 1075-1075.5	NC 1763 .S5	N 8241.5
Sports	GV 561-1198.995	NC 1763 .S7	N 8250
Tobacco pipes	TS 2270	NC 1763 .T6	N 8253 .T6
Writing	Z 40-104.5	NC 1763 .W7	N 8265
Youth	HQ 793-799.2	NC 1763 .Y52	N 8266

Fishing (Sport):	**799.1**
Humorous treatment of fishing	**799.**102 07
Audiovisual treatment of fishing	**799.**102 08
Tobacco pipes	**688.42**
Humorous treatment of tobacco pipes:	**688.420** 207
Audiovisual treatment of tobacco pipes	**688.420** 208

Figure 8.18. Above the horizontal line: Examples of LCC groupings by what searchers for the topic itself would probably consider a minor characteristic.

These topics (Columns 1 and 2) are scattered throughout the classification, A to Z. Caricatures of the same subjects (Column 3) are concentrated under *NC 1763,* which is part of *NC* (*Drawing, Design, Illustration*). The same subjects as depicted in the visual arts (Column 4) are concentrated under *N 8217-N 8266*. LCC notations like *TS 2270* cannot be searched hierarchically or through scrolling to find topical, caricaturistic, and visual arts treatment of the topic together. Other devices, such as keywords or subject headings, must be used. **Below the horizontal line: In DDC the standard notation is added to the basic topical notation to indicate, for example, *Humorous treatment,* or *Audiovisual treatment.*** This permits scrolling of the topic and, because the DDC notation is expressive, it permits broadening a topical search by right truncation or narrowing it by "exploding" a notation—if the program permits it.

Missing Links

Missing links in the LCC structure do not affect scrolling but do impede hierarchical searching. Because LCC uses cardinal integers without synthetic devices and, so far, does not have standard uniform (Cutter) tables for formats, forms of presentation, time periods, or geographic areas, it can express the concept of one topic in several formats only by means of different notations, which vary from case to case. The previously shown example of *Geomagnetism (QC 811 - QC 849)* in Figure 8.15 illustrates this point: Nine notations, from *QC 811* to *QC 816*, all mean *Geomagnetism in general,* but written at different times, in various formats or manners of treatment. There is a missing hierarchical level, a "missing link," for *Geomagnetism in general.*

Although a missing hierarchical link may not be a problem in assigning class numbers—one can always, by convention or directive, use one of a span of numbers for the general concept—and although a span of numbers can be used for scrolling, it does cause problems if one tries to use it for hierarchical searches. Truncating does not answer the query "Find Geomagnetism in general"; *QC 81?* would cover too much because it would include *QC 818-QC 819 (Observatories* and *Instruments).*

Conversely, if the question "What is available on geomagnetism in general?" is addressed to the DDC, the system can answer with one topical notation, *538.7.* To this number can be added a series of standard subdivisions that describe many, but not all, of the categories listed in LCC's *QC.811* to *QC 822,* and some additional, even more specific ones. With its decimal notation and limited synthetic ability, DDC can usually use the notation to broaden or to narrow down a search via right truncation.

538.7	Geomagnetism and related phenomena
538.7<u>02 8</u>	Apparatus, equipment, materials
538.7<u>02 88</u>	Maintenance and repair of apparatus and equipment
538.7<u>05</u>	in the form of a serial
538.7<u>09</u>	historical and/or geographical treatment
538.7<u>09 494 56</u>	in the Swiss canton [state] of Aargau

OPACs and LCC's Notation

Nonexpressive LCC Notations and Hierarchical Searching

The use of cardinal sequential numbers and of decimals that have no hierarchical meaning results in a nonexpressive notation. (Only most of the letters signifying major topics and disciplines, and some Cutter numbers, are expressive to the initiated.) This, along with the lack of rigid standardization in structure and notation, prevents hierarchical searching by class notation alone.

For example, merely by looking at notation *QC 835* in Figure 8.15 one cannot know that logically it is a subdivision of *QC 830*. To use another example, the notation *LC 1503* (*Vocational education of women in the United States*) does not express that it is, conceptually, a subdivision of *LC 1500* (*Vocational education of women in general*).

OPACs and Right, Left, or Central Truncation of LCC Notations

LCC's nonexpressive notation of cardinal numbers prevents broadening a search by means of truncation or making it more specific by asking the system to "explode" a notation by adding to the original notation digits that indicate the next, more specific level of the hierarchy.

Right truncation of the basic LCC number (that is, the symbols to the left of any alphabetical subdivision) will typically not permit broadening a search effectively. For example, searching under truncated notation *ML 93?* will deliver only some of the literature on *wind instruments* (*ML 930-990*), because much of it is classed in *ML 940-990*. Conversely, searching under the truncated notation *M 152?* will provide access to notations *M 152[0] to M 152[9]*, which includes an array far too miscellaneous to be useful: on the one hand, vocal music for ballets, motion pictures, radio, and television; on the other duets, trios, and so forth for solo voices.

Conversely, in Figure 8.15 the indentions of the captions show that, at least in the minds of LC classifiers, *Sunspot periods* (*QC 836*) is a subdivision of *Geomagnetism and related aspects*, which, in turn, is a subdivision of *Magnetic observations* (*QC 830*). The notation, however, does not permit the system to answer the command, "Explode (that is, show the next more specific array of) *QC 830* by listing it with the next digits added" because the subdivisions of *QC 830* have no more digits than *QC 830* itself.

Left or central truncation is usually equally ineffective. For example, truncating *QC 811* (*Geomagnetism*) into *QC ?11* calls up a motley array, including notations such as *QC 111* (*Density and specific gravity*), *QC 311* (*Thermodynamics*), and *QC 711* (*Electric discharge through gases*). Truncating as *Q? 811* calls up an equally useless array, including notations such as *QB 811* (*Proper motion of stars*) and *QL 811* (*Anatomy*). Truncating as *?C 811* calls up an even wilder assortment, including notations such as *GC 811* (*The Yellow Sea*) and *PC 811* (*History of Romanian drama*).

It is also usually meaningless to truncate to the left of any alphabetical subdivision, because alphabetical subdivisions are not necessarily consistent. For example, the subdivision *.R4* means different things under the class notations *QC 373* and *QC 454* (*Reticles* for the one, *Reflectance spectroscopy* for the other). Even if the user has access to these subdivisions for the purpose of limiting the search outputs, their use in searching will produce unpredictable results.

Alphabetical Subdivision and Missing Links

Alphabetical subdivision quite often impedes effective hierarchical searching, sometimes as the result of a "missing link" in the hierarchy. On the other hand, the many notations that use alphabetical, rather than classed, subdivision are probably the only places where the LCC schedules permit truncation and "explosion" of a notation, that is, automatic display of more specific or less specific arrays. This can be very useful where the alphabetical subdivisions are limited to one category or concept. For example, in Figure 8.16, *JN 5985* leads to the group as well as to individual political parties in the Netherlands.

Again in Figure 8.16, alphabetical subdivision permits an answer to the queries, "What do we have on *QD 181 .H4 (Helium)*?" and "What do we have on *QD 181 (Individual inorganic chemical elements)*?" But these elements also form groups. For example, helium, neon, and argon are part of the group of *inert*, or *noble*, gases. Direct alphabetical subdivision of *QD 181* into chemical elements omits an essential step in a hierarchical display and therefore prevents retrieval of these elements by groups.

Searching Geographical Subdivisions

LCC's device of arranging geographical subdivisions of a subject alphabetically has been mentioned (see Figure 8.16). A second device that impedes hierarchical geographical searches is the use in many schedules of different notations for different levels of geographical division. The cities of a region are in such cases not listed as subdivisions of that region. For example:

```
HC 398 (subdivided A-Z): Economic history and
                         conditions of the regions and
                         cantons (that is, states) of
                         Switzerland.

HC 399 (subdivided A-Z): Economic history and
                         conditions of the cities of
                         Switzerland.
```

Therefore, the economic conditions of the city of *Baden* is *HC 399. B3*, but the economic conditions of the canton (state) of *Aargau,* in which the city of *Baden* lies, is *HC 398. A2*. The searcher who has found *HC 399. B3* cannot use right truncation to expand the search to the economic conditions of the next larger political unit, the canton of Aargau. The query *HC 399?* will lead to a display of the economic conditions of *all* Swiss cities in the file, not just of the cities in the canton of Aargau. The query *HC 39?* will lead to a display of economic conditions in Switzerland—and in Spain, Andorra, Gibraltar, and Portugal, because the numbers for the economic conditions of these countries range from *HC 381 to HC 390* for Spain and *HC 390.5 to HC 400* for the other countries.

In this particular case, the DDC would also not have permitted broadening the search from city to canton, because the notations are not worked out in enough detail to separate Swiss cities. However, the notation and machinery permit it, and right truncation of the DDC notation would permit an ever-broadening search from economic conditions in the city of Baden, to the economic conditions of Europe, or economic conditions in general.

```
330.9        Economic situation and conditions
330.94          in Europe
330.949 4        in Switzerland
330.949 45         in the Swiss Plateau cantons [that is, states]
330.949 456          in the canton [that is, state] of Aargau
330.949 456 3          in the city of Baden
     [hypothetical notation, not yet assigned]
```

MARC 21 FORMAT
FOR CLASSIFICATION DATA

It was recognized early on that the LCC notations, and notations of other library classification schemes, could not just be encoded automatically, number for number. To make the schedules electronically functional, every notation must be shown in one way or another in context, as part of a total hierarchical and coordinated structure. For LCC, several possible techniques were suggested (Cochrane and Markey 1985; Chan 1986). Nancy J. Williamson (1995) identified and made recommendations regarding LCC problem areas that had to be considered when converting the LCC schedules to machine-readable format. (Many of these problem areas were touched on previously in this chapter.)

In close consultation with LCC and DDC, and with input from UDC and the National Library of Medicine (NLM) Classification, LC's Network Development and MARC Standards Office began in 1987 to develop the *MARC 21 Format for Classification Data* (MARC 21 cf). It is a machine-readable format for classification data to allow for the communication of classification records between systems and to provide a standard for the storage of classification data in the computer. Although intended as authority format for every class number in any classification system, some of its features are clearly designed to accommodate LCC characteristics, and others are designed for DDC characteristics. It has the potential of circumventing classification system flaws.

This is basically a helpful, even essential, feature, but it may also calcify the respective classification system's basic structure and thereby make conceptual development and improvement less likely than heretofore. However, both DDC and LCC have recently made, and are continuing to make, quite a few changes and standardizations in their schedules, tables, and policies to make assigning class notations in OPACs easier and notational searching more effective, for example by coordinating indexing and caption terms and by beginning to standardize the use of tables (in the case of LCC) and precedence instructions (in the case of DDC).

In 1990 the ALA's Machine Readable Bibliographic Information (MARBI) Committee approved MARC 21 cf. In 1991 LC tested it, and by 1996 had converted all LCC schedules, mostly with the help of contractors, after hundreds of thousands of hours of work, and earlier than expected. In 1996 LC began to explore a mechanism needed to link the data in its online MARC 21 cf database (the authority file for class notations) with its online bibliographic and authority files. Linking bibliographic records files with their respective authority files infuses syndetic features and structure into the bibliographic records file and opens up potentially powerful new search strategies. It can also help to integrate, automate, and expedite cataloging functions.

The format of the individual MARC 21 cf authority record is based on the format of other MARC records such as the *MARC Bibliographic Format* (described with the other MARC formats in Chapter 2), in which fields for call numbers also exist, for example,

```
050   Library of Congress call number

055   Call numbers/class numbers assigned in Canada

060   National Library of Medicine call number

086   U.S. Government Documents Classification number
```

as well as fields for "locally assigned" LC-type, DDC-type, and other numbers. These call numbers, however, are basically part of the bibliographic description of a specific document. Provided the individual library's computer system permits it, they can be used for retrieving the document by call number and even for scrolling the shelflist. But they cannot be used for sophisticated input or retrieval functions such as number building, a record of past classification decisions, hierarchical searching, referral to other pertinent numbers, explanation of a number's scope, retrieval by indexing or caption terms, or linking to a subject heading or an uncontrolled vocabulary system. For that, MARC 21 cf is needed.

MARC 21 FORMAT FOR CLASSIFICATION DATA: SEARCHING CAPABILITIES[1]

As of 1999, only LC had implemented MARC 21 cf, and it has used most, but not all of its wide range of capabilities. The format allows for great specificity in coding and for explicit identification of data elements that can be manipulated for a variety of functions. MARC 21 cf does not provide a record of a document or of a call number but is an authority format for individual class numbers and their captions. Manipulation of document surrogates, including manipulation by call numbers, is possible through linking the respective authority files with the document (bibliographic) files, that is, the catalog and the shelflist. Generally, each line that includes a caption in a classification schedule receives a separate MARC 21 cf record. The record's basic structure resembles that of the other USMARC systems, with leader, directory, and variable fields that are grouped by function, each with indicators and subfields.

Although it is difficult to predict the limitations that a local system might encounter in using the MARC 21 cf data, the literature as well as experts working with MARC 21 cf stress repeatedly that local implementation largely determines how, and how well, the various possible functions are carried out. Local library policies, finances, and system capabilities will determine the nature and extent to which the format's considerable capabilities are used. As authority for class numbers the format is a cataloging aid and has been used as such, but it is equally versatile as a searching tool. Developing its use locally as a sophisticated subject retrieval tool will require great commitment but will also enrich subject retrieval techniques.

For retrieval purposes several fields hold great promise, among them the following variable fields ("NR" means "Not Repeatable"; "R" means "Repeatable"):

153: CLASSIFICATION NUMBER (NR): The classification number or number span for which this is the authority record, its associated caption, and superordinate levels of the caption hierarchy. (Described in greater detail below.)

154: GENERAL EXPLANATORY INDEX TERM (NR): A general explanatory term (not associated with one classification number or span) from the index to the classification scheme used.

253: COMPLEX SEE-REFERENCE (R): The explanatory text and classification number traced from field 153 to field 253, when a more simple cross-reference generated from a 453 or 553 tracing field is insufficient (e.g., needed for a reference to a span of numbers that does not have a corresponding caption, for a reference to more than three numbers, for a general textual reference).

353: COMPLEX SEE-ALSO REFERENCES (R): The explanatory text and classification number referred to, when a more simple cross-reference generated from a 553 tracing field is insufficient (e.g., as for field 253). (Described in greater detail below.)

453; 553: TRACING FIELDS: Fields leading directly from one number to another number. They can be used to refer from an old to a new number or for references such as "For [topic] see [topic]" or "See also [topic]".

453: INVALID NUMBER TRACING ("see") (R): The tracing for a cross-reference from an invalid to a valid classification number, that is, from field 453 to field 153.

553: VALID NUMBER TRACING ("see-also") (R): The tracing for a cross-reference from a valid classification number to another valid classification number, that is, from field 553 to field 153. May be coded to show that the number and caption refer to a broader or narrower topic in the hierarchy to facilitate online browsing.

680: SCOPE NOTE (R): If needed, explains the topic classed in field 153.

684: AUXILIARY INSTRUCTION NOTE (R): Information from, or a citation to, documentation intended to be used with a classification schedule, for example the *DDC Manual*, which is intended to describe policies and practices.

685: HISTORY NOTE (R): Information about the history of the use and meaning of a classification number listed in field 153 or referred to in fields 453 or 553. Allows for indicating the type of change recorded and the old and new class numbers. Can be used to indicate whether the number referred to is a new or an old number.

700-751, 754: CONTROLLED INDEX TERMS. Controlled subject access terms.

700: INDEX TERM—PERSONAL NAME (R)

710: INDEX TERM—CORPORATE NAME (R)

711: INDEX TERM—MEETING NAME (R)

730: INDEX TERMS—UNIFORM TITLE (R)

750: INDEX TERM—TOPICAL (R): Controlled subject access terms (from thesauri such as LCSH or MeSH).

751: INDEX TERM—GEOGRAPHIC NAME (R)

753: INDEX TERM—UNCONTROLLED (R): Uncontrolled subject access terms, used to supplement the terms in the record and to generate an alphabetical index; keywords such as terms in captions, notes, and in an index to a classification schedule, which provide subject access to a classification number or span in field 153 or an index term in field 154. Separately identified subfields are used in this field to establish hierarchical relationships between terms or for references to other terms within the classification index.

754: INDEX TERM—FACETED TOPICAL TERMS (R): Contains a topical subject constructed from a faceted vocabulary. Each term is identified as to the facet/hierarchy in the thesaurus from which the term came. In addition, the focus term of the expression is identified.

761-768: NUMBER BUILDING FIELDS (R): Intended for the computer, and/or the classifier, to perform the necessary computations to create synthesized numbers. The information in some of these fields is not written in a form adequate for public display. In some cases, rephrasing these fields into end-user language could make them useful for searching. This is also true for some other fields such as 681: CLASSIFICATION EXAMPLE TRACING NOTE (R).

Two typical MARC 21 fields are shown below in greater detail:

153 CLASSIFICATION NUMBER (NR): The classification number or number span for which this is the authority record, its associated caption, and superordinate levels of the caption hierarchy. This structure gives a context for the classification caption which in some cases may be meaningless (such as, "General works"), and also provides for a hierarchical display online or in print.

Indicators: Undefined; each contains a blank (#)

Subfield Codes

$a   Classification number element—single number or beginning number of span (R)

$c   Classification number element—ending number of span (R)

$h   Caption hierarchy (R): The superordinate caption hierarchy in descending order, that is, all captions to which the caption representing the number in subfields a and c is subordinate. By counting the number of subfield h's the system can calculate the indention level of the caption.

$j   Caption (NR): The lowest caption in the hierarchy for a classification number or number span. That is, the specific caption for the number represented in subfields a and c.

$k   Summary number span caption hierarchy (R): Contains the caption at a level higher than the last for a summary number span in the DDC.

$z   Table identification—table number (NR): Used by catalogers for input.

EXAMPLES:

153 ##$aQL638.E55 $hZoology $hChordates. Vertebrates $hFishes $hSystematic divisions $hOsteichthys (Bony fishes) $hFamilies $jEngraulidae (Anchovies)

153 ##$a306.36 $hSocial sciences $kSpecific topics in sociology and anthropology $hCulture and institutions $hEconomic institutions $jSystems of labor

353 COMPLEX SEE-ALSO REFERENCE (R): The explanatory text and the classification number referred to, which are required when see-also relationships exist between classification numbers that cannot be adequately conveyed by one or more simple cross-references generated from a 553 tracing field. As in many fields, for searching purposes the phrasing must be revised for end-users, unless neutral phrasing

can be developed that serves both input and
searching purposes.

<u>Indicators</u> Both undefined; each contains a blank (#)

Subfield Codes

$a   Classification number referred to—single number or
      beginning number of span (R)

$c   Classification number referred to—ending number of
      span (R)

$i   Explanatory text (R): Contains a special reference
      instruction phrase that may be used when the
      generation of a standard phrase is not appropriate.

$z   Table identification—table number (R): Used by
      catalogers for input.

EXAMPLE:

353 ##$z1 $a07155 $ifor in-service training and
residency, $a331.21 $ifor wages, $a331.255 $ifor
fringe benefits

Although this listing does not spell out the searching capabilities of individual fields in detail, it hints at the system's overall capabilities—always with the proviso that actual use is closely linked to the implementing library's policies and system capabilities. MARC 21 cf's overall searching potential is awesome although, as of this writing, very few, if any, libraries take advantage of it. Even when the classification system itself does not permit a feature that is listed in the section "Desirable Features of Online Classed Retrieval Systems" at the beginning of this chapter, or does so only imperfectly, MARC 21 cf (2000) often enables it, or at least ameliorates a shortcoming. (While reading the next few paragraphs it should be helpful to refer to previous sections of this chapter.)

It can, in effect, superimpose to some extent an improved hierarchy over an existing classification system and thereby permit hierarchical numerical searches that otherwise might not be possible. (This should help overcome, among others, the problems of false links and unsought links, and often the problem of missing links.) It permits browsing and forward and backward scrolling; it shows the relative position of a topic in a hierarchy; it permits referring to related aspects or to a subject in other disciplines; and it permits explaining relocations and the scope, or changing scope, of a notation.

It permits (for example in the LC implementation) showing a hierarchy in a window while the number in question is on the main screen and jumping from one number to another directly. It permits alphabetical access by terms and numbers from a variety of sources, linking to bibliographic files, and using them in alphabetical or classed order, like a classed catalog.

But MARC 21 cf cannot overcome all flaws and irregularities in a classification system. For example, it cannot truncate unless the notation permits it. (But the words leading to class notations can be truncated.) It cannot accommodate interdisciplinary subjects any better than the classification system itself can. (But the alphabetical index features combined with Boolean searching can overcome the lack of a meaningful insertion of multidisciplinary topics into an existing scheme.) It does not permit notational synthesis unless the notation permits it. (But the alphabetical index fields

700 to 754 may help to ameliorate this shortcoming.) Although it can often create a meaningful missing hierarchical link, this is usually not possible when LCC employs alphabetical subdivisions (See *QD 181* in Figure 8.16 for an example). MARC 21 cf also seems unable to override the use of different notations for different levels in LCC of the same geographical unit, described in "Searching Geographical Subdivisions" in this chapter. This prevents hierarchical searches in such situations from city to district to country.

Following are some examples. Field 153 can be helpful for hierarchical searching, as can fields 453 and 553. The caption hierarchy (153 subfield $h) can be displayed (or printed) in a box, with or without the corresponding numbers, while the notation itself (153 subfields $a or $a and $c) is on the screen, so that the searcher always knows the notation's relative position. One function of field 154 is to serve as a general explanatory term from the index to the classification scheme used. In libraries that use more than one classification scheme (for example LCC for most works and the U.S. Superintendent of Documents scheme for federal government documents) it helps searchers to switch from one scheme to another as needed.

Fields 253, 353, 453, and 553 are used to refer from one classification number to one or more other numbers. The generated display text is aimed at input and must be revised for searching purposes by the public. Fields 253 and 453 can be used to direct searchers to another classification number, for example when a number is invalid or when its scope has changed or was partly transferred to one or more other numbers. Fields 353 and 553, also with built-in text suitably revised for searching, can help to explain to searchers where different aspects of a topic can be found or where to search for related concepts.

Along with their primary use as input aids for catalogers, note fields 680, 685, and possibly even 684, can also be important searching aids. They are intended to explain the current and past scope of the notation listed in field 153 and the history of its use, including implementation dates. These fields can be useful indications of other notations that searchers may want to explore.

Field 765 (Synthesized Number Components) (R) would provide all the information needed for sophisticated searching on Dewey numbers, *if* there were a full MARC database, including a MARC record for every built Dewey number, and *if* there were a search engine to exploit the possibilities. Neither, apparently, exists as of this writing, although both could. If they did exist one could search separately on any of the pieces used to build a number, and if the search engine provided the proper linkage, one could search on either the numbers or the words associated with these numbers.

CONCLUSION

Subject retrieval by class notations is underused in OPACs, even though it has been known for a long time that searching by classed terms tends to provide somewhat different results than searching by alphabetical terms and that both approaches tend to result in overlapping but not duplicating results. As long as the classed approach was only available through the shelflist (on cards) or through shelf browsing, physical obstacles made classed subject searching difficult, especially since the shelflist was typically not publicly accessible. Electronics have removed the physical obstacles, and the MARC 21 cf format, in conjunction with the other MARC 21 formats, provides the means for subject searching in a far more sophisticated and multifaceted way than was possible heretofore. This type of searching may well go beyond what the casual user in an "everyday situation" wants or needs, but it should be available when exhaustive or thorough subject searches are called for.

NOTE

1. For much of the factual information on *MARC 21 Format for Classification Data* we are indebted to Julianne Beall, Rebecca S. Guenther, and Mary K. D. Pietris., in addition to the cited references. Any errors or misinterpretations are our own.

REFERENCES

Chan, Lois Mai. 1986. Library of Congress classification as an online retrieval tool: Potentials and limitations. *Information Technology and Libraries* 5 (September): 181–92.

———. 1990. The Library of Congress classification system in an online environment. *Cataloging & Classification Quarterly* 11 (1): 7–25.

———. 1999. *A Guide to the Library of Congress Classification.* 5th ed. Englewood, CO: Libraries Unlimited.

Cochrane, Pauline Atherton, and Karen Markey. 1985. Preparing for the use of classification in online cataloging systems and in online catalogs. *Information Technology and Libraries* 4 (June): 91–111.

Cutter, C. A. 1901. *C. A. Cutter's three-figure author table.* Chicopee, MA: Huntting Co.

———. 1969. *C. A. Cutter's three-figure author table (Swanson-Swift revision).* Littleton, CO: Libraries Unlimited.

Dahlberg, Ingetraut. 1977. Major developments in classification. *Advances in Librarianship* 7: 41–103.

[DDC]. 1951. *Decimal classification devised by Melvil Dewey.* Standard (15th) ed. Lake Placid Club, NY: Forest Press.

———. 1958. *Dewey decimal classification and relative index.* 16th ed. Lake Placid Club, NY: Forest Press.

———. 1965. *Dewey decimal classification and relative index.* 17th ed. Lake Placid Club, NY: Forest Press.

———. 1971. *Dewey decimal classification and relative index.* 18th ed. Lake Placid Club, NY: Forest Press.

———. 1979. *Dewey decimal classification and relative index.* 19th ed. Albany, NY: Forest Press.

———. 1989. *Dewey decimal classification and relative index.* 20th ed. Albany, NY: Forest Press.

———. 1996. *Dewey decimal classification and relative index*. Edition 21. Albany, NY: Forest Press.

Guenther, Rebecca S. 1992. The development and implementation of the USMARC format for classification data. *Information Technology and Libraries* (June): 120–31.

———. 1996a. Automating the Library of Congress classification scheme: Implementation of the USMARC format for classification data. *Cataloging & Classification Quarterly* 21 (3–4): 177–203.

———. 1996b. Bringing the Library of Congress classification into the computer age: Converting LCC to machine-readable form. *Advances in Knowledge Organization* 5: 26–32.

Hill, Janet Swan. 1984. Online classification number access: Some practical considerations. *Journal of Academic Librarianship* 10 (March): 17–22.

Maltby, Arthur. 1984. Dewey decimal classification: A liability. *Catalog and Index* 72: 45.

Mandel, Carol A. 1986. *Classification schedules as subject enhancement in online catalogs: A review of a conference sponsored by Forest Press, the OCLC Online Computer Library Center, and the Council on Library Resources*. Washington, DC: Council on Library Resources.

Mann, Thomas. 1991. *Cataloging quality: LC priorities, and models of the Library's future*. (Opinion Papers, no. 1). Washington, DC: Library of Congress, Cataloging Forum.

———. 1993. *Library research models: A guide to classification, cataloging, and computers*. New York: Oxford University Press.

[MARC 21 cf]. 2000. *MARC 21 concise format for classification data*. 2000 edition. Prepared by Network Development and MARC Standards Office. Washington, DC: Cataloging Distribution Service, Library of Congress. (*See also* Update No. 1, October 2000, available: http://lcweb.loc.gov/marc/classification/, accessed May 15, 2001.)

Markey, Karen, and Ann N. Demeyer. 1986. *Dewey decimal classification online project: Evaluation of a library schedule and index integrated into the subject searching capabilities of an online catalog*. Dublin, OH: OCLC.

Miksa, Francis. 1984. *The development of classification at the Library of Congress*. (Occasional Paper No. 164). Urbana: University of Illinois at Champaign Urbana, Graduate School of Library and Information Science.

Mitchell, Joan S. 1995. DDC 21 and beyond: The Dewey Decimal Classification prepares for the future. *Cataloging & Classification Quarterly* 21 (2): 37–47.

Sanborn, K. C. 1896. *C. A. Cutter's alphabetic-order table: Altered and fitted with three figures by Miss Kate E.Sanborn*. Chicopee, MA: Huntting Co.

Statement on types of classification available to new academic libraries. 1965. *Library Resources and Technical Services* 9 (Winter): 104–11.

[UDC]. 1993. *Universal decimal classification. International medium edition: English text*. 2d ed. (BS1000M). London: British Standards Institution. (See also I. C. McIlwaine, *Guide to the use of the UDC*. (FID 703). The Hague: FID, 1993; G. Robinson, *UDC in brief*. London: British Standards institution, 1994.)

Vizine-Goetz, Diane. 1996. Classification research at OCLC. Available: http://www.oclc.org /oclc/research/publications/review96/class.htm. (Accessed May 12, 2001).

Williamson, Nancy J. 1995. *The Library of Congress classification: A content analysis of the schedules in preparation for their conversion into machine-readable form.* With the assistance of Suliang Feng and Tracy Tennant. (LC 30.2:C 56). Washington, DC: Library of Congress, Cataloging Distribution Service.

9

Users and
User Needs

INTRODUCTION

The purpose of an information system is to link documents and users in a relevant manner. Typically, this purpose has been construed as enabling users to meet their information needs by retrieving relevant documents. The success of an information system is dependent to a significant extent on the skills, backgrounds, and needs that users bring to the system. Realizing that it is virtually impossible to serve all of the information needs of all users all of the time, we strive to fulfill most of the needs of most of the users most of the time. To do so, we have developed ways of viewing users and their needs and have studied users to better understand how they go about seeking information.

The study of users and their needs makes up a major part of the corpus of library and information studies (LIS) (for reviews of this literature see Dervin and Nilan 1986; Hewins 1990; and Sugar 1995). Therefore, it is impossible to do it justice in one chapter. In addition, although this research pertains to the whole process of linking people and information, much of it is not more specific to subject access in online catalogs than to other aspects of library work.

Hence, this chapter does not attempt to discuss or even summarize this important body of work but instead introduces two particularly pertinent areas. First, it looks at three different schools of thought or paradigms that have arisen within the field of LIS to explain how we link users and information. Second, it examines the concrete characteristics of catalog users that have been identified in research and how these characteristics relate to development and use of information systems. Some specific studies of catalog use are discussed in relation to evaluation in Chapter 11.

PARADIGMS AND USERS

Three paradigms have developed in LIS to help us explain the interaction between users and information via retrieval systems: the physical, the cognitive, and the social constructionist.

The Physical Paradigm

The physical paradigm is derived from the importation of the scientific method into LIS. It views information as flowing from a source to a destination, the user, who is relatively passive. The focus is on the process of translating information into a message that the system can convey to the user, as suggested by Claude Shannon's Communication Theory (Shannon and Weaver 1998). Shannon described this process in five stages: 1) Information in the form of a message comes from a source; 2) It is encoded into a signal by a transmitter; 3) The signal passes through a channel and is received by a receiver; 4) The receiver decodes the signal back into the message and sends it to a destination; 5) The destination in this model, as it is applied to catalogs, is the user. The direction of movement is from the information source to the user. This model is useful for examining the encoding and decoding process. In the case of subject access in library catalogs the process is the creation of a catalog record. A document comes into the library system and a catalog record is created to represent it. That act of representation is the encoding. It is then sent through the channel—the system—to be retrieved for a user.

Shannon's complementary Information Theory somewhat ameliorates the implication of a passive user. In his Information Theory, Shannon sees the message as made up of two separate parts: entropy and redundancy. Entropy is the new part of the message that conveys something to the user, whereas redundancy is that part of the message that is already known by the user (note that this notion of entropy bears no relation to the use of the same term in the field of physics). Therefore, the informational content of the message is determined by a given user's existing situation. It is possible to construe from this theory that an effective transmission of information will result in fulfillment of a user's information need. However, the focus in this physical paradigm is on the system rather than on the user.

Research that adheres to the physical paradigm typically compares systems to a relatively arbitrary notion of what a successful search might be. For example, Cyril Cleverdon's Cranfield studies (discussed in Chapters 4 and 11) compared different forms of subject representation using predetermined searches with predetermined results. If the predetermined results were retrieved, a search was considered successful. Cleverdon's studies were among the most influential, but many other studies follow this same paradigm.

The Cognitive Paradigm

In the 1970s, LIS researchers began to use concepts drawn from cognitive psychology to discuss information seeking. The model used for understanding users' information processing presumes that each individual has a mental knowledge structure. The knowledge structure is made up of concepts that are organized into schema which, in turn, fit together into a more or less coherent whole. The individual sees the world through this knowledge structure, which is built up through the individual's interaction with the world. As a person encounters the world, he or she will identify gaps in that knowledge structure and seek to fill them. Information retrieved in this search will be filtered through the knowledge structure and add to and shape the knowledge structure. So the relationship between information and the user is one of reciprocal change. A user's knowledge structure will affect that person's perception and processing of information and the information will, in turn, change the person's knowledge structure.

In a cognitive approach, users' formulations of information requests will consist of a number of internal processes:

Perception

Conceptualization

Verbalization

Choice

Translation

Listing the processes might imply that they are discrete, separate, and conscious. If that were so, it might be very much easier to create artificial intelligence systems. However, it is not so, which suggests that the cognitive model is a useful one for discussing user needs (as the physical paradigm is useful for discussing systems) but is not necessarily the only valid approach.

The first internal process, according to the cognitive approach, is perceiving or recognizing that a need exists. The perception may be immediate, in which case movement to the next step is direct. Sometimes, however, the perception is gradual, in which case it seems likely that the processes of perception and conceptualization operate simultaneously. The user gradually becomes aware that she or he needs additional information to complete her or his mental knowledge structure, to make it work better, or to have it better match the individual's context.

When a need has been perceived to exist, the next stage in the cognitive model involves the recognition of the nature of that need, determining as best as possible what the need is. The process of conceptualizing a need involves examining the knowledge structure and determining the nature of its incongruities. In what way do its pieces, the concepts that make it up, not fit together? Where are the gaps in the structure? Conceptualization of a need may involve reconsidering the concepts and the ways in which they are linked (Belkin, Seeger, and Wersig 1983).

The end product of conceptualization is the existence of a need that is not only recognized but also inwardly identified and described, at least by the person involved. Such recognition may be in negative terms, in that the person can think clearly only about what is missing; only the gap is known. The problem is how it should be filled. The word "want" describes the end product of the conceptualization process. A want may consist of lack of concepts, lack of links between concepts, or both.

Verbalization is the cognitive process of deciding how to say what it is a person wants, what words will be used to express the want. In the physical paradigm the verbalization that describes the want is considered the equivalent of the need, the want, and the translation (described below). However, the cognitive paradigm recognizes that there may be a discrepancy at any of these stages that can cause a mismatch between the need and the information ultimately retrieved.

The next stage in the processing of a need by a potential user is deciding which system or person to ask. Although in many instances the user reaches the decision to use the library or its online catalog, it is worthwhile to point out that most inquiries never reach such a "formal" information system as a library *and* many of those that do not should have. The final consideration with respect to choice of source made by the user is that the choice may relate more to what the user thinks can be obtained than to what is actually wanted.

Once an information source is chosen, the user tries to express his or her information need in terminology that can be understood by the system. This translation process is not always perfect, and may result in retrieval failures. In an online catalog, the system terminology is two-layered: 1) the system's command language and 2) the system's indexing language, as represented by both the controlled vocabulary assigned to the bibliographic records and the keywords acting as indicators of the topical contents of the record. The verbalization and translation processes include all of the vagaries of language regarding semantics and syntax discussed as problematic for information retrieval in Chapter 3.

The implication of the cognitive view of the formulation of an information request is that many of these processes—perception, conceptualization, verbalization, and choice—are beyond the control of online catalog designers. Nevertheless, user errors in these stages will result in retrieval failures. The only area where the system designer has some control is the process of translating the user information need into terminology that is understood by the system. It is only at this point that the user is interacting with the system and can benefit from (or be hindered by) its content and design. It is, therefore, not surprising that the physical paradigm focused on the system as a fruitful area for study. Nonetheless, knowledge of users' information seeking and processing can enhance both system design and subject representation as seen through the cognitive paradigm.

The Constructionist Paradigm

Social constructionism as a critical perspective asserts that individuals and their realities are constructed by powerful forces within society. These forces are referred to as "discourses." They are the political, economic, cultural, and social sets of ideas that prescribe how we see our world. Because we each experience these discourses differently and are exposed to both complementary and competing discourses, our worldviews may be different. A constructionist view of information retrieval suggests that discourses construct our information needs. Whereas the cognitive paradigm is grounded in psychology and focuses on individuals, the constructionist paradigm comes from a largely poststructural perspective and focuses on social, political, and economic processes (Frohmann 1992). The poststructural aspect of constructionism is to question the existence of innate qualities in users. It examines the environment in which users' identities, and therefore their needs, are constructed.

The construction of users' identities is apparent in the categorization of users in most user needs studies (Frohmann 1994). For example, a study examining the needs of scholars in various disciplines may try to define the needs of a philosopher compared to a scientist. A librarian working to meet the needs defined by such a study will have a superficial notion of the field of philosophy and how scholars generally operate in it. Such an understanding will only fit mainstream scholars. It will not allow support of innovative work that questions the mainstream or takes the discipline into new, creative areas. For an in-depth understanding, a librarian will need to understand the discourses within philosophy that shape the status quo as well as those that are at odds with it.

To relate this view to subject access, it is important to recognize that the constructionist paradigm rejects the possibility of a neutral or objective representation of information. Rather, it views our subject access standards as constructed by and reinforcing the most powerful discourses in our society. As our standards make mainstream information representable, they also make it easiest for users to retrieve information within these same discourses. Users discover that the questions most readily answered are the most conventional ones. In this manner the system reinforces the same discourses that create it and encourages users to define their needs within those discourses. Understanding how our information systems can construct users' needs can help us avoid a simple reinforcement of the status quo and allow us to support critical and innovative use of information as well.

USERS' CHARACTERISTICS

Users' characteristics that seem to affect their information-seeking behaviors in online catalogs include demographic traits (gender and age), background traits (education, training, and experience), and situational traits (purpose, research stage, etc.). Much of the research on who uses online catalogs and who uses them most effectively is built on the Council on Library Resources online catalog studies of the early 1980s (for a summary see Matthews, Lawrence and Ferguson 1983). These studies had wide-ranging findings that have had an enormous impact on the development of online catalogs and on the research into how people use them. Among these findings are links between different user traits and catalog use. Although some of these findings may now be dated, they set the stage for further work, as described in the following sections.

Demographic Traits

Two factors that have been suggested as correlated with information seeking in online catalogs are gender and age. The relationship between gender and computer use has been a controversial issue for some time. Two problems arise in analyzing this relationship: 1) the constant change of computers and their interfaces, which makes research quickly obsolete; and 2) the many other characteristics that affect computer use that may or may not also correlate with gender, thus complicating its analysis. However, it is still worth bearing in mind that existing research suggests that women use computers less than men and that girls are less comfortable with computers than boys. There is also evidence indicating that this discomfort may relate to context and that computers are commonly found in situations in which boys find them more accessible than do girls (Jacobson 1991).

There is also evidence suggesting that technology as we currently use it has been designed and constructed primarily by men and is probably more suited to the ways in which men are more likely to approach it than are women (Pritchard 1993). These issues are complex, and there exists a large and relatively inconclusive literature on gender and technology. In terms of online catalogs it is useful simply to bear in mind that gender differences exist at least in some contexts and that a variety of modes of access are more likely to appeal to a range of users than one "ideal" approach.

Age has also been raised as a factor in the use of online catalogs. Children demonstrate difficulties with online catalogs such as problems with reading and spelling, conventions of the catalog (such as use of plurals in subject headings and use of spacing and punctuation in searching), and confusion over categorization (such as what is an author and what is a subject) (Solomon 1993; Sandlian 1995). Older adults are more likely to have difficulty conceptualizing how computer searching operates than in being able to perform particular operations or using appropriate technology. Their problems most commonly relate to keyword searching, Boolean searching, and searching across databases (Sit 1998).

This brief overview of both age and gender factors suggests that much of the difference relates to factors of background rather than to the demographic traits themselves. For example, older adults are more likely to have less computer experience because they may have had less contact with computers during their careers. Children will not only have had less experience but also may not have reached developmental stages necessary for some of the conceptual structures of a catalog. Female-intensive occupations such as secretarial work and homemaking may depend on technology, but it is typically in transparent forms (one does not need to know how a vacuum cleaner is engineered to be able to clean a carpet).

Traditionally, boys have been the ones encouraged to take apart and understand technology. Although these legacies from the past are changing, they still have a significant effect. Therefore, one might speculate that as online catalogs are becoming more "user-friendly" with interfaces that take less practice to use effectively, women may find them more convenient to use without having to make that use an avocation. These same factors may make online catalogs more accessible to children and older adults or to any other people with limited experience or limited time in which to gain familiarity.

Background Traits

An individual's background may affect how he or she goes about information searching. Three factors in particular have emerged as relevant from research in this area: education, training in the use of information systems, and experience.

The amount and kind of education that a user has is likely to affect her or his behavior in relation to an information need. Education may assist users in being able to articulate their information needs. It correlates with the ways in which users learn to use online catalogs. For example, undergraduates are more likely to ask friends for assistance or to use trial and error than graduate students, who are more likely than undergraduates to ask library staff for help (Cherry and Clinton 1992). Further, education in different fields is likely to influence information seeking in different ways (Borgman 1986 and 1989).

For example, on a simplistic level one might reasonably say that scientists are more likely to require recent literature, probably published in journals, whereas historians are more likely to need literature not limited by publication date and to use monographs as well as journals. This difference will probably lead to different searching techniques using different bibliographic tools. One can speculate that users who are trained to locate information place more demands on a subject retrieval system than those who have not received such training.

The nature and extent of training in the use of information systems and services that a user has had affect both the likelihood that formal information systems will be used and the probability that they will be used only when appropriate, as well as the degree of skill and expertise with which they are used. At present, user training may be divided into three separate areas:

1. Bibliographic and library skills: the use and exploitation of collections of printed and other materials and of the secondary sources that make it possible to find them. Familiarity with the conceptual basis of organization of information in libraries will assist users in using new as well as familiar bibliographic tools.

2. Computer skills: basic practical abilities such as keyboard use, the ability to sign on to a system (especially as remote access becomes more common), and the ability to take at least limited remedial action when things go wrong. Obviously, greater skill will enhance users' ability to interact with a system, especially when encountering anything outside of the routine.

3. Understanding of computer systems: conceptual understanding of the manner in which information retrieval systems operate to provide access to stored data, for example, an understanding of the differences between free text searching of keywords and controlled vocabulary searching, including what types of information (in professional terms, what fields of the MARC record) are being examined in a given search, and a comprehension of Boolean logic.

User training has both affective and cognitive aspects. It impinges both on the desire to use a particular information system (or indeed to use any system at all) and on the knowledge and skills brought to bear in system use.

A user's training is likely to help in a number of ways. It will help the user form a mental model of the online catalog (Borgman 1982). The mental model can help a user to conceptualize various activities performed in the online catalog as a series of related activities with specific purposes and specific results. In the absence of a mental model, the user may not be able to understand the significance of various commands and procedures and, therefore, may not be able to evaluate the search results.

Users with prior training are likely to better understand and implement effective search strategies. Although searching for known items by author and title is straightforward in most catalogs, subject searching involves more complex intellectual activities. Search strategies become especially important if the online catalog has a number of diverse features. An effective search strategy will enable the searcher to retrieve information efficiently in terms of time and system resources while at the same time meeting search requirements such as the desired levels of recall and precision. The more options the catalog presents, the more responsibility is on the searcher to devise an efficient strategy; otherwise, the user will be inundated with documents or retrieve little or nothing of relevance.

Not surprisingly, experience with online catalogs has an influence on searching online catalogs. Online catalog users are likely to develop either positive or negative attitudes based on the success of previous experience. Frequency of use is also a factor, with more frequent users being more effective users. In computing, three different categories of users are identified: experienced, naïve, and casual. Experienced users may require little help from the system. Naïve users are those who require help but may be expected to acquire sufficient knowledge and skills to become experienced users. Casual users, unlike naïve users, are not expected to make sufficiently frequent use of the systems and therefore will always require assistance.

Some factors regarding users' experience have implications for subject access. Most notably, experienced users tend to do more subject searches. Because users also generally have more difficulty with subject searches than with other types of searches, it is worth asking whether subject access might be more complex than is necessary. The current combination of free text and controlled vocabulary and the need to perform Boolean searches have become too complicated if only experienced users feel that it is worth trying or can achieve reasonable results.

Situational Factors

Three types of factors relate to the situation of the information need: purpose, research stage, and other factors. They are concrete in nature and relate to a specific instance.

The purpose of an information search will determine the kind of results a user wants. If the user is involved in formal research, an exhaustive search requiring high recall may be necessary. However, if a user is interested in obtaining a practical answer to a practical question, high recall will be a nuisance requiring wading through too many results. Each of these would be quite different from a search based on personal curiosity, which may require some basic information along with possibilities for further inquiry.

The stage of an individual's search on a given topic will also influence what results will be desired. Carol C. Kuhlthau's research (1993) suggests that a broad (i.e., high recall) search is what a user wants at the beginning of an information search to be able to survey all possibilities, whereas a precise search is more useful at a later stage when the information want has been narrowed down.

Finally, there are other factors in relation to an information need: the level of urgency felt by a user, the anticipated form of information likely to satisfy the need (e.g., a bibliography or a manuscript), and/or the availability of an information source (e.g., local access versus interlibrary loan).

CONCLUSION

The different views of users' information needs reflect very different traditions within our culture (Hjørland 1998). The physical paradigm grows from an empiricist tradition, focusing on the measurement of information transferred from documents to users and on the degree to which that information satisfies users' needs (usually measured as recall and precision, discussed in Chapter 11). This perspective views users' needs as discrete and identifiable and presumes that they can be addressed by particular pieces of information. User characteristics such as degree of computer skills might be viewed as potential noise to be eliminated by particular measures from this perspective.

The cognitive paradigm comes from the tradition of rationalism, which presumes the supremacy of logic over experience. Users are viewed as having individual knowledge structures built on the basis of inherent rules and governing both input and output in a logically definable manner. Research from the cognitive paradigm takes on the task of identifying the factors influencing user/system interactions, in particular, educational and experiential factors that would have contributed to individuals' knowledge structures.

The social constructivist paradigm is related to the tradition of historicism, which focuses on a society or culture rather than on individuals. It sees individuals' information needs as being constructed by social forces and the factors identified by cognitive research as constructed by the research itself as well as by larger cultural discourses. For example, the demographic characteristics of age and gender would be viewed as products of society rather than essential to being female or older.

Each of these paradigms offers interesting theoretical and useful pragmatic insights, but their coexistence suggests to us that like other social sciences, LIS depends on an imperfect knowledge of human behavior.

REFERENCES

Belkin, N. J., T. Seeger, and G. Wersig. 1983. Distributed expert problem treatment as a model for information system analysis and design. *Journal of Information Science* 5: 153–67.

Borgman, Christine L. 1982. Mental models: Ways of looking at a system. *ASIS Bulletin* 9 (December): 39.

———. 1986. Why are online catalogs hard to use? Lessons learned from information-retrieval studies. *Journal of the American Society for Information Science* 37(6): 387–400.

———. 1989. All users of information retrieval systems are not created equal: An exploration into individual differences. *Information Processing and Management* 25: 237–51.

Cherry, Joan M., and Marshall Clinton. 1992. Online catalogs at five Ontario universities: A profile of users and user satisfaction. *Canadian Library Journal* (April): 123–33.

Dervin, Brenda, and Michael Nilan. 1986. Information needs and uses. *Annual Review of Information Science and Technology* 21: 3–33.

Frohmann, Bernd. 1992. The power of images: A discourse analysis of the cognitive viewpoint. *Journal of Documentation* 48: 365–86.

———. 1994. Communication technologies and the politics of postmodern information science. *Canadian Journal of Information and Library Science* 19: 3–22.

Hewins. Elizabeth T. 1990. Information need and use studies. *Annual Review of Information Science and Technology* 25: 145–72.

Hjørland, Birger. 1998. Theory and metatheory of information science: A new interpretation. *Journal of Documentation* 54: 606–21.

Jacobson, Frances F. 1991. Gender differences in attitudes toward using computers in libraries: An exploratory study. *Library & Information Science Research* 13: 267–79.

Kuhlthau, Carol C. 1993. *Seeking meaning: A process approach to library and information services.* Norwood, NJ: Ablex.

Matthews, Joseph R., Gary S. Lawrence, and Douglas K. Ferguson, eds. 1983. *Using online catalogs, a nationwide survey: A report of a study sponsored by the Council on Library Resources.* New York: Neal-Schuman.

Pritchard, Sarah. 1993. Feminist thought and the critique of information technology. *Progressive Librarian* 8 (Fall): 1–9.

Sandlian, Pam. 1995. Rethinking the rules. *School Library Journal* (July): 22–25.

Shannon, Claude E., and Warren Weaver. 1998. *A mathematical theory of communication.* Urbana–Champaign: University of Illinois Press. Originally published 1949. Available: http://cm.bell-labs.com/cm/ms/what/shannonday/paper.html. (Accessed May 10, 2001).

Sit, Richard A. 1998. Online library catalog search performance by older adult users. *Library & Information Science Research* 20: 115–31.

Solomon, Paul. 1993. Children's information retrieval behavior: A case analysis of an online catalog. *Journal of the American Society for Information Science* 44: 245–64.

Sugar, William. 1995. User-centered perspective of information retrieval research and analysis methods. *Annual Review of Information Science and Technology* 30: 77–109.

10

User-System Interfaces

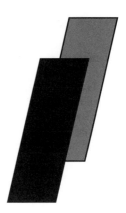

INTRODUCTION

Emerging developments in computer technology have dramatically changed the user-system interaction in recent years. In particular, the growth in use of the World Wide Web (WWW), the popularity of windows environments, and the general acceptance of the Z39.50 standard (described in this chapter) have introduced radical changes for the interface between catalogs and users. Additionally, the increasing speed, power, sophistication, and reliability of computer technology have enabled types of searching that were limited to experimental contexts only a decade ago.

Not long ago, online catalogs looked and acted much like card catalogs and required several steps to request even a direct match for a heading. Subject searching was limited or nonexistent in these catalogs, which Charles Hildreth refers to as first generation online catalogs (1995). However, second generation catalogs have escaped these narrow limits to take much fuller advantage of the electronic medium. They provide more access points, multiple approaches to searching, and far more information when records are retrieved.

Some of the attributes that Hildreth defines for third generation online catalogs are now becoming available, such as ranked retrieval and relevance feedback loops. They will make searching online catalogs a more interactive process for users. This chapter deals primarily with the interfaces of second generation online catalogs but also looks to the future, particularly in the sections on search facilitation and browsing. It is in these areas that the potential of third generation online catalogs is most likely to emerge.

The user-system interface is the point at which the system interacts with those searching it with a view to retrieving documents or their surrogates (such as bibliographic records). It is dependent on a variety of different factors. Most notable among these are the content of the individual records themselves and the connections between them that make up a database. No system can completely overcome the principle of "garbage in, garbage out." An ineffective interface is a waste of time and money, but it can be replaced. An ineffective database is almost irremediable because its upgrading, usually record-by-record, is beyond the resources of nearly any institution. It is important to recall that interfaces can be fluid.

What is discussed in this chapter can change quickly and, indeed, it has changed radically in just the past few years. As a result, this chapter includes the devices that are currently being used to enhance user-system interfaces, but it also examines the conceptual perspectives that are shaping the use of these devices. Further, it deals with the technicalities of user-system interfaces only in general terms (with references to other sources for fuller explanations) except as they relate to subject access. Because subject access is probably the most problematic aspect of interfaces, that aspect alone is sufficiently challenging and complex.

User-system interfaces have the same goal as other aspects of catalogs: to connect people and information in a useful manner. Generally, a user-system interface should achieve this goal through an interaction that is self-evident, smooth, and flexible so that users need not learn arcane procedures, spend time in awkward dances with the system, or conform to some predetermined model of what searching should look like. It is important to remember that the "user" part of a user-system interface (as surveyed in Chapter 9) is not a monolithic concept. "The user" of an online catalog is a mythical character. In reality, the users of online catalogs differ widely in their interests and abilities in using online catalogs in particular and information systems, including libraries, in general. What is self-evident to one user may be complex to another. What is smooth to one user may be overly simplistic to another.

The "system" part of a user-system interface is made up of hardware, software, and databases. The separation between a user and a system is not always obvious. Some functions will be performed by users in one instance and by a system in another instance. In fact, this blurring of the boundaries, the possibility of delegating tasks to the system or reclaiming them from it, is one of the most interesting areas in recent research and development of interfaces.

Another blurring of boundaries is the real or virtual location of systems. Interfaces that operate through the Z39.50 protocol and via the WWW expand the range of users searching any one system beyond the confines of a particular institution. One of the traditional characteristics of library catalogs is that they reflect the holdings of one library or of a consortium of libraries. However, library catalogs now go well beyond physical location in their contents, which frequently include virtual documents and databases not located in the institution reflected in the catalog. Further, library catalogs are now expanding to include other databases and are available in turn to other locations.

The Z39.50 protocol is a standard of the National Information Standards Organization (NISO) and the American National Standards Institute (ANSI). Its purpose is to allow searchers using a particular interface to search other databases via that interface (Lynch 1997). That is, by using one's local catalog, one can search external databases without learning new search techniques or needing to becoming familiar with different displays. This arrangement requires systems to be structured in a common manner so that their elements can be reconfigured into a form familiar to local users. Both the local system or client and the remote system or server must be compatible with the Z39.50 standard. This arrangement allows users to become more adept at searches through a locally standardized interface. Because of the complexity of effective subject searching, such standardization can be a considerable asset (Payette and Rieger 1997). However, accomplishing the standardization required for implementation of Z39.50 is predictably complex. Not all Z39.50-compatible systems are equally effective (*Survey of Z39.50 to Web gateways* 1996). Z39.50 can be implemented at several different levels, and there are several different versions of it. It will be interesting to observe the effect of this kind of standardization on interfaces and databases in relation to subject access as libraries gain more experience with Z39.50.

The other major factor affecting online catalog interfaces is that a rapidly increasing number of catalogs is available on the WWW. The existing infrastructure of the WWW offers a convenient medium for libraries to use for off-site access to their catalogs—far more convenient than previous systems requiring dialing in (Yee and Layne 1998). More important for subject access, WWW use of Hypertext Markup Language (HTML) provides the opportunity for linkages within catalogs that facilitate useful browsing features. It also makes the catalog available to a wider range of users, even more diverse than local users. That diversity makes it even more difficult to provide adequate flexibility in the interface between system and users.

This chapter explores the present state and future possibilities of user-system interfaces for subject access in three parts: modes of access, search capabilities, and display. Modes of access are the means of communication between systems and users. Search capabilities are the techniques available in a system for facilitating communication between users and databases. Displays are the visual manifestations of this communication.

MODES OF ACCESS

The interaction between a user and an online catalog may take place through any of several modes. The two basic modes of operation are the command-based and menu-based interfaces. These two modes are useful as conceptual models for the control of the interaction between user and system. In this sense, the command-based interfaces might be more broadly considered as user-initiated and the menu-based interfaces as system-initiated.

User-Initiated Interfaces

The command mode was the first to be used in online catalogs. In the command mode an individual user initiates and controls the dialogue between the user and the online catalog. A command is issued to the system and the system responds. Each command is made up of two parts: an "operator," which tells the system what kind of command it is, and an "operand," which gives the content of the particular command. For example, a command to search for a subject in an online catalog might be:

SU cats

with SU being the operator explaining to the system that it is a subject search and *cats* being the operand specifying the content of this particular subject search. The command mode can be a very powerful device. However, it does require that a user become familiar with a wide range of commands. For example, in the University of Alberta's "Direct Search" mode (telnet dra.library.ualberta.ca) there are lists of commands to tell the system what files to search and how to navigate through the system. In Figure 10.1 (page 278) the basic search commands for simple searches are shown with the search *s=cats* shown. To activate the search it is necessary to hit <enter>, and the screen in Figure 10.2 will appear. This screen offers headings for the searcher to choose from and a selection of possible commands for navigating the system at the bottom of the screen. This format is quite characteristic of early second generation online catalogs.

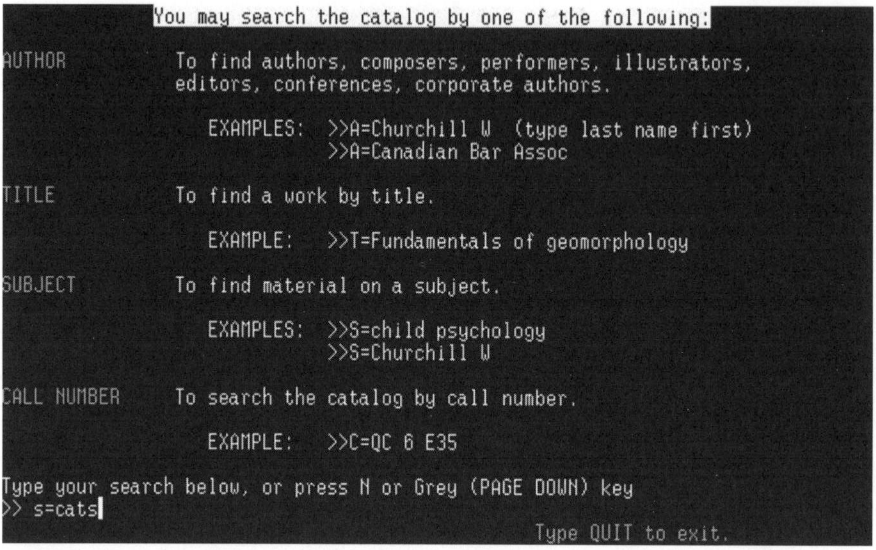

Figure 10.1. University of Alberta direct search.

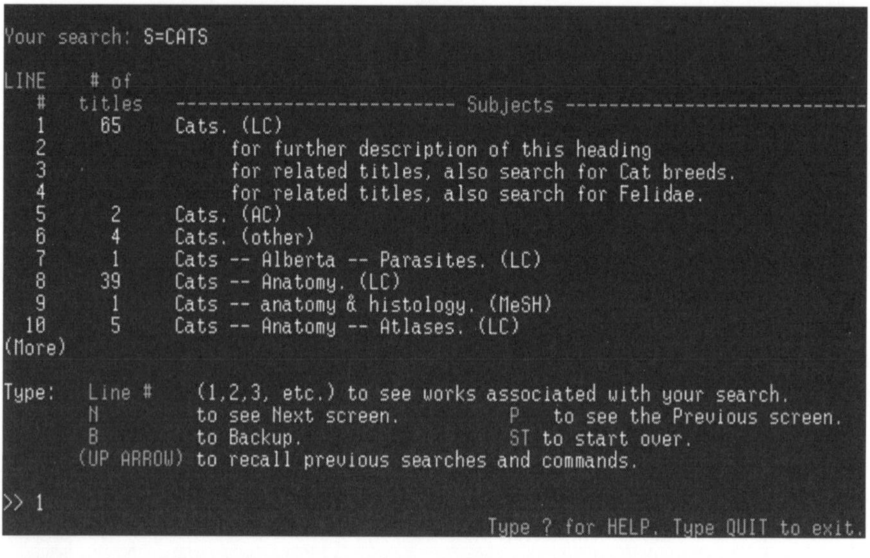

Figure 10.2. University of Alberta direct search subject display.

Figure 10.3 shows more recent sample searches from the Library of Congress (all of the examples from the Library of Congress in this chapter are from its WWW-based catalog, available at http://lcweb.loc.gov/catalog/ unless otherwise specified). It is both more sophisticated and more complex.

LIBRARY OF CONGRESS ONLINE CATALOG

Return to: Command Keyword Searching or Information on Index Codes
Detailed Help for Command Keyword

Command Keyword Search Examples

Use punctuation, boolean operators and/or codes.	
Quotes should surround exact phrases:	"tax reform"
Boolean AND, OR, NOT (upper case):	(mars OR venus) AND mission
Index codes can refine searches:	KSFG western *(finds western as a subject form/genre term)*
? indicates truncation:	ecumen? *(finds ecumenical, ecumenism, etc.)*
EXAMPLE: (wood? OR forest) AND "resource manage?"	

NUMBER SEARCH EXAMPLES:

To retrieve LCCN 89-456:	010a 89000456
To retrieve ISSN 1094-1304	KISN "1094-1304"
To retrieve ISBN 0-553-37783-3	KISN 0553377833

* Search results sort order varies with index choice.

Figure 10.3. Library of Congress command keyword search.

In both cases, a user needs to know the operator for each command she or he wants to employ. Further, a user must be able to construct the operand in such a way that the system understands it. Therefore, command mode interfaces are generally favored by experienced users who use a particular catalog frequently.

Many catalogs no longer have a command mode interface because they have not been considered to be user-friendly. However, the presumption behind this decision is that users do not want to spend the time to become adept at searching a particular catalog. This presumption will certainly be true for large numbers of users, but intense users, those who use the catalog frequently and with sophisticated search techniques, may well prefer the control they can have in a command mode interface. For a knowledgeable searcher, a command approach will be quicker and more accurate than interfaces in which the workings of the system are less visible. The major advantage of the command mode is the power and flexibility it offers to users. Unfortunately, command mode is difficult for many users because the major responsibility of conducting the user-system dialogue is placed on the users.

System-Initiated Interfaces

The alternative chosen to augment or replace command mode in most online catalogs was the menu-based interface. In the menu mode, commands are hidden from users. A list of choices is offered to the system's users, who select from the list to implement their searches. Users need not remember the operator for a given function, making menu-based interfaces easier to use for novice and infrequent searchers. Nearly all catalog users will be familiar with the concept of using a menu to implement functions. Menus are ubiquitous in computer software and in most online catalogs.

Word processing, spreadsheet, electronic mail, and other programs have used menus for years. One comes across menus in other settings as well, including banking, television, and, most exasperating of all, when attempting to interact with various services by telephone. Experience with such telephone menus explains the major shortcomings of menus: They limit one's options and take longer than a more direct approach. That is because in the menu mode, the system initiates and controls the communication. Of course, a computer keyboard is a more versatile instrument than a telephone number pad and menus can be well-designed to be understandable and to offer the options that users are most likely to want or need.

Older menu-based interfaces required navigating the keyboard with directional keys to highlight a choice and then pressing the <enter> key or keying in a one- or two-character code. With the establishment of graphical user interfaces (GUIs), menus can be opened in a window, and a mouse or other device can be used to point and click to activate a particular choice on the menu. This arrangement has become so common that for most computer users it is now intuitive. The entry screen to the University of Alberta's WWW-based catalog (http://gate.library.ualberta.ca) is a typical example (see Figure 10.4).

The GATE Catalogue via the Web

Click on one of the following to begin a search.

Keywords	Call Numbers
Titles	Reserve Room
Authors	Other Numbers
Subject Headings	Borrower Information

The GATE:
NEOS Libraries' Catalogue

Figure 10.4. University of Alberta GATE initial screen.

Such an interface is useful in making catalog searching a smooth process. However, if the menus are not well designed, the problem of limitation of choices and the time required to work through nested windows of menus will still arise, especially if the WWW connection is a slow one.

A variation on the menu-based interface is the fill-in form commonly found on the WWW. Like a menu, it offers options, but instead of a command from a menu, a searcher will select blanks on a form to fill with the requested information (operand). So, in searching a library catalog on the Web, the form might include typical fields (each of which will be linked to fields in a MARC record) such as author, title, subject, and keyword. A user can fill in any or all of these fields, which then become commands to the system to initiate a search. The example in Figure 10.5 is from the Library of Congress online catalog. It shows a typical fill-in form set up for basic Boolean searching. Figure 10.6 (page 282) shows the drop-down menu that allows searchers to select fields to search. Again, the balance of control is with the system in terms of what it offers as options and how those options are sequenced.

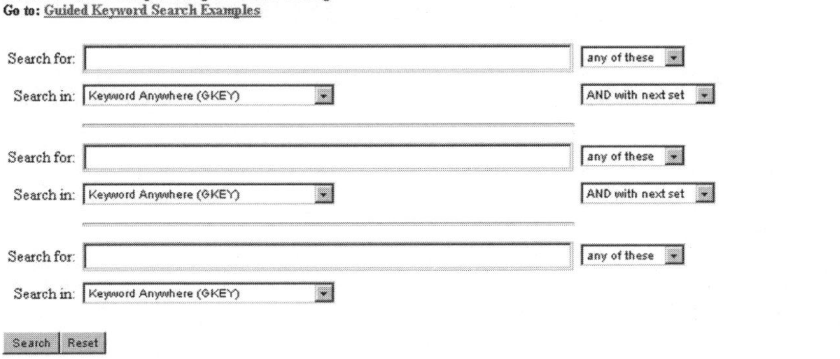

Figure 10.5. Library of Congress keyword form.

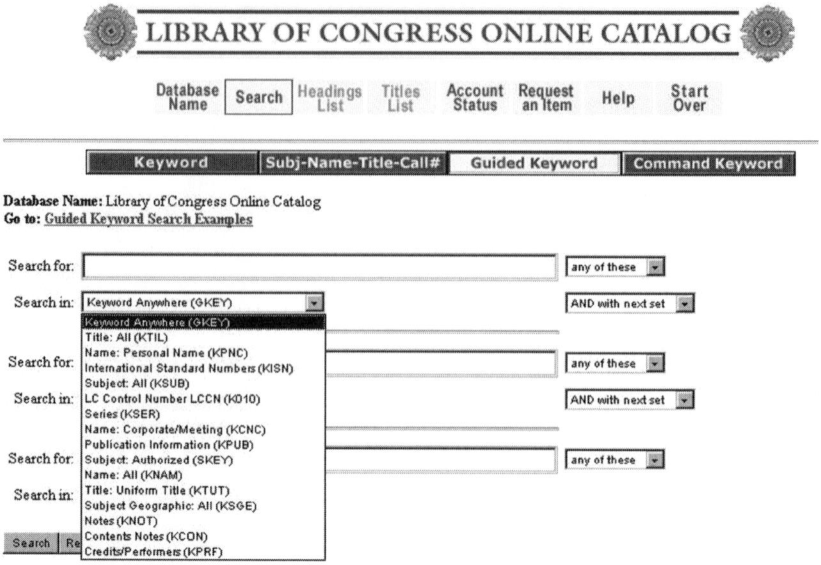

Figure 10.6. Library of Congress keyword dropdown menu.

Combinations of Interface Modes

Because subject searching is complex, it may require the power and flexibility of a command-based interface to achieve optimal results. However, its complexity also means that users find it potentially frustrating and can benefit from the firm-handed guidance of a menu-based or fill-in form interface. As noted previously, the responsibility of the system and the responsibility of the user can become blurred and will certainly vary between interfaces.

Most typical today are systems that allow different approaches. A common example in the current windows environment is the procedure for saving a file. Typically, a user can pull down the *File* menu usually found in the upper left corner of the screen. In that menu will be an option to *Save*. When the user "clicks" on *Save*, a window will be opened and he or she will be prompted to enter a file name, and so forth. However, it is also possible in most situations to use a two-key combination of <Ctrl-S> to receive the same window. The latter is more like a command mode. Another type of hybrid system especially common in library catalogs is to have more than one interface available. For example, the University of Alberta catalogs shown in Figures 10.1 and 10.4 are typical of the kinds of choices available in many libraries' online catalogs.

As systems become more hybridized, offering various options of interaction modes, what they can do is far more important than how the interaction is initiated.

SEARCH CAPABILITIES

The actual search may be initiated through commands or menu choices or forms, but the strategies that can be used for searching depend on the interface's capabilities. As discussed in Chapter 3, the two major approaches to subject access are controlled vocabulary and natural language. The problem to be overcome in searching controlled vocabulary is for users to find the preferred or authoritative term used for the subject they are seeking. Therefore, an interface that assists users in finding such terms will be effective for controlled vocabulary subject searching.

The problem to be overcome in searching the natural language found in various fields of bibliographic records is that that vocabulary has not usually been designed to be readily searchable. Therefore, the searcher is responsible for including all relevant word forms and synonyms and for differentiating homographs. Interfaces include various capabilities to address these problems directly or to work around them. The capabilities generally used in library catalogs fall more or less into four categories: authority control, free text searching conventions, browsing, and search facilitation.

Authority Control

Authority control to guide the searcher in an online catalog operates in roughly the same manner as in a card catalog. References from unused forms and synonyms (*USE* or *see* references) lead to the forms that are used, and references between authoritative headings show the relationships between them as defined in the subject headings list used for the catalog—usually broader terms, narrower terms, and related terms. Scope notes may also be made available through the interface. Figure 10.7 shows an example from the University of Alberta online catalog. Searching the phrase *equal pay* resulted in this screen, which sends the searcher from the non-authoritative heading, *Equal pay for comparable work,* to the authoritative heading *Pay equity.* For the similar heading *Equal pay for equal work* it includes a scope note (here called a *Search also note*) explaining the difference between these two concepts and a reference to the related heading *Women—Employment.*

Assuming that the authority records are included in the database, all of this information is readily available in coded form to be identified for inclusion in the interface. In a study of failed subject searches in a catalog without authority control, Adeline Wilkes and Antoinette Nelson (1995) found that nearly three-quarters of these failures linked to references in a catalog with authority control. These results strongly suggest the efficacy of including the references from authority records. That

---

EQUAL PAY

- Equal pay for comparable work. (LC)
  - *Search under:* Pay equity.
- Equal pay for equal work. (LC) (about) (31 titles)
  - *Search also note:* Here are entered works on equal pay for jobs that require identical skills, responsibilities, and effort. Works on comparable pay for jobs that require comparable skills, responsibilities, effort, and working conditions are entered under Pay equity.
  - *Search also under:* Women -- Employment.
- Equal pay for equal work -- Alberta. (LC) (2 titles)
- Equal pay for equal work -- Alberta -- Edmonton. (LC) (1 title)

Figure 10.7. University of Alberta GATE subject heading display.

many libraries have migrated to systems that display references indicates that experience tells librarians the same thing.

The one question that arises in regard to *USE* references is whether they should be displayed or users should simply be taken directly to the entries under the authoritative heading. Again it is a question of user control (displaying the *USE* references) or user ease (saving the extra steps, but hiding the process). For all of the references, as well as the scope notes, the major difficulty is how they should be displayed (discussed further in the section "Display").

Even when references are included, it is unlikely that users will always be able to key in the text of controlled vocabulary entries. It is for that reason that free text searching has become so popular.

Free Text Searching Conventions

The standard conventions for overcoming the problems of word forms, synonyms, and homographs in free text searching are truncation, Boolean logic, and proximity operators (limiting is a similar device, but it is of less utility for subject searching). For clear discussions of all of these techniques in greater detail, see Martha M. Yee and Sara Shatford Layne (1998).

Truncation

Truncation is intended to gather different forms of the same word or a family of words: singular with plural (*cat* and *cats*; *child* and *children*), verbs or adjectives with nouns (*feminist* and *feminism*), worker with institution (*librarians* and *libraries*), and so forth. Interfaces offer two types of truncation: explicit and implicit.

Explicit truncation requires a user to think of what should be truncated and at what point. Explicit truncation is accomplished by inserting a character such as an asterisk or question mark in place of one or more letters. For example, if a searcher wanted to gather everything on both librarians and libraries, he or she might search *librari?* if the system allowed a question mark to represent more than one character. However, this search would not gather records with the word *library*. The searcher would need to anticipate this problem and search *librar?*. Although not a major problem, this does require the searcher to be aware of all of the possible difficulties that might arise. If a searcher wants to gather *cat* and *cats,* the search *cat?* would be disastrous because it would also retrieve everything about *catalogs, catacombs, catatonia, catscans*, and so forth The searcher would need to know the truncation character representing only one letter, perhaps an asterisk, to search *cat**.

Implicit truncation, on the other hand, does not ask the searcher to think about whether or not to truncate but does it for her or him. Therefore, it will search on the basis of where the searcher stops inputting, a certain predetermined number of letters into the word, or on the basis of a stemming algorithm. A stemming algorithm built into the search interface will truncate automatically according to grammatical conventions. So, plurals ending in -*s* will typically be truncated, as will other common endings such as -*ed* and -*ing*. Obviously, implicit truncation can have problems similar to those of human searchers, even with sophisticated algorithms. If searching an online catalog for the process of creating an index, one wants to search on *indexing*. If it is truncated automatically to *index* the search will retrieve every catalog record with a note that says "Includes index," which would probably be the majority of the database.

As with other issues previously discussed in this chapter, the problem is that control and responsibility go together. If the user controls the search, including the truncation, then he or she must account for all the vagaries of language that might skew the search. If the system controls the truncation, then the results will follow standardized rules rather than the context of the particular search. In either case, truncation is a capability that is useful for free text searching but is not foolproof.

Boolean Logic

Boolean logic, based on set theory, can help address all three of the potential problems of free text searching: variant word forms, synonyms, and homographs (for a fuller discussion of Boolean logic see Pao 1989, 176–85). It can also combine concepts expressed in controlled vocabularies. It is the basis for postcoordinate subject access. That is, it uses terms to qualify each other during searching rather than during indexing.

The three standard Boolean operators are AND, OR, and NOT (sometimes stated AND NOT). AND is used to make a search more specific by calling for the intersection of two sets. If seeking a book about pigs in outer space one might create the search statement *pigs AND space*. The system will then search for all records with the word *pigs* and extract from that set all of the records that also include the word *space*. It is a narrower search than either term alone. Of course, in addition to retrieving documents on pigs in outer space it may also retrieve documents on how big pig barns should be. The results will, however, be a more limited set for the user to wade through than all of the records on *pigs* without limiting to those also including *space*.

If this search does not retrieve enough material it would be possible to expand it with a Boolean OR operator. OR gives an alternative for an element in a search. A user might decide to include hogs as well as pigs because the distinction is fuzzy for most of us. So a search on *pigs OR hogs* would retrieve the material using either term. To combine this with the idea of pigs in space the rules of logic would have the searcher create the query: *(pigs OR hogs) and space*. The parentheses indicate that the OR function should be performed first.

To eliminate the material on porcine barns, the searcher might use the NOT operator. NOT excludes homographs from the search by excluding a word associated with the meaning not intended. In this case the intended meaning of *space* is outer space rather than living space on hog farms. Therefore, adding *NOT barns* would exclude that material. Of course, if the pigs' barns were in outer space then the NOT would exclude something desired by the searcher. NOT is a risky operator because it is difficult to anticipate what will be inadvertently excluded.

As in the case of truncation, Boolean operators can be an effective means for refining a search, but to do so the searcher needs a clear understanding of what is likely to be in the database and exactly how the operators work. One thing that has been clearly established by research in this area is that users generally have difficulty constructing effective Boolean searches and rarely attempt to use them (see, for example, Borgman 1986; Ensor 1992a and 1992b; Hildreth 1995; Norgard et al 1995). To help users, most catalogs will have implicit Boolean operators. Typically in library catalogs they will be a Boolean AND or a proximity operator (described below). In some WWW search engines it will be a Boolean OR. Interfaces may or may not state these defaults. Users may readily deduce that AND is implied in a fill-in form that does not specify otherwise, but in a menu-based or command-based system it will not be obvious. An interface that gives searchers some control is shown in Figure 10.8. This "guided keyword" search of the Library of Congress catalog allows users to choose between explicit Boolean operators. However, they will still need to know how Boolean logic operates. Again, users can either be in control and required to have sufficient knowledge or can have assistance, but not necessarily realize the ramifications of it.

Proximity Operators

Various types of proximity operators can assist in making searches more precise and in excluding undesired homographs. Proximity operators are similar to Boolean AND, but require that two words not only occur in the same record but near each other. They may specify words next to each other, within a prescribed number of words of each other, or just in the same field. They may also specify the order of words next to each other. Proximity operators have much the same implications for searchers and systems as do Boolean operators.

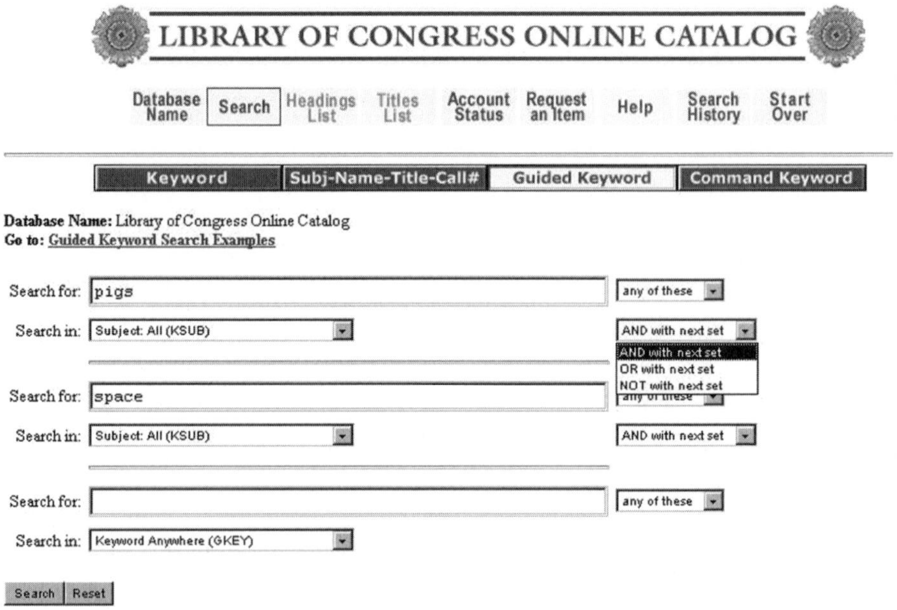

Figure 10.8. Library of Congress guided keyword search form.

Browsing

The traditional free text searching capabilities grew out of a recognition that users cannot be expected to know the authoritative headings of the controlled vocabulary. However, the idea of free text searching is not actually a radical change from conventional controlled vocabulary searching. As Charles Hildreth says, we have accepted a limiting paradigm for information retrieval in the past:

> Unfortunately, most present-day operational and experimental retrieval systems, including most online catalogs and CD-ROMs, reflect in their design and operation a partial, inadequate conceptual model of information retrieval activity. This model describes the exact or best-match, product-oriented approach of most IR [information retrieval] systems. The model assumes the presence of a known, specifiable information need (or subject topic) to start with. Materials that are relevant to that need or topic are represented by index terms such as keywords or subject descriptors, and the need is represented in a well-specified query. These representations are then "best-matched" by the retrieval system . . . to produce the best output set of retrieved materials or information. A second presumption is that for any given query there exists a single best output set that should be targeted for retrieval. . . . This "known-subject need, best-match, end product-oriented" information retrieval paradigm accounts for only part of the subject searching story. It is conceptually inadequate for explaining a variety of information seeking situations or for describing different actual subject searching behaviors (Hildreth 1995).

The alternative paradigm that Hildreth proposes is browsing, a "primary, frequent or preferred mode of subject searching for many individuals."

Browsing is an activity with a long history in libraries and other contexts (Chang and Rice 1993). Users browse the shelves of libraries "instead of" using the catalog. Of course, in this practice they are using the classification applied by catalogers for this very purpose. Users will often find a place to begin browsing by finding one or a few relevant-looking catalog records and following up at the shelves. Librarians have traditionally relied on shelflists, which are catalogs in call number order. Further, the flipping through subject card catalog drawers that was a regular practice of many users was a form of browsing. Now this has been transferred to online catalogs to varying degrees. Perhaps the "known-subject need, best-match, end product-oriented" paradigm that Hildreth describes is responsible for a lack of recognition of the importance of browsing.

Defining browsing, Hildreth invokes the idea of an animal with a purposive search for edible vegetation: "Browsing takes place in a patch of interest and is characterized as tentative nibbling, at least at the start" (1995). He discusses purposive browsing, suggesting that although browsing in a catalog is not well-defined searching, it nevertheless has a purpose. A. C. Foskett goes somewhat further in describing searching by browsing as being "unplanned" and following a "casual train of thought" or even serendipity (1996, 26). A reasonable definition might be that browsing, in the context of the user-system interface, is an exploration of the database with the idea that something interesting or useful might be encountered by following connections.

There may or may not be an articulable purpose although there is likely to be an area or areas of interest at least as starting points.

Some online catalogs still have virtually no browsing capabilities. Often what is called a browse search is not characteristic of the paradigm shift that Hildreth describes or the traditional activities of library users and librarians. Yee and Layne describe five different types of browse searches, only one of which engages users in the type of browsing activity described here (1998, 39–41). This type of browsing responds to a search with lists including the closest match and following (and sometimes a few previous) entries. A conventional browsing interface is shown in Figures 10.9 and 10.10. Searching the term *cats* in LC's "subject browse" mode retrieves a list of subject headings beginning with the word *cats*. However, because the Library of Congress displays headings for several different controlled vocabularies, the list from the first screen (Figure 10.9) shows a range of headings from the *Thesaurus for Graphic Materials* before getting to the LCSH subdivisions on *Cats* on the next screen (Figure 10.10).

Database Name: Library of Congress Online Catalog
YOU SEARCHED: Subject Browse = cats
SEARCH RESULTS: Displaying 1 through 25 of 25.

◀ **Previous   Next** ▶

#	Titles	Headings	Heading Type
[MORE INFO]₁	421	Cats	LC subject headings
2	242	Cats	LC subject headings for children
3	6	Cats	Medical subject headings
4	1	Cats.	Thesaurus for graphic materials: TGM I, sub. terms
5	1	Cats 1620-1650.	Thesaurus for graphic materials: TGM I, sub. terms
6	1	Cats 1770-1780.	Thesaurus for graphic materials: TGM I, sub. terms
7	1	Cats 1770-1790.	Thesaurus for graphic materials: TGM I, sub. terms
8	1	Cats 1860-1870.	Thesaurus for graphic materials: TGM I, sub. terms
9	2	Cats 1870-1880.	Thesaurus for graphic materials: TGM I, sub. terms
10	1	Cats 1880-1890.	Thesaurus for graphic materials: TGM I, sub. terms
11	1	Cats 1890-1900.	Thesaurus for graphic materials

Figure 10.9. Library of Congress subject browse results.

◀ Previous   Next ▶

#	Titles	Headings	Heading Type
1	7	Cats Aging.	LC subject headings
2	52	Cats Anatomy	LC subject headings
3	1	Cats anatomy & histology.	Medical subject headings
4	2	Cats anatomy & histology laboratory manuals.	Medical subject headings
5	1	Cats Anatomy and histology Atlases.	Medical subject headings
6	1	Cats anatomy and histology laboratory manuals.	Medical subject headings
7	7	Cats Anatomy Atlases.	LC subject headings
8	2	Cats Anatomy. [from old catalog]	LC subject headings
9	1	Cats Anatomy Juvenile literature.	LC subject headings
10	12	Cats Anatomy Laboratory manuals.	LC subject headings
11	1	Cats Ancedotes, facetiae, satire, etc. [from old catalog]	LC subject headings
12	72	Cats Anecdotes.	LC subject headings
13	2	Cats Anecdotes.	LC subject headings for children
14	3	Cats Anecdotes, facetiae, satire, etc.	LC subject headings
15	4	Cats Anecdotes, facetiae, satire, etc. [from old catalog]	LC subject headings
16	3	Cats Anecdotes Juvenile literature.	LC subject headings
17	2	Cats Antarctica Fiction.	LC subject headings

Figure 10.10. Library of Congress subject browse results; next screen.

A more sophisticated display referred to as "Browse Search" was available in the Library of Congress Web-accessed catalog for a period of time (http://lcweb .loc.gov/catalog/browse/; accessed July 8, 1999). It offered a compact and interactive display, in which entering the term *cats* as a subject retrieved the following:

```
Subject Search For: CATS
```
You may *either* select a link to see more subject in-
formation, or check one or more boxes and then select
"Display":

☐ **Catroux, Georges, 1877-1969--** (2 items)
   Browse subdivisions of: Catroux, Georges, 1877-1969

☐ **Catry, Solange** (1 item)

☐ **Cats--** (3,485 items)
   Browse subdivisions of: Cats
   See other search suggestions for: Cats

Cats (in religion, folk-lore, etc.)
   See Cats--Folklore

Cats (in religion, folk-lore, etc.)
   See Cats--Mythology

Cats (in religion, folk-lore, etc.)
   See Cats--Religious aspects

☐ **Cats as laboratory animals--** (2 items)
   Browse subdivisions of: Cats as laboratory animals
   See other search suggestions for: Cats as
      laboratory animals

Selecting the link to *Browse subdivisions of: Cats* allows browsing at a more specific level:

> **CATS--**
>
> You may *either* select a link to see more subject in-
> formation, or check one or more boxes and then select
> "Display":
>
> ☐ **Cats** (3,485 items)
> > *See* other search suggestions *for:* Cats
>
> ☐ **Cats--Abstracts** (1 item)
>
> ☐ **Cats--Addresses, essays, lectures** (3 items)
>
> Cats--Adoption
> > *See* Cat adoption
>
> ☐ **Cats--Aging** (7 items)
>
> ☐ **Cats--Anatomy** (38 items)
>
> ☐ **Cats--Anatomy--Atlases** (6 items)
>
> ☐ **Cats--Anatomy--Juvenile literature** (1 item)
>
> ☐ **Cats--Anatomy--Laboratory manuals** (12 items)
>
> ☐ **Cats--anatomy & histology** (3 items)

Selecting the link to *See other search suggestions for: Cats* retrieves its hierarchical references, augmenting browsing with the authority control capability described previously in this chapter:

> **Other Search Suggestions For: Cats**
>
> Here are entered works on domestic breeds of cats.
> Works on the family of cats are entered under Felidae.
>
> **Narrower Topic(s):**
> - Cat breeds
> - Cretin (Cat)
> - Eyra
> - Feral cats
> - Games for cats
> - Jones (Cat)
> - Kittens
> - Longhair cats
> - Misty (Cat)
> - Morris (Cat)
> - Photography of cats
> - Princess (Cat)
> - Ruby (Cat)
> - Scarlett (Cat)
> - Socks (Cat)

· Tinkle (Cat)
· Toys for cats
· Working cats

Broader Topic(s):
· Domestic animals
· Felis

Selecting the link to the narrower term Princess (Cat) puts the searcher into another list for browsing:

PRINCESS (CAT)

You may either select a link to see more subject information, or check one or more boxes and then select "Display":

☐ **Princeses--**(3 items)
Browse subdivisions of: Princeses

☐ **Princess--**(6 items)
Browse subdivisions of: Princess

☐ **Princess (Cat)** (1 item)
See other search suggestions for: Princess (Cat)

Princess Aloha orchid
See Vanda Miss Joaquim

☐ **Princess and princesses** (1 item)

☐ **Princess Anne** (1 item)

☐ **Princess Anne (Md.)**— (2 items)
Browse subdivisions of: Princess Anne (Md.)

☐ **Princess Anne Co** (1 item)

☐ **Princess Anne County** (7 items)

☐ **Princess Anne County (Va.)**—(11 items)

Similar searches can be performed by other subject retrieval standards such as classification. Searching for the *Dewey Decimal Classification* (DDC) number for *cats, 636.8,* retrieves the following:

Dewey Number Search For: DDC 636.8

Check one or more boxes and then select "Display":

☐ **636.77** (1 item)

☐ **636.770896** (1 item)

☒ **636.8** (317 items)

☐ **636.80014** (1 item)

☐ **636.80019** (4 items)

☐ **636.800207** (8 items)

- ☐ **636.800222** (6 items)
- ☐ **636.80028** (1 item)
- ☐ **636.800284** (2 items)
- ☐ **636.800294** (2 items)
- ☐ **636.800296** (1 item)
- ☐ **636.8002967471** (1 item)

Selecting *636.8* brings up a screen with the first twenty brief records (full records can also be requested), but here browsing becomes more problematic because there seems to be no particular order to the records displayed.

Another classification browse is currently available from the Library of Congress. Figure 10.11 shows a search on the Library of Congress Classification number for specific breeds of cats, *SF 449* followed by a topical Cutter number for the breed. This figure shows the range from *Abyssians* to *black cats*. Classification numbers can be reached by links from individual bibliographic records.

These examples from the Library of Congress illustrate some of the options for browsing interconnected parts of a database. The ability to create hypertext links in Web-mounted catalogs like the links from a heading (in this case, *Cats*) to its subdivided forms and its references has virtually infinite potential for browsing. Other types of links can also be made by the database creators, the interface, and users. Now

☐ 12	SF449 A28 S76 1999	Stone, Lynn M.	Abyssinian cats / Lynn M. Stone.	1999
☐ 13	SF449 A45 D38 1999	Davis, Karen Leigh, 1953-	American shorthair cats : everything about purchase, care, nutrition, health care, behavior, and showing / Karen	1999
☐ 14	SF449 A45 Q36 2000	Quasha, Jennifer.	Shorthaired cats in America / Jennifer Quasha.	2000
☐ 15	SF449 A45 U75 1992	Urica, Ingeborg.	American shorthair cat / Ingeborg Urica.	1992
☐ 16	SF449 A63 H46	Hendrickson, Aletha Staunton.	Turkish Angora : revival of an ancient breed / by Aletha Staunton Hendrickson with Beverley Amos ... [et al.].	1976
☐ 17	SF449 B3	Baker, Hettie Gray, 1881-1957.	Your Siamese cat.	1951
☐ 18	SF449 B4	Becker, May Lamberton, 1873-1958.	Five cats from Siam, photographs by Thurman Rotan.	1935
☐ 19	SF449 B45 J64 1991	Johnson, Gene.	Getting to know the Bengal cat / Gene Johnson.	1991
☐ 20	SF449 B45 R535 1995	Rice, Dan, 1933-	Bengal cats : everything about purchase, care, nutrition, breeding, health care, and behavior / Dan Rice ; illus	1995
☐ 21	SF449 B45 S76 1999	Stone, Lynn M.	Bengal cats / Lynn M. Stone.	1999
☐ 22	SF449 B5 M34 1996	Maggitti, Phil.	Birman cats : everything about acquisition, care, nutrition, breeding, health care, and behavior / Phil Maggitti	1996
☐ 23	SF449 B55 T38 1000	Taylor, David, 1934-	Little black cat book / David Taylor.	1990

Figure 10.11. Library of Congress classification search results.

that some catalogs include such elements it seems likely that this will be an area of creative development.

Further, there is likely to be a demand for browsable catalogs. People have always liked to browse, and as they surf the WWW they are becoming accustomed to various types of online browsing, following links of various types. The classifications used in most WWW search engines foster browsing around a hierarchy, an activity for which cataloging databases might have been designed. Going from one type of browsing tool to another is the type of freedom needed for encompassing the bibliographic and, increasingly, full-text-linked databases that online catalogs now represent.

Search Facilitation

The fourth type of capability found in online catalog interfaces is facilitation of users' searches. Many of the sophisticated search capabilities of online catalogs are seldom used, mainly because of their complexity of execution (Borgman 1986; Ensor 1992a and 1992b; Hildreth 1995; Norgard et al. 1995; Payette and Rieger 1997). As mentioned previously, Boolean searching is difficult for many users to use effectively, but other capabilities are also shunned. Because of the complexity of subject searching, these capabilities are, perhaps, most important in that context. To return to the idea that the interface should be self-evident, smooth, and flexible, there should be some way to design interfaces so that they can be simple and easy to use without losing the capability for sophisticated searching in a variety of ways. Attempts to accomplish this goal have been with us for some time, but are becoming more interesting and effective through recent research and developments.

The earliest efforts at facilitating effective searches were online help devices such as screens summarizing commands, help screens, and so forth. Such features have become more effective in later interface development but are still not heavily used by searchers, probably because they require searchers' initiative and interpretation. Other features are being developed to either address a particular problem or create paths that searchers can follow, rather than just giving them online instructions.

An example of addressing a particular problem is the introduction of features to deal with the problem of misspelling. Although misspelling accounts for a small proportion of search failures (less than 10 percent), it is a problem that can cause total failure in an otherwise good search strategy. Karen M. Drabenstott and Marjorie S. Weller (1996c) found that most users notice spelling errors, but some do not and go on to compound the problem with other efforts at "fixing" the search strategy. Automatic spelling-detection routines, similar to spell-checkers in word processing software, can prompt searchers with options that match the spelling in the catalog.

A more complex problem is the mismatch between the terms users input and the vocabulary in catalog records. As mentioned previously, users' difficulty in matching subject headings contributed to the popularity of free text searching and the complex search strategies it requires for effectiveness. Another approach to this problem is to not require users to input terminology at all, but to let them choose paths to follow. Browsing is one such option. Browsing classification sequences, as shown with the LCC in the Library of Congress interface in Figure 10.11, is a reasonable search facilitation if captions (labels saying what each number represents) are included with the classification numbers.

Tree structures based on the hierarchies of classification or subject headings offer another navigational tool that users can follow without knowing the classification numbers or terms to input. World Wide Web search engines often use this approach. Being able to choose a subject heading or classification number from a relevant bibliographic record found by some other means allows users to find more records on the same general topic. More sophisticated features can combine a number of factors from a bibliographic record to find "more like this one." All of these features are available in at least some online catalogs.

A very sophisticated example that goes much further than these capabilities is proposed by Drabenstott and Weller (1996a). They suggest that the interface be programmed to identify the most effective type of search for a given query. Drabenstott and Weller describe these as "search trees" (not to be confused with tree structures) because the system uses a decision tree. In their model (see Drabenstott and Vizine-Goetz 1994 for a full description), if the query exactly matches a subject heading, then the search is performed in the subject heading file; if not, the system searches one-word queries against the main headings in the subject headings file. If it does not match there, titles will be searched for a keyword match. Multiple-word queries that do not match subject headings exactly will be searched as keywords in subject headings, then in titles, and so forth. All failed searches will be checked for spelling errors.

The actual search trees are obviously more complex than this description. Each decision is based on a combination of knowledge about how subject headings are constructed, empirical evidence, and logic. Drabenstott and Weller (1996b) found preliminary evidence to support the efficacy of this approach. Whether precisely this model or something similar is used, this is the type of search facilitation that can codify our professional knowledge of searching for the benefit of users through the user-system interface.

DISPLAY

The actual point of interface between users and systems is the screen. How things are displayed on a computer screen will affect the manner in which people perceive the capabilities of the system. Various checklists have been put forth for the attributes of a good online catalog display. However, online catalog displays are still open to criticism. Joan M. Cherry (1998) amalgamated these checklists and tested the result against a range of online catalogs, both on the WWW and not, and found them to be generally wanting, fulfilling on average only 60 percent of the desired characteristics. Generally, these characteristics involve screen layout, the content and sequence of elements displayed, vocabulary, typography, spacing, and punctuation (Matthews 1991).

Recently, work in this area has reached a sort of culmination with the draft *Guidelines for OPAC Displays* prepared for the International Federation of Library Associations and Institutions (IFLA) Task Force on Guidelines for OPAC Displays by Martha M. Yee (1998). These guidelines are receiving considerable attention through a consultative process instigated by IFLA and the task force's chair, Dorothy McGarry. The *Guidelines* treat all aspects of an online catalog display whether WWW-based or not, some aspects of which are especially pertinent to subject access in online catalogs.

The *Guidelines* include thirty principles solidly grounded in the foundations of cataloging and in international agreements and standards. Following is a discussion of those that relate in a major way to subject access:

Principle 2, The Headings Principle.

The following are usually better represented by a list of headings than by an immediate display of bibliographic records:
a particular author
a particular work
a particular subject (Yee 1998, 7)

In Principle 2 the *Guidelines* suggest a browsable list compatible with the ideas of browsing discussed previously.

Principle 3, Assume Large Retrievals.

All but the smallest of catalogues should assume large retrievals as the norm. Popular authors publish many works. Popular subjects have lots of works written about them. Popular works go into multiple editions. All OPACs should be capable of summarizing, sorting, and displaying thousands of headings and records quickly and efficiently. (Yee 1998, 14)

Principle 3 is more of a warning than a directive. However, its point is well taken. It suggests sorting results of searches in some efficacious order and facilitating the limitation of searches to make them more manageable.

Principle 4, Display What Was Searched.

Whatever data elements have been searched should appear in the resultant display. For example, if the user does a search that searches note fields, all indexed note fields should appear in the display of the retrieved records. (Yee 1998, 15)

The idea in Principle 4 is that users should be able to see readily what caused a particular record to be retrieved. Examples of what this might look like are in Figures 10.7 (page 283) and 10.9 (page 288). The wider implication is that users should be able to understand where they are in the system and why.

Principle 7, Integrate Cross References in Displays.

Displays of headings should always integrate "see" and "see also" references from any available authority file(s) into one alphabetical sequence of headings, "see" references and "see also" references. (Yee 1998, 15)

As discussed previously in this chapter, references from authority records should be displayed for use in searching. The *see* and *see-also* references may be *USE* references and *NARROWER TERMS, BROADER TERMS*, and *RELATED TERMS*, but the principle is the same. Figure 10.7 is a good example of the fulfillment of this principle.

Principle 11, Provide Compact Summary Displays.

Designers of displays should try to summarize the results of a user's search as compactly as possible, to minimize the need for the user to scroll through many screens to select the author, work or subject he or she desires. (Yee 1998, 20)

Once again, Principle 11 dictates that displays should be convenient for browsing, which means that users should be able to scan a reasonable amount of material on a single screen.

Principle 13, Provide Logical Sorting.

Sorting of headings in a headings display should be done as logically as possible. (Yee 1998, 21)

Principle 13 posits that browsing is also easier if the entries are in some order that makes sense to users.

Principle 15, Do Not Truncate Headings.

Never truncate the display of a particular heading in a headings display. Always display the full heading, including any subdivisions or qualifiers. (Yee 1998, 23)

Lists of headings with their differentiating subdivisions cut off by the edge of the screen were a constant problem in early online catalogs. Newer systems that avoid this problem are an asset to searching, particularly to browsing.

Principle 19, Display the Hierarchical Relationship Between Headings and Their Subject Subdivisions.

It should be recognized that a heading has a hierarchical relationship to another heading that begins with the same main heading, but has subsequent subject subdivisions. Whenever the main heading is displayed, all of its subject subdivisions should be available for display as well. (Yee 1998, 31)

Principle 22, Display the Hierarchical Relationship Between a Classification Number and the Entire Classification.

It should be recognized that a particular classification number has a hierarchical relationship to the entire classification from which it is derived. Whenever the particular classification number is displayed, its context in the classification as a whole should be available for display as well. (Yee 1998, 34)

Principles 19 and 22 reflect the favored status of hierarchical relationships over other types of relationships in the subject standards used in most online catalogs. Hierarchical relationships provide the contextual meaning for headings and classification numbers in our organization of information so that it makes sense that online catalogs should demonstrate that structure. One critique of principle 22 is that it could be difficult to achieve, but in both instances the electronic records representing headings and classification numbers should make this information available for display.

Principle 24, Highlight Terms Matched.

In all displays, the words used in the user's original search should be highlighted in any subsequent displays of headings or bibliographic records matched. (Yee 1998 34)

Principle 24 is another effort to keep users oriented to why they have retrieved something and where they are within the system. Figure 10.12 shows the results of a Boolean search on *pigs* and *space,* with the relevant search terms highlighted in bold and italics.

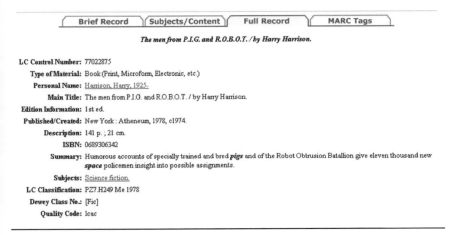

Figure 10.12. Library of Congress bibliographic record full labeled display.

The themes running through these principles are the browsability of the displays and the ability of users to understand how the system is operating. It is interesting that the paradigm that Hildreth sees as a contrast to traditional information retrieval research has effectively emerged in the official guidelines produced by a committee of an international body. Further, it is notable that the *Guidelines*, although advocating user-friendliness, do not suggest that the interface be made transparent. Rather, the *Guidelines* suggest that users should not be shielded from what is actually happening in the retrieval process; that they be made aware of why they retrieved what they retrieved and, at least to a degree, how.

Drabenstott and Weller (1994) again offer a suggestion for aiding users while keeping them apprised of what is going on. It coincides with most of the principles discussed here and serves as a good example of a display. The IFLA draft principles indicate a great deal of material to be displayed for users' understanding of the catalog. Long lists of subdivisions would be required to satisfy principle 19, and these headings with subdivisions are difficult to fit on the screen, as implied by principle 15. Further, references from authority records should be made available to users as well as lists of headings coming before or after the heading retrieved in a given search (principles 2 and 7). However, displays should also be compact (principle 11) so that users can take in the information without having to relate it over several screens.

The answer that Drabenstott and Weller suggest, at least once a subject heading has been identified, is similar to the devices used in the Library of Congress searches recorded above, but goes further. Listed in relation to a particular heading would be the heading itself and links to lists of synonyms (*USE* references); relationships (*BROADER, NARROWER,* and *RELATED TERMS*); and the heading with topical subdivisions, with geographic subdivisions, with chronological subdivisions, and with form subdivisions. Further, Drabenstott and Weller's suggestion would offer the possibility of expanding the search using other strategies (see the discussion of search trees above). From one screen in such a system, users can choose from several options a search strategy suited to their interests. It might be similar to a traditional Boolean search, an authority controlled linkage, or the system's best guess on what might come next.

Drabenstott and Weller's model is not the only one likely to prove fruitful, but it does offer an example of the manner in which a range of features can be put into a compact display with clarity and efficacy. The display needs to make the search capabilities of the system clear and to lead users to the features that will facilitate their searches.

CONCLUSION

Overall, user-system interfaces in online catalogs present searchers with a range of options, from those designed for a virtuoso searcher in perfect control of each keystroke to the novice being carefully led through basic techniques. Either of these categories of users might have clearly articulated information needs but also might be browsing through the connections made in the catalog with little or no idea what will produce satisfaction in a given search. Ideally, a selection of search capabilities will meet the needs of users with different skills and purposes but will never leave a user unable to proceed in some way and will never leave a user uncertain of where she or he is or has been or why a particular item was retrieved.

A good user-system interface will not assume the traditional paradigm of "known-subject need, best-match, end product-oriented" information retrieval, but will also offer the opportunity for browsing that is greatly enhanced by technology now widely available. If user-system interfaces can maintain flexibility in terms of who initiates the dialogue—users or systems—and in terms of the specificity of the approach to searching, they will do much to accommodate the wide range of searches that might produce an effective link between people and information.

REFERENCES

Borgman, Christine L. 1986. Why are online catalogs hard to use? Lessons learned from information-retrieval studies. *Journal of the American Society for Information Science* 37 (6): 387–400.

Chang, Shan-Ju, and Ronald E. Rice. 1993. Browsing: A multidimensional framework. *Annual Review of Information Science and Technology* 28: 231–76.

Cherry, Joan M. 1998. Bibliographic displays in OPACs and Web catalogs: How well do they comply with display guidelines? *Information Technology and Libraries* 17(3) 124–37.

Drabenstott, Karen M., and Marjorie S. Weller. 1994. Testing a new design for subject searching in online catalogs. *Library Hi Tech* 12 (1): 67–76.

———. 1996a. The exact-display approach for online catalog subject searching. *Information Processing & Management* 32 (6): 719–45.

———. 1996b. Failure analysis of subject searches in a test of a new design for subject access to online catalogs. *Journal of the American Society for Information Science* 47(7): 510–37.

———. 1996c. Handling spelling errors in online catalog searches. *Library Resources & Technical Services* 40 (2): 113–32.

Drabenstott, Karen M., and Diane Vizine-Goetz. 1994. *Using subject headings for online retrieval: Theory, practice, and potential.* San Diego: Academic Press.

Ensor, Pat. 1992a. Knowledge level of users and nonusers of keyword/Boolean searching on an online public access catalog. *RQ* 31 (1): 60–74.

———. 1992b. User practices in keyword and Boolean searching on an online public access catalog. *Information Technology and Libraries* 7: 210–19.

Foskett, A.C. 1996. *The subject approach to information.* 5th ed. London: Library Association Publishing.

Hildreth, Charles R. 1995. *Online catalog design models: Are we moving in the right direction: A report submitted to the Council on Library Resources August, 1995.* Available: http://www.ou.edu/faculty/H/Charles.R.Hildreth/clr-opac.html. (Accessed May 9, 2001).

Lynch, Clifford A. 1997. The Z39.50 information retrieval standard. Part I: A strategic view of its past, present and future. *D-Lib Magazine* (April). Available: http://www.dlib.org /dlib/april97/04lynch.html. (Accessed May 9, 2001).

Matthews, Joseph R. 1991. Use of knowledge about users in software development. *Canadian Journal of Information Science* 16 (1): 42–45.

Norgard, Barbara A., et al. 1995. The online catalog: From technical services to access service. *Advances in Librarianship* 17: 111–48. Also available: http://ic-www.arc.nasa.gov /people/plaunt/advances.pdf. (Accessed May 9, 2001).

Pao, Miranda Lee. 1989. *Concepts of information retrieval.* Englewood, CO: Libraries Unlimited.

Payette, Sandra D., and Oya Y. Rieger. 1997. Z39.50: The user's perspective. *D-Lib Magazine* (April). Available: http://www.dlib.org/dlib/april97/cornell/04payette.html. (Accessed May 9, 2001).

Survey of Z39.50 to Web gateways. 1996. Version 3.0. DSTC Pty Ltd. Available: http://www.dstc.edu.au/RDU/reports/zreviews/z3950-gateway-survey.html. (Accessed May 9, 2001).

Wilkes, Adeline, and Antoinette Nelson. 1995. Subject searching in two online catalogs: Authority control vs. non-authority control. *Cataloging & Classification Quarterly* 20 (4): 57–79.

Yee, Martha M. 1998. *Guidelines for OPAC displays.* Prepared for the IFLA Task Force on Guidelines for OPAC Displays by Martha M. Yee. Available: http://ifla.org/VII/s13/guide/opac.htm. (Accessed May 9, 2001).

Yee, Martha M., and Sara Shatford Layne. 1998. *Improving online public access catalogs.* Chicago: American Library Association.

11

Evaluation of Subject Retrieval in Online Catalogs

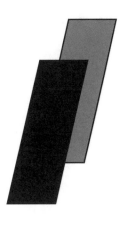

INTRODUCTION

Evaluation of subject access in online catalogs means the evaluation of every component of the online catalog that has a bearing on subject retrieval. However, it is difficult when evaluating to tease out the effect of any single component because they all interact intimately to produce the result. The contents of the collection, the indexing of the documents, the system, the users, and the searching are all factors that affect the subject access retrieval.

Furthermore, the paradigmatic differences described in Chapter 9 have an affect on the evaluation of catalogs. Most catalog evaluation has accepted the model of a user searching a catalog with an information need or want in mind and the ability of that user to identify the items that fulfill that need. The idea that a catalog might or might not be a fruitful place for less goal-oriented searching such as browsing has received little attention. The concept of a "successful" search is difficult to determine even in the predominant paradigm. It is much more difficult if there is no specific goal. However, a wide range of techniques has been used for evaluation of catalogs, and among them there are many opportunities for adapting the evaluation procedures already established in the literature to be helpful in pursuing various purposes for evaluation.

This chapter approaches the problem of evaluation by examining the variables that are measured, the methods that are used for data collection, and the interpretation and application of research results. It is not a comprehensive summary of catalog use studies but rather describes a selection of such studies to illustrate different aspects of evaluating catalogs and their use. Review articles offer a more complete overview of available research; see James Krikelas (1972); Karen Markey (1980); Pauline A. Cochrane and Markey (1983); Christine L. Borgman (1986); David W. Lewis (1987); Sharon Seymour (1989); Thomas A. Peters (1993); William Sugar (1995); and Borgman, Sandra G. Hirsch, and John Hiller (1996).

VARIABLES

A variable is simply one factor that is characteristic of something. If sampling a group of people one might consider the variables of age, sex, or education. The variables used for evaluation of online catalogs that are discussed in this chapter are the three types that are most commonly used and most specific to catalog research:

- Relevance and its derivatives, precision and recall;

- Term matches; and

- Search types

and a sample of the wide range of other variables that have been helpful in this area and others.

Relevance, Precision, and Recall

Relevance

Relevance has been the primary variable for testing information systems for decades. Broadly speaking, the degree of relevance is the degree to which a document retrieved fulfills a user's information need. Tefko Saracevic (1975) identified relevance as the basic concept in information science that began in the context of experimental research. Because experimental research tries to focus on as few variables as possible to isolate their impact, researchers using this technique in information retrieval often leave out people. The result of this tendency in information science is that much of the early work on relevance measurement reflects a focus on the system as opposed to the searcher.

Cyril Cleverdon's Cranfield studies, discussed in Chapter 4 and throughout this chapter, were the major contribution to this research and, not surprisingly, caused the greatest controversy. Although the Cranfield studies were performed on manual rather than electronic databases, their results heavily influenced the development of online catalogs in the following decades. The controversy over the omission of real people with real information needs from the experimental research resulted in two general views on relevance that Don Swanson (1986) calls objective and subjective relevance. For a fuller discussion see Linda Schamber, Michael B. Eisenberg, and Michael S. Nilan (1990).

"Objective relevance" relates to the subject of the document retrieved vis à vis the subject of the query. That is, a particular document will always be relevant to a particular query no matter who asks the question, when, or why. Objective relevance grows from the physical paradigm discussed in Chapter 9. The greatest advantage of objective relevance is that it is easy to measure and is consistent. For example, if a user is seeking an understanding of Plato's *Sophist*, then William S. Cobb's translation accompanied by notes on the work, notes on the translation, a synopsis, a topical index, a discussion of important Greek words, and voluminous endnotes must be "objectively" relevant.

In the Cranfield studies and other similar research, a search was deemed to be successful when a specific document, predetermined to be relevant to a query, was retrieved. As a result, it was easy to compare the success of different methods of indexing. Searches were standardized as well as the relevance of documents so the experiment could focus on differentiating the results of these different indexing methods. Without the artificial context of an experimental study (discussed further in the section "Experiments") it would have been impossible to isolate the variable of indexing method. The Cranfield studies also identified solutions to some major subject retrieval problems, especially relating to the use of authority control and Boolean logic. These results are still useful.

"Subjective relevance," on the other hand, is a user's judgment of whether the document fulfills the need. It is more closely related to everyday reality and the actual usefulness of a particular document to a particular user in a particular instance. It is therefore dynamic and situational, based in users' perceptions. So a particular user wanting to understand Plato's *Sophist* might find Cobb's translation just the thing, or he or she might already know the conventional interpretation of *The Sophist*, or might already have read Cobb's translation, or might want secondary interpretation instead of primary text, and find something like Adriana Cavarero's *In Spite of Plato: A Feminist Rewriting of Ancient Philosophy* to be relevant.

Subjective relevance will be better for finding out if the total combination of components in subject retrieval is operating effectively. It will be affected by factors that allow and encourage users to be flexible in their searches and to include browsing as well as goal-oriented searching. However, subjective relevance is difficult to interpret. Because it will be different for different users and even for the same user at different times, it limits how much the effectiveness of a catalog can be generalized from research results.

Subjective relevance is actually an entire family of perceptions of relevance growing largely from the cognitive paradigm discussed in Chapter 9. D. J. Foskett (1972) viewed relevance (or what we have discussed as objective relevance) as part of public knowledge, but added another factor, pertinence, which is drawn to the specific pattern of a user's mind or private knowledge. Foskett's "pertinence" is another interpretation of subjective relevance. Patrick Wilson (1973) proposed situational relevance as a type of relevance that is logical or objective but at the same time individual as it relates documents to the individual's "stock of information."

William Cooper (1973) developed the concept of "utility," which asks the user to place a theoretical monetary value on retrieval of documents and, in turn, his "Gedanken" or "utility-theoretic" indexing asks the indexer to anticipate the value users will give to retrieval of documents relative to particular access points. Stephen Harter (1992) developed the idea of "psychological" relevance, which he defines as incorporating the other types of subjective relevance, effecting a change in a user's cognitive state. This idea is similar to the cognitive paradigm of users' information-seeking behavior noted in Chapter 9 in that relevance can be taken to relate to an individual's knowledge structure.

Research into users' judgments of relevance indicates that users' points of view (even when assigned to them by researchers) affect relevance judgments (Cuadra and Katter 1967). The order of presentation of documents also affects relevance judgments (Eisenberg and Barry 1988), as does the amount of information about a document that is revealed (Janes 1991). Most important are abstracts, then titles, bibliographic information, and indexing. Carol Barry's (1994) research suggests that factors affecting relevance judgments include aspects as personal as beliefs, as practical as how difficult the material would be to obtain, and as political as the searcher's relationship to the author. This work confirms that subject is only one of many factors in relevance decisions, keeping those of us who focus on subject access as a primary concern at least a little bit humble. All of this research has been done in an academic setting, which is very narrow compared to the larger world of information seekers. It is not clear that these conclusions about relevance are transferable to other contexts.

Precision and Recall

Relevance is an interesting concept, but to make it useful in evaluation of subject access in online catalogs it must be put in a form enabling comparison. The usual way of making relevance judgments, whether objective or subjective, useful for evaluative purposes is to derive the precision and recall ratios of these data. "Recall" is defined as the percentage of relevant documents retrieved; "precision" is the percentage of retrieved documents that are relevant. These relationships are shown diagrammatically in Table 11.1.

Table 11.1. Recall-Precision Diagram

A. Relevant documents retrieved	B. Nonrelevant documents retrieved	A + B Retrieved documents
C. Relevant documents not retrieved	D. Nonrelevant documents not retrieved	C + D Documents not retrieved
A + C Relevant documents	B + D Nonrelevant documents	Total documents

Recall can then be mathematically defined as

$$\frac{\text{Relevant documents retrieved}}{\text{Total relevant documents}} \times 100$$

or

$$A \div (A+C) \times 100$$

Precision can be mathematically defined as

$$\frac{\text{Relevant documents retrieved}}{\text{Total documents retrieved}} \times 100$$

or

$$A \div (A+B) \times 100$$

So if a database contains 155 relevant documents on a topic and 278 documents are retrieved, of which 86 are relevant, the calculations of recall and precision would be

```
recall = 86 ÷ 155 = 55.5%

precision = 86 ÷ 278 = 30.9%
```

Recall gives an idea of how much of the relevant material was retrieved (just over one-half in this case) and how much was missed (here, just less than one-half), so it reflects how inclusive the search was. Precision gives an idea of how much of the retrieved material is actually of use (less than one-third in this instance), so it reflects the efficiency and exclusivity of the search.

Precision and recall have been used in measuring the effectiveness of searches since the 1950s, but the Cranfield studies were key in establishing precision and recall as evaluative measures. Perhaps most important is that the first Cranfield study established the existence of an inverse relationship between precision and recall, generally confirmed by later research (for a different argument, see Fugmann 1994). That is, when precision goes down, recall is likely to go up, and vice versa.

Precision is reasonably easy to derive, but recall presents the significant problem that one is not likely to know exactly how many relevant documents exist in a given database. Online catalogs contain thousands to millions of records. How is a researcher to determine how many are relevant? The answer is to develop a formula that compares relative recall ratios rather than absolute measures of recall. Typically, two or more types of indexing, databases, or types of searching will be examined, and the figure for the total number of relevant documents (A + C in Table 10.1) will be replaced by the total number of relevant documents retrieved in all cases combined. So, for example, if one were comparing free text searching and controlled vocabulary searching in a particular online catalog, each type of search would be performed and the results for comparison might look like this:

```
Relevant documents retrieved only in free text search = FT

Relevant documents retrieved only in controlled vocabulary
    search = CV

Relevant documents retrieved in both searches = B

Relative recall for free text, Rᶠᵀᵀ = (FT + B) ÷ (FT + CV + B)

Relative recall for controlled vocabulary, Rᶜᵛ = (CV + B)
    ÷ (FT + CV + B)
```

Comparing R^{FT} and R^{CV} suggests which type of searching has higher recall. If R^{FT} is the higher number, then free text searching has higher recall in this instance. If R^{CV} is the higher number, then controlled vocabulary searching has the higher recall in this instance.

The same concept can be used for searches by different users to compare user characteristics, or with different types of controlled vocabularies or different search techniques available in different interfaces (see Martyn and Lancaster 1981, 163–69). Any type of comparison will allow use of this approach.

Precision and recall do seem to be measures that relate to the problems real searchers have with databases. Markey (1984), in the CLR-OPAC studies (large-scale research sponsored by the Council on Library Resources, referred to in Chapter 1 in the section "Subject Analysis") identified two basic retrieval problems:

- Retrieval of sets that are too large and

- Retrieval of sets that are too small.

Raya Fidel (1985) linked the two problems with precision and recall (emphasizing that the correspondence is not absolutely clear cut):

- Need for greater precision and

- Need for greater recall.

It is easy to see why precision and recall have become standard measures of the effectiveness of indexing, databases, interfaces, and searching.

Term Matches

A second type of variable used in evaluating online catalogs is matching. Various instances of matching have been tested, and they usually relate to the terminology used for retrieval in the database itself and in searching.

One area in which matching has been used is in assessing consistency (discussed in Chapter 5 in the section "Indexing Consistency"). To determine whether subject indexing has been consistent it is necessary to match both concepts and terms found in bibliographic records. Lois Mai Chan's (1989) consistency study is an excellent example of such a matching study and the problems encountered with matching as a variable. She compared *Library of Congress Subject Headings* (LCSH) assigned to bibliographic records by the Library of Congress to those assigned by other libraries.

In this study, Chan needed to determine the definition of a "match." If the main heading and any subdivisions were all the same, then the two obviously matched. However, if only the main heading or the main heading and perhaps one of two subdivisions matched, how is that to be characterized? It is more of a match than if the records have no headings in common at all. What if two records for the same document have one heading in common and one different? Chan had to develop a veritable classification of matches, each with its own definition, to address this problem.

Matching of terms has also been useful in comparing vocabulary in bibliographic records with the vocabulary used by users in searching. Allyson Carlyle (1989) reviewed matching studies as far back as the 1940s to set up categories of matches between users' search terms and controlled vocabulary in library catalogs. Tschera Harkness Connell (1991) varied this model by using descriptions of books from the *Book Review Digest* to test how well bibliographic records represent the aboutness of books as users might search for them. She matched words from the reviews to words in the titles, subject headings, and other parts of the record.

Matching studies presume that a user has something in mind, a particular topic if not a particular document. They test systems effectively for that type of information need. However, they will not be effective tests of less formulated forays into databases using techniques such as browsing.

Search Types

A third variable is the type of search performed, which can indicate how users prefer searching and how an interface might encourage one type of searching over another. Type of search might be author, title, subject, or other, or it might be more specific such as controlled vocabulary subject searches compared to free text subject searches. One problem is that if evaluative studies do not actually ask users to specify the type of search but take the type from observation of users' actions, it is possible that users may not realize what type of search they are performing. As interfaces become more conducive to moving from one approach to another, and when the interface design is intended to lead users without their having to make decisions, users are less and less likely to know what aspect of the catalog they are using.

Another type of search often studied is the use of various search techniques. Because vendors are increasingly making more sophisticated search techniques available, it is important to know which ones are being used, which are ignored, and which might actually confuse users. As discussed in Chapter 10 in the section "Boolean Logic," one finding of this type of study is that users frequently do not make use of Boolean and other similar search capabilities.

Other Variables

The variables that might be used in evaluating online catalogs are limited only by the ingenuity of researchers. Raya Fidel and Dagobert Soergel (1983) identified variables relating to eight elements of the retrieval process:

Setting (e.g., type of institution)

User (e.g., amount of experience)

Request (e.g., level of specificity)

Database (e.g., nature of the vocabulary, controlled and/or uncontrolled)

System (e.g., search capabilities available)

Searcher (e.g., attitude)

Search process (e.g., degree of modification)

Search outcome (e.g., user satisfaction)

They then identified ten categories of variables that applied more or less across these elements, for example, the category of complexity related to users' ability to handle complexity, complexity of the system, and so forth. These general categories still provide a useful survey of possibilities even though the roles of user and searcher have been largely collapsed with the rise of end-user searching. Although the variables of relevance, precision, and recall; term matches; and search types are prevalent in much research on online catalogs, there is no practical limit to the variables that might be worth measuring for useful results.

METHODS

A range of methods is available to gather and analyze data on these various variables. The most commonly used are

Experiments

Questionnaires

Interviews

Focused group interviews

Observation/protocol analysis

Transaction log analysis

Database analysis

Textual analysis

Each has advantages and disadvantages and, as in other research, use of more than one method makes the results more reliable. The following discussion introduces these methods and provides selected examples. Further information on their application in catalog use studies may be found in review articles such as Krikelas (1972); Markey (1980); Cochrane and Markey (1985); Borgman (1986); Lewis (1987); Seymour (1989); Peters (1993); Sugar (1995); and Borgman, Hirsch, and Hiller (1996). Further information on specific methods can be found in basic research methods texts in library and information studies such as Charles H. Busha and Stephen P. Harter (1980); Ronald R. Powell (1991); and Jack D. Glazier and Ronald R. Powell (1992).

Experiments

Experimental research, as mentioned previously, isolates a few variables in a controlled context to test their interaction with each other. In evaluation of library catalogs this method has been used in what might be called laboratory experiments, such as the Cranfield studies, to test concepts. The Cranfield studies tested types of indexing by indexing each document in a test collection in several different ways and then comparing the results. The Cranfield studies were performed in a manual environment, but this method has proven useful in an online environment as well. For example, Ray R. Larson (1992) used a test catalog to compare the exact matches required when using Boolean logic to the partial matching that can be identified using vector and probabilistic models of searching. This type of experiment is very artificial, but it is also the most effective at eliminating extraneous data and focusing only on the variables of interest.

Other research in online catalogs might be considered quasi-experimental in that it takes place in the less predictable environment of actual libraries with actual users. For example, Sharon Baker (1988) tested differences in shelf browsing between fiction classified according to genre and fiction shelved alphabetically by author. She had different degrees of each variable in three different public libraries and compared their circulation to find that the fiction arranged by genre circulated more often than that arranged alphabetically (although not directly related to online catalogs, Baker's results do have implications for browsing). This kind of experiment is more subject to extraneous variables, so the connections it makes between variables are not as solid. However, it is more naturalistic and therefore may be better for generalizing to real life situations.

Questionnaires

Questionnaires have been one of the standard means of gathering data in library contexts for most of the last century (Krikelas 1972). They are an efficient means of gathering large amounts of data and effective when well-constructed and carefully administered. Joan Cherry and Marshall Clinton (1992) used a questionnaire to study nearly 3,000 participants, a representative mix of users in terms of academic status. Users were asked by librarians to fill out the questionnaire as they left the workstation. Cherry and Clinton compared user satisfaction with various aspects of the system to user characteristics. They concluded that academic users are generally both computer literate and OPAC-experienced.

Their learning is independent, mainly trial and error, and, except for faculty who consult librarians, few use traditional library instructional means in learning to use online public access catalogs (OPACs). To collect data on a wide range of variables in a consistent manner a questionnaire is a very useful tool. It is relatively inexpensive and easy to administer (even to a large sample of users) and relatively easy to analyze (although not necessarily to interpret). Its drawbacks are that it can be written so that users will not all interpret the questions in the same way, it can be skewed by a poor sampling of users or by poor timing (for example, exam week in a university library), it may get few responses, and it generally gathers only the information requested.

Interviews

Interviews have also been used as a data-gathering method for a long time. They may be highly structured (virtually an oral questionnaire), completely unstructured (letting interviewees direct the discussion), or somewhere in between. Interviews have a better chance of gathering unexpected data than do questionnaires. The interviewer can follow up on a user's answers for a more rounded picture. Alexandra Dimitroff (1992) explored users' views of systems from a cognitive perspective. She identified whether users had developed their own mental models of an online catalog through unstructured interviews (except for personal data, she asked users only two questions, on which they were to expand). She combined the interview data with data about searches done by the same users and found that users with an accurate mental model of how the system worked had a higher success rate in their searches. In Dimitroff's study, interviews were able to show her very subjective data that a questionnaire could not have obtained. However, interviews are very labor-intensive, so large groups of users cannot be sampled as with questionnaires.

Focused Group Interviews

Focused group interviews were introduced to catalog evaluation in the 1980s in OCLC research and were used in the CLR-OPAC studies. A focused group interview involves a group discussing predetermined questions with the help of a facilitator who records their discussion and decisions (for a fuller description, see Drabenstott 1992). The participants bring their own views to the discussion but also interact with each other to produce a more synergistic discussion than in an individual interview.

On the other hand, some participants may be less frank in a group than they would be individually. Focused group interviews often allow inclusion of more participants than is possible in individual interviews. Focused group interviews are good sources of data describing people's feelings and beliefs on a topic. In that way they can identify problems for future research or help to explain data gathered by other methods. For example, in the CLR-OPAC studies, focused group interviews were used as a follow-up to a questionnaire. The groups were carefully constructed with the idea that online catalog users and nonusers in different demographic groups be represented as well as several categories of library staff. The interviews were done at six libraries, again reflecting different constituencies: public, academic, and research. Between ten and sixteen group interviews were conducted at each library, for a total of seventy.

The sessions were transcribed for analysis. Obviously this kind of interview creates a lot of text, which was analyzed manually in the CLR-OPAC studies but can now be analyzed using specially designed software. In addition to generalizations that might be drawn from a project the size of the CLR-OPAC studies, the comments of individual group members are also potentially significant. Karen Markey (1983) summarized the results of the focused group interviews in the CLR-OPAC studies and reinforced them with typical and often creative or pithy quotes. Most of her conclusions still apply to online catalogs even in their new environments such as the World Wide Web.

Observation/Protocol Analysis

Observation by researchers of users searching catalogs was used to evaluate card catalog use and has continued with online catalogs. The observation may be with or without users' knowledge. If it is with users' knowledge, they may search differently knowing that they are being observed. However, ethical issues arise in observation without users' knowledge. Observation can provide data on what users actually do, but not on why. Protocol analysis supplies this information. A typical protocol analysis in evaluating online catalogs asks users to speak aloud what they are thinking as they search or to describe it immediately after they search. In this way, researchers can get a clearer picture of why users choose to perform particular searches in particular ways.

S. J. Hirst and Jan Corthout (1999) used verbal protocols to compare users' interactions with the same online catalog using both old and new (hypertext) interfaces over the Internet. The users were students at the University of Loughborough in England and were using the interfaces to access the catalog of the University of Antwerp. They were given eight tasks to perform in each interface and asked to speak their thought processes aloud as they went along. Their verbal comments and their interactions with the systems were recorded by an observer and videotaped for later analysis. These rich data were combined with statistics on usage of the systems, questionnaire data, and comparison against a standardized checklist. In the protocol analysis/observation section of the study, the new hypertext system was actually less satisfactory than the old system. Such data can lead to design modifications when discovered in the evaluative stage of development (as was the case in this study).

Transaction Log Analysis

Online catalogs have added the opportunity for a new type of method in the tradition of observation. Most catalogs have the capacity to log the transactions (searches, displays of records, etc.) between users and the system. These logs are a rich source of data. This data-gathering method has the advantage of being quick and inexpensive. It is also unobtrusive, so searchers do not search differently because someone is watching, as may be the case with protocol analysis.

The major problems with transaction log analyses are in the analysis, not in the data gathering. First, transaction logs produce far more data than any other collection method used before in catalog research. Finding ways to sift through this data to identify what is pertinent to a particular research question is challenging to say the least. Second, it is not always easy to tell what is happening in a given transaction. For example, it is difficult to separate author or title from subject searches when users employ free text searching. Third, transaction logs have typically been completely separated from users. In a conventional transaction log it is impossible to tell when one user stops searching and another starts, much less anything about why a user is performing a particular search in a particular manner. If a user enters the word "power," is she or he interested in electricity or politics? There are some ways of getting around these problems, although they, too, have their pros and cons.

Thomas A. Peters and Martin Kurth (1991) used a relatively straightforward transaction log analysis. They collected seven months' worth (representing different aspects of the academic year) of online catalog transactions using dial access (that is, searchers who were not actually in the library but used a modem to connect to the catalog). Dial access sessions could be defined by logon and logoff, addressing the problem of other transaction log research, which cannot distinguish between users. They were looking for shifts between controlled and uncontrolled vocabulary subject searches but found it difficult to interpret what was and was not a title keyword search employed as a subject search (rather than a known item title search). They logged 1,972 search sessions, but only 131 used both subject approaches, according to Peters and Kurth. Their findings suggested that linkage of controlled vocabulary to users' terms and uncontrolled vocabulary be enhanced to facilitate searching.

In a study at four libraries (two in the United States and two in the United Kingdom; two public and two academic), Micheline Hancock-Beaulieu (1993) used a software package that allows online questionnaires to be linked with transaction log analysis to supply personal data linked to the logs. An online questionnaire both pre- and post-search supplied some of the data, especially regarding satisfaction, which supplemented the transaction logs. The method was, therefore, more obtrusive than other transaction logs, risking errors from the respondents' reactions to the measurement. But it avoided at least some errors in interpretation of the data. It was an opportunity to collect the kind of contextual data other transaction logs cannot. An interesting aspect of Hancock-Beaulieu's study is that through this methodology she was able to identify that users preferred online browsing of subject headings to keyword searching where the former was available (three of the four libraries).

Transaction log analysis, especially combined with other methods, offers considerable potential in the evaluation of online catalogs. The application of results from transaction logs is discussed in the section "Interpretation and Application" in this chapter.

Database Analysis

The data-gathering method discussed here is, for lack of a well-recognized name, called database analysis. This method is very widely used in studies of catalogs. It encompasses a range of techniques, all of which analyze the content of databases, including bibliographic and authority records and elements of such records. The consistency studies mentioned earlier are often types of database analysis, such as Lois Mai Chan's (1989) comparison of different catalog records for the same documents. Indeed, most studies that match terms fall into this category. Studies of errors in cataloging are also in this group.

Elaine Svenonius and Dorothy McGarry (1993) looked at OCLC bibliographic records to see whether their LC subject headings were accurate in comparison to the documents cataloged (for aboutness) and the Library of Congress's *Subject Cataloging Manual: Subject Headings* (SCM:SH). They were seeking an objective way to evaluate the assignment of subject headings and concluded that by identifying obsolete headings, incorrectly constructed subject heading strings, and blatantly inappropriate aboutness, they could, indeed, assess most headings without concern for the differences that perspective might bring. Their study had a small sample (100 records), which is characteristic of most database analysis when it requires human assessment of each piece of text, although Chan and Vizine-Goetz (1996) examined 9,422 headings for analysis of incorrect and obsolete headings.

The analysis used a combination of manual and automated tools (SCM:SH and MARC authority records). The results of this and other studies led to development of a computerized validation file (Chan and Vizine-Goetz 1998, discussed in Chapter 5) that can greatly improve the accuracy of subject cataloging. Retrieving a representative sample may be difficult and analyzing a large sample may require ingenuity, but this type of study has been very fruitful and will, undoubtedly, continue to be so.

Textual Analysis

Textual analysis uses theoretically based methods often drawn from critical work in the humanities. Recent theorization on domain analysis in classification and indexing offers an environment for this research. Instead of pretending to be a "value-free ethics of dissemination of knowledge" in which we adopt a "prudent objectivity," Hanne Albrechtsen (1993, 223) suggests that indexers and classificationists need to recognize that social and cultural realities call for subjectivity in taking responsibility for information access for different groups. Domain analysis analyzes the cultural, historical, and linguistic characteristics of specific knowledge domains—traditional disciplines and other discourses—with a view to understanding how knowledge is constructed within those domains (Hjørland and Albrechtsen 1995). It has been used successfully to map two very different knowledge domains: fiction studies (Beghtol 1995) and mathematics (Iyer and Giguere 1995).

In a different type of textual study, Hope A. Olson (1998) used the text of the *Dewey Decimal Classification* (DDC) as the basis for a theoretical analysis of the treatment of marginalized groups and topics in mainstream classification schemes. She employed theory from feminist philosophy and geography to better understand the cultural biases inherent in standardized subject access tools. This theoretical analysis was then applied to identify problem areas in DDC and provide a search mechanism for improved access for a particular group of users (Ward and Olson

1998). Texts can be used for any type of theoretical discussion, be it deconstruction, hermeneutics, discourse analysis, postcoloniality, or any of the other critical stances that can help us understand how our practices and standards have come about and how they operate at a metaphysical level (see, for example, Frohmann 1994 and Olson 1997).

INTERPRETATION AND APPLICATION

Interpretation of most of the data gathered about online catalogs is similar to that in any research. It may be quantitative analysis (e.g., determining precision and recall values), qualitative analysis (e.g., interpreting the transcripts of verbal protocols), or theoretical analysis (e.g., uncovering the underlying assumptions of classification). Finding out how effectively online catalogs work is not simple, but neither is it the most difficult of research problems. What is very difficult is to locate what is causing both the successes and failures of online catalogs.

As mentioned at the beginning of this chapter, the effectiveness of online catalogs is a combination of the standards for subject access, their application, the nature of the collection being cataloged, the policies of the library in relation to cataloging, the structure of the database, the interface between the database and the user, the search techniques used, the characteristics of the users, and who knows what else. If a study discovers low precision in searches in a particular catalog, any one of these factors or, more likely, a combination of several, could be responsible. Perhaps the vocabulary is not specific enough or is not applied to the optimal level of specificity. Perhaps the authority control mechanisms in the database do not lead users to search for the most specific term. Perhaps the interface confuses users regarding what and how to search. Perhaps the users do not know how to narrow a search, which may be because they do not understand Boolean logic or because they have not been instructed in how to use the particular interface.

The design of a research project can help to overcome this confusion by collecting data on a variety of variables and using different methods as cross-checks to each other. The example of Hancock-Beaulieu's (1993) study using both an online questionnaire and transaction logs suggests that such combinations are worth the extra effort. Similarly, the questionnaires and focused group interviews used in the CLR-OPAC studies complemented and supplemented each other for richer results (Matthews, Lawrence and Ferguson 1983).

In spite of the problems of doing research on online catalogs, the results are worthwhile. Application of the findings can enhance the services of libraries in relation to subject retrieval in their catalogs. Taking transaction log analysis as an example, Beth Sandore (1993), in an excellent review article, categorized its usefulness for all aspects of a library system. Administrative applications of this method can indicate what staff training is needed. Public service applications can inform librarians on effectively assisting users in searching. Systems applications can address issues of effective screen display. Cataloging and classification applications can detect errors, estimate the value of adding elements to catalog records for free text subject searching, and identify frequent term mismatches that might be addressed via additions to authority records. Collection management applications can note the parts of the collection in most demand. In addition to providing data on which to base development of new features, changes to catalogs can be assessed using before-and-after data (as in the Hirst and Corthouts 1999 study described previously).

How a library actually used transaction logs to diagnose and solve problems is described by Nirmala S. Bangalore (1997) and Deborah D. Blecic et al. (1998). They explain the collection of a sample of transactions (nearly 40,000) taken from the catalog of the University of Illinois at Chicago during a four-day period in 1995. These logs were divided up among a group of librarians who reviewed them systematically to identify patterns that caused users problems in searching. As a result of this analysis, changes were made to the introductory screens of the catalog. Then just over 20,000 transactions from a similar period in the following academic term were logged and the analysis was repeated.

The analysis for each period included eight well-defined categories of problems that were recognizable in transaction logs alone. The result was improved user success in these categories. The library has now set up a regular monitoring and feedback loop to continue this process, realizing that one improvement will not answer for the long term. There will be changes in users' interactions with the catalog, and ongoing analysis and application are essential to effective service.

CONCLUSION

Online catalogs are complex applications, so it is not surprising that their evaluation is not simple. Standard variables such as relevance, precision, and recall still have value in showing the performance of an online catalog, but they will not always pinpoint what is responsible for a particular aspect of that performance. Adding more general variables to the mix and using a variety of methods to gather and analyze those variables will offer the possibility of sophisticated evaluation if the research design is carefully crafted. Application of research findings should be tested after implementation to ensure that changes made are, indeed, addressing the perceived problem as intended.

The complexity of catalogs makes research difficult but it also makes research imperative. Too often we presume that we know how users are searching the catalog. With the rapid changes in nearly every element of the online catalog, there is no room for presumption. Reading existing research and performing both generalizable and case-specific research is essential to fulfilling our goal of linking people and information via online catalogs.

REFERENCES

Albrechtsen, Hanne. 1993. Subject analysis and indexing: From automated indexing to domain analysis. *The Indexer* 18 (4): 219–24.

Baker, Sharon L. 1988. Will fiction classification schemes increase use? *RQ* 27 (3): 366–76.

Bangalore, Nirmala S. 1997. Re-engineering the OPAC using transaction logs. *Libri* 47: 67–76.

Barry, Carol L. 1994. User-defined relevance criteria: An exploratory study. *Journal of the American Society for Information Science* 45 (3): 149–59.

Beghtol, Clare. 1995. Domain analysis, literary warrant, and consensus: The case of fiction studies. *Journal of the American Society for Information Science* 46 (1): 30–44.

Blecic, Deborah D., et al. 1998. Using transaction log analysis to improve OPAC retrieval results. *College & Research Libraries* 59 (1): 39–50.

Borgman, Christine L. 1986. Why are online catalogs hard to use? Lessons learned from information-retrieval studies. *Journal of the American Society for Information Science* 37 (6): 387–400.

Borgman, Christine L., Sandra G. Hirsch, and John Hiller. 1996. Rethinking online monitoring methods for information retrieval systems: From search product to search process. *Journal of the American Society for Information Science* 47 (7): 568–83.

Busha, Charles H., and Stephen P. Harter. 1980. *Research methods in librarianship: Techniques and interpretation*. New York: Academic Press.

Carlyle, Allyson. 1989. Matching *LCSH* and user vocabulary in the library catalog. *Cataloging & Classification Quarterly* 10: 37–63.

Chan, Lois Mai. 1989. Inter-indexer consistency in subject cataloging. *Information Technology and Libraries* 8: 349–58.

Chan, Lois Mai, and Diane Vizine-Goetz. 1996. Feasibility of a computer-generated validation file based on frequency of occurrence of assigned LC Subject Headings, Phase II, Nature and pattern of invalid headings. *Annual Review of OCLC Research, 1996*. Available: http://www.oclc.org/oclc/research/publications/review96/feas.htm. (Accessed May 9, 2001).

———. 1997. Errors and obsolete elements in assigned Library of Congress Subject Headings: Implications for subject cataloging and subject authority control. *Library Resources & Technical Services* 41 (4): 295–322.

———. 1998. Toward a computer-generated subject validation file: Feasibility and usefulness. *Library Resources & Technical Services* 42: 45–60.

Cherry, Joan M., and Marshall Clinton. 1992. OPACs at five Ontario universities: A profile of users and user satisfaction. *Canadian Library Journal* 49 (2): 123–33.

Cochrane, Pauline A., and Karen Markey. 1985. Catalog use studies—since the introduction of online interactive catalogs: Impact on design for subject access. *Library & Information Science Research* 5: 337–63.

Connell, Tschera Harkness. 1991. Techniques to improved subject retrieval in online catalogs: Flexible access to elements in the bibliographic record.. *Information Technology and Libraries* 10 (2): 87–98.

Cooper, William S. 1973. On selecting a measure of retrieval effectiveness. *Journal of the American Society for Information Science* 24 (2): 87–100 and 24 (6): 413–24.

Cuadra, Carlos A., and Robert V. Katter. 1967. Opening the black box of "relevance." *Journal of Documentation* 23 (4): 291–303.

Dimitroff, Alexandra. 1992. Mental models theory and search outcome in a bibliographic system. *Library & Information Science Research* 14: 141–56.

Drabenstott, Karen Markey. 1992. Focused group interviews. In *Qualitative research in information management*, edited by Jack D. Glazier and Ronald R. Powell, 85–104. Englewood, CO: Libraries Unlimited.

Eisenberg, Michael, and Carol Barry. 1988. Order effects: A study of the possible influence of presentation order on user judgments of document relevance. *Journal of the American Society for Information Science* 39 (5, September): 293–300.

Fidel, Raya. 1985. Moves in online searching. *Online Review* 9 (1): 61–74.

Fidel, Raya, and Dagobert Soergel. 1983. Factors affecting online bibliographic retrieval: A conceptual framework for research. *Journal of the American Society for Information Science* 34 (3): 163–80

Foskett, D. J. 1972. A note on the concept of 'relevance.' *Information Storage and Retrieval* 8 (2): 77–78.

Frohmann, Bernd. 1994. Discourse analysis as a research method in library and information science. *Library & Information Science Research* 16: 119–38.

Fugmann, Robert. 1994. Galileo and the inverse precision/recall relationship: Medieval attitudes in modern information science. *Knowledge Organization* 21 (3): 153–54.

Glazier, Jack D., and Ronald R. Powell. 1992. *Qualitative research in information management*. Englewood, CO: Libraries Unlimited.

Hancock-Beaulieu, Micheline. 1993. A comparative transaction log of browsing and search formulation in online catalogues. *Program* 27 (3): 269–80.

Harter, Stephen P. 1992. Psychological relevance and information science. *Journal of the American Society for Information Science* 43 (5): 602–15.

Hirst, S. J., and Jan Corthouts. 1999. Hyperlib Deliverable 5.1: Evaluation of the Hyperlib Interfaces. Hyperlib Electronic Document Store. Available: http://143.169.20.1/MAN/WP51/root.html. (Accessed May 9, 2001).

Hjørland, Birger, and Hanne Albrechtsen. 1995. Toward a new horizon in information science: Domain-analysis. *Journal of the American Society for Information Science* 46 (6): 400–425.

Iyer, Hemalata, and Mark D. Giguere. 1995. Towards designing an expert system to map mathematics classificatory structures. *Knowledge Organization* 22 (3/4): 141–47.

Janes, Joseph W. 1991. Relevance judgments and the incremental presentation of document representations. *Information Processing & Management* 27 (6): 629–46.

Krikelas, James. 1972. Catalog use studies and their implications. *Advances in Librarianship* 3: 195–220.

Larson, Ray R. 1992. Evaluation of advanced retrieval techniques in an experimental online catalog. *Journal of the American Society for Information Science* 43 (1): 34–53.

Lewis, David W. 1987. Research on the use of online catalogs and its implications for library practice. *Journal of Academic Librarianship* 13 (3): 152–57.

Markey, Karen. 1980. *Research report on analytical review of catalog use studies.* Columbus, OH: OCLC.

——. 1983. Thus spake the OPAC user. *Information Technology and Libraries* 2 (4): 381–87. (Reprinted in *Information Technology and Libraries* 12 (1) (1993): 87–92.

——. 1984. *Subject searching in library catalogs: Before and after the introduction of online catalogs.* (OCLC Library Information and Computer Science Series No.4). Dublin, OH: OCLC.

Matthews, Joseph R, Gary S. Lawrence, and Douglas K. Ferguson. 1983. *Using online catalogs: A nationwide survey: A report of a study sponsored by the Council on Library Resources.* New York: Neal-Schuman.

Martyn, John, and F. Wilfrid Lancaster. 1981. *Investigative methods in library and information science: An introduction.* Arlington, VA: Information Resources Press.

Olson, Hope A. 1997. The feminist and the emperor's new clothes: Feminist deconstruction as a critical methodology for library and information studies. *Library & Information Science Research* 19 (2): 181–98.

——. 1998. Mapping beyond Dewey's boundaries: Constructing classificatory space for marginalized knowledge domains. *Library Trends* 47 (2): 233–54.

Peters, Thomas A. 1993. The history and development of transaction log analysis. *Library Hi Tech* 11 (2): 41–66.

Peters, Thomas A., and Martin Kurth. 1991. Controlled and uncontrolled vocabulary subject searching in an academic library online catalog. *Information Technology & Libraries* 10 (3): 201–11.

Powell, Ronald R. 1991. *Basic research methods for librarians.* Norwood, NJ: Ablex.

Sandore, Beth. 1993. Applying the results of transaction log analysis. *Library Hi Tech* 11 (2): 87–97.

Saracevic, Tefko. 1975. Relevance: A review of and a framework for thinking on the notion in information science. *Journal of the American Society for Information Science* 26 (6): 321–43.

Schamber, Linda, Michael B. Eisenberg, and Michael S. Nilan. 1990. A re-examination of relevance: Toward a dynamic, situational definition. *Information Processing & Management* 36 (6): 755–76.

Seymour, Sharon. 1989. Online public access catalog user studies: A review of research methodologies, March 1986–November 1989. *Library & Information Science Research* 13 (2): 89–102.

Sugar, William. 1995. User-centered perspective of information retrieval research and analysis methods. *Annual Review of Information Science and Technology* 30: 77–109.

Svenonius, Elaine, and Dorothy McGarry. 1993. Objectivity in evaluating subject heading assignment. *Cataloging & Classification Quarterly* 16 (2): 5–40.

Swanson, Don R. 1986. Subjective versus objective relevance in bibliographic retrieval systems. *Library Quarterly* 56 (4): 389–98.

Ward, Dennis B., and Hope A. Olson. 1998. A shelf browsing search system for marginalized user groups. In *Information access in the global information economy: Proceedings of the 61st annual meeting of the American Society for Information Science, October 25–29, 1998, Pittsburgh, Pennsylvania,* 342–47. Medford, NJ: Information Today.

Wilson, Patrick. 1973. Situational relevance. *Information Storage and Retrieval* 9 (8): 457–71.

12

Conclusions

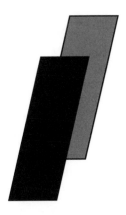

This book will have made clear the complexity and dynamism of subject analysis in online catalogs. This conclusion highlights the technological factors that instigate change and the means of meeting future demands and improving representation of and access to the subjects of information-bearing documents.

TECHNOLOGICAL CHALLENGES

As we look to the future we can expect change from at least three technological challenges: the further development of metadata, the presence of catalogs on the World Wide Web (WWW), and the use or lack of use of the Z39.50 standards.

Simple formats for metadata may well become a serious rival of the bibliographic MARC record. Because metadata are basic data about a document that may accompany the document or be held in a separate database like a catalog, they are more flexible than the stringent standards hitherto used for library cataloging. If less-developed metadata standards do take over from MARC or even gain reasonably wide application, we may see opportunities for subject representation that is not tied by the strictures of LCSH, DDC, and LCC.

We must be wary of a repetition of the simplistic claims initially made for keyword searching of free text. Metadata need to offer more if they are to surpass the current capabilities of uncontrolled vocabulary. The achievements of automated authority control should not be side-stepped as metadata are made easy enough for the creators of documents to apply. Rather, we need to find creative ways of using existing authority control principles and technologies to enable effective subject access in this different environment.

One of the main reasons that simpler conceptions of metadata are being sought is the enormity of the WWW. Suggestions that librarians catalog the WWW recognize only one of our professional functions—organization of information—and fail to note that the information we organize is typically selected for its credibility and utility before we organize it. We do not yet have an effective means of collection development for the WWW. It is not a parallel situation to print publishing. The WWW is far more fluid, more immediate, and more spontaneous than print publishing. Therefore, it does not lend itself to the same kind of control. Databases link to each other and later disconnect, users are not readily identifiable, and technical capabilities vary constantly. We do not know what we are organizing or for whom. At the same time that the task seems overwhelming, the possibilities seem limitless.

The Z39.50 standards present a somewhat similar though more limited scenario. The purpose of these standards is to allow users to search alien databases using the familiar interfaces of their own catalogs. If the Z39.50 standards achieve this goal, they could offer opportunities for reaching a wide range of audiences similar to those presented by the WWW. However, those users and their information-seeking contexts will be just as unknown as on the WWW. The difference will be that there is a standardization required of the local online catalogs and other databases that may make Z39.50 less popular. The complexity of standardizing a competitive arena like online catalog vendors makes the success of Z39.50 uncertain. However, if Z39.50 or something like it is successful, it offers far more immediate opportunity for the use of authority control and other subject analysis aids.

All three of these factors—metadata, the WWW, and Z39.50—have arisen very quickly, and undoubtedly there are other technological innovations just over the horizon that will affect subject analysis and subject access.

SUBJECT ANALYSIS AND
THE FUTURE

In meeting the challenges and opportunities that technological changes present and in creating opportunities for improved subject access, it is important to consider the knowledge gained in the rich tradition of subject analysis at the same time that we go beyond the current boundaries of that tradition. The principles explained in Chapters 3 through 5 can be applied to subject analysis in any environment. Issues of semantics and syntactics that we understand from print catalogs and the first two generations of online catalogs, as well as from experimental work in information retrieval, also apply to catalogs and other kinds of organization of information on the WWW. As an example, the creators of hierarchical browsers in Yahoo!, AltaVista, and other similar search engines would do well to build on this understanding. The topic *Cannibalism* is classified in Yahoo! hierarchically under *Eating Practices* and in the same category as *Macrobiotics, Raw and Living Foods, Vegetarianism*, and *Wild Foods*. In AltaVista, *Feral Cat Control* is classified under *Lifestyle* via *Pets & Animals* or indirectly via *Hobbies* (examples viewed on May 9, 2001). A clear conceptual knowledge of subject analysis principles would avoid such foibles.

The pros and cons of authority control and controlled vocabularies also relate to the range of different types of databases now being brought together under the umbrella of online catalogs. Use of vocabulary across as well as within databases presents new challenges, but the principles are the same. As different kinds of searching are performed in databases with blurred edges, it is important to know what levels of exhaustivity and specificity are involved because those factors affect the results of searches in terms of precision and recall. For example, we seem to want higher levels of both exhaustivity and specificity as we add tables of contents and various other text to bibliographic records.

However, it is not clear that the ramifications of doing so have been carefully weighed to ensure that more positive (higher recall) than negative (lower precision) results are produced or that there is not a better way to gain the positive results. Exhaustivity and specificity also affect the consistency that can be expected within a given database. Database and interface designers, catalogers and indexers, and searchers and search intermediaries need to know these principles developed over generations.

In the 1940s and 1950s new storage and retrieval techniques were invented such as "peek-a-boo cards" and "uniterms" that have not been significant elements for decades. These early efforts to implement postcoordination did not achieve popularity at least partly because librarians did not see the need for quicker and deeper analysis of a new type of material, research reports, which started appearing by the thousands. Factors such as these led to reinvention by trial and error. Not only do we want to avoid reproducing what the past can already offer us, at the current rate of change we do not have time for such duplication of work. It is imperative that we understand very clearly what has gone before so that we can select and adapt what will work in the fluid world of information technology.

An important product of this tradition is relevance ranking. Previous experiments that could be carried out only on small databases can now be more effectively implemented due to the increasing power and reliability of computer systems. Relevance ranking is being used on the WWW with mixed success. The algorithms developed and tested in the information retrieval literature over the past several decades have led to conceptual notions of how word occurrences and co-occurrences may or may not reflect aboutness. Simple word counts are poor substitutes for more sophisticated subject analysis. Free text searching of keywords has become commonplace as a supplement or option to controlled vocabulary, but many searchers avoid Boolean logic due to its complexity or implement it ineffectively. Relevance ranking is a useful device for making retrieval manageable in large databases.

One of the things that relevance ranking does is to make large sets of retrieved surrogates browsable. It is a step in the direction of fostering browsing and facilitating searching so that searchers can understand what is happening in the database but not be required to spend time developing sophisticated search techniques such as Boolean logic. Cyril Cleverdon (1987), after his Cranfield studies illustrated the efficacy of Boolean searching, regretted that it had become so dominant. Facilitating searches with prompts can assist searchers in achieving effective Boolean searches. Browsing can go further and allow searchers to wander about well-organized databases to achieve useful results, whether in a focused search or through what one might call "assisted serendipity."

Key to effective browsing are the semantic relationships between concepts in a database. Controlled vocabularies create these relationships most effectively. Subject headings manage them through the syndetic structure of references between terms, but they still scatter topics according to the alphabet. Classification, on the other hand, arranges topics in proximity to other related topics and structures broader and narrower topics for effective browsing. The popular use of hierarchies for locating pages on the WWW suggests the accessibility of this method for searchers, especially given the haphazard hierarchies that are often tolerated.

A renaissance of classification for organizing information along subject lines seems both appropriate and imminent. Classification is attracting more interest both intellectually, as a topic of study, and practically, as a device for facilitating both finding and browsing, especially the latter. The classifications used on the WWW demonstrate a reinvention of the classed catalog (discussed in Chapter 7) that uses multiple classification numbers to provide hierarchically arranged entries for subject access.

For example, in Yahoo! the topic *Vegetarianism* is listed not only under *Eating Practices,* a subdivision of *Food and Drink,* but also under *Vegetarians,* which is a subdivision of *Cultures and Groups.* Both *Food and Drink* and *Cultures and Groups* are subdivisions of *Society & Culture. Vegetarianism* is also listed in the completely separate hierarchy of *Nutrition* within the broader area of *Health.* As a result, searchers browsing the Yahoo! classification do not need to know the one "right" way that Yahoo!'s indexers have classified *Vegetarianism,* but can approach it from different directions.

This approach is similar to using subject headings in online catalogs, but with the added browsability of a classification. The authors of this book strongly urge consideration of classification for new efforts in online subject access and better capabilities for browsing classification in online catalog interfaces.

Using classification, creating new interfaces, facilitating searching, and browsing all need more research. In addition, it is important to develop a range of research in the field: experimental research testing cutting-edge ideas, empirical research assessing the status quo, critical research to raise fundamental questions and keep ideas from stagnating, and research in individual institutions to develop and assess local solutions. We also suggest some specific directions for research, most notably, more research on the coordination of alphabetical and classified controlled vocabularies, on enhancing use of relationships between concepts other than hierarchical relationships, and a continuation of the current research focus on interfaces.

Furthermore, it is not enough to do research. In the rapidly changing environment of online subject analysis it is essential to work at application without necessarily waiting for research directly related to a specific problem. It is necessary to extrapolate carefully, but creatively, from existing research, experience, and common sense. We need to balance control and flexibility, supporting users and offering them a range of well-constructed tools while allowing them to direct their own searches. Applications in our current context need to be ingenious and even a bit subversive. We cannot afford to play with our toys only as they were meant to be played with. Finding solutions and improvements will be increasingly challenging—and perhaps fun.

REFERENCES

Cleverdon, C. W. 1987. Historical note: Reminiscence from Cranfield. *Journal of the American Society for Information Science.* 38 (May): 152–55.

Index